Black Wave

Black Wave

How Networks and Governance Shaped Japan's 3/11 Disasters

DANIEL P. ALDRICH

The University of Chicago Press   Chicago and London

The University of Chicago Press, Chicago 60637
The University of Chicago Press, Ltd., London
© 2019 by The University of Chicago
All rights reserved. No part of this book may be used or reproduced in any manner whatsoever without written permission, except in the case of brief quotations in critical articles and reviews. For more information, contact the University of Chicago Press, 1427 E. 60th St., Chicago, IL 60637.
Published 2019
Printed in the United States of America

28 27 26 25 24 23 22 21 20 19   1 2 3 4 5

ISBN-13: 978-0-226-63826-3 (cloth)
ISBN-13: 978-0-226-63843-0 (paper)
ISBN-13: 978-0-226-63857-7 (e-book)
DOI: https://doi.org/10.7208/chicago/9780226638577.001.0001

Library of Congress Cataloging-in-Publication Data

Names: Aldrich, Daniel P., author.
Title: Black wave: how networks and governance shaped Japan's 3/11 disasters / Daniel P. Aldrich.
Description: Chicago: The University of Chicago Press, 2019. | Includes bibliographical references and index.
Identifiers: LCCN 2018052337 | ISBN 9780226638263 (cloth: alk. paper) | ISBN 9780226638430 (pbk: alk. paper) | ISBN 9780226638577 (e-book)
Subjects: LCSH: Tohoku Earthquake and Tsunami, Japan, 2011. | Fukushima Nuclear Disaster, Japan, 2011. | Disaster relief—Japan—Tōhoku Region—Citizen participation. | Disaster relief—Government policy—Japan. | Disaster victims—Social networks—Japan—Tōhoku Region. | Social capital (Sociology)—Japan—Tōhoku Region.
Classification: LCC HV555.J3 A54 2019 | DDC 363.34/9580952090512—dc23
LC record available at https://lccn.loc.gov/2018052337

♾ This paper meets the requirements of ANSI/NISO Z39.48-1992 (Permanence of Paper).

Contents

List of Tables and Illustrations vii
Preface ix

1 Introduction
   The Story of Three Disasters — 1

2 Individual Level
   Neighbors Saving Lives — 29

3 Village, Town, and City Level
   Vertical Ties Bringing Resources — 72

4 Prefectural Level
   Networks Making a Difference — 102

5 National Level
   Governance Challenged — 128

6 International Level
   How Institutions Save Lives — 158

7 Conclusions and Recommendations
   Building Trust and Tying Us Together — 177

Appendix 1: Interviewees and Surveyed Residents 195
Appendix 2: Statistical Tables 199
Notes 207   Sources 233   Index 259

Tables and Illustrations

TABLES

4.1. Comparative Damage across Prefectures 103
4.2. Social Connections in the Three Prefectures 126
5.1. National Reconstruction Progress 130
6.1. Four Disasters and Their Outcomes 173
A.1. Descriptive Statistics for Mortality Dataset 200
A.2. Mortality Regression Analysis Results 201
A.3. Logistic Regression Coefficients for Council Member Outreach 202
A.4. Descriptive Statistics for Recovery Study 203
A.5. Components of NIRA Recovery Index 203
A.6. Sources for Recovery Data 204
A.7. Estimated Regression Coefficients for Recovery by 2012 205
A.8. Estimated Regression Coefficients for Recovery by 2013 206

ILLUSTRATIONS

1.1. Map of affected cities and prefectures in Japan 27
2.1. Comparison of mental distress between the general Japanese population and Futaba evacuees after 3/11 52

2.2. Comparison of mental distress between Futaba evacuees and residents of other Tōhoku villages 52

3.1. Variation in mortality outcomes across communities 74

3.2. Correlation of tsunami height with mortality 75

3.3. Relationship between pre-tsunami crime rate and mortality 80

3.4. Predicted probabilities of municipal council members reaching out to members of the national House of Representatives 88

3.5. Conditions immediately after the disaster and two and three years later 91

3.6. Relationship between number of powerful politicians representing a municipality and speed of recovery 95

4.1. Recovery after 3/11 in Iwate, Miyagi, and Fukushima 122

6.1. Relationship between government expenditure on social safety nets and disaster mortality 161

6.2. Relationship between Polity IV Democracy Score and disaster mortality 162

Preface

The tragic events that we know colloquially as 3/11 began the afternoon of March 11, 2011, but have continued to affect survivors and rivet the world for more than seven years. A trio of disasters[1]—an earthquake, tsunami, and nuclear meltdown—paralyzed Japan, a country ranked among the world's most advanced, industrialized democracies with some of the best building regulations and best-trained engineers. Hundreds of miles of breakwaters and seawalls defended the coastal population of Tōhoku, the region most affected by the disaster. Concrete barriers and planted pine forests along nearly half the shoreline served as additional layers of protection against massive waves. But the tsunami set off by the 9.0 Great East Japan Earthquake not only killed more than 18,400 people[2] but also caused full fuel meltdowns in three of the six reactors at the Fukushima Dai-ichi nuclear power plant.

Estimates put the disasters—known in Japanese as the Higashi Nihon Daishinsai—among the costliest in recorded human history with more than $235 billion in losses.[3] In the affected area, 125,000 homes were destroyed, and 270 railway lines and hundreds of roads were closed.[4] Beyond loss of life and property damage, the cost of radioactive decontamination and compensation for evacuees from Fukushima Prefecture will probably run more than ¥21.5 trillion ($202 billion).[5] Fukushima Dai-ichi's owner and operator, a private utility called the Tokyo Electric Power Company (TEPCO), and the central government face some 2,000,000 individual claims for compensation along with 500,000 claims from corporations and smaller

PREFACE

firms.[6] Radioactive cesium and iodine spread to some 14,000 km² (5,400 square miles) of land. Microparticles of uranium and cesium have been found miles from the plant. At the peak of evacuation, some 470,000 people left their homes in the Tōhoku region due to the nuclear meltdowns and the tsunami,[7] including 160,000 from Fukushima Prefecture alone, nearly 10% of its population.[8] As of fall 2018, more than seven years after the earthquake, 75,000 people remain in interim housing, including temporary housing units, government-owned housing, and the homes of relatives.

This book tackles several pressing mysteries. Perhaps the biggest one is how so many people survived one of the most catastrophic events of the last decade. Despite the massive height and broad impact of the tsunami, some 96% of those living and working in the inundated areas in Tōhoku made it through. Smaller-scale earthquakes and tsunami have killed far more people in nearby countries such as China and India. Yet even with such a high survival rate overall, some towns and cities in northeastern Japan suffered significantly more than others. Accordingly, I investigate why survival and mortality rates varied so much across the Tōhoku region.

Further, the rebuilding process has not moved in lockstep across the area, nor has it proceeded according to government mandates. As one resident told me when talking about the variation across his prefecture, "You can't reduce our cities' recoveries to a simple pattern."[9] At the same time, the Japanese government has highlighted signs of recovery such as the upcoming 2019 Rugby World Cup matches,[10] the 2020 Summer Olympic Games, and the closing of disaster recovery budgets.[11] But these artificial milestones remain unconnected to the day-to-day needs of survivors and the speed of their recoveries.

Since that moment in 2011, Tōhoku residents, regional and national decision makers, nongovernmental organizations, and scholars alike have struggled to make sense of the events and their aftermath. As someone who lost my home, car, and possessions to Hurricane Katrina in 2005, I have long been interested in what makes individuals, communities, and regions resilient to disaster. How people from the hardest-hit prefectures (Miyagi, Iwate, and Fukushima) made it through the tsunami and rebuilt their lives remains a critical question for scholars and governments alike. Few agree on what allowed some residents to escape the deadly 20 m (65-foot) tsunami while others succumbed. Some commentators have argued that geography was destiny, as certain coastal areas were more exposed to the waves than others.[12] Others have pointed to demographics, seeing the very young and very old as the most likely to perish.[13] A few scholars have stated that the best recoveries from disaster depend on strong and competent national leadership.[14] But these arguments are at best partially correct.

Further, some survivors returned to their hometowns, while others decided to begin their lives afresh elsewhere. People who lived near the Fukushima Dai-ichi nuclear power plant in communities such as Futaba cannot yet return, although the government has lifted evacuation orders for towns farther away, such as Namie, Iitate, Hirono, Naraha, and Kawauchi. The central government has promised repopulation for other Fukushima villages, such as Ōkuma, by 2020.[15] Some evacuees from Fukushima and elsewhere remain in temporary housing (*kasetsu jūtaku*) scattered across Japan as of late 2018. Even if the government lifts entry bans and helps rebuild housing near the damaged nuclear power plant, a large-scale return seems unlikely. Radioactive decontamination of the soil and homes continues, and decommissioning the nuclear reactors in Fukushima Prefecture will take at least four decades. The few industries left operating in the region near the ruined nuclear plant focus on radioactive waste and cleanup, for which the costs are enormous.

Scholars have argued that it would be far cheaper to relocate and buy homes for all evacuees than to decontaminate properties in an attempt to convince them to return.[16] Similarly, relocating the homes of people who lived in vulnerable coastal villages to higher ground would cost around ¥80 million ($730,000) per person.[17] Despite the economic inefficiencies of its approach and broad public opposition to atomic energy, Japan's government continues to encourage relocation to higher elevation areas, invest in radiation cleanup, and push for new nuclear power plants and reactor restarts.[18]

Beyond the individual and neighborhood levels of survival and recovery, some towns and cities seem to be doing quite well, while other communities have yet to reopen railroad stations and downtown businesses. A handful of cities and towns in Tōhoku—such as Rifu and Sendai—have attracted new residents and actually grown, whereas most cities along the coast have lost population. Many former residents have abandoned coastal villages and moved inland to larger cities, accelerating two long-term trends that have vexed most of Japan: rural depopulation and aging.[19] To attract new residents and convince evacuees to return, communities near the ocean have built seawalls, moved residential areas to higher ground, and launched programs promoting return and economic recovery. One popular attempt to increase livelihoods in these peripheral communities involves promoting local foodstuffs, handmade local crafts, and specialty alcoholic drinks through what one observer has called "rebuilding through rebranding."[20] TEPCO itself has sought to jump-start Fukushima revitalization by building "clean coal" energy facilities and sending in employees to clean up the community and interact with local residents.[21]

Some cities have sought to work independently on their rebuilding plans, ignoring recommendations from the regional and national governments and moving quickly to institute their own visions. A number of towns, such as Watari in Miyagi Prefecture, have used the disasters as a chance to upgrade local industries such as agriculture. Hoping to keep strawberry production as a core industry, Watari invested in high-tech greenhouses complete with computer-controlled irrigation, automated light systems, and in-house beehives. Other towns followed the guidelines offered by Tokyo-based national bureaucrats for their economic development and rebuilding. Similarly, prefectures—the Japanese equivalent to North American states—have experienced varying levels of ongoing recovery. Fukushima Prefecture lags behind Miyagi Prefecture, with Iwate Prefecture in second place, in terms of restoration and recovery.

Despite the variation and nuances in recovery, media coverage of the disaster and ongoing rebuilding has ignored the diversity of experience among prefectures, communities, and individuals and has been hamstrung by stereotypes and well-worn cultural tropes. Popular media stories in the West about Japanese resilience in the face of the 3/11 disasters regularly emphasized *cultural* attributes as contributing to recovery at the national level and ignored local and regional variation in outcomes and responses. We hear of Japanese stoicism[22] from observers who watched residents waiting patiently in food or water distribution lines and saw evacuees waiting hours to use phones set up at nearby mobile NTT East offices.[23] But they may have missed angry residents publicly challenging government officials at what had previously been "rituals of assent"[24] and cursing TEPCO executives who came to shelters to bow and apologize for causing inconvenience after the meltdowns. Few have remarked on the use of rock music, cartoons, and public performances to mock both Tokyo's attempts to reassure citizens over radioactive exposure and the government's insistence on restarting nuclear power plants.[25]

Observers content to use a culture of acceptance as their frame have also overlooked lawsuits seeking ¥100 million ($96,000) per child filed by bereaved families whose children died at the Okawa Elementary School in Ishinomaki.[26] Outsiders may have ignored the litigation[27] from those whose loved ones perished at the 77 Bank in Onagawa[28] and the demands for compensation from the residents of Iitate, some 45 km (28 miles) from Fukushima Dai-ichi, for psychological distress and radiation exposure.[29] Whatever role a national Japanese culture has played in the recovery process after the triple disasters, it has not been consistent across the affected region. As one study argued, "Focusing on the characteristics and qualities of the Japanese people and Japanese society as a whole is highly problematic as an intellectual framework" for understanding the response to and recovery from the 3/11 disasters.[30]

Claims about the importance of Japanese culture during crises also fail to acknowledge the importance of the governance structures and formal institutions undergirding outcomes at the individual, town, and prefectural levels. We need to understand Japan's experiences with the disaster and its social and political consequences in broader, international comparison as well. Certainly residents of Japan facing a mass catastrophe encounter different challenges than those living in Haiti, India, or China. Whereas Haiti was a failed state before its devastating earthquake, struggling to deliver the most basic of services to its residents, Japan sat among the OECD nations and had invested heavily in education, health care, and transportation systems. Its rigorous building codes, solid governance framework, and highly professionalized bureaucracy[31] put it head and shoulders above struggling countries facing similar, or even less severe, catastrophes. Viewing Japan's experiences side by side with those of other disaster-affected nations can illuminate important aspects of its regulatory and political systems.

Recognizing the shortcomings of telling the story of survival and recovery at any one level of analysis, this book uses data from a variety of levels, beginning with the individual and moving up through the city, prefectural, national, and international levels to place the story of the 3/11 triple disasters in context. Grasping the nuances of Tōhoku's recovery process will require an in-depth focus on formal and informal institutions as well as the choices made by, and the connections among, individuals. Where earlier it was challenging to grasp the long-term arc of policies and recovery,[32] now, some seven years after the tragedies of 3/11, we have better data and a clearer view of what has come since then. To look into these questions at multiple levels of recovery and rebuilding required a new approach to the questions of survival and recovery.

My earlier studies of social capital and resilience in the United States, India, and Japan, for example, rarely touched on the stories of individuals whose decisions and experiences drove broader patterns

PREFACE

of recovery.[33] The books and articles I wrote on nuclear power plant host communities[34] and the response of civil society to the Fukushima Dai-ichi nuclear accident[35] rarely used the voices of local residents. In the past, when looking into how social networks influenced the ability of people and places to bounce back after crises, I focused almost exclusively on micro-level data and decisions without investigating the ways that towns, prefectures, and national political institutions influenced those outcomes. Engaging with residents and using their words and opinions is critical not just because it is the ethical thing to do. It's important because it reminds us, as Andrew Littlejohn has pointed out, of the real suffering and emotions that accompany events like Japan's 3/11 disasters. Many investigations of the Tōhoku disasters have not placed their research in this broader perspective.

Interviews with and anthropological studies of survivors tell us a tremendous amount about the lives of a handful of people before and after the disaster; however, we lack a broader understanding of how their experiences compare with those of others across the affected area.[36] Many newspaper articles on the disaster focus on the missing, the dead, and the heroic. These reports are important. But surely the geographic, political, and social context influenced residents' decisions and altered their lives before and after the earthquake, tsunami, and meltdowns. Scholars have emphasized how strongly the broader "context of reception" influences the decisions made by survivors about return, migration, and recovery.[37] The social ties and institutional context in Japan—that is, networks and governance, which vary from city to city, prefecture to prefecture—have proved important factors in influencing rebuilding, and it is on them that my focus remains throughout this book.

Villages, towns, and cities sit one level of analysis up from individual experiences. Yet many descriptions of town recoveries make it difficult to understand whether the experiences of often-referenced towns are the result of their efforts or of less obvious factors.[38] Journalists have spent hours in towns that set up businesses in temporary buildings downtown, relocated residences to higher ground, built new railroads and stores, and put people back in homes and workplaces. But reporters have demonstrated less interest in looking into the ways that prefectural spending decisions and interactions between town officials and regional and national decision makers shaped town recoveries. Observers also have few insights into the ways that connections between local leaders in Tōhoku communities and power brokers in Tokyo and abroad helped accelerate reconstruction.

Some may expect this book to focus on only a single aspect of the triple disasters, whether the earthquake, tsunami, or nuclear meltdowns. Instead, I write about all three crises, as their effects often overlapped.[39] Along with looking at the casualties and physical recovery from the events, I also analyze the mental and psychosocial consequences of radioactive exposure for residents. Biological studies of species in the area have revealed genetic abnormalities.[40] The results of ongoing cancer screenings across Fukushima are still coming in, but they show higher than expected rates of thyroid carcinoma among the 300,000 people who have been tested.[41] Some argue that there is no direct link between these testing outcomes and the nuclear accident,[42] but parents have voted with their feet, moving out of the area with their children in droves. One mother from Iitate said that she "believes only half of what the doctors say" about the risks she and her children face.[43]

Further, residents from the area face not just the potential of death from radiation-induced cancer and leukemia, but measurable physical and mental illness caused by anxiety about their health, separation from friends and family, and uncertainty about their old homes and their livelihoods. When some locals from towns such as Futaba evacuated the area near Fukushima Dai-ichi due to government orders, they unintentionally relocated to towns, such as Iitate, in the plume of spreading radioactivity. That town, like several other destinations for evacuees, had no such mandate to depart, but was also exposed to radiation. Hypertension and diabetes, along with childhood obesity, have risen across the area.[44] Residents face the accompanying challenges of alcoholism, mental illness, depression, and suicide. I hope that this research on these less visible but palpable health outcomes can bring the social consequences for Japanese society as a whole, and for the residents of Fukushima in particular, into better focus.

While my past articles, chapters, and books have included extensive tables of numbers and difficult-to-grasp social science terms, I wanted to take a different approach for this work. This book moves between qualitative and quantitative methods in what scholars call a *nested analysis* to fill in the gaps of each method and to better guide the analysis.[45] No single approach, whether interviews, participant observation, focus groups, case studies, or regression analysis, can provide a holistic perspective on complex issues. Further, publishers, editors, and critics alike point out that social scientists can make the most interesting subjects dull and lifeless. Overemphasizing methodology—*how* we know what know—rather than what we have learned may be partially responsible. So in this book I've tried to submerge the methodologi-

PREFACE

cal skeleton underlying the claims by placing it in the appendices. For those readers with an interest in ordinary least squares regression analysis coefficients, you'll find them buried there. Similarly, I've put a list of the people with whom I or my colleagues have spoken (identified by name, if possible, or by organization if not) there as well.[46] Throughout the text I've used maps, figures, and graphs, instead of lists of numbers, to make my points.

This project has grown out of a series of visits and several extended stays in Japan, beginning with a short trip in the late spring of 2011 following the disasters and culminating in a year-long stay as a Fulbright Fellow from late summer 2012 through fall 2013, a full summer (May–August) in 2015, and fieldwork and teaching in Tōhoku in 2017 and 2018. I was also fortunate to go on a variety of fact-finding missions over the past few years with organizations such as the Earthquake Engineering Research Institute (EERI), the United Nations International Strategy for Disaster Reduction (UNISDR), and the Federation of Electric Power Companies of Japan (FEPC). I interacted with local nongovernmental organizations in Tōhoku, including Ibasho, Ishinomaki 2.0, and PlanMiyagi. Speaking with survivors, interviewing heads of NGOs and decision makers in Japanese, carrying out fieldwork in many Tōhoku villages, gathering quantitative data through surveys, and reading local newspaper and blog accounts of the disaster underscored for me how often our research lacks depth and background. For details on the many people I've spoken with and interviewed through summer 2018, see the list of interviewees and institutions in appendix 1.

As all authors know, books are never the products of their writers working in isolation. Instead, I have been fortunate to benefit from the help, mentorship, and guidance of a large number of individuals who have given of their time and expertise. Thank you to Howard Aldrich, Yael Aldrich, Simon Avenell, Leo Bosner, Jinko Brinkman, Kent Calder, Stephanie Chang, Rosie Clawson, Kyle Cleveland, Kevin Crook, Christian Dimmer, David Edgington, Shin Fujihira, Mariko Gakiya, Ted Gilman, Kazuaki Hagi, Ken Hartman, Dan Homsey, Laurie Johnson, Rieko Kage, Machiko Kamiyama, Emi Kiyota, Kathy Krauth, Claire Leppold, Kaori Linderman, Andrew Littlejohn, Liz Maly, Peter Matanle, Tomoko Matsushita, John Morris, Hiroyuki Nakata, Dan Neely, Ilan Noy, Eiji Oguma, Rob Olshansky, Yoshikuni Ono, Susan Pharr, Jim Platte, Liesel Ritchie, David Satterwhite, Yasuyuki Sawada, Jennifer Sklarew, David

PREFACE

Slater, Gavin Smith, Amina Sugimoto, Ezra Suleiman, Kathleen Tierney, and Irwin Weiser.

I had excellent research assistance from Elicia Cousins, Saki Kitadai, Yusuke Kuroishi, Kai McGuire, Keishi Nambara, Violet Ranson, Yuto Sakakibara, Masayuku Sawada, Takahiro Yamamoto, and Daisuke Yoneoka in Japan. Jennifer Adams, Gavriel Tzvi Aldrich, Ben Averbuch, Anne Culbertson, Allie Hastings, Michele Hemler, Masayoshi Miura, Keishi Nambara, Ishra Noor, Courtney Page-Tan, and Miyuki Tsujikawa supported this research in the United States. Thanks especially to the graphic artists who helped make the ideas come alive: Rachel Faibish, Steven Braun, and Bahare Sanaie-Movahed. John Morris and Machiko Kamiyama provided a sanctuary for good conversations, rest, and regrouping while I was in Sendai. Courtney Schley helped point out all of the ways I could say things more clearly.

Several different institutions supported the research necessary for this publication. The Colorado Natural Hazards Center under the direction of Kathleen Tierney provided a Quick Response Grant for research in the summer of 2011. I was honored to receive a Fulbright research fellowship under the auspices of the Japan-U.S. Educational Commission (JUSEC) during the 2012–2013 academic year; thank you to Jinko Brinkman, Mizuho Iwata, and David Satterwhite for great administrative support. The East Asia Institute under the guidance of Young-Hwan Shin provided support for comparative research in China in the summer of 2013. Purdue University's Kinley Trust grant supported me in the summer of 2014. I appreciate the institutional support provided by Rosie Clawson and Irwin Weiser at Purdue University and by Mitchell Orenstein, Uta Poiger, John Portz, Matthias Ruth, and Tom Vicino at Northeastern University. The Center for International Research on the Japanese Economy (CIRJE) at the University of Tokyo's Faculty of Economics provided funding for writing and research during the summer of 2015.

I received feedback from colleagues at presentations at the Japan International Cooperation Agency (JICA), the German Institute for Japanese Studies (DIJ), the National Graduate Institute for Policy Studies (GRIPS), the University of Tokyo, Tōhoku University, Taisho University, Academica Sinica, Beijing Normal University, Fudan University, Harvard University, Lincoln University, Canterbury University, Brookings Institute, Ishinomaki Senshu University, the Program on US-Japan Relations at Harvard, the Natural Hazards Conference, Oxford University, Northeastern University (especially the students in my Dialogue

PREFACE

of Civilizations course on disasters and recovery), and the University of Wellington. Talks at the UNISDR Conference on disasters in Sendai, the Southern Political Science Association (SPSA), and the World Bank helped to refine and clarify my ideas, as did informal and formal talks with colleagues at Northeastern University, including Max Abrahms, Steve Flynn, and Jennie Stephens. A Mercatus Center–sponsored book conference under the leadership of Virgil Storr brought together Stefanie Haeffele, Arnold Howitt, Tonya Neaves, Eileen Norcross, William Siembieda, and Solomon Stein, who put hours into helping me up my game. I appreciate their input and the work of Rob DeLeo, Tim Fraser, Liz Maly, and Courtney Page-Tan in improving the final drafts.

The *chesed* of the Borei Olam sustains us often in ways that we fail to sufficiently appreciate. My wife, Yael, remains the core of my world and the reason I've been able to relocate our family some 14 times over more than 20 years of marriage. Her strength, sense of humor, intelligence, and dedication to our shared vision make it a delight to be married to her. All that I have—personally and professionally—comes from her.

Our children, Gavriel Tzvi, Yaakov, Yehudis, and Dov Ber, are a blessing and we should continue to *shep nachas* from them. My immediate family—Howard and Penny Aldrich, Steven, Allison, and Jackson Aldrich, Dalia Carmel, Suncha and Louis McCoy, Michael Spring, and my various uncles and aunts—Carol, Craig, Cheryl, Chuck, Chris, Curt, and Cathy, among them—help me stay focused on what matters. My grandparents, Fifi and Jack Daum, Howard and Dorothy Aldrich, and my great-uncle Herb Goldstein have left this world but remain in our thoughts. My sister-in-law, Nicole McCoy-Spring, passed away after a long battle with cancer before I could finish this project. She lived a life of optimism, giving, and outreach to others across racial and religious lines. Our memory of her should continue to be a blessing and her resilience should inspire us. I hope this book can refocus our research and spending priorities on factors that make a difference in reducing mortality, building resilience, and accelerating recovery.

ONE

Introduction: The Story of Three Disasters

At 2:46 p.m. on March 11, 2011, a magnitude 9.0 earthquake shattered the chilly afternoon in Tōhoku, the northeastern region of Japan's main island, Honshu. Seconds before the ground would jolt, Japan's earthquake early warning system (*kinkyū jishin sokuhō*) detected the oncoming seismic P-waves and sent an alert: a quake was coming. Some people standing near municipal loudspeakers in Tōhoku heard a prerecorded announcement about the danger,[1] but most residents did not. Rather than dissipating quickly, like most of the hundreds of small but noticeable earthquakes that hit the country each year, the shaking continued for what many told me felt like eternity. A force equal to 600 million times the energy released over Hiroshima by the atom bomb in 1945 discharged over six minutes some 130 km (80 miles) off Japan's coast. That undersea megathrust earthquake remains among the top five most powerful ever recorded, and its power measurably slowed the earth's rotation and moved Miyagi Prefecture some 5 m (15 feet) to the east. In Tokyo, the nation's capital, hundreds of miles from the quake's epicenter, skyscrapers swayed slowly like palm trees to the sound of groaning metal.

In Tōhoku itself—the region closest to the epicenter—windows shattered, steel girders bent out of shape, and computer monitors and files toppled from desks. Shelves collapsed, sprinkler pipes burst, floating ceilings caved in, and bricks fell off the front of buildings in Sendai and other Tōhoku cities. Salespeople ushered customers outside, and teachers gathered their pupils in schoolyards and baseball fields dusted by snow. Many homes and buildings lost power. People hid under desks and tables, shielding their heads from falling debris; many outside lay down on the ground or hugged trees to keep from falling over. In Tokyo, water bubbled to the surface in parks built on reclaimed land as liquefaction turned the ground to mud. Once the shaking subsided, roughly 2.5 million people hurried from their office buildings in Tokyo to begin the long commute home, which for many, with trains and subways shut down, would involve hours of walking or waiting in taxi lines that stretched for hundreds of meters.

Three minutes after the earthquake stopped, the Japanese Meteorological Agency (Kishōchō, or JMA) issued tsunami alerts via several different channels. Authorities broadcast warnings in Chinese, English, and Japanese. Their tsunami warnings overrode television broadcasts and blared on loudspeakers, radios, and cellular phones. Mobile phones in the coastal region operated by all of Japan's networks, including the most popular phones from NTT and SoftBank, emitted a disconcerting squeal followed by a series of messages predicting potential wave heights.

While intended to motivate people to evacuate low-lying areas of the Tōhoku region, the JMA's warnings radically underestimated the tsunami heights. The 6 m (20-foot) forecast sent for the city of Onagawa, for example, underestimated what would actually be a 20 m (65-foot) wave. Similarly, the first JMA tsunami warning sent to Otsuchi predicted a 3 m (10-foot) wave, although the agency later doubled that figure to 6 m as more data came in. Other cities and villages in Tōhoku also received wave height forecasts that did not match future reality. By the time the JMA revised its tsunami warnings to give more accurate wave heights, many residents had lost power for their radios and televisions or had stopped paying attention.[2] Surveys by Japan's Cabinet Office showed that as many as 74% of residents did not hear about the changes in the predicted tsunami heights.[3]

Along with the broadcast messages, police officers and firefighters began driving around coastal towns telling residents to evacuate (*hinan shite kudasai*). Many residents in the Tōhoku region began to evacuate schools and businesses, following the protocols drilled into them by teachers and disaster managers. Many schoolchildren had been taught the concept of *tsunami tendenko*: fleeing after an earthquake without stopping.[4] Elementary and junior high school students in Kamaishi had just received a lecture on precisely this topic from Toshitaka Katada, an engineering professor who had studied how 10-year-old Tilly Smith saved some 100 lives on a beach in Thailand during the 2004 Indian Ocean tsunami.[5] Smith, who was vacationing with her family from the UK, had learned the warning signs of impending tsunami in a science class. When she recognized those signs—deeply receding tide and frothing waters—she yelled for other beachgoers to flee to higher ground. Inspired by the young girl's impact, Katada wanted to share those lessons with students in tsunami-prone areas in Japan. The students in Kamaishi who heard Katada's lecture escaped successfully, inspiring stories of the "Kamaishi miracle." Photos taken just prior to the tsunami at the school showed older students helping younger children flee to safety.

Japanese children's books[6] and training for older students and adults alike emphasize that residents in coastal areas should not stop even to check on family members following an earthquake; they must save themselves. For decades, authorities have held an annual Disaster Prevention Day with large-scale evacuations and simulations across Japan. Beyond training and drills, cities in Tōhoku have faced actual tsunami multiple times over the past two centuries. The city of Ofunato, for example, saw 3,000 people killed in the June 16, 1896, Meiji Sanriku tsunami (more than 21,000 died in the region overall). Another 405 Ofunato residents perished in the March 3, 1933, tsunami and fires; 53 died in the May 24, 1960, Chilean tsunami. Residents across Japan, and especially those in the Tōhoku region, have been exposed to the concepts and realities of disaster and have been trained to escape it.

But on March 11, 2011, not everyone immediately moved to higher ground. Close to half the residents of the coastal areas in Tōhoku delayed their evacuation. Some did not think the waves could reach their homes. Several tsunami in the years and even days before March 2011 had been minuscule. A very small tsunami—some 10 cm (4 inches) high—washed up in Iwate Prefecture on March 9, setting up some residents to see the March 11 tsunami two days later as similarly harmless.[7] Other residents recognized the potential danger but lost critical time by first checking on their loved ones or picking up children from elementary school. Some people who lived in cities surrounded by multiple lines of defense, such as thick concrete seawalls and pine forests, believed they were safe from incoming waves. In many cases, the JMA's initial warnings predicted tsunami heights that were far lower than the seawalls in those communities, so locals stayed put, figuring the walls would easily keep the water out.

A surprising number of people reported that they neither heard

CHAPTER ONE

warnings via any medium nor were spurred to evacuate by the intense earthquake. In some communities, disaster announcement systems were damaged or silenced by the quake itself.[8] In Natori, for example, the emergency municipal radio system failed completely.[9] Many elderly and infirm residents did not hear warnings from loudspeakers, radios, or televisions. Fewer than 33% of those over 70 used mobile phones,[10] so their access to the mobile alerts issued by the Area Mail Disaster Information System was limited.[11] Even if they were aware of the danger, disabled and older residents needed assistance to leave low-lying areas and evacuate to higher ground. One scholar underscored that victims "who were over the age of 60 accounted for 64% of all male and 68% of all female casualties."[12] The mortality rate of disabled and infirm people was roughly 2.5 times greater than that of other residents.[13]

Many who did immediately flee to higher ground remained in danger. The earthquake thrust the ocean floor 16 m (52 feet) upward. All that energy, in the form of multiple tsunami, propagated from the epicenter, reaching the coastal cities of Tōhoku roughly 40 minutes later. Beginning around 3:15 p.m., the tsunami overran or destroyed almost all of the seawalls and concrete barriers that were supposed to hold back the water from downtown districts in Tōhoku. When they came ashore, these tsunami were not clear: they were black waves. Their dark, often oil-like color came from the material that they swept up as they smashed into the coast, pulling up homes, cars, electrical poles, trees, and everything in their way. The tsunami were higher than 20 m (65 feet) in many places at landfall, and they traveled as far as 10 km (6 miles) inland up riverbeds and water channels. As a result, even towns and cities not directly on the coast faced the danger of inundation. Buildings and homes shuddered, swayed, and then broke free of their foundations, crunching loudly as plaster and wood gave way to the water, which pulled them into whirlpools and ground them together.

Towns with high seawalls, such as Iwanuma (which had a wall 7.5 m, or 24 feet, tall), Taro (12 m, or 39 feet) and Miyako (10 m, or 32 feet), saw the black waves pick up massive concrete blocks from the seawalls and smash them into buildings.[14] Kamaishi's 10 m walls, built at a cost of more than $1.6 billion, made the *Guinness Book of Records* for their size, but were similarly destroyed by the waves and then swept into the downtown area.[15] At Shiogama Port, the sea breached the seawall easily, pouring over the barrier as if it were a child's blocks. Expensive coastal infrastructure did little to stop the destruction as houses were lifted from concrete slabs in coastal towns such as Rikuzentakata and Onagawa. In Kesennuma, the downtown was flooded in seconds as 30-meter-long boats were yanked free of their anchors and hurled into structures.

Seawalls, berms, and other defensive physical infrastructure weren't the only facilities toppled by the power of the tsunami. The Onagawa hospital—located at the top of a hill overlooking the downtown area— had its first floor flooded; many patients, medical personnel, and residents who had fled there seeking shelter drowned. Onagawa's hospital tragedy was not unique. In the three-story Ogatsu Municipal Hospital in Ishinomaki, all but 6 of the 40 patients and 24 doctors and nurses died. The disaster prevention manual written for the hospital assumed that tsunami would not reach more than 6 m (19 feet) above sea level. As a result, hospital staff believed the black waves would not reach the top floor of the hospital and painstakingly moved patients there by hand to wait out the rising floods.[16] When the water broke through the windows of the third-floor patient rooms, staff tried to save patients in the chaos, but to no avail.[17]

Those who fled to designated evacuation sites—areas the government had set up for residents fleeing tsunami and other disasters—were not necessarily safe. Many evacuation sites were susceptible to both tsunami and quake. In fact, only 60% of them remained undamaged after the triple disasters.[18] Scores of emergency shelters, fire stations, and public schools across the region that served as priority tsunami evacuation sites were washed away. The tsunami inundated more than 100 evacuation sites,[19] turning safe havens into traps for those fleeing the waves.

Yet neither evacuating nor staying in place guaranteed survival. Some who tried to flee in their cars found themselves carried swiftly down flooded streets and buffeted by debris; others became trapped inside houses or on the roofs of homes and buildings. The official death toll from the National Police Agency (Keisatsu chō) stands at 15,895, with 2,539 people remaining missing, for a total of 18,434 lives taken. The tsunami destroyed 129,423 buildings and inundated 300,561 km^2 (some 116,000 square miles) of land with salt water and debris. Some 250,000 people lost their homes to damage from the tsunami and the earthquake. The tsunami created 22 million tons of rubble—the equivalent of 20 years of municipal waste from cities across Japan—in an afternoon.[20] Despite preparation, strong building codes, and miles of concrete along Tōhoku's shores, the events of March 11 showed how vulnerable even Japan remained to disaster.

CHAPTER ONE

Nuclear Catastrophe

At the moment the earthquake struck, ground sensors in the Fukushima Dai-ichi nuclear power plant complex run by TEPCO in Fukushima Prefecture recognized the seismic activity. Instruments triggered an automatic emergency shutdown of the nuclear reactors, known in the industry as a SCRAM.[21] Of the six reactors at the complex, three had been operating before the earthquake while the other three had been shut down for standard maintenance. To ensure the cooling of operating reactors 1, 2, and 3, which were still generating heat despite being turned off, pumps circulated water through the complex to transfer heat outside. Engineers built the pumps to operate for several days in a crisis to reduce the temperature in the reactors and prevent a meltdown. When the power flowing into the plant failed because of the earthquake, 13 backup emergency diesel generators kicked in to push water through the reactor cores.[22] Large packs of batteries stood ready to help move water should the generators run out of fuel.

The existing layers of protection at the plant, had they been installed and operated properly, might have been enough to stop the tragedy that followed. While the quake and waves damaged some equipment at the plant, the nuclear meltdowns that followed were not inevitable. A lack of foresight, poor risk evaluation, and faulty disaster management choices by TEPCO officials resulted in a large-scale nuclear catastrophe.[23] Government regulators, too, bear responsibility for this manmade disaster, as no emergency response manuals provided guidance for a compound crisis of this magnitude.[24] Nor did civil servants push utilities to upgrade safety in the years before the 3/11 events.[25]

At 3:37 p.m. on March 11, after a series of smaller waves arrived, a 13 m (42-foot) tsunami overtopped the 5.5 m (18-foot) seawalls at Fukushima Dai-ichi and flooded the entire site, which sat at sea level right next to the ocean. Decades before, TEPCO had worked with central government bureaucrats to site the facility on the coast because the area was sparsely populated and had few civil society organizations that could organize opposition to the plant.[26] TEPCO was among the first energy firms in the nation to build a commercial nuclear power plant, and others—including Chubu, Hokuriku, and Kansai—followed suit, placing their facilities along the coast where population density and potential antinuclear sentiment were low.

Engineers had built small-scale seawalls between Fukushima Dai-ichi and the ocean, recognizing that a large wave could disrupt operations. But they placed the machinery that could prevent a meltdown in a vulnerable location because of the engineering culture where the reactors were designed: the United States. In the late 1960s, TEPCO engineers located the backup cooling mechanisms at Fukushima Dai-ichi based on the kind of disaster a North American plant was most likely to face: tornadoes.[27] As a result, the diesel generators sat on the first floor of the seaside building and the batteries in the basement. The waters flooded and destroyed these secondary systems that could have prevented the cores from overheating.

With power out, and with active backup systems damaged by inundation, a third line of defense remained. Passive cooling mechanisms known as isolation condensers at reactor 1 and throughout the Fukushima Dai-ichi site could have continued to cool the reactors even without power.[28] Unfortunately, TEPCO personnel had shut them off just before the plant lost electricity. Without indicator lights to confirm their status, engineers in the control room mistakenly believed that the devices were still working as temperatures rose for several hours, losing a chance to slow or halt the progressing meltdown in reactor 1.[29]

At this point, water was no longer circulating through the reactors to cover the fuel rods, and because active and passive backup systems were offline, the temperature inside the reactors began to surge upward. The plant experienced what engineers call "total station blackout" without any source of power to operate pumps or sensors.[30] Because TEPCO engineers never thought this could happen, there was no manual or protocol for dealing with the situation.[31] The plant operators struggled to reduce the massive heat buildup in the reactors without full sensor readings, external power, or clear communication channels to one another or the outside.

Further, TEPCO engineers lacked training and experience to effectively manage such a complex and novel scenario. They did not recognize that the weak puffs of steam coming from the "pig snouts" of the isolation condensers indicated that they were not working.[32] Staff at Fukushima Dai-ichi had never practiced pumping water into the reactor cores using external means such as fire trucks, and they had not set up the internal pipes to deliver water into the reactors efficiently. Efforts to open safety release valves to vent pressure and radioactivity and to pump water into the reactors from fire trucks brought in to assist early in the morning on March 12 had little effect. Despite these inadequate preparations for emergencies, a lack of training, and poor choices, TEPCO later defended its personnel, arguing that they had made no errors in their responses during the crisis.[33]

CHAPTER ONE

A chemical reaction between the fuel rods and salt water caused hydrogen explosions, blowing the facades off reactors 1, 3, and 4. This made for impressive television news loops, but the more pressing environmental problems at the plant were not visible to the world. Without cooling water for more than 14 hours, the radioactive fuel inside the Fukushima Dai-ichi reactors melted through the 7-inch steel containment vessels into the basements as temperatures in the reactor cores reached 2,800°C (5,000°F). The fuel rods broke apart and pellets spilled into the interior of the reactors. Reactor 1 had melted down by 1:10 a.m. on March 12; reactor 3 melted down on March 13; and reactor 2 on the evening of March 14.

More than seven years later, nuclear engineers continue to try to pinpoint precisely where the melted nuclear fuel sits within and beneath the primary containment vessels that surround the reactor cores. Lethal levels of radioactivity make it impossible for humans—and even many robots—to enter the lower levels of concrete where it is probably resting, although a few probes have survived the interior conditions long enough to relay blurry images. Engineers have turned to more exotic methods, such as muon scans, to better understand those conditions.

Wherever the radioactive materials sit, cooling water sprayed into the complex, as well as groundwater, rain, and floods flowing through it, have carried radioactive cesium, iodine, and tritium particles into the water table and out to sea. Even though the intensive cooling efforts have stopped, tons of water still flow daily through the site and need to be recaptured using wells and pumps and then stored on-site until cleaned. Given the reluctance of local fishermen and communities to accept TEPCO's dumping of this water out in the ocean, storing it has become the interim solution. Since 3/11, authorities have tried various methods to reduce environmental damage, such as storing contaminated water in large, ad hoc steel storage tanks (which have proved leaky[34]) that hold more than 1 million tons of it. TEPCO continues to tinker with an expensive experimental underground ice wall to stop water from leaving the site.[35] The efficacy of the underground ice remains unclear, and engineers have since constructed a steel wall between the plant and the ocean. The company continues to filter out radioactive cesium and iodine and reduce the volume of polluted water flowing out through the ice and steel walls. Nevertheless, there is no known technological means of resolving the contamination at the reactor sites.[36]

Nuclear experts soon classified the Fukushima Dai-ichi meltdowns as a level 7 event on the International Nuclear Event Scale (INES), representing the highest level of danger—the same rating they gave the 1986 Chernobyl meltdowns in Ukraine, which spread radioactivity as far as Denmark and France. As the government and TEPCO struggled to formulate consistent plans for managing the disaster and evacuating people in harm's way, some mayors in Fukushima Prefecture used their legal authority to order evacuations directly.[37] Other local elected officials, afraid that their lack of data on actual conditions could lead to poor decision making, waited for guidance from the top, which did not always arrive speedily.

The Fukushima governor ordered an evacuation of residents within 2 km (1.2 miles) of the plant at 8:50 p.m. on March 11. At 5:45 a.m. on March 12, the Nuclear Emergency Response Headquarters issued a mandatory evacuation order for those within 10 km (6 miles) of the plant and later expanded it to 20 km (12 miles).[38] As the disaster unfolded, responses from one of Japan's closest allies indicated a higher level of concern. United States officials including Ambassador John Roos recommended that US residents within 80 km (50 miles) of the plant evacuate. The United States also set up a voluntary evacuation for families of diplomats and military personnel at bases far from the Fukushima Dai-ichi site in locations such as Tokyo (some 240 km, or 150 miles, away). The US military flew some 10,000 dependents of armed services personnel out of the country.[39] The US aircraft carrier *George Washington* pulled out of Tokyo, ostensibly traveling to Sasebo (nearly 600 miles away) for repairs that would take until mid-April.[40] Experts in the US Nuclear Regulatory Commission received little useful information from their counterparts in Tokyo and struggled to make sense of the accident from afar. Eventually, some American scientists, including experts under the aegis of the American Association for the Advancement of Science (AAAS), traveled to Japan to try to assist the US embassy in its efforts to advise Japan.

On March 15, the Japanese government told those living 20–30 km (12–18 miles) from the plant to shelter indoors, and nearly two weeks after the disaster, on March 23, urged those still residing within 30 km of the nuclear facility to leave. On March 26, Greenpeace encouraged the government to evacuate areas farther from Fukushima Dai-ichi based on data indicating high levels of radiation exposure.[41] By the end of the month, more than 150,000 residents of Fukushima Prefecture had evacuated due to the threat of radioactive contamination.[42] Some

CHAPTER ONE

78,000 of the evacuees had lived within a 20 km radius around the plant, and another 10,000 had lived near the village of Iitate, which sat in the center of a plume of radiation that had drifted north and west.[43] On April 22, 2011, the government set up the 20 km evacuation zone as a restricted or no-entry area guarded by police while establishing a larger area as a "deliberate evacuation area." Nearly a month after Greenpeace's initial warnings, the government finally urged those still in the village of Iitate to leave as well, and by June 2011, the village had fully emptied.

More than seven years after the meltdowns, the central government continues decontamination efforts near residences and schools, with contractors bagging hundreds of thousands of tons of radioactive topsoil and washing down roofs and walls.[44] Initial reports on these expensive efforts to reduce contamination have concluded that the government's efforts have reduced cumulative radiation exposure by a maximum of 27% beyond natural decay.[45] As time has gone on, natural decay of elements such as cesium has reduced radiation levels in forests by some 70%.[46] Whether communities see the government's efforts as sufficient is a separate question.[47] The national government has allowed some survivors to return to decontaminated communities near the nuclear plant, including parts of the town of Minamisoma (some 30 km north of Fukushima Dai-ichi). It has also promised repopulation for some evacuated communities by 2020, the date when Japan will host the Summer Olympics.

But tens of thousands of evacuees still reside far from their original homes without a clear return date. The residents of Tōhoku—especially those from Fukushima—had to survive the quake and tsunami and then try to resume the rhythms of daily life against a backdrop of potential radioactive exposure, uncertainty, and loss of homes, jobs, and contacts. The government's choice to hold back information about radiation levels ushered in what some observers have called a "new era . . . based on distrust of the government."[48] As one scholar reported, nearly 60% of respondents to nationwide polls "identified the central government as the least reliable source of information after a disaster."[49] While outsiders may have seen Japan as a nation with a deep sense of respect for government authority, 3/11 revealed fractures between civil society and the state. But before looking closely at issues such as distrust in chapter 5, I want to focus on how Japanese residents and communities have (and have not) built resilience to catastrophe.

Theories of Recovery and Resilience

When talking about recovery and rebuilding after a disaster, we may think of a linear path with certain regular steps. A textbook on disaster recovery might argue that after the disaster, authorities first carry out search-and-rescue missions, helping the living and burying the dead. That first phase involves providing medical attention, food, water, and mortuary services. Then, decision makers and first responders transition from the emergency to the recovery phase. A more sophisticated model might start with damage assessment and repair, move to infrastructure and public services recovery, then housing and social recovery, followed by reconstruction management and financing.[50] As the chapters that follow demonstrate, the realities on the ground in Tōhoku have been less clear.

We also slip into vagaries when talking about the status of recovery in areas affected by the 3/11 disasters. Visitors to certain metropolitan areas such as downtown Sendai might argue that Japan is doing well, as signs of distress or damage in that bustling prefectural capital are hard to spot. Alternatively, visitors to areas near the Fukushima Dai-ichi nuclear power plant would encounter towns that have progressed little, if at all, since the day of the earthquake and tsunami. Government officials in Tokyo would point to the forthcoming 2020 Summer Olympics and various other well-publicized sporting events as signs of resilience. Bureaucrats would enforce this sense of progress in reconstruction by highlighting the upcoming closure of various supplementary budgets dedicated to infrastructure rebuilding. But these rather casual methods of analysis overlook the fact that there is considerable variation in levels of survival and recovery.

Although some 18,400 people died, these lives were not lost primarily in the communities hit by the tallest and most powerful tsunami. In some communities struck by very high waves—such as Tanohata, which faced a 19 m (62-foot) tsunami—roughly 3% of the population died in the disaster. While tragic, Tanohata experienced a far lower death rate than many communities struck by lower waves. The places that experienced literal decimation of their population—with more than 10% killed, such as Rikuzentakata and Onagawa—faced waves nearly 7 m (20 feet) shorter than the maximum measured black waves. A number of communities in Tōhoku's hardest-hit prefectures of Iwate, Miyagi, and Fukushima had no casualties at all. So we cannot talk

CHAPTER ONE

about all of Tōhoku "doing well" or "doing badly" when the tsunami struck; the variation in mortality forces us to look more closely at patterns across the dozens of coastal cities and towns.

Further, long after the waters had receded and people began to pick up the pieces of their lives, recovery efforts across towns and prefectures did not show parity. The processes of moving people from temporary to permanent housing on higher ground, repairing gas and electricity lines, returning pupils to classrooms, and other steps in recovery have not moved in unison across Tōhoku. A handful of towns, such as Rifu and Fudai, completely restored infrastructure and opened schools within two years of the disasters. Other communities have rebuilt most homes, reopened schools and businesses, and restarted gas, electricity, and rail lines. In still other communities—especially those near the Fukushima Dai-ichi reactors—8-foot weeds grow out of cracks in unused roads while the roofs of blighted houses slowly sag to the ground. Ostriches, packs of boars, and other wildlife have become the only visible residents along deserted streets.[51] Journalists, animal rescue workers, and thrill seekers sneak into these ghost towns while security officers chase them away from the irradiated woods and valleys. Even cities farther out from the site of the nuclear meltdowns have not bounced back to pre-disaster levels of population, business, and civil society.

Some towns find themselves unable to kick-start their business districts or bring children back to local schools. Others have invested in expensive physical infrastructure—for example, by literally raising the ground using earthmoving machinery—to better prepare the community against future tsunami. Despite a variety of attempts to reinvigorate Tōhoku, local residents have rarely praised the recovery process, often feeling ignored and left out of decision making. Some communities were able to formulate and initiate their own recovery plans without support from prefectural or national authorities. Onagawa, for example, came through the recovery process without a seawall, an outcome matched by few other localities despite local opposition to the structures. Other cities and towns gave up when their creative attempts to carry out less standard approaches, such as building shorter seawalls than recommended by the government, were rebuffed.

These more nuanced findings about survival and recovery raise important questions about the political and social dynamics of disaster recovery. Why such a high percentage of residents were killed by the tsunami in some towns in Tōhoku, while others lost only a handful of citizens, is chief among them. In addition, it is unclear why some towns were able to quickly build temporary shelters, restart fish canning factories, and bring in new residents, while others continue to struggle. Understanding what allowed some survivors of the disaster to resume normal lives relatively quickly while others struggled with depression and mental illness is also critical.

Scholars of disaster have long tried to derive lessons from mass-casualty events and catastrophes and deduce laws for recovery by echoing the work of their colleagues in the biological and chemical sciences. Some, like Voltaire, began looking for patterns in these events as early as the mid-eighteenth century, when an earthquake and tsunami sacked Portugal. Experts began more systematic attempts at data collection with the massive Halifax maritime explosion in 1917 and have continued their efforts through recent North American disasters such as Hurricanes Katrina, Sandy, and Harvey. In trying to track such patterns, they have often focused on factors such as the power of the disaster itself, the strength of the physical infrastructure, gender and demographics in affected communities, leadership capability, economics and financial resources, and national culture. While some of these approaches have merit, others, such as studies of national culture, do not hold much water.

Intensive empirical studies have implicitly undermined many pearls of folk wisdom. For example, it is intuitive that a more powerful disaster (such as an earthquake that levels half a city) would create a slower recovery than a less powerful one (such as a tornado that damages a narrow swath of the countryside). But that has not been the case. Nor does having more money from public or private sources guarantee that neighborhood stores will resume business as usual and that residents will restart daily life quickly.[52] Nor is being wealthier or healthier a silver bullet to deal with the post-traumatic stress disorder, anxiety, and depression that often accompany survivors, including those evacuated from Fukushima.

Rather than relying on my impressions or the stories of a few survivors, this book uses qualitative and quantitative data to illuminate two critical factors during and after the 2011 Great East Japan Earthquake: *networks* and *governance*. These elements played essential roles at various levels of the recovery, from the individual to the global, and I follow the advice of those who have called for researchers to frame studies of disaster using local and government networks.[53] I designed this book with a multilayered framework, focusing on international, national, regional, local, and personal responses to and recoveries from the 3/11 events. Individuals and communities with stronger networks and better governance had higher survival rates and accelerated recoveries. In neighborhoods and towns whose residents had strong ties to one another and to decision makers, people worked together to push past bureaucratic obstacles and support innovative leadership. Less connected communities with fewer such ties faced harder recovery processes and lower survival rates. Such communities also found themselves in the iron grip of top-down, standardized recovery plans.

Networks

I use the term *networks* to describe connections between people, whether thin (as between people who may meet only occasionally, if at all) or thick (as between family, kin, and neighbors who have regular contact). Scholars have categorized such connections—also known as social capital—into three main types.

Bonding social capital is a horizontal connection between people who are quite similar. Friends who speak the same language, attend the same cultural and religious events, and share similar worldviews are connected via bonding social capital. So, too, are immediate and extended family members (even ones you'd prefer not to see). One scholar illustrated these thick bonds with the case of a neighbor who comes into your home without knocking and takes a soda from your refrigerator without asking. Maybe few of us have friends like these in the early twenty-first century, but the example illustrates the deep trust potential for such relationships. We would give such a neighbor a key to our home and ask her to watch our plants or pets when we are away. People who interact regularly over a shuffleboard court, share casual meals, compete over card games, and who feel a mutual sense of place, have higher levels of bonding social capital. They also have more trust in their neighbors and believe that the community can solve problems without involving a third party, such as lawyers or the police. Such kin and engaged neighbors might join an occasional community police patrol, help out on moving day, and pick up trash together at the nearby river or schoolyard. As chapter 2 shows, the relationship between Mr. Shimizutani and his wife—residents of the Arahama hamlet in Tōhoku—fits squarely in the category of bonding social capital. Higher levels of bonding social capital can help people recover from shocks and rebuild lives after a crisis.[54]

In contrast, those with lower levels of bonding social capital may not know their neighbors' names, play chess and *shogi* outside with community regulars, or leave their apartments for walks in the park.

They may not be able to distinguish the faces of strangers from those of the people who live next door. If a neighbor played music too loudly, they would call a security guard or police officer before or rather than speaking to the guilty party directly. If they had a disagreement with a business partner, entrepreneurs with shallow levels of bonding social capital might rely on lawyers, rather than the actual participants, to hash out a solution. Older men whom I encountered when visiting temporary shelters near the Fukushima Prefecture city of Minamisoma who rarely left their FEMA trailer–like shelters fall into this group.

A number of factors have been shown to undermine bonding social capital. High levels of ethnic diversity may create the perception, especially among older residents, that the neighborhood is unsafe, pushing them to hunker down in their homes. People who feel uncomfortable around people of different nationalities, races, or religions may avoid contact altogether. Alternatively, people in the community may be introverts and less interested in the company of others. Shut-ins, known as *hikikomori* in Japanese, may not even venture outside their homes to meet next-door neighbors or go shopping, instead relying on the internet to have goods and services delivered to them. Another explanation for low levels of connections may be negative interactions with authority figures, whether police officers or other first responders, that weaken residents' attachment to their community and their belief in its importance. It may also be that long driveways, high fences, and a lack of sidewalks have created a physical environment that makes interacting and creating thick social ties challenging.

Bridging social capital, which some have labeled a weak tie, involves horizontal connections between those who are dissimilar and only tenuously connected, such as through a shared interest in a social activity (e.g., a sports team, acting guild, or book club) or a common institutional affiliation (such as a faith-based group, school, or workplace). These ties bridge ethnic, religious, class, and caste differences. Weekend warriors who meet only to engage in paintball war or parents who catch up at monthly PTA meetings fit here. Similarly, a friend of a friend would constitute a bridging social tie. While "weaker" than bonding social capital, these kinds of ties can be very helpful during critical moments, whether trying to find a babysitter on short notice or learn about the best restaurants in a new town.

Hindu and Muslim communities in Gujarat, India, for example, that had set up bridging social capital to cross the ethnic gaps between them had fewer riots and less violence during contentious political periods.[55] When looking for that first job, we are much more likely to see success by talking with friends of friends and distant acquaintances than by searching an anonymous website or asking only our immediate family for help.[56] Survivors of the Great Sichuan Earthquake in China with broader *guanxi*—the personal relationships and social networks that help facilitate business dealings—had better recoveries than those with fewer connections.[57] After the 1995 earthquake, communities in Kobe, Japan, with higher levels of bonding and bridging capital restarted businesses and gained employment more quickly.[58]

Individuals with higher levels of bridging capital have many friends across industries and fields and are known to be "well connected." They also have access to more information, which increases their potential for finding creative solutions that come from outside their field. People with lower levels of bridging social capital may know only a limited number of colleagues beyond their immediate circle of friends; their news sources are limited to a small number of channels, and thus their perspective on solutions to pressing problems is more limited. Immediately after the 3/11 disasters started, the bridging tie between the Inagakis and their neighbors —as discussed in chapter 2—saved lives at a time of danger.

Linking social capital, in contrast to the horizontal ties laid out above, describes a vertical connection, such as that between a typical resident and someone with political power and authority. It might be a connection to the head of the regional Federal Emergency Management Agency (FEMA) office or the head of constituent services at an elected official's office. Residents may know their town's mayor through participating in a community workshop on zoning, or they may have the phone number or email address of someone working for an NGO or regional government agency from chance meetings at past events. Local government officials in Japan and around the world may be able and willing to reach out to powerful politicians or ex-politicians who can manipulate the levers of power (especially because research has shown that local residents tend to blame mayors when they suffer from disasters).[59]

These linking connections are harder to create and maintain, but they can provide strong benefits, primarily to the citizen.[60] While few citizens have elected officials on speed dial, these types of linking connections are critical to accessing resources and information that cannot be found locally. Indeed, as noted in chapter 3, the relationship between a powerful and well-connected local decision maker in a Tōhoku community I will call Coastal Town and members of the Cabinet helped the city acquire a windfall of money from the national government, expediting the rebuilding process.

INTRODUCTION

All three types of network connections and the trust that accompanies them are critical during and after disaster.[61] These types of social capital provide information, resources, motivation, the ability to work collectively, and a sense of belonging and well-being. While they are not a panacea, and also have a documented dark side,[62] these ties can provide assistance at pivotal moments throughout the emergency management cycle.[63] In the pages ahead I will provide real-life examples of how social connections made a difference to Tōhoku residents. Data on mortality rates, for example, showed that physical infrastructure systems such as seawalls and pine forests did little to save lives during the tsunami. Instead, social infrastructure—the ties between people living in the same community—measurably saved lives as the tsunami bore down on the coast. How did these connections make a difference at that critical moment?

People in Tōhoku communities with higher levels of trust and engagement worked cooperatively and collectively to rescue the elderly and infirm during the 3/11 disasters, often carrying the most vulnerable citizens to safety. Neighbors knocked on nearby doors and helped people to safety. As chapter 2 details, they extricated their neighbors from trapped cars as the water rose and provided them with food and water as they awaited rescue from official first responders. Some even carried elderly neighbors on their backs until they reached safer ground. People who felt connected to their neighbors and helped them went against the tsunami *tendenko* principle—the teaching that each person should flee for their lives rather than stop to help others. In some cases, helping out put the helper at risk, and some Tōhoku residents who went to the aid of family, friends, and neighbors paid the ultimate price for their altruism.

Conversely, residents who did not know if anyone lived next door, or had no friends in the neighborhood, were less motivated to seek out and offer aid to those in need of help. Those in towns and villages where trust was low and where fear of crime kept people inside during normal circumstances might not even think to endanger themselves to help someone living nearby. Then, when the waves receded, communities that could work collectively cleared roads for emergency vehicles, distributed food to the hungry, and self-organized to handle the ongoing crisis. Communities unable to mobilize collectively often sat waiting for help until the authorities arrived and then accepted direction from above.

We may believe that damage, wealth, and health would best predict the levels of anxiety felt by evacuees from communities near the

17

Fukushima Dai-ichi nuclear power plant. We could imagine that if we were facing an uncertain future, the dread of potential illness caused by radiation, and worries about our livelihoods, money, and well-being would reduce our anxiety. Wealthier or healthier people might be better able to feel confident about their futures and focus on immediate tasks at hand, such as completing paperwork for aid, finding a job, or setting up child-care arrangements. But that wasn't the case. Rather, strong social ties acted as a shield against such anxieties. After controlling for other factors that could influence their mental health, we found that evacuees from towns and villages near Fukushima reporting higher levels of connection to neighbors felt less stress and depression after the disaster.

Bonding social capital also proved important in maintaining and improving physical health after the catastrophe.[64] Individuals cooperating in group activities, such as small-scale urban farming and local knitting groups, showed better physical health during and after the crisis than similar individuals who did not venture out of their homes.[65] Connected individuals worked collectively to plan their futures and cheered on iconoclastic leaders with visions that challenged the central government's. These neighborhoods turned down government attempts to impose high seawalls, thought creatively about ways to bring back residents, and pushed for space to implement innovative rebuilding schemes. Individuals with high levels of social capital gave more aid and mutual help to others and in turn received more assistance to help them weather the crisis.[66]

Finally, given the importance of social ties, this book will also show how various interventions and programs can strengthen social networks. Far from being set in stone, our reservoirs of social capital can be deepened and broadened through deliberate effort. People who may have few friends or know only a handful of faces can become more social and develop a stronger attachment to place and neighbors. Such ties, though, can also be damaged by relocation and extended separation. When evacuees are resettled randomly, far from their old communities and from friends and family, they may prefer to hunker down rather than reach out. Thus the decision to place elderly evacuees in isolated areas, severing them from their connections, often worsened health outcomes.

Some residents of Tōhoku, such as those living in Ofunato, have created new community centers, such as the Ibasho project, led by elderly survivors, which provides communal spaces and events. As I will discuss in chapter 7, the Ibasho project has measurably broadened the social ties of local residents and improved their sense of efficacy—the degree to which they believe they make a difference. Other Tōhoku communities sought to maintain existing social ties by moving neighboring families together to new housing rather than assigning individuals and families randomly to temporary shelters.[67] A few evacuees created tighter bonds with their new neighbors in temporary shelters than they had back home.

Some towns and villages created programs in which locals with cars shopped for the elderly and infirm, building social connections and ensuring that people had access to important material resources.[68] Tōhoku communities have also created community garden projects to engage elderly residents of nearby temporary shelters; similarly, group farming projects such as Hamarassen Farm have strengthened bodies and minds.[69] Finally, disaster managers conscious of potential *kodokushi* (lonely deaths) worked to ensure that housing built for evacuees was no more than 1 km (0.7 miles) away from important network members and locations. Past disasters showed that many evacuees separated from friends, doctors, and family passed away because of this lack of connections even when in relatively safe accommodations. Network-focused urban planning made a difference in maintaining existing ties and preventing their disintegration post-disaster. Connections are one part of the survival and recovery equation; governance is the other.

Governance

Vertical social networks—the linking ties between local residents and those in the corridors of power in city halls and parliaments—overlap strongly with what political scientists call *governance*.[70] Many of us are vaguely familiar with the textbook descriptions of how states such as Japan and the United States are structured. The Japanese government, for example, consists of a unitary framework with three levels of actors in which the central government in Tokyo has final say in administrative matters and can overrule mayors and governors despite their elected status.[71] Some 1,700 cities, towns, and villages (*shi, cho, machi, son,* and *mura* in Japanese) sit within 47 prefectures (*ken*, similar to states in the United States or *länder* in Germany, which are run by governors). As with other advanced industrial democracies, the central government handles issues such as defense and diplomacy while local and regional governments handle day-to-day issues such as roads, education, garbage disposal, and police and fire services.[72]

Japan's prime minister heads the executive branch and the Cabinet and shares power with the National Diet (the bicameral national legislative assembly made up of the lower house, the House of Representatives, and the upper house, the House of Councilors) and the judicial branch (with the Supreme Court at the top). Japan has no equivalent to the American FEMA. Instead, during a crisis, the prime minister forms either a Major Disaster or Extreme Disaster Management Headquarters on an ad hoc basis, which is supported by the Disaster Management Section within the Cabinet Office, drawing members from the ministries.

The core ministries—most of which have branches throughout the country—include the Ministry of the Economy, Trade, and Industry, the Ministry of Land, Infrastructure, Transport and Tourism, the Ministry of Health, Labor, and Welfare, and the Ministry of Internal Affairs and Communications, and they sit at the top level of Japan's government. Japan created new national organizations, namely, the Reconstruction Agency (Fukkōchō) and the Nuclear Regulation Authority (Genshiryoku Kisei Iinkai, or NRA), after the 3/11 triple disasters to ensure better coordination between local authorities and national agencies and to provide tighter control over atomic energy. The national government, its ministries, and its agencies sit at the top, with the prefectures in the middle and the villages, towns, and cities at the bottom.

But the phrase *governance* moves beyond static textbook descriptions to capture the quality of formal and informal interactions at the local, regional, and national levels by which politicians and civil servants deliver services and make and enforce rules.[73] Governance measures citizen participation, feedback, and adaptive learning, along with flexibility,[74] fairness, and accountability[75] in decision-making processes.[76] Since the end of World War II, the Japanese political system has been undergirded by high-capacity horizontal and vertical networks. Horizontal connections stretch between local governments and civil society organizations such as unions, food and agricultural cooperatives, and religious groups in cities, towns, and villages. These ties allow people, as both citizens and consumers, to make their wants and needs known to politicians and agents of the government.

Vertical networks extend between these local government units and organizations and the regional (prefectural) and national (central) government agencies, bureaucracies, and politicians.[77] Such structures help the public sector deliver goods and services such as quality health care, education, and assistance in a timely manner to all who need them. Good governance means that citizens who need help paying their medical bills, whose children need special assistance in school, or who require housing aid will receive them thanks to the work of their local, regional, and national governments. Well-governed societies demonstrate flexibility and responsiveness while ensuring that roads and hospitals are safe and infrastructure up-to-date.

As even the best internally connected local communities lack the resources to rebuild infrastructure, medical facilities, and businesses from scratch following a major catastrophe, they need connections to regional and national institutions and agencies that can help. Post-disaster, Japanese prefectures are responsible for providing temporary housing, while local governments are in charge of public welfare and family and community support. The central government provides the majority of funding for large-scale public works projects such as seawalls, roads, dams, and ports.

Just as social networks can be strong or weak, governance varies across and even within countries. While Japan's local, regional, and national governments stand out among the advanced democracies in terms of transparency, responsiveness, and public goods provision, there has been great variation within its system, especially after the triple disasters. Strong governance involves local leaders, mayors, and governors who are motivated to serve the public and all of their constituents, not line their pockets or protect only those partisans who support them politically. When I lived in New Orleans during and after Hurricane Katrina, the arrest of local leaders such as ex-mayor Ray Nagin on bribery and corruption charges inflamed my already cynical perspective on the government's recovery efforts. While examples of poor governance and tone-deaf leaders abound during and after Japan's 3/11 disasters, some communities and elected officials have worked to create models of grassroots-driven planning and progress. Examples of strong governance include mayors who independently decided to evacuate communities and distribute potassium iodide pills to citizens living near the Fukushima Dai-ichi nuclear power plant without an official mandate to do so.

Good governance embraces politicians who reached out directly to multiple targets, including the national government, the international private sector, and civil society organizations, for assistance when the wheels of government bureaucracy turned too slowly. After the disasters, some local mayors, such as Minamisoma's Mayor Katsunobu Sakurai, used social media platforms like YouTube to appeal for help when they felt overlooked or ignored by the central government.[78] Some local bureaucrats also showed flexibility by providing services to evacu-

CHAPTER ONE

ees, even those not registered as residents in the town providing assistance.[79] Normally, access to services comes from proven registration, but sympathetic Japanese local governments provided medical care, school attendance, and financial assistance even to unregistered evacuees after 3/11.[80]

Local and regional governments in Japan stepped in to provide critical logistic and administrative support. Preexisting sister-city agreements, under which towns, cities, and villages from outside the disaster area assisted Tōhoku communities during the disaster, provided a great deal of aid.[81] After the 1995 Great Hanshin-Awaji Earthquake, which rocked the city of Kobe near Osaka in central Japan, Hyogo Prefecture moved to create reciprocal aid agreements with Hokkaido and other prefectures in case of a large-scale disaster. Other areas soon took on the practice, and 3/11 provided a broad-scale test of this framework. Yokohama, for example, dispatched local government personnel to Sendai, while Ebina, in Kanagawa Prefecture, sent many officials to assist the city of Shiroishi, in Miyagi Prefecture.[82] Even as of August 2018, employees of the Nagoya City Hall were working in Rikuzentakata. At one point, roughly 1 in 40 local government officials within Tōhoku were from outside the region, "on loan" from other cities and towns that had sent them over to help after the crisis. Sister cities also sent money and volunteers to Tōhoku towns and cities.

Further, some prefectures worked as bridges between domestic and even international organizations during the chaotic search, rescue, and recovery periods. Miyagi Prefecture, for example, began with more economic and political power, but also far outshone Iwate and Fukushima in its ability to connect to Japanese NGOs, bureaucracies, and even foreign governments. These broader connections helped the regional government carry out more focused, sophisticated, and expensive efforts to rebuild the lives of its citizens. Social network analysis data, as we will see in chapter 3, shows how the prefecture could serve as a node connecting various disaster relief and recovery groups from Japan and around the world that had rarely interacted face-to-face. Such connections showed Miyagi's superior governance and ability to serve its residents.

While the process of rebuilding is often frustrating, democratic governance requires that speed be sacrificed for local agreement, and that urban planners and government agencies relax expectations about pace to ensure that residents are part of the process. While some may be pushing to return to damaged areas immediately, well-governed communities can work collectively to plan for a future driven by residents, not professional planners. With middling or poor governance, decision makers ignore the voices and views of local residents and rapidly push a top-down, standardized agenda. Strong governance comes from town council members who change their political behavior after a disaster to better connect to political, administrative, and financial resources necessary for recovery. With good governance, creative systems are in place to assist disaster-struck communities that have lost many of their civil servants and bureaucrats. These systems might include sister-city partnerships in which towns in the affected areas receive help from pre-designated partners outside those areas.

The governance approach to disasters also looks closely at whether political representatives mirror the demographics and interests of their electorate. In the majority of Japanese political arenas, women are vastly underrepresented, and the post recovery process has been no different. Women may feel that their disaster-related issues, including radiation avoidance, health care for children and family members, and long-term medical surveillance are being ignored.[83] Disenfranchised by the system, they often engage in community and political affairs through other, often informal, channels.[84]

Further, networks and governance interact regularly. When unresponsive government officials overlook the desires and vision of local residents, they damage the trust that had sustained the vertical connections between them. Delaying the release of important information about levels of radioactivity, for example, hurt vertical relations between local residents and Tokyo's bureaucrats and politicians, as chapter 5 lays out. Because they believed that the Fukushima Dai-ichi disaster was being covered up, and were angered by the media's and TEPCO's refusal to recognize the events at the plant as a meltdown, many residents resorted to citizen science to get answers.[85] Engineers, coders, and Japanese residents across the nation created open-source repositories on radiation levels, which anyone could add to or analyze. Websites such as Safecast[86] have become the go-to institutions for accurate, up-to-date, and transparent data on radiation levels.

Bureaucratic insistence on standardized, cookie-cutter rebuilding solutions—such as re-creating or building the controversial seawalls along the coast—pushed many to dream of more creative, bottom-up ways to mitigate the dangers from future tsunami. Rather than rebar and concrete, a number of communities have sought to develop infrastructure resilience through strategic forest planting and innovative urban planning using railway lines and roads as buffers against future waves. Instead of building massive 14.5 m (47-foot) seawalls under cen-

CHAPTER ONE

tral government pressure, well-organized communities that benefited from responsive governance structures set up multiple lines of defense in ways that did not block gorgeous views of the ocean, kill off tourism, or impede fishermen who needed access to the water. While engineers may see these shorter walls as increasing risk for local coastal communities, residents view them as signs of successful citizen participation in planning.

A final type of governance structure that interacts with social capital is the clientelism still found in a number of policy spheres in Japan, including disaster recovery. Communities that have more long-serving representatives in the National Diet found themselves doing better than similar communities whose representatives had shorter tenure. The boons are not limited to incumbent politicians, however: a powerful ex-politician can continue to interact with colleagues in bureaucracies and large-scale construction firms, working to sway those organizations to the direct benefit of his hometown.

Similarly, ex-mayors, such as Otsuchi's Yutaka Ikarigawa, who resigned from their positions in disaster-struck communities but feel connected to the people there, continue to serve, using their resources and skills to help local people file their taxes and make their way through complicated legal appeals to the ministries. Other local leaders in communities such as the city I will be calling Coastal Town have reached out to contacts in the Cabinet Office and in neighboring countries to raise money for special reconstruction projects and ensure that already swamped construction firms take an interest in their constituents. Where strong social connections have saved lives and reduced anxiety, good governance has been able to create effective, bottom-up plans built on the visions of residents.

Structure of the Book

This book seeks to understand the processes of survival and recovery in social and political context. It explores a spectrum of actors from households to the national government. With multiple levels of players involved in the triple disasters, it does not make sense to talk about recovery at a single level. Instead, recovery as a society begins with the individual, taking place person by person, house by house, and neighborhood by neighborhood. Their choices build into and simultaneously depend on the choices made by towns and cities, then prefectures, and finally the national government. Local residents in a disaster-affected

INTRODUCTION

community may be waiting for trustworthy information from known sources before they make decisions about investing in rebuilding and return.[87] While central governments and regional decision makers can definitively declare a disaster over or encourage locals to return, residents look to people with whom they have interacted in the past before taking the plunge.

Each level has its own actors, governance structures, and laws. Whatever the level of focus, I weave together the factors of networks and governance throughout the analysis. Networks among residents and their fellows (horizontal) and between residents and decision makers (vertical) measurably influenced outcomes. Similarly, the quality and choices of leadership and the institutions and laws in place altered the trajectories of survival and recovery.

The choices and struggles of individuals in Tōhoku during and after the disaster are the foundation for the book, and chapter 2 seeks to capture some moments of their lives as they faced the unimaginable. Chapter 2 focuses on residents of Iwate, Miyagi, and Fukushima Prefectures, drawing on interviews with residents, NGO staff, and decision makers from across Tōhoku to understand both survival (and mortality) and recovery (and stagnation). Even relatively isolated individuals who had altruistic, involved neighbors found themselves being rescued from water-trapped cars and roofs, while those with a sense of community and place returned as quickly as possible to start rebuilding. Students from the high school in Taro, for example, carried the elderly on their own backs out of homes and shelters to keep them safe.[88]

After the disaster, some communities moved quickly to clear roads for rescue helicopters and food drops well before the arrival of uniformed personnel from the fire departments, police departments, or Japanese Self Defense Forces (SDF). In some cases it was a week before SDF troops arrived with food and up to three weeks before local residents saw the return of organized local government. In the meantime, many towns took care of their wounded and elderly, created latrines, distributed food according to needs, and self-organized governance systems to handle short-term needs. Most such individuals lived in larger political and administrative units and were embedded socially in their communities.

Chapter 3 moves up one level of analysis to the perspective of the village, town, and city. Some municipalities saw high levels of mortality in the tsunami, while others did not. Exposure to the coast, tsunami height, demographics, and other factors cannot explain these outcomes, but connections among locals can. Why a few cities rebounded

CHAPTER ONE

quickly from the event while others struggled to recover population and businesses is an equally important question. Some cities and towns had strong connections to powerful politicians or ex-politicians in Tokyo, ties that simultaneously embody governance and connections. With a shortage of construction firms and available labor, bureaucratic impediments to rapid zoning changes, and a variety of large-scale, top-down construction projects in the area, a deft political touch came in handy.

Town council members—a group typically overlooked by experts on Japanese politics—served as links between local residents and national-level politicians and bureaucrats. Whereas before the disaster, few council members had reason to reach out to agencies and Diet members, afterward, those in the most damaged cities and towns began doing so. Tōhoku's cities—even those with strong cohesion and vertical ties—still face devastating depopulation.[89] Their long-term futures remain grim and will depend heavily on the ability of their leaders to undertake creative and outside-the-box recovery strategies, and on residents who share strong mutual norms and broadly held visions of their futures.

These Tōhoku cities themselves are based in regional Japanese political units called prefectures, which are covered in chapter 4. Shifting one step up from cities, I use chapter 4 to investigate the three prefectures most affected by the 3/11 disasters: Fukushima, Miyagi, and Iwate (known in Japanese as the *Tōhoku sanken*). Some prefectures built strong social networks with external and domestic NGOs and organizations, which accelerated their recoveries; others did not. Fukushima, host of the Fukushima Dai-ichi nuclear power plant, continues to struggle. Choices made by administrators and politicians in Miyagi and Iwate Prefectures also influenced the trajectory of their recoveries. Prefectural administrators often made suggestions to local governments based on central government recommendations that they interpreted as mandates, narrowing the options for reconstruction projects and reducing local autonomy in the process. At this level of analysis, local social networks mattered less than prefectural governance.

The prefectures and cities I focus on throughout the book are illustrated by the map in figure 1.1, which highlights Fukushima, Iwate, and Miyagi Prefectures along with their towns, cities, and villages.

Chapter 5 steps one level up from prefectures and looks at the national context of the 3/11 triple disasters. This chapter focuses on the decisions made by the central government before, during, and after the disasters. At the national level, while the government was reasonably

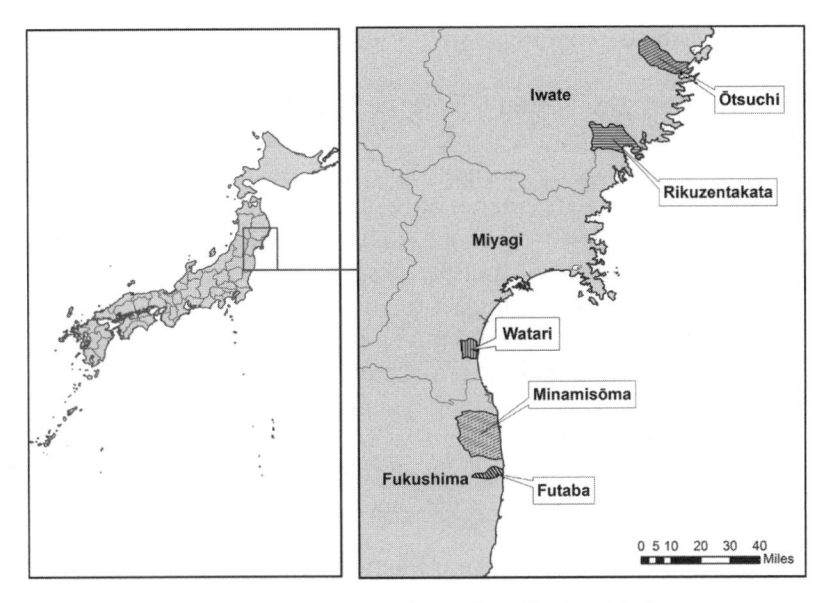

FIGURE 1.1. Map of cities and prefectures in Japan affected by the triple disasters.

well prepared for standard disasters such as earthquakes and tsunami,[90] it was not prepared for a nuclear disaster and lacked administrative resources, such as legal frameworks and knowledgeable personnel, to respond quickly and effectively. Further, choices made by government agencies, including the choice to withhold information about radiation exposure during the crisis and the choice to apply top-down, one-size-fits-all rebuilding frameworks, showed poor national-level governance. The government's seemingly arbitrary and capricious selection of acceptable radiation exposure levels rattled many from Fukushima and around the country.

Chapter 5 traces how the Japanese central government, which had long struggled to build trust with its people, retreated, despite an innovative start after the 3/11 disasters—including the creation of several new institutions that showed flexibility on certain issues[91]—to standard operating procedures soon after. While the central government handled reconstruction elements involving large-scale projects well, such as the removal of debris and the building of seawalls, it has faltered on issues of societal trust and permanent housing. Similarly, scholars have pointed out that Tokyo performed ably in areas where it had established institutions for handling the disaster and recovery processes, but in new issue areas—such as dealing with a nuclear melt-

27

down and the decontamination process that has followed—it showed ineptitude.[92]

Chapter 6 leaves behind a domestic focus to place the experiences of Japanese residents in a global context through data gathered from crises in China, Haiti, and India, among other nations. This chapter shows the power of governance at the international level. Despite the challenges to governance laid out in chapter 5, Japan's track record of representative democracy, transparency, and spending on social safety nets helped mitigate the impact of the 3/11 disaster. Other nations without such policies have fared far worse during similar disasters. I use a dataset on disaster deaths from around the world, along with case studies of disasters in developing nations, to illustrate the safety nets and protection systems in place that helped Tōhoku residents facing the triple disasters. Residents of countries with more democratic and responsive systems have better outcomes than those in more repressive and closed ones.

I conclude the book in chapter 7 with concrete policy recommendations for residents, NGOs, and policy makers in Japan and around the world. Drawing on the experiences of residents, cities, prefectures, and the national government, I use this chapter to illustrate how Japan's experiences can inform and assist other vulnerable communities around the world. Building on the calls of those who have advocated for developing both "disaster culture" and "disaster institutions,"[93] I provide residents, NGOs, and governments with specific ways that they can improve resilience using both bottom-up and top-down approaches. Rather than hoping that physical infrastructure will buffer future risks, vulnerable communities can take control of their futures and invest in social infrastructure and programs that deepen social ties and enhance resilience.

TWO

Individual Level: Neighbors Saving Lives

Mr. Shimizutani,[1] a spry and spirited man in his late 60s, was puttering in the living room of his compact home mid-afternoon Friday, March 11. He and his wife lived in a wooded area near the small Shinto shrine that he managed in the Arahama area outside the center of Miyagi Prefecture's Watari village. The flat patchwork of small farming plots sits just 2 km (1.2 miles) west of the ocean. The couple was home that afternoon when the earthquake struck at 2:46 p.m. Almost all Japanese residents experience dozens, if not hundreds, of minor earthquakes during their lives. Most temblors end quickly, in less than a minute, and are little more than nuisances. But this one was different, he said. As the violent rocking stretched on, and more and more household items and books fell from shelves, Mr. Shimizutani and his wife tried to hide under their dining room table. They managed to squeeze only their heads under it because—as in many Japanese homes—piles of goods and books stored there took up all the space.

This chapter investigates the survival and recovery processes at the level of the individual. Following the 3/11 earthquake, some Tōhoku residents evacuated their homes to seek higher ground, while others stayed in place or were slow to leave. How people survived the tsunami—the most severe physical hazard they faced in the triple disasters—depended on a combination of chance, choices, and connections. Many survivors, especially the elderly and

CHAPTER TWO

infirm, survived because of their strong links to neighbors and kin. Some, like Mr. Shimizutani, were able to get through the catastrophe because they were physically able and followed authorities' instructions. Others required strong social connections to individuals willing to put themselves in harm's way.

Escape from the Tsunami

Once the shaking subsided, Mr. Shimizutani went outside to begin cleaning up the shrine. "Right after the earthquake, and I believe it was the same for everyone else, all of the household goods were scattered about. I was cleaning up the mess, and right after that the television shut down; it made a noise like *'putsun.'* After I tried to clean up inside the house, I went outside. I am the priest, so I was worried about the shrine. When I saw the copperplate roof of the hand-washing station outside had collapsed like *bam*, I thought to myself, 'This is something very serious,' and I went immediately to the shrine, and cleaned all the scattered festival material."

The Shimizutanis were among the more than 8.7 million households that lost power following the earthquake. Like the majority of Tōhoku households, the Shimizutanis received information about the initial stages of the disaster primarily from television (and not from other sources such as mobile phones or social media). With the power out, the family's portable battery-operated radio soon began to broadcast calls to evacuate the area due to an impending tsunami.[2] The first two appeals for evacuation didn't alarm Mr. Shimizutani or his wife. Earthquakes in Japan regularly trigger tsunami warnings from the JMA. Some past warnings had proved to be false alarms or, if accurate, announced tiny tsunami that had no real impact on the area. But after the third call from authorities, he and his wife quit their cleanup attempts and got in their car to drive to the nearby Takaya elementary school, the designated evacuation area for several local hamlets outside the main town area. Like some 80% of people interviewed in a study of Tōhoku disaster behavior, the Shimizutanis were well aware of the location of their nearest evacuation shelter.[3]

Sometime around 3:00 p.m.—hardly 15 minutes after the shaking had started—the Shimizutanis found themselves at the school with about a hundred other dazed-looking residents. From the raised grounds of the school, Mr. Shimizutani gazed toward the ocean and saw what looked like a cloud of sand in the distance. Other survivors described the tsunami as looking like a *tsuchikemuri*, a cloud of dust, or a thundercloud, or a mist.[4] Some thought that the white disturbance they saw in the distance was smoke from a fire.[5] It took Mr. Shimizutani a moment to recognize that what he saw was in fact a tsunami.

Realizing the size of the tsunami, the teachers in charge at the Takaya elementary school feared they weren't safe at the present location, and they briskly told the evacuees to leave their cars and possessions behind and head to higher ground, at the Watari elementary school. It was cold, and Mr. Shimizutani considered disobeying the instructions and returning to the school to reclaim and drive his car, but he stayed with the group during the hour-long trek to the second shelter. "I think it would have been better for us to use the car to evacuate, since we would've gotten there faster, and it would have prevented us being outside in the cold weather. And the cars left at the Takaya elementary school were ruined by the salt water. We went to retrieve our cars two or three days later, and although the engine was able to turn on, all the cars were pretty badly ruined. But the people who were giving the evacuation orders were probably trying to avoid confusion and panic by making us leave our cars at the schoolyard." Not everyone listened to orders to avoid using cars for evacuation.

En route to the new evacuation site, Mr. Shimizutani and the other evacuees saw the Abukuma River swelling within its low earthen banks, and he realized the seriousness of the situation. Throughout Tōhoku, numerous inland communities located several kilometers from the coast nonetheless experienced massive flooding when the tsunami swept up rivers and streams. Many houses outside the boundaries of Watari sat close to the river; as Mr. Shimizutani passed them, he noticed that many residents seemed to be watching the water rise rather than fleeing. As his walk dragged on, Mr. Shimizutani began to realize that those who had not heeded the evacuation order might now be dead.

During his interview, Mr. Shimizutani speculated about a number of reasons why people may have ignored the order to evacuate. Some lived along embankments that had proved to be sufficient protection in past tsunami—which had been only centimeters tall. Some said they couldn't leave because they were waiting to join up with family. A neighbor he passed on the road while evacuating told him, "I still have my grandson who's not back from his daycare, and we can't evacuate without him." Others seemed surprised that he took the order seriously, asking, "Are you really going to take shelter in the elementary school?" They implied that sheltering in place would be a better option.

CHAPTER TWO

After an exhausting trek, Mr. Shimizutani, his wife, and their group arrived at higher ground, where they waited out the tsunami in safety. Mr. Shimizutani and his wife survived because they were able-bodied, had access to evacuation information, and moved quickly despite ignoring the first requests to evacuate. While the car they abandoned at the Takaya elementary school turned into junk, and while it took several days to clear the debris from their home and shrine, they managed to save the *omikoshi* (portable shrine) to use in local festivals. Mr. Shimizutani learned later that 25 people from his community were washed away in the tsunami.[6] Mr. Shimizutani's evacuation involved little obvious assistance from others, such as neighbors or friends, and his story might be similar to those of many younger and healthier residents along the coast.

Mr. Tanaka, a retiree in his early 60s, lived with his wife, daughter, and elementary-school-aged grandson in a coastal village in Miyagi Prefecture, just a bus ride away from the Shimizutanis. Mr. Tanaka had been relaxing at home when the earthquake struck. Once the shaking ceased, he turned on the television to try to get information about what had happened. But a flash of insight stopped him: his fourth-grade grandson was at the nearby elementary school. Without pausing to clean up, Mr. Tanaka drove to pick up his grandson, joining a group of anxious parents and caregivers who sped to the area to find their children waiting outside at the school's playground. Relieved, Mr. Tanaka collected his grandson and returned home.

Mr. Tanaka's relief was short-lived as he parked his vehicle and began getting out. His grandson more quickly leapt from the car and chanced a look down the street toward the downtown area. The young boy began screaming, "The tsunami is here! The tsunami is here!" Mr. Tanaka believed that those screams from his grandson may have saved the lives of neighbors. "The neighbor living behind my house heard my grandson scream and he escaped to higher ground. We met a few days ago and talked about how we were glad to see each other alive. And I told him my grandson's name and our story, and he told me that my grandson's yell helped him escape. Without it, he would have not known about the tsunami."

Still halfway in the car, Mr. Tanaka shouted for his wife, daughter, and grandson to run up to the second floor of their home. But he faced a daunting challenge: an earlier handicap had left his legs severely weakened, and he walked with a cane. He knew he would not be able to climb the stairs to the upper floor quickly enough. He decided to chance it in the car, and he sped away toward the main street some 400 m (1,312 feet) away. As Mr. Tanaka drove down his street, he passed a number of people watching the rising tide from nearby embankments and homes. Mr. Tanaka tried to warn them to flee. "From the car, I told those people, 'What are you doing! The tsunami is coming!' And I said, 'Hurry and run!'"

As he approached the main street, Mr. Tanaka's car was swept up in the rush of the tsunami. "The car I was riding in, the car floated, and it was washed away, like it was being pulled. And, during the time I was riding in the car, if I was to say which emotion I felt, I felt fear. It is because all the wood, like pine trees, and more and more debris, were smashing the car over and over again. I had no words. But I used to work where a lot of crisis management was involved, and I also had training, so I knew I wasn't supposed to panic, and I decided to let the tsunami carry me away."

As his car was pulled along with other debris, Mr. Tanaka realized he was floating past the local village administration office and that the employees inside might see him. Mr. Tanaka tried waving to get their attention, but did so cautiously, out of fear for upsetting the balance of the floating vehicle and capsizing. Later, he met some of the civil servants who had seen his car as it was caught by the tsunami. "They said when they were watching me wash away in the car as the tsunami came, they saw me wave my hands, and they knew I wanted help, but there was nothing they could do. They said all they could do was to watch in that situation. They said they were not expecting to meet someone who was washed away like that. Some of them were crying and talking through their tears."

Mr. Tanaka forced himself to be calm as the tsunami carried him away. "It was more of a 'I don't care what happens' way of thinking than feeling of calmness. I had emergency training and learned never to panic. That was stuck in my head. I was thinking that I will deal with this situation calmly. And wherever I end up is where I'm destined to go to. If I'm still alive by then, then everything is OK. And if I die . . . if the car couldn't withstand the tsunami, then that is the end to my life."

Mr. Tanaka's car floated like a leaf on the water, washing some 2 km (1.2 miles) away from his home, eventually getting stuck in the debris from a collapsed hotel near the Jōban railway line. Trying to remain still, Mr. Tanaka turned on his portable radio as three cycles of waves washed around his impromptu life raft and then pulled back. The car

CHAPTER TWO

held fast beneath the wooden beams, household debris, and floating garbage, but Mr. Tanaka could not get out of the car. He had brought his cell phone and found the network was still operational. "My cell phone had reception till the next morning. And I was able to contact my daughter. My daughter told me her location and cried on the phone as she heard my voice, since she was able to find out that I was alive." While for the first hour or so the insides of the vehicle were dry, water slowly began to trickle inside. Wearing waterproof boots, which were now sitting in rising water inside the vehicle, he did his best to sit upright and avoid tipping the car or splashing water on his clothes. Sleepy, but desperate to stay awake in order to avoid hypothermia, he spent the night nodding off, upright inside the trapped car.

Around 5:30 a.m. on Saturday, March 12, the morning after the tsunami, help arrived. "Near the area where I was stuck, actually on the house right there, I saw a nearby homeowner but I forgot his name. He was there with his son, and he yelled, 'Is there anyone in the car?' And I replied, 'Yes there is. Please help me!' He said, 'All right, I will help you so hang in there.' He brought hammers and other tools to break the windshield for me to escape as the doors wouldn't open. And since I had spent the night focusing on staying calm and awake, I was very tired. I became very sleepy. And the person who came to help, he thought he had to break the glass. But I owned the car, so I was kind of hesitant about the idea of breaking it open. I asked if they were able to move the debris and the beer case near the door which blocked my exit. And they did, and the door opened."

Mr. Tanaka asked his rescuers to call the authorities on their radios, and by 11:00 a.m. Saturday morning three local firemen showed up. "They figured it would be very difficult to get me to walk, so the firemen carried me on their backs, switching the role between the three of them and carrying me all the way to the nearest road where there was no flooding. From there, they drove me on the fire truck to Yoshida elementary school, which was the evacuation spot. And that time, my body was very cold. I was very cold, until next morning." A physician from Yamashita treated Mr. Tanaka at a makeshift clinic for hypothermia and exposure. Without the firemen to carry him, and the neighbors who noticed him trapped in the car, things could have turned out very differently.

Mr. Tanaka wasn't the only person in his family whose life was saved by others during the tsunami. Back at his home, Mr. Tanaka's wife, daughter, and grandson spent an anxious night in beds on the second floor, unsure of the fate of their patriarch and of what would happen to them in a cold, dark house without water, power, or heat. Japan's Self Defense Forces (SDF) began sending helicopters to the area to try to rescue residents, as local roads had been washed away or were covered in debris and impassable. Roughly 70% of victims of the triple disasters received assistance via the SDF over the first month after 3/11.[7] Yet the troops initially overlooked Mr. Tanaka's family waving and signaling from the house, and the helicopter passed by to search for survivors elsewhere.

Within hours, a neighbor who had found another way into their block on foot came around to check on the home and found the family. The neighbor used his still-working cell phone to contact the SDF helicopter search party, which soon returned and rescued them.[8] The actions of the homeowner who saw Mr. Tanaka trapped in the car certainly saved his life; sitting in water in his car, afraid to move for fear of upsetting the vehicle, he faced hypothermia and exhaustion. Further, without the assistance of the neighbor who contacted the authorities to pick up his family, they would have been stranded without food, water, or electricity.

Mr. Inagaki, a farmer in Nishikigura in his late 70s, had been working in his greenhouse sowing carrot seeds when the earthquake hit. He first tried grabbing on to the structure to stay upright, but as the shaking continued, he lay flat on the ground. Like a number of other evacuees interviewed about their experiences, he was not immediately aware of the impending tsunami and did not hear any sirens, cell phone warnings, or radio announcements. "I knew the disaster prevention alarm was announcing something, but other noises interfered, and I couldn't catch the announcement at all."

Mr. Inagaki, like Mr. Tanaka, is unable to walk without assistance, and he stood up and slowly used his walker to return to his home. He and his wife went inside, unsure what to do. Then, his sister, who lived nearby, arrived. "The one person who came to my house was my sister, and she told me, 'Brother, we have to evacuate.' And I told her, 'I'll catch up later so you go on and escape on your own,' and let her escape before me. And then, young officers from the neighborhood association (*chōnaikai*) came to my house and told us to evacuate. They were standing in front of our entrance telling us to evacuate. And that moment, I saw in front of our house, around 150 meters ahead, a lot of water running through the area carrying cars and many other things."

After this first view of the impending tsunami, Mr. Inagaki and his wife—like Mr. Tanaka—decided to escape via car, but soon after they closed the doors and tried to drive off, they were caught up in the tsunami. The car floated only a short distance from their home and stopped when it hit the side of their home, trapping the couple inside. "We tried to break the car's window, and we tried so many times, but the window wouldn't break. I tried hitting it with my normal cane, but it didn't work. But we also had an aluminum cane, so we used it to break the car window." The car began to shake, and the Inagakis feared it would float farther away or overturn. "I got my hand out and, and grabbed on to the pole of the greenhouse and the line, there is this line that connected with a solid anchor, and we attempted to wait until the strength of the flowing water decreased." After an hour the water subsided, but the car wouldn't start, and the electric windows were stuck. The water had either short-circuited the electrical systems or choked the tail pipe. In any case, the car was dead, and they were trapped inside by the debris.

The Inagakis faced cold and isolation trapped in their vehicle and feared drowning or injury from the water and debris outside. But an officer from the neighborhood association—one of the same men who had originally told them to evacuate—soon spotted them as he patrolled the neighborhood looking for those who needed help. The young man had climbed a stack of debris to reach the roof of the Inagakis' house. "This young man saw us from the roof, and he came down from there, and carried us both on his back from the car and helped us. We were saved because there was a third person, but if there were only the two of us, then we might've not been able to make it, for sure." Carried into the house, Mr. and Mrs. Inagaki moved up to the second floor to escape the water pooling on the first floor. They spent a difficult night there without power, gas, or water, but had the company of their rescuer.

The next morning, SDF troops came by, and the young man asked them to call in a helicopter, which arrived by midday. Mr. Inagaki, his wife, and the neighbor were taken to South Miyagi Medical Center in Ōgawara, where they were treated by doctors. All recovered fully. Mr. Inagaki later learned that three people in his neighborhood died during the tsunami.[9]

These three individual stories of evacuation during the tsunami drive home several key points. First, many people across Tōhoku did not immediately evacuate after the massive earthquake, for a variety of reasons. Some did not register the possibility of an impending tsunami despite warnings across a variety of channels, including television, radio, mobile phones, and loudspeakers. The elderly and those with disabilities may not have had cell phones or other means of accessing information after their power failed. Others expected a milder tsunami that would come very quickly; when 30 minutes passed without a tsunami, they assumed it wasn't coming.[10] Many residents did not evacuate because they believed that the various physical infrastructure protections in place—including massive concrete seawalls, earthen berms, and pine forests—would protect them. Some residents may have returned to their homes for belongings or gone to check on family members rather than following the *tendenko* approach, fleeing without delay. Those who evacuated immediately had a much better chance of surviving the event; only 3% of residents who immediately left Rikuzentakata, for example, died, while nearly 29% who did not leave died in the wave.[11]

Second, among those who recognized the imminent danger of the tsunami and wanted to evacuate, many needed physical assistance to do so safely, whether they left immediately or later. A survey of more than 4,200 people in Tōhoku found that 60% of elderly and disabled people did not immediately evacuate to shelters after the earthquake. Of those who required help, roughly one-third said that they could not leave because they did not have assistance; another third said that they did not receive sufficient information to decide what to do.[12] A smaller study of Tōhoku residents with disabilities found that the majority of those who survived did so because they received direct help from institutions, neighbors, or family.[13] Connections to neighbors and friends were a critical resource for those unable to escape by themselves.

Third, despite standard evacuation procedure, which instructs residents not to flee by car, many people used private automobiles to try to escape the flood. One survey found that in Iwate, 43% of respondents had used a car to evacuate; in Miyagi, 63%; and in Fukushima, 84%.[14] An observer in Otsuchi stated, "The majority used their cars in order to flee from the tsunami. . . . [W]e can surmise that many of those who remained stuck in the crowds of stationary cars were engulfed by the waves."[15] Evacuating by car presents a number of connected hazards, including traffic jams and the possibility of the car being overturned by the tsunami itself.[16] A number of communities reported gridlock, cars becoming stuck or being washed away, and car accidents that compromised the ability of people to flee safely and efficiently.[17] In two of our narratives, residents who chose to flee by car

CHAPTER TWO

became trapped in their vehicles and survived only because of the altruism of neighbors.

Finally, these stories underscore the critical role played by family, neighbors, and NGO members in the initial period after a crisis. Individuals who needed assistance—whether they needed to be freed from a vehicle or given information about what to do—looked to other people, not websites or social media, especially among the elderly. Neighbors, family members, and volunteers delivered information, helped victims out of their vehicles, arranged for them to be taken to shelters, and went house to house searching for trapped neighbors. Local volunteer fire corps, known as *shobo dan*, assisted the elderly, shut tsunami gates, rang fire bells, and carried the helpless to safety.[18] By contrast, it took hours or even days longer for the SDF to reach affected residents across Tōhoku via helicopter. Local social connections proved critical during the Tōhoku tsunami itself and also during the process of providing more shelter.

Evacuation

The scale of the evacuation following the March 11, 2011, triple disasters was massive. More than 470,000 people left their homes across Tōhoku after March 11 due to the earthquake, tsunami, and nuclear meltdowns.[19] Some 321,000 evacuees—some 70% of the total—remained outside their original homes by December 2012, most still in temporary shelters and hotels or with friends and family.[20] For example, evacuees in Iwaki, in Fukushima, which accepted residents displaced from cities near the nuclear power plant, faced an extended stay at schools and public halls; many were still stuck there a full year after the disasters.[21] More than two years after the tsunami, as of September 2013, 290,000 people were still in temporary shelters.[22]

After fleeing their homes, many evacuees first moved into designated emergency shelters, as seen in the three narratives above. Most residents sought shelter at their local public schools, but others ended up at shelters in private buildings run by faith-based organizations such as the Buddhist religious movement Soka Gakkai, which set up cots or sleeping bags in its facilities.[23] Still other evacuees headed to the homes of friends and family who lived outside the affected areas.

Emergency shelters at schools, public halls, and government buildings provided no privacy and little in the way of creature comforts. Evacuees often slept on blankets or futons directly on the floor, with only crude cardboard dividers or polyester curtains to separate their space from their neighbors'. This lack of privacy especially affected women, who could not access "private spaces where they could change their clothes or breast-feed their babies."[24] Observers pointed out that relatively easy fixes could create temporary shelters that met the specific needs of women.[25] Shelters could provide separate rooms for breastfeeding women, supply feminine products in restrooms, and work to create spaces where women would feel safe and be free from harassment. Food, especially in the weeks following the event, was scarce. Evacuees were often provided just small balls of rice and bottled water once or twice a day;[26] more nutritious fare, such as fruits and vegetables, was unavailable. Most emergency facilities had few, if any, showers and no public baths nearby.

Very few displaced people moved from their homes directly into a residence where they would stay for an extended period. Instead, most evacuees moved multiple times over the first week or two, while others continued to move over the first few years. One 50-year-old woman from Miyagi Prefecture, far from the nuclear accident, moved four times during the first year after the earthquake. She spent five days at her designated evacuation center (a local school), then five days with a friend, roughly four months at her brother's home, and then a year and a half in a prefabricated temporary housing unit.[27] One researcher reported that 80% of the evacuees he interviewed had moved more than three times in the first six months after 3/11. That was on the low end of the spectrum. Another study found that some Tōhoku residents changed evacuation centers and living spaces more than ten times over six months.[28]

Prefectural authorities—legally responsible for providing temporary accommodation to residents displaced by disaster[29]—followed Japanese precedent in designating schools and community centers as short-term solutions. This was not only because evacuees needed more permanent, homelike accommodations, but also because those facilities had regular uses. Government officials hoped to reopen schools, city halls, and other community centers for normal operations as soon as possible, and the hundreds of evacuees housed in each building made such plans challenging. But the demand for more permanent shelters—such as prefabricated temporary homes or public or privately owned apartments—was higher than the supply. Vacant private apartments in rural areas were few, and there was a delay as prefabricated shelters were built.[30] In disasters, the central government provides a subsidy of up to ¥2.4 million (some $29,000) per emergency shelter provided by local governments. This subsidy covered the cost of the modular, FEMA trailer–like structures used most commonly by Tōhoku municipalities, but would not cover the far higher costs of more permanent, higher-quality housing.

As temporary or permanent housing gradually became available, some local bureaucrats used a lottery system to decide which evacuees would move out of emergency shelters first, despite a directive from the Ministry of Health, Labor, and Welfare that said that people from the same neighborhood should be kept together when relocating to temporary housing.[31] By using a lottery to determine when evacuees entered available permanent housing, authorities cut residents and children off from their friends and communities.[32] Randomly placed in the first available housing, sometimes far away, these evacuees had no one nearby whom they knew or could rely on for help. In short, dispersing evacuees through random relocation reduced social ties and safety nets, especially for the elderly who lacked vehicles and broader mobility. A study in 2018 identified roughly 240 people who died lonely deaths, or *kodokushi*, because they were separated from family, friends, and community by relocation after the tsunami.[33] In contrast, some local governments tried to keep neighborhoods, or at least groups of three to four households, together. Displaced residents who were kept together with others from their immediate communities through group relocation experienced more socializing and participation in civic and neighborhood events.[34]

Many extended families that had previously lived together in a single home were split up during the evacuation and rehousing periods. As one study of the relocation reported, "Nearly 30 percent of families who originally lived together were separated by the earthquake. Especially large families with three or more generations were affected with nearly half experiencing separation."[35] Households with two adults served as the model for technocrats designing temporary housing frameworks. Larger families had to split into groups to fit within the cramped temporary accommodations. For example, grandparents who had lived with their adult children and grandchildren were sent to separate housing units, often far away from those family members. One study of eight villages and towns in Fukushima found that only half of the families that evacuated areas near the nuclear power plant were able to stay together in one household. In many areas, larger families had to split into two, three, or even four different households, depriving many of their core social support at a time of crisis.[36]

Many families with small children decided to leave Tōhoku completely out of concerns about space, radiation exposure, and long-term safety; therefore, many of those left in shelters and temporary housing were the elderly and those without jobs or immediate family. Studies of communities in Tōhoku showed that adults with children showed a stronger desire to relocate from disaster-affected communities than similar adults without kids.[37] Over time, the proportion of temporary prefabricated shelters occupied by the elderly has increased as those with young dependents and employment have moved elsewhere.[38]

The nuclear accident made evacuation and rehousing especially challenging for those in Fukushima. Residents faced tremendous uncertainty in the initial days and weeks after the triple disasters, which was compounded by contradictory and shifting information. Interviews with officials from five town governments near the stricken nuclear power plant showed that only two of them ended up receiving official evacuation orders from the central government as the meltdowns unfolded. The other three officials learned of the ongoing disaster via television news and had to make their own determinations about what to do.[39] Younger Tōhoku residents and concerned observers turned to social media, especially Twitter, to try to lobby authorities for assistance and to get information to those who needed it.[40] But few of the middle-aged and elderly people with whom I spoke relied on social media during or after the disaster. Many instead relied on community radio or emergency FM radio transmitted by 30 *saigai* (disaster) radio stations across Tōhoku, which were slower to update information.[41]

Some 110,000 people across 12 cities, towns, and villages in Fukushima had to relocate as a result of the evacuation orders.[42] But it took more than a month after the meltdowns for the central government to set up three official evacuation zones around the nuclear power plant. The zone closest to Fukushima Dai-ichi encompassed the area within a 20 km (12-mile) radius around the plant; neighborhoods within it were "evacuation designated areas" due to high radiation levels. All residents in this zone had to leave, and entry—except perhaps for hour-long visits arranged later—would be forbidden for years to come. No one could live or work in these areas, which included the towns and villages of Futaba, Namie, Tomioka, and Ōkuma. The next zone encompassed communities 20–30 km (12–18 miles) from the plant, which were labeled "emergency evacuation preparation areas." These areas— such as Minamisoma and parts of Kawauchi—were seen as facing up to 20 millisieverts (mSv) a year in cumulative radiation exposure, and while evacuation was strongly encouraged, it was not initially required. (A 20 mSv annual dose is the international limit for those who work with radiation.) Residents of this zone were encouraged to stay inside and be ready should they need to leave at the government's request, which came later. The final zone set up by the government involved certain towns and villages greater than 30 km (18 miles) from the plant, which were labeled "deliberate evacuation areas." These areas included Katsurao, whose residents were given up to a month by the government to settle their affairs and leave their homes. The government canceled evacuation orders for this zone—the farthest from the plant—by September 30, 2011, allowing residents to return.

The government used concentric circles drawn on a map to set up these zones to keep residents from what officials saw as the most critical risks. Yet residents in some communities, such as parts of Minamisoma, were told to evacuate even though they were farther away than the 20 km specified by the central government. Further, residents in areas located outside the three official evacuation zones, such as those in Iitate, discovered that they nonetheless faced high levels of radiation exposure. By 2016, the Reconstruction Agency had given the zones slightly more optimistic names,[43] and by 2018, Tokyo had relaxed entry and visitation requirements for some towns (e.g., Iitate, Namie, Hirono, and Kawauchi), lifted the evacuation orders for others (e.g., Tomioka and Naraha), and promised return for still others (e.g., Ōkuma) by 2020.

Many residents in Fukushima felt left in the dark about the accident due to a lack of detailed information about the ongoing meltdowns and levels of radiation exposure. Few felt they could make informed decisions about evacuating (and, eventually, returning) because the Japanese government did little to guide them. This was despite attempts by Japan's foreign allies to provide it with helpful information for affected citizens. Within days of the nuclear meltdowns, the United States had generated detailed radiation maps of the nearby areas using sensors on its military aircraft and shared them with Japanese nuclear agencies, including the Ministry of Education, Culture, Sports, Science and Technology, or MEXT.[44] The US-made maps showed that towns and villages such as Iitate, 25 km (15 miles) northwest of the nuclear plant, were squarely in a plume of radioactivity producing a dangerous 125 microsieverts (μSv) per hour. Spending eight hours in such a location would expose someone to the annual permissible dose of radiation. Yet local, regional, and national authorities neither publicized the maps nor used them to evacuate residents being exposed to high levels of radiation.[45] After waiting several days with no action from the Japanese authorities, the US government publicly released the data on March 23.

Japanese government authorities had other ways of mapping potential radiation exposure for Fukushima residents through the Nuclear Safety Division of the MEXT's System for the Prediction of Environment Emergency Dose Information (SPEEDI) computer system. SPEEDI, first introduced in 1993, used information about wind patterns, particle release levels, and other data to try to estimate exposure levels across areas.[46] The system cost some ¥13 billion ($120 million).[47] But again, Japanese bureaucrats did little to provide information from SPEEDI in a timely or useful way to local residents. The Nuclear and Industrial Safety Agency (NISA), the regulator for nuclear power plants at the time of the disasters, did not provide information from SPEEDI to the public or residents of potentially affected communities, even though it sent data to officials in Fukushima Prefecture as early as March 12, 2011.[48] Media reports claimed that prefectural bureaucrats in Fukushima received SPEEDI files and then deleted them.[49] Initially, bureaucrats responded to criticism of their failure to help inform residents with the dubious claim that the radiation exposure information was lost due to power failure across the area.[50] Others, such as Deputy Chief Cabinet Secretary Tetsuro Fukuyama, argued that the desire for accuracy—rather than swiftness—led to slow releases of information from the government.[51]

Such post hoc excuses did not survive deeper scrutiny. Referring to the radiation maps available through SPEEDI and the US government, the head of MEXT's Science and Technology Bureau admitted some four years later that "there was no thought of taking advantage of the offered data for resident evacuations."[52] Goshi Hosono, special adviser to the prime minister, later explained that authorities deliberately held back information on radiation from the public "to avoid panic among the population."[53] One study concluded that the withholding of information about the Fukushima Dai-ichi meltdowns was actually due to "elite panic,"[54] not inflated worry among the public.[55] Politicians and bureaucrats feared what would happen should they provide accurate and up-to-date information to residents. In several Fukushima towns, including Tomioka and Kawauchi, mayors moved ahead to voluntarily evacuate their villages by March 16 rather than waiting for clear information and orders from prefectural or national authorities.

TEPCO itself did little to assuage concerns that local residents were not in the loop. For months, the company refused to describe the events at Fukushima Dai-ichi reactors 1–3 as meltdowns, instead proffering the more ambiguous phrase "core damage."[56] The Japanese media followed TEPCO's lead for months, preventing the public from understanding the seriousness of the accident.[57] TEPCO eventually recognized the events as meltdowns on May 12, perhaps because the foreign press covering the story in Japan had quoted experts who had been using the more accurate phrase for some time. Only in December 2011 did the Japanese government and TEPCO acknowledge that they had underplayed the severity of the event.[58]

Other events convinced local residents that TEPCO was not consistently sharing information and warnings. Several stated that Fukushima evacuees with relatives or friends who were TEPCO employees received private warnings on their cell phones on March 11 advising them to leave the area. These evacuees left their evacuation centers, "pulling away quietly to Niigata or Yamagata Prefectures."[59] Watching a neighbor of hers sneak out of the Futaba evacuation shelter after receiving a phone call from a friend who was a TEPCO worker, one resident told a researcher, "After she left, I realized that her house had been completely destroyed by the tsunami and so it was impossible for her to go back home. Then, I understood that she did not want to tell me that she was actually fleeing from the town. I felt I was going crazy with fear when I saw people sneaking out of the evacuation center in the middle of the night, one by one."[60] TEPCO's refusal to share these warnings more broadly no doubt harmed trust among local residents.

Further, because of concerns about the health effects of potential radiation exposure, evacuation procedures were often rushed and poorly planned.[61] The initial moves out of Fukushima homes were often rapid ones, and evacuees had little time to prepare themselves or think through which items they could take in the single bag or suitcase they were allowed. As new information on radiation plumes came in, some who fled their homes during the initial evacuation had to evacuate a second time when it was discovered they were still in danger of exposure. For example, some 2,200 residents from Futaba fled on March 12 to Kawamata, approximately 40 km (25 miles) away from the plant. But with local levels of radiation rising, about half of these evacuees then moved again, to Saitama Prefecture, 200 km (124 miles) away.[62]

Residents in the town of Namie, which was less than 4 km (2.5 miles) from the nuclear plant, evacuated to a shelter thought to be sufficiently distant from the danger outside the 20 km perimeter. Yet less than a day later, officials urged them to move farther to the village of Nihonmatsu, located 50 km (31 miles) from the plant. Within hours of arriving, they were told to move yet again due to prevailing winds that were blowing radioactivity into the area. Similarly, Tomioka residents first moved to Kawauchi, some 30 km (18 miles) from the plant, but were then forced to move again to Koriyama, which was 60 km (36 miles) from the plant.[63] Because of such relocations, Fukushima residents moved an average of nearly five times between the 3/11 events and 2016.[64] The mayor of Futaba moved with 1,200 evacuees from his town five times; the group eventually settled in classrooms and gyms in an unused high school in Saitama Prefecture, where people lived 10 to a room. As space became available in government-run public housing nearby, evacuees moved out to more permanent shelter.

While younger residents may have been able to handle the stresses of constant relocation, elderly and vulnerable populations suffered measurable health consequences because of them. Many of the Fukushima-based hospitals and nursing homes within 20 km of the nuclear accident evacuated their patients the evening of March 13 and the morning of March 14. Often placed by themselves without accompanying medical personnel, these elderly patients suffered trauma and lost access to care due to the panicked move. A number of those patients were left in health-care offices for up to 24 hours without heaters or medical supplies before being admitted to hospitals outside the area.[65] Patients farther away also faced health consequences from rushed evacuations. According to one study, many patients died as a direct result of the evacuations.[66] Authorities classified these evacuation deaths as "mental and physical fatigue from moving to shelters" or "mental and physical fatigue from life in the shelter."[67] For example, nursing home residents some 20–30 km (12–18 miles) from Fukushima Dai-ichi were initially told to shelter indoors. However, the government then designated their zone as an area that needed to be ready to evacuate due to the ongoing radiation leaks from the plant. Rather than staying in the area, which was permitted under the government order, many nursing home managers decided on their own to evacuate their patients. The multiple evacuations that followed, as the patients were moved from place to place, took their toll on the residents.[68] Studies have shown that many patients died as a result of the stresses suffered during the evacuations themselves rather than from any radiation-related maladies.[69] Scholars estimated that between one and two thousand elderly evacuees died because of the shock and rush of their unnecessary evacuations.[70]

For Fukushima residents who evacuated to areas outside the prefecture, prejudice and misunderstandings made their lives harder. Observers reported that cars with Fukushima Prefecture license plates were denied service at gas stations and hotels in other prefectures.[71] Displaced children also faced bullying in their new schools, ostracized for being "contaminated."[72] One 13-year-old boy who had evacuated with his family to Yokohama said that "many times, I wished to die" due to the bullying he faced while in his new school.[73] A classmate told a child evacuated from Fukushima, "You'll probably die from leukemia soon."[74] One 9-year-old girl told her mother that she did not want to attend the new school she had moved to in Tochigi Prefecture because the other students had told her to stay away.[75] Others have spoken of engagements broken off by men from outside the area because of concerns about the health of the brides, who were from Fukushima.[76]

In a 2013 documentary, a mother living in Date, a town in Fukushima, told an interviewer that even an NGO that offered evacuees a short vacation made them feel like they were lepers through its exhaustive list of precautions they would have to take to spend time at the retreat.[77] The instructions included bagging all textiles, such as bedding and clothing, they brought with them from their homes in Fukushima. Some evacuees mentioned they stopped telling people they were from Fukushima and told their children to lie about their origins. More than two-thirds of evacuees from Fukushima remained within the prefecture after the evacuation,[78] probably due to a combination of connection to their hometowns and financial incentives provided by the government, but also because of concerns about discrimination. In an attempt to bring wary students and their families back to Fukushima, local schools have offered free lunches and after-school lessons, and proof of decontamination.[79]

Further complicating the evacuation, the central government divided evacuees into two groups: people from evacuation designated areas (often referred to as "forced evacuees") and those who "voluntarily" evacuated. Residents within 20 km of the nuclear plant who had no choice but to evacuate due to government orders received different benefits than those who lived outside the 20 km radius and left because of health or livelihood concerns. Some 40,000 to 50,000 people voluntarily left areas that were not evacuation designated areas.[80] Forced evacuees received greater benefits and compensation if they stayed within Fukushima Prefecture instead of departing for other prefectures. For example, forced evacuees who stayed in the prefecture were offered financial assistance with temporary housing, medical services and radiation scanning, and recovery housing help. On top of those benefits, the government provided forced evacuees (whether they stayed in the prefecture or not) with decontamination assistance, some compensation, and eligibility for designated temporary housing.[81] Thus government officials built incentives to keep Fukushima residents local after the disaster.

But voluntary evacuees—sometimes referred to as *jishu hinansha*, or self-evacuees—who lived beyond the 20 km zone received little, if any, support from the government.[82] In many cases, voluntary evacuees were mothers who fled with their children while their husbands remained in Fukushima to work.[83] Some faced accusations of abandoning or running away from their families, particularly by Fukushima kin into whose families they had married. Relatives labeled these wives disloyal and overly sensitive. "Every time I go up to visit my hometown in Fukushima for a funeral or a traditional holiday, I'm always asked the same question by my relatives," one woman said to a reporter. "'When are you moving back home?' they ask. 'It's safe now.' The relationship I have with my family has become distant."[84] Another woman cried continuously when speaking of the dissolution of her marriage; her husband insisted on staying in Fukushima, but she was anxious over the health of their only child and separated from him to move with their daughter to Tokyo.[85]

Nonetheless, for those who have left, new social networks, new jobs, and distance from the nuclear site have created feelings of connection and a sense of belonging to their new homes and communities. A recent survey of more than 3,000 ex-Fukushima residents in 2015 found that roughly two-thirds of them did not desire to return. Fewer than 20% indicated that they hoped to return to Fukushima in the future,[86] and that number has decreased as time has gone on. Across the board, the number of people indicating that they do not plan on returning to towns near Fukushima Dai-ichi has increased each year.[87]

Life in Shelters and Temporary Housing

Prefectural and local governments worked to set up temporary housing units across Tōhoku as required by law.[88] Locating shelters and temporary housing on or near the coast meant that evacuees and survivors had to live in landscapes of devastation. Entire neighborhoods of homes and businesses had been wiped out, and many residents were still missing. Downtowns were often covered in piles of debris and rubble. Some communities lost 80% of their infrastructure and capacity, leaving no open businesses, gas stations, child-care centers, schools, or city halls nearby.

In this environment, the quality of life in emergency shelters depended on a combination of social networks and self-governance. For example, for three weeks following the disasters, the city of Otsuchi had no working local government and few, if any, professional first responders to handle medical emergencies. Yet in cohesive, mobilized communities, local residents organized the distribution of food, water, and heat and even the delivery of supplies from outside agencies.[89] Local social networks substituted for more formal medical and social welfare organizations in communities with high cohesion and trust. In Otsuchi, local residents self-organized to handle all of the community's needs, including food, water, and medical care provision. They retrieved the bodies of victims and even created an emergency helicopter landing pad using available heavy machinery. With bulldozers and backhoes, local construction workers created a place where SDF and private helicopters could land to pick up the most critically wounded and deliver supplies.

As one resident told a researcher, "We decided to set up the Emergency Council by ourselves. If we had not done that, if we had waited for help from the authorities, then nothing would have been accomplished."[90] The collective action they were able to achieve because of their social cohesion showed through in a number of their activities. For two nights after the tsunami, Otsuchi residents believed that thieves had been breaking into homes, ransacking valuables, and removing whole safes. They set up a checkpoint at the entrance to the neighborhood of Kirikiri to ensure that only residents and authorized responders entered the area. Residents also created a community patrol. Later, they worked with a donor to set up a gender-segregated community bath, a critical resource in an area where there was no running water for two months. These residents had built trust and cohesion well before 3/11, working together on volunteer projects, cleanup days, and school sports days to create connections.

Despite stereotypes of group-oriented harmony and avoidance of conflict in Japan, not all short-term shelters and communities self-organized and demonstrated social cohesion. Shelters where individuals did not have strong social connections beforehand found themselves unable to effectively create leadership and committees to run things smoothly.[91] One volunteer who worked at such a shelter said that "it was remarkable how much of a selfish attitude the people there had. People were just concerned about their own survival. I saw that several times. In a state of panic, people just seek self-protection. But then I also saw things that went beyond that, people fighting."[92]

A lack of trust in others spilled into interactions with outsiders; in some cases, volunteers trying to bring in food or use kitchens were yelled at by locals. These residents, fearing that nonlocals were using up scarce resources, pushed them to stop. Within shelters lacking strong social cohesion, evacuees argued over who deserved aid. "When someone from a partially destroyed house came to an evacuation center to get food and relief items, the evacuees in the center openly complained that the person did not have the right to receive assistance because her house was not completely destroyed."[93] Without ties to bind them and smooth over differences during a period of high stress, individuals who had no home to return to saw those with still-standing houses as less worthy of assistance.

Despite massive challenges and traumatic conditions, some communities rallied collectively to restart the rhythms of a normal life. Local communities wanted to reopen schools as soon as possible; in Otsuchi, one school opened on April 21, 2011, even while evacuees still bunked in the facility's gym and classrooms.[94] By putting children back in the classroom, the town provided parents with a chance to work on rebuilding their homes and lives and also restored a sense of normalcy to the children. Despite the reopening of schools, many observers worried about the clear negative impact of the events on local kids.[95] Some Tōhoku schools had nurses who could look carefully at children for stress symptoms and evidence of mental illnesses such as post-traumatic stress disorder (PTSD), which manifested, according to some reports, in as many as 30% of children.[96] Nurses could quietly pull such children from group activities to counsel them and work to restore normalcy.[97]

As survivors sought to piece together their lives in emergency shelters and temporary housing, they simultaneously struggled to deal with the psychological consequences of the disasters. Mental health experts have stressed the importance of psychological first aid after a major crisis, urging "an empathic and pragmatic approach to assist persons in distress to stabilize and begin their own practical and emotional recovery."[98] One 64-year-old survivor revisited the site where his home used to be, but said he could not go twice. "When I come here, I see all the faces of the people being washed away, every single one of them, my neighbors, my friends. I can't shake them."[99] For some, the desire for closure after the tsunami became intense, especially the families and friends of the more than 2,500 victims whose bodies still have not been recovered. A handful of survivors in the town of Onagawa, for example, have learned to scuba dive in order to search for the remains of their loved ones. Some of them have entered deep, dangerous waters hundreds of times looking for wives and daughters who disappeared during the tsunami.[100]

While the most obvious psychological shocks involved the deaths, disappearances, or injuries of family and loved ones, long-term evacuees also had to face uncertain futures as well as losses of their homes, property, and livelihoods. Additional sources of worry included survivor guilt and anxiety about radiation. For example, studies done the year after the triple disasters revealed that some 81% of residents in Tōhoku feared radioactive contamination.[101] When asked about the reasons for their anxiety, Fukushima evacuees focused on three main causes: economic reasons (losses of jobs and livelihoods), uncertainty (not knowing if they could return to their pre-disaster lives and homes or would face health problems in the future from radiation), and a loss of social networks (loss of neighborhood connections, friendships, and community groups).[102] Similarly, the mayor of a town in Fukushima mentioned four main reasons for delays in returning to the area: anxiety about long-term exposure to low-level radiation, lack of accessible infrastructure such as medical facilities and shops, lack of employment opportunities, and concerns about quality of education.[103] One-quarter of respondents in Fukushima said that they had lost their jobs following the disasters, while two-thirds reported a loss of or decrease in income.[104] These concerns and worries had measurable health effects on the population. Among some 200 patients admitted to the Tōhoku University Hospital after 3/11, more than 25% had generalized anxiety disorders, and more than 10% showed symptoms of PTSD.[105]

Mental anxiety, distress, and depression were quite high among evacuees and especially high among those from Fukushima Prefecture. One research group, which carried out five surveys of more than 500 Fukushima evacuees between March 2012 and March 2015, found that PTSD symptoms surfaced in about two-thirds of the population within the first year after the nuclear accident. The percentage of those with PTSD symptoms shrank to about half of the respondents by 2015.[106] In a study of student mental health three years after the tsunami, 10% to 40% of health teachers surveyed indicated that their students had not adapted successfully to the disaster. Some pupils manifested these behavioral changes through truancy, while other teachers saw increased obesity, injury, and stress.[107]

Our own studies of the mental health of evacuees from towns near the nuclear plant showed that they had far higher levels of anxiety than is typical in modern Japan. Further, their depression and mental health issues were worse than for other evacuees from Tōhoku who had lived through the trauma of the earthquake and tsunami, but not a nuclear evacuation. That is, the nuclear disaster added a more serious

INDIVIDUAL LEVEL

level of concern and dread than was found in those surviving the crises of the earthquake and tsunami.

In 2013, my Japanese colleagues and I surveyed evacuees from the village of Futaba, one of the communities that hosted the Fukushima Dai-ichi nuclear power plant and which had 7,000 residents before the disaster.[108] Futaba, like Ōkuma, Namie, and other nearby towns, was evacuated soon after the 3/11 disasters. The Futaba city government operates out of Iwaki, overseeing some 3,000 people from Futaba who have resettled there, 70 km (44 miles) away from their hometown. We measured levels of anxiety and depression in over 580 respondents using the Kessler 6, or K6, survey, which asks six simple, easy to understand questions such as, "Over the past month, how often have you have felt nervous? Hopeless? Unable to get out of bed?" We then aggregated responses to the six questions—each of which could score a maximum of four points—into a single score with a maximum of 24 points. Most Japanese people (and people from other advanced industrial democracies) in normal situations have scores in the lowest range of the scale, between 0 and 4.

Across Japan, roughly 68% of respondents have scores in this lowest range, from 0 to 4. Around 18% have scores from 5 to 9, 7% from 10 to 12, and fewer than 3% above 13. In Futaba, fewer than 25% of the residents reported anxiety and depression at the lowest measurable levels. Some 15% had scores in the highest range on the K6 survey, that is, higher than 15. Figure 2.1 illustrates the stark differences in mental health between Futaba residents and Japan as a whole.

Recognizing that a comparison between those in Futaba and in the rest of the country may be like comparing apples with oranges, we then looked at the anxiety levels of those who faced the nuclear meltdowns, earthquake, and tsunami compared with those who experienced only the earthquake and tsunami. Figure 2.2 shows that residents of disaster areas that did not face radiation exposure had lower levels of anxiety and depression than those that faced the nuclear disaster as well. In the towns of Yamada and Rikuzentakata, which were devastated by the tsunami but relatively unaffected by the nuclear disaster, residents had higher levels of anxiety and depression than respondents from Japan overall. Ex-Futaba residents, however, displayed higher mental distress levels than evacuees who suffered through the earthquake and tsunami but not the meltdowns.

Survivors' financial concerns were compounded by the gaps between insurance and compensation and the actual costs that evacuees faced.[109] One Onagawa resident, for example, received ¥10 million

Japan and Futaba (2013)

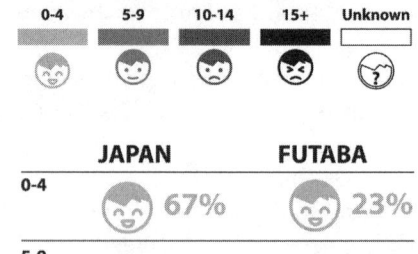

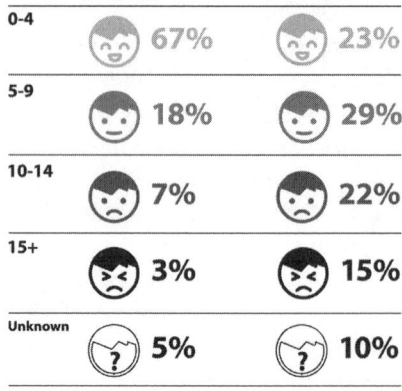

	JAPAN	FUTABA
0-4	67%	23%
5-9	18%	29%
10-14	7%	22%
15+	3%	15%
Unknown	5%	10%

FIGURE 2.1. Comparison of mental distress between the general Japanese population and Futaba evacuees after 3/11. Higher numbers indicate higher reported levels of anxiety and depression on the Kessler 6 (K6) survey. (Data from Iwasaki, Sawada, and Aldrich 2017.)

Level of Mental Health

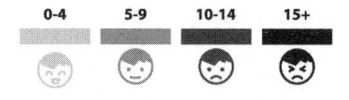

	RIKUZENTAKATA	YAMADA	FUTABA
0-4	59%	55%	26%
5-9	29%	29%	33%
10-14	7%	8%	17%
15+	6%	7%	24%

FIGURE 2.2. Comparison of mental distress between Futaba evacuees and residents of other Tōhoku villages (Rikuzentakata and Yamada) that experienced the 3/11 earthquake and tsunami, but not the nuclear disaster. Higher numbers indicate higher reported levels of anxiety and depression on the Kessler 6 (K6) survey. (Data from Iwasaki, Sawada, and Aldrich 2017.)

(roughly $94,000) in compensation for the property he left behind within the contaminated zone in Fukushima, but his new house was projected to cost ¥26 million ($245,000).[110] The gap between compensation and actual costs was only one of a set of financial challenges facing evacuees. Many of them had to negotiate with banks unwilling to let them stop payments on damaged or devastated properties still under mortgage.[111] Residents in many areas had to borrow money from municipal authorities to make ends meet, adding to their strains.[112]

Survivors of the earthquake, tsunami, and/or nuclear disaster altered their outlooks and daily behaviors, focusing less on the future and more on the present.[113] Scholars studying past catastrophes have observed that people who have experienced harm to themselves or their property become more focused on the present and tend to discount the future.[114] This shift can have significant short- and long-term consequences. For example, disaster survivors may be willing to take smaller government and insurance payouts immediately, rather than waiting for larger payouts in the future. Further, survivors may engage in riskier behaviors, focusing on short-term pleasure and ignoring long-term detriment. These behaviors and decisions could manifest because, having faced a deadly risk and prevailed, survivors see themselves as lucky or invincible. Or they may experience anger, guilt, and depression, which can reduce their concern about hazards and risks and the future. Scholars observed such changes in risk behaviors of Tōhoku disaster survivors: men (but generally not women) became more risk tolerant. In their daily lives, male survivors from Tōhoku three years after the triple disasters were more likely to engage in behaviors such as drinking, gambling, and lack of exercise than similar males who had not experienced such stress.[115] Risk behaviors such as heavy drinking, engaging prostitutes, and gambling had broader social consequences. One local observer described the social scene after the disaster: "We've watched families break apart. Domestic abuse is on the rise too, it's just a mess."[116]

The next stage of recovery—moving from emergency shelters into temporary housing units—brought additional social, emotional, and physical health problems. By the end of 2011, most evacuees had moved out of public emergency shelters, such as gymnasiums, schools, and shrines, into temporary housing (*kasetsu jutaku*) set up by local and regional governments. The temporary houses were typically prefabricated rectangular boxes with little to no insulation, as they had to be cheap enough to fit within the ¥2.4 million (some $29,000) subsidy range set by the central government. (Americans might recognize them as cousins of the FEMA trailers that dotted the landscape of New Orleans after Hurricane Katrina.) Tōhoku residents described them as uncomfortable year-round: cold in the winter and hot in the summer.[117]

In interviews, residents said that the thin walls and close proximity to neighbors made them refrain from engaging in marital intimacy. One year after the disasters, a journalist described life for one survivor: "These days, Mr. Sasaki wakes up every morning in a room the size of a parking space inside a prefabricated home provided by the government. His father sleeps in an adjoining room, separated by a curtain."[118] While existing laws stipulate that temporary housing is intended to be used for up to two years,[119] decision makers have admitted that a lack of permanent housing options means that many evacuees will continue to stay in these less-than-optimal homes far longer. Fukushima Prefecture, for example, extended the initial two-year deadline for occupying temporary shelters to March 2017,[120] and site visits to the area showed many displaced residents still living in them in summer 2018. Some towns, villages, and cities, including many in Fukushima, have not been able to forecast when local residents will be able to leave temporary housing complexes for permanent ones.[121]

City planners struggled to find sufficient space for thousands of these structures outside city cores, which were often clogged with piles of debris and massively damaged infrastructure. Typical locations for these FEMA trailer–like modules included school playgrounds, vacant lots on the periphery of towns, and unused agricultural land. The government provided more than 52,000 prefabricated housing units; most were made from aluminum, but about a quarter (13,000) were constructed from wood. But some local communities sought to build alternative, more localized, communal shelters instead of housing people in prefabricated, anonymous boxes. In the city of Soma, in Fukushima, for example, local communities pushed to create cooperative housing units with shared food preparation, eating, and interaction areas along with space for volunteers to stay in. These wooden shelters provided a feeling of more permanence than the flimsy aluminum prefabricated modules. Prefectural governments also paid the rent for some 67,000 normal apartment rental units occupied by evacuees; these survivors avoided the strains of the standard prefabricated units.[122]

The vast majority of the temporary shelters were far from the original clusters and neighborhoods where their residents had lived in their hometowns and original villages. Few downtown residents of Tōhoku cities, for example, could move into temporary shelters in the city core. The placement of temporary shelters in remote locations had a measurable effect on the residents, especially the elderly and infirm. Research showed that in cities such as Rikuzentakata, elderly evacuees placed in shelters more than 1 km (0.7 miles) from stores, bus stops, medical offices, and other places of interest were far more likely to remain homebound.[123] Residents saw walking farther than that as a strain, so rather than continuing their past practices of walking to visit friends, stores, and doctors, they hunkered down at home instead. By placing the shelters in convenient open locations rather than in the heart of urban communities, authorities inadvertently further isolated their occupants during a period of strain and trauma. Scholars have underscored that residents of temporary housing units in Tōhoku faced physical deterioration and health risks due to a lack of physical activity.[124]

Studies of other post-disaster recoveries have similarly emphasized that distance to facilities constrains feelings of recovery and resilience. When new housing sits far from business, recreation, and social facilities, communities participate less in communal life and see diminished recoveries.[125] One Tōhoku woman in her 70s spoke about living alone, without a car, some 500 m from the nearest neighbor. The nearest grocery store is 15 km away, and even the closest convenience stores are a 30-minute walk for her.[126] These distances make interactions unlikely and increase the social isolation of those in already poor conditions.

One door-to-door survey recorded responses from more than 4,100 households in Ishinomaki about their social conditions while living in temporary or rental housing units after the disasters. Interviewers who asked about their social interactions found that men over the age of 65 who lived alone were the ones most likely to have little or no contact with family, friends, or neighbors.[127] Such social isolation can have serious consequences. As one survivor in Rikuzentakata said, "When you're alone with your thoughts, it never goes in the right direction."[128]

The disasters ended the normalcy of life for many Tōhoku residents. For example, as of 2017, some 75% of men over the age of 65 were not working (compared with 59% of women), despite the fact that many had at least part-time jobs before the disasters. And, as discussed earlier, the process of evacuation and finding temporary housing broke up many families, especially those from rural parts of Fukushima, where extended families were common. Middle-aged women have demonstrated higher anxiety and concern, which may be attributed to a lack of people to talk with and reduced opportunities for physical activities and participation in community events. More than half of women surveyed in damaged areas of Tōhoku reported going out less frequently, with 18% going out less than once per week (compared with a national average of 8%). Further, the majority (close to three-quarters) quit hobbies and personal activities after the earthquake.[129] A 52-year-old woman who formerly lived in Iwanuma talked about her feelings of helplessness when she went to visit her old, devastated neighborhood of Hasegama. "I was filled with extreme anxiety, thinking, 'How will I live from now on?'" she said.[130]

With many survivors struggling with depression and anxiety, suicides rose in the area. While overall suicides throughout Japan as a whole were down in the year 2011 (fewer than 30,000 nationwide), Tōhoku-based suicides in May 2011 were 20% more frequent than in the year before (a two-year high). The suicide rate in Miyagi Prefecture rose 39% over that in the previous year by June 2011.[131] The National Police Agency reported that some 68 people ended their own lives in Fukushima Prefecture by May 2011, up from 19 in May 2010. Many of the cases connected to losses of agricultural livelihoods became widely known. A cabbage farmer from Fukushima hanged himself some two weeks after the 3/11 events.[132] A dairy farmer in Soma, Fukushima, left the message, "If only there weren't a nuclear power plant."[133] In 2013, TEPCO settled with relatives of a farmer after he hanged himself from a tree in a vegetable field when authorities banned the shipment of Fukushima farm products.[134]

Workers at the Fukushima Dai-ichi nuclear power plant faced a particularly complex set of stressors, ranging from work-related anxiety to social backlash from community members who blamed them for the disaster.[135] TEPCO officials nevertheless encouraged employees to volunteer in towns near the plant to help improve the company's image and attempt to start rebuilding trust with locals. Many company employees plucked weeds from abandoned gardens, cleared brush, and removed snow from temporary shelters to help portray the company as a positive contributor to the area.[136]

While there are tremendous psychological strains on survivors and TEPCO personnel alike, social connections play a significant mitigating role in reducing mental strain. Using the data that we collected on Futaba residents, we looked into the factors that might help mitigate the very high levels of anxiety and depression captured by the Kessler 6 questions. Initially, we believed that wealth and health might reduce these and other signs of poor mental health. Perhaps having a more solid financial base would erase some of the worries about the future and about the potential need for medical assistance. Being healthy, we speculated, might also serve as a buffer against worry. But the data did not support these suppositions. Instead, after controlling for factors such as age, sex, and other demographic characteristics, we found that having more neighbors and friends reduced measured reported signs of depression, anxiety, and PTSD significantly. Specifically, individuals who still had more than eight contacts from their old communities had far lower levels of anxiety than similar individuals with fewer such connections.[137]

Further, social connections can help survivors make positive choices. Individuals' decisions to reenter the workforce after the disaster, for example, were driven by the choices of their peers and neighbors. Many nuclear evacuees faced anxiety about the future, did not know when they could return to their homes, and were also receiving regular compensation payments from the authorities. With monthly payments coming in and jobs relatively scarce, their incentives to return to work were low. Evacuees from Fukushima received approximately ¥1,000,000 (some $9,500) per household in April 2011 and then another ¥300,000 ($2,800) per person in July 2011 from TEPCO. These payoffs were followed by monthly payments of ¥100,000 ($945) per person per month until evacuation orders are lifted. In a study of some 558 individuals randomly assigned to temporary shelters, scholars found, after controlling for a number of potentially confounding characteristics, that those who were placed near peers who returned to work were more likely to do so themselves. That is, members of networks who worked had a positive influence on other members, perhaps through sharing information or changing norms and expectations about work after crisis.[138]

A final way in which social ties assisted as survivors moved from emergency to temporary shelters and then to more permanent housing was through volunteers. In the two months after the triple disasters, some 300,000 volunteers came into the area to assist through disaster volunteer centers, NGOs, and NPOs.[139] By the fourth month, nearly 500,000 had registered as volunteers.[140] Many outsiders spent time with survivors, assisting them with menial chores (such as clearing out mud from damaged homes and cleaning photographs) or helping with routine household activities (such as shopping and washing clothes). Others worked with children to ensure that they had time and space to play. Some volunteers helped assemble or maintain the temporary shelters while others provided entertainment, dancing, and physical activities for the elderly. Such contact, while irregular, provided human interaction for evacuees who otherwise might have had little. Further, research showed that individuals who were supported by others were more likely themselves to volunteer and help.[141] Whether short-term

Returning Home

In the town of Rikuzentakata, where 10% of the population was killed and 80% of businesses washed away, a baker named Masayuki Kimura was willing to return to the destroyed area to bake sweets, breads, and snacks for his community. He returned cognizant of the fact that turning a profit was unlikely and that his startup costs would be high. Rather than returning because of his love for the business or because he had no other options, he moved back to his hometown because of his personal ties to the area. Kimura had saved his own life and that of his mother by evacuating to higher ground soon after the earthquake struck. From a hilltop nearby, they watched as their home and bakery shop were destroyed; the tsunami, as high as 14 m (46 feet) in some places, swallowed much of the city of Rikuzentakata.[142]

The $370,000 worth of business loans that Kimura had taken on before the disaster remained, though, and he considered leaving the area to start afresh elsewhere. Had he left, he would have been among many making similar choices; more than 1,200 people had left the city to move elsewhere by the end of 2011.[143] The costs of returning to start up a business in a tsunami-affected municipality were obvious. Beyond the financial costs of re-creating the bakery, Kimura and other would-be returnees faced opportunity and psychological costs. There was little chance that many of his old customers would be there to purchase his products. And much of the town he would be moving to was a wasteland of rubble and cranes.

Despite the tremendous psychological, opportunity, and financial costs of returning to their homes, many Tōhoku residents, at least initially, stated that they wanted to return. In one survey some two years after the disaster, 70% said that they loved their hometowns, 65% expressed a connection to their land, house, and ancestral graves, and 45% said that they wanted to participate in the recovery process with neighbors.[144] Feelings of connection to Fukushima areas were typically strongest among the elderly who had lived there the longest and who no longer had younger children with them. "The young people have already given up on Namie," one elderly women reported. "It is only the old people who want to come back."[145] As we shall see, social ties worked both ways after the disasters. Nostalgia and years of interaction with neighbors drew elderly residents back to their damaged Tōhoku hometowns. But new social ties and the chance to build connections kept others interested in staying in their new homes, even in temporary shelter communities.

The Fukushima town of Hirono provides additional insights into the decisions made by survivors following the triple disasters. Pre-3/11, Hirono had a population of 5,500, and jobs with TEPCO at the nearby Fukushima Dai-ichi nuclear power plant provided a major source of income. In a relatively small study of 30 people done shortly after the disasters, 70% of respondents planned on returning to Hirono. But as of 2015, only half of the community had returned. By mid-2018, the number had barely risen, as just 2,900 out of 5,490 residents had returned home.

One core reason why people—even those who expressed an interest in returning—did not return to their original towns had to do with social networks. Back in the fall of 2011, after Hirono residents had been living in emergency shelters for six months, the local government, which had prioritized temporary housing for the elderly and those with children, moved people from Hirono together to temporary housing in the nearby city of Onagoe. Once in their new housing, many felt that those temporary homes—which actively promoted activities such as hula hoops, arts and crafts, and group outings—provided a more densely populated community of friends and contacts than they would have if they returned to Hirono. In such a tight-knit community, when people did not show up for events, their neighbors came knocking to check on them. People reported that they were worried that returning to Hirono would result in social isolation. Other reasons for staying away from their hometown included the conveniences provided by the temporary housing (better access to medical care, stores, and so forth), a sense of injustice (towns nearer to the nuclear power plant were providing incentives for returnees, while Hirono was not), worries about radioactive contamination, and concerns that if they actually returned to their homes, they would not be eligible for compensation as displaced residents.[146]

While citizens from Hirono and other cities in Tōhoku may not be returning in large numbers, they are maintaining their registration in their hometowns out of concern that they may lose future compensation if they change their residency. Japanese government officials have relied on village records in determining who is (and is not) eligible to receive assistance payments. Residents, even those who move away, have a strong interest in maintaining at least an administrative connection to those record keepers.

Along with concerns over losing social ties, the rising cost of construction and rebuilding has kept many families from returning to their homes. Multiple large-scale reconstruction projects in Tōhoku, along with projects for the 2020 Summer Olympics, have raised the cost of materials and labor. As the *Japan Times* reported, "Before the quake, in certain parts of Miyagi Prefecture the average cost of building a house was ¥90,000 [roughly $800] per tsubo [3.3 m², 35 square feet]. It is now almost ¥500,000 [$4,400] per tsubo."[147] Even with compensation from TEPCO and rebuilding assistance from the government, skyrocketing labor and materials costs have kept many from rebuilding homes in the area.[148] This may be in part due to the bid rigging discovered by Japan's Fair Trade Commission, which fined eleven road pavers some ¥1.4 billion ($13 million) and issued cease-and-desist orders to another nine for illegal activities.[149]

Stronger social ties in the temporary shelters of Onagoe may have kept some residents of Hirono from wanting to return. But social ties—the original friendships and connections that people had to their old neighbors and neighborhoods—also proved a powerful draw for some to return home. The story of Masayuki Kimura, the baker from Rikuzentakata, helps illustrate these connections. Although he was returning to a devastated community and saw no signs of potential customers, Kimura's sense of place and connections to his family and neighbors brought him back to take a risk and reopen. His baking business had been started in 1926 by his grandfather, who had had specifically brought Kimura's father into the family to keep the enterprise going. Even while sitting in temporary housing following their evacuation, Kimura's mother soon began telling reporters that she wanted to rebuild and begin making sweets for the community again.

Spurred by her words, Kimura found secondhand baking gear and moved into a temporary location, discovering that many of his suppliers of equipment and foodstuffs refused to take his money when they found out where he was living. While distributing supplies at evacuation centers, he heard many people discussing their nostalgia for the flavors of normal life: "People are longing for our local taste." Recognizing the draw of his community and the ways in which his sweets could help others rebuild their lives, Kimura committed to rebuild whatever the costs.[150]

Once the waters had receded, other survivors, like Kimura, had to decide whether or not to return to their damaged homes and communities. Social ties and a sense of belonging heavily influence the choice between exit—departing a damaged community to start over—and returning to a damaged area to invest time, energy, and money in rebuilding.[151] Kimura's personal ties to the town motivated him to move back to the wasteland that was Rikuzentakata, even though he understood the process would be costly and slow. In rebuilding his business, aid from and ties to colleagues and acquaintances proved critical; financial and emotional support from social network members cemented his desire to move forward. Individuals and localities bounced back from tragedy and hardship not through wealth, government aid, or top-down leadership, but through their neighbors, connections, and social networks.

Social Ties and Quality of Life

Along with serving as an incentive for individuals to rebuild in damaged areas (or stay in new ones) and as a shield against mental health problems, social ties (or a lack thereof) have strongly affected quality of life for survivors. Post-3/11, for example, social ties have become one 70-year-old evacuee's focal point for activities and have helped her redevelop a zest for life. "I invite the volunteers who have been passing out newspapers into my house and offer them tea. I enjoy connecting with volunteers who come from different places and to my close friends. I am planning on learning Chinese again, and I am excited to interact with more foreign Chinese students."[152] Whereas before she knew few foreigners and focused mostly on her own family, the disaster provided the chance to build a wider social network. Another evacuee had the chance to return to Fukushima Prefecture despite concerns about radiation and livelihoods. When asked why she chose to come back, she said, "I missed my vegetable garden, my flower beds, the mountains."[153] These ties to place come from a sense of belonging and community.

A number of communities have formed formal and informal groups that provide strong social ties to survivors who may be feeling isolated, especially in temporary housing. In Shichigahama, a group of volunteers has been meeting to knit together almost daily since they began a new local club one year after the disasters. The Keito Iki-Iki (Yarn Alive) group, made up primarily of women 65 and older, has helped people feel a sense of connection as the area struggles to rebuild. The

CHAPTER TWO

group serves as a place where knitters can share tips and materials. But one member commented on how the club helps to keep people healthy and safe. "When I wasn't there, they called me and said, 'Why aren't you here?'" Ms. Kasuya said. "It feels so good when they say things like that."[154]

A 60-year-old woman from Ishinomaki spoke about the role of social connections in helping her through the crisis. "Through this hardship, many people have supported me, and I don't know how to repay them. I don't need anything. Everyone told me that I don't need anything as long as I get to live. Those words supported me. It is true that their things and their love have been supporting me. People who trust are truly kind and soft. . . . I am glad I have many friends. Friends I could talk to. I won't be able to do anything alone. Trust is important. I have friends who ask me to stay at their places."[155]

One 70-year-old evacuee preferred to live with family in a crowded home without running water rather than in a prefabricated temporary shelter. "I evacuated to the house of my daughter-in-law. They had wells for their water and a log stove for cooking, and I started living with 23 others in the house." Her social connections provide tangible and intangible resources. Old friends and classmates sent her care packages after her evacuation. She said that after evacuating, she found meaning in work and interacting with new acquaintances. Despite the challenges of moving into temporary housing, she has found it fun.[156]

But for those in temporary housing who have been without social connections, the impact has been life threatening. Nearly 240 evacuees have died solitary deaths (*kodokushi*) over the past five years, with 51 dying in 2015 alone. A newspaper article reported that a social welfare official in Miyagi said that these deaths are occurring because there are fewer neighbors checking on elderly residents. "As contact with neighbors has decreased, it has become difficult for neighbors to watch over them."[157] Most of the solitary deaths have been among older men. Further, as permanent housing slowly opens up and people depart from temporary shelters, newly formed social networks are disrupted, with dwindling numbers attending communal events such as barbecue parties. Of one shelter in Tōhoku, a 2015 article reported, "When university volunteers throw get-togethers for the community, there are times when there are more staffers than residents."[158]

Some NGOs and civil society groups sought to help restart the rhythms of normal daily life in the area for evacuees living in challenging conditions. One Tokyo-based religious nonprofit organization (NPO) brought food trucks to temporary shelter camps, handing out

INDIVIDUAL LEVEL

ice cream in the summer and *yakiimo* (roasted Japanese sweet potato) in the fall.[159] By re-creating the patterns of seasonal foods even when the evacuees were sheltered in unfamiliar, flimsy homes, the NPO recognized the possibility of activating a sense of community and belonging. Other civil society organizations have helped local restaurants that lost their buildings to rebuild their businesses by helping them set up food trucks and "kitchen cars."[160] Faith-based organizations, along with festivals held at local Shinto shrines, have been anchors for community attachment and group activities.[161]

In disaster-affected areas, shared spaces not at home or at work—known as "third spaces" by scholars of urban planning—have been few and far between. Survivors in Rikuzentakata have found a third space at one of the few open pubs, named the Bar Lemonheart.[162] The entire establishment—perhaps named for a popular Japanese manga (animation) series that began in the mid-1980s—has only six stools and a table and would probably fit into the kitchen of most US bars. Nevertheless, it provides a haven where locals can drink and talk quietly. Some NGOs and civil society organizations, such as Ibasho in Ofunato, moved to create new shared spaces that could help local residents maintain or generate new ties.[163] I will discuss the measurable effect of programs such as Ibasho on cohesion and a sense of belonging in the final chapter, but in short, these social capital strengthening or building programs have been lifesavers for many who would otherwise be isolated.

Obstacles to Individual Recovery

Several types of obstacles to individual recovery remain serious barriers to community revitalization and recovery. These obstacles include concerns about radiation exposure, uncertain livelihoods, and red tape. The reactor meltdowns at Fukushima Dai-ichi created widespread fears about radioactive contamination in Japan and abroad, and public opinion on nuclear energy underwent a sea change.[164] Before the meltdowns, the majority of Japanese citizens hoped to expand the country's domestic use of nuclear energy; afterward, more than two-thirds wanted to curtail it.

Because of potential health risks, Fukushima residents have received a series of free internal radiation screenings, and children across the prefecture have had yearly health monitoring. To date, few residents have developed visible health problems that doctors are willing to link to exposure to high levels of radioactivity. Surveys of nearly 10,000 mothers in Fukushima Prefecture carried out after the 3/11 disasters, for example, found no significant adverse outcomes in their babies, whether stillbirths, congenital anomalies, or preterm births, that could be linked to radiation exposure.[165] Internal radiation scans of tens of thousands of Fukushima residents in the hospitals of Minamisoma have turned up very few individuals with measurable levels of radiation due to consumption of contaminated food and drink.[166] Most of those with measurable contamination are locals who foraged for mushrooms and other wild food items, which absorb large amounts of radionuclides from their environment.[167] Attempts to track the radiation exposure of tens of thousands of TEPCO contractors, employees, and part-time workers on the site of the Fukushima Dai-ichi plant have been less successful. Of 20,000 people who entered the plant, only 35% have followed through with radiation screenings.[168] This lackadaisical approach to worker safety resonates with the fact that until 2015, Japan was one of a handful of nations using nuclear power that had no checks on workers in nuclear facilities in place.[169]

Authorities have had better success with screening children because of the concerns of their parents. While larger-than-normal numbers of thyroid abnormalities were detected in children in the prefecture, some have argued that was the result of the larger number of children being screened[170] as opposed to the consequence of exposure to the Fukushima Dai-ichi meltdowns. Nevertheless, the mothers of those children, many of whom have been found to have A2 level cysts—which are typically harmless—in their thyroids, remain quite anxious,[171] and their fears have manifested as rashes, tiredness, and depression.[172] Concerns about the safety of their children have resulted in a mass exodus from Fukushima Prefecture. By the spring of 2018, fewer than 4% of the children originally in communities near Fukushima Dai-ichi—including Namie, Tomioka, Iitate, and Katsurao—were enrolled in local schools.[173]

In response to concerns about health and livelihoods, the Japanese government has sought to decontaminate the areas near the nuclear plant by digging up radioactive topsoil and placing it in black garbage bags for temporary storage. With a goal of limiting radiation exposure to 0.23 μSv per hour,[174] the Japanese government has cleaned up 9 million m^3 of soil and leaves and has used water to spray down residences and businesses in towns such as Naraha, Tomioka, and Futaba.[175] Critics have pointed out that the government decontaminates only the ground, trees, and rocks within 20 m (65 feet) of homes, along with the walls and roofs of the homes themselves. This leaves a great deal of the inhabited space around homes untouched by decontamination and therefore provides a way that additional radioactive particles may end up in contact with residents. Government workers have also sought to clean off roads, shrines, and other well-traveled public places.[176]

While these efforts are important, decontamination around homes and businesses may miss critical areas. As rain and condensation carry radioactive particles from roofs, for example, they tend to collect at drains and footpaths near roads, houses, and schools. As a result, the septic tanks of car washes in Fukushima have been found to have very high levels of radiation due to particles being trapped there after being sluiced from cars.[177] The government does not plan to decontaminate mountains and forests near Fukushima towns, even though they are likely to remain hotspots for radioactive particles. A visit in July 2018 showed the highest levels of radioactive contamination coming not from streets or abandoned homes, but rather from the nearby forests and trees. The Fukushima Dai-ichi site itself continues to spread radioactive cesium, iodine, tritium, and strontium through groundwater contamination. TEPCO is trying a number of strategies to reduce the spread of radionuclides, including an experimental underground ice wall that has yet to demonstrate efficacy, a steel and concrete wall along the shore, and an underground bypass.[178] While TEPCO has reduced the flow of contaminated water into the ocean, it still faces the challenge of removing tritium and other radioactive contaminants from the millions of gallons of stored water on-site.

Whatever the status of the radiation leaks over time, the reactors onsite will not be used again and must be disassembled, and the highly radioactive components and spent fuel rods must be stored somewhere. TEPCO has predicted it will take four decades to decommission the reactors at Fukushima Dai-ichi, although this prediction may be optimistic. Residents of towns near Fukushima Dai-ichi who have been allowed to return to their homes have expressed concerns that the decommissioning process itself may bring more accidents and radiation exposure.[179] A resident from Namie said in 2016, "We do want to return—we were born and raised there. But can we make a living? Can we live next to radioactive waste?"[180] A survey of several hundred Fukushima residents by Japan's Reconstruction Agency found that more than half of those between the ages of 10 and 29 did not select their hometowns as where they want to be living in 30 years.[181]

In Ōkuma, another city near the Fukushima Dai-ichi nuclear power plant, the elderly make up the small number of evacuees who have expressed a desire to return to what is currently a "no residence zone." Local officials quoted one elder as saying, "In the final years of my life, I want to live in my hometown where I was born and grew up."[182] Two years after the disaster, officials in the town of Namie, just 4 km (2.5 miles) from Fukushima Dai-ichi, reported that roughly 30% of residents had no intention of returning, another 30% hoped to return, and another 40% were unsure.[183] By early 2016, only 18% of Namie residents said they wanted to go back to their town, 48% said they did not want to return, and the remainder were undecided.[184] As of summer 2016, only a few hundred of the 21,500 residents had actually returned, and by the fall of 2018, only 700 were living full-time in town.[185]

When other cities in Fukushima have been opened to repopulation, they have not seen a large influx of returnees either. For example, after authorities lifted the evacuation order for the city of Naraha on September 5, 2015, only a handful of its more than 7,300 former residents returned home, and by March 2016, only 459 had come back.[186] By summer 2018, Fukushima Prefecture reported that only 9% of the original population was living in Naraha. Similarly, a section of the town of Kawauchi was partially reopened to its residents (and newcomers) in April 2012, and was completely opened to resettlement by October 2014, but only 19% of its pre-disaster population returned. Of those who did, 40% were over the age of 65.[187] (Hotels, inns, and other lodgings are quite full, though, in the open towns closest to the Fukushima Dai-ichi nuclear power plant due to the out-of-town workers there for decontamination work in and around the nuclear plant.[188])

Beyond the issues caused by radiation, bureaucracy and red tape have created friction and resentment for those hoping to rebuild their damaged towns.[189] For communities hoping to relocate to new, safer areas, establishing ownership of the land they once occupied and negotiating a government buyout has been stalled by the exodus of population and the destruction of paper records by the tsunami.[190] The reconstruction process has further stalled due to required authorizations from multiple levels of government across various agencies. Rebuilding the Ishinomaki port, for example, involved organizing permission from the Fisheries Agency (in charge of the port), the Miyagi prefectural government (for permission to raise the sunken land), and the city government (to restore sewer and water lines to the site).[191] Those agencies and governments rarely communicate directly with one another, and while the Reconstruction Agency has attempted to serve as a node for kick-starting permitting and licensing, many city agencies have lacked the expertise and personnel to move projects through quickly.

Similarly, in Sendai, which had comparatively little damage, the process of constructing new private housing for evacuees began with the local government seeking approval from the Ministry of Land, Infrastructure, Transport and Tourism (MLIT) to zone land for residential use. Next, Sendai requested financial assistance from the central and regional governments to set up a budget to assist with the process. Hiring consultants and city planners, the city also negotiated with the owners of the land it wanted to acquire. Residents planning on moving to the new homes had to secure bank loans and, depending on the case, negotiate directly with construction firms—which have been in high demand since the disasters—individually or in groups. One city hall official told me that negotiating the bureaucracy could take years of full-time work by would-be residents.[192] Many locals looking for strong signs of recovery in quick infrastructure redevelopment have remained disappointed.

Mayor Futoshi Toba of Rikuzentakata has written and spoken publicly about bureaucratic obstacles that have impeded recovery for the residents of his town.[193] Given the town's success in using its social ties to accelerate recovery through large-scale public works projects, his commentary is telling. In 2013, he talked about a plan to develop high-rise housing units in the hills behind the city, which had been stalled for more than two years. "The first problem is that it involves clearing the forest, which means we have to get special dispensation for the plan under the stipulations of the Forest Act [Shinrinhō]. After that, we need to get official clearance to level the land, and then to build anything on the wide area that the city would gain as a result of that leveling, since it would be classified as a major development project [*dai-kibō kaihatsu*]. In addition to this, the town's plans for rezoning and reconstruction to mitigate the loss of life in the event of future tsunamis have to be approved by various agencies at various levels of government."[194] Further, Mayor Toba has argued that "Rikuzentakata was unable to build a supermarket because of zoning laws aimed at protecting small shopkeepers."[195] In conversation, he pointed out that beyond the annoyances of the central government's conservative bureaucratism, local residents refusing to go along with reconstruction plans have cost the city months, if not years, in delays.[196] More recently, he told me that he still believed the central and regional governments had not provided sufficient timely help in the city's quest to rebuild.

A lack of qualified personnel in local civil service, along with associated administrative challenges, has added to the problems slowing individual recovery. Municipalities in Tōhoku lack the capacity

CHAPTER TWO

to simultaneously handle relocation, rehousing, and rebuilding projects.[197] Typically, bureaucrats in local governments have training as generalists, not specialists, especially in areas such as reconstruction law and administration. Many of the departments and agencies at the city, town, and village level remain understaffed, as personnel were killed in the tsunami or left soon after. For Tōhoku residents who want to sever connections to their old homes in areas such as Fukushima, the compensation being offered for land is low, and many land registry and family records are out-of-date. Lacking records, neither bureaucrats nor residents can move forward on land sales. Further, the tsunami itself wiped out many obvious borders, and towns have yet to completely resurvey the areas to create the necessary administrative and financial maps.[198]

With these various bureaucratic obstacles in place, the quality of governance provided by local decision makers has made a major difference after the disaster. Where local residents have not felt listened to, they have been discouraged and turned away from participating in the rebuilding process. Many citizens have felt disenfranchised by the reconstruction and recovery plans. A 60-year-old woman said, "I was also concerned with the way city reconstruction was proceeding without listening to the local citizens' opinions and ideas. People from somewhere else are in charge of the reconstruction."[199]

Where local leaders—both laypeople and elected officials—have demonstrated strong and responsive governance, things have been different. The town of Yamada in Iwate Prefecture, for example, has been offering disaster victims seeking to rebuild private houses on their own unified housing designs that bring down overall building costs. In other cities, residents of a particular neighborhood have moved simultaneously to newly developed, higher land; this reduced the costs of the process, as firms constructed all the homes at the same time.[200] Similarly, Mayor Toshiaki Honda of the city of Tono has pushed his civil servants to offer extended administrative and material assistance to the neighboring city of Kamaishi.[201] Working against the often top-down nature of the Japanese bureaucracy requires dedication and persistence.

Strong local leaders have had to adapt to changing times and take on new skills to help their communities move forward. Local elected officials often had to deal with tremendous personal tragedy as they sought to lead their town's recovery. Mayor Toba of Rikuzentakata, for example, lost his wife to the tsunami and slept next to his desk on the floor in his office following the disaster to coordinate the recovery.[202]

He mentioned that his sense of place and desire to help his town provided him with the emotional strength to persevere.[203]

One ex-mayor in Tōhoku has become a legal adviser, known in Japanese as a scrivener (*shihō shoshi*), to ensure that his constituents can proceed through the complicated bureaucracy involved in recovery. "As evacuees now living in temporary housing move into their newly built homes, they need help in producing documents to be handed in to the town government," he said.[204] Town residents across the area have had to prepare mountains of documents. The simplest financial compensation form initially produced by TEPCO for evacuees ran to 60 pages; with instructions, it was more than 160 pages of dense type and extended blanks. Due to complaints, TEPCO eventually reduced the forms required for compensation to roughly 34 pages with more than 1,000 sections to be filled out.[205] Applications for temporary housing similarly ran into the dozens of pages. Further, because many bureaucrats in city halls refused to show flexibility and accept incomplete or incorrectly filled out applications, residents often had to return multiple times to receive permits and licenses. While some local governments have embraced electronic governance, placing many forms online, this has been a particular challenge for the elderly who lack knowledge of such systems.[206]

Other local decision makers have moved beyond standard operating procedures to more flexible and innovative approaches. Rather than placing survivors in prefabricated temporary shelters, for example, Fukushima Prefecture decided to skip the FEMA trailer–like facilities and instead create higher-quality temporary homes made from wood. Officials accomplished this by using local builders, incorporating local (often repurposed) timber, and allowing residents to modify the homes to meet their needs.[207] Despite the best efforts of government and NGOs, though, the supply of permanent housing in Tōhoku remains low. While many individuals were moving out of prefabricated temporary shelters by the spring of 2016, their destinations were not necessarily permanent private or public housing. Instead, hundreds of families moved from their previous temporary shelter or housing unit to a new temporary home. Five years after the disasters, 172 families in Miyagi Prefecture from the towns of Kesennuma, Sendai, Shichigahama, Tagajo, and Natori had to leave their temporary housing due to closings, but moved to other temporary houses rather than actual permanent housing. Rikuzentakata still had some 500 families in temporary shelters as of summer 2018.

A final issue that has slowed recovery has been uncertain livelihoods and economic futures in Tōhoku. During one discussion in the Fukushima town of Minamisoma, a local fisherman compared his plight and that of his industry with the results of another industrial accident: Minamata. In one of the widely publicized Big Four pollution cases in Japan, the city of Minamata experienced broad communal health damage, including congenital birth defects and nerve damage, because of the dumping of ethyl mercury into the ocean. "Just like no one buys fish from Minamata," the Minamisoma fisherman told me in 2013, "even though the Chisso company long ago stopped putting mercury into the water, so too no one will want to buy fish from Fukushima even if proven clean."[208]

Nuclear power plant host communities in Fukushima Prefecture face severe livelihood challenges; many relied on nuclear power, the accompanying government aid, and small- to medium-scale fishing to support their few residents. In Onagawa, for example, the catch has declined by 20% in the years since 3/11, and "the once lively port district remains eerily vacant"[209] despite the creation of a new seafood processing plant.[210] The mayor of Onagawa has said that with its nuclear power plant offline because of the meltdowns, and the fishing industry still recovering, his community's revenues are down.[211] He has also underscored the uncertainty facing his town, wondering whether sufficient funds and businesses will be available in the area to complete reconstruction.[212] A visit to Onagawa in summer 2018 found a community that has rebuilt its downtown, created an attractive new railroad station, and managed to push off government plans for a seawall. But its lack of economic diversity and reliance on fishing and nuclear power remain a challenge. In short, there is little economic diversity in coastal Tōhoku communities, especially in Fukushima, where radioactive contamination and out-migration have cut off standard employment opportunities.

This chapter has focused on the individuals living in Tōhoku who faced the massive challenges of the triple disasters. Their decisions, as we have seen, were influenced both by their connections to others and by the kinds of governance mechanisms in place. Social ties and cohesion allowed many to survive the event and then begin working collectively, even while living in temporary shelters. The elderly and infirm, especially, relied on social ties and connections to carry them from danger and provide assistance during the evacuation. These social connections helped them to restart the rhythms of their lives and their businesses. Even in the emergency shelters, whether schools or government buildings, better-connected communities managed to organize food deliveries, provide shelter and temporary medical care, make space for helicopters to drop off supplies, and work collectively to solve problems. Tōhoku communities with strong stocks of social capital had stronger recoveries, while those divided by mistrust and a lack of coordination struggled to come back.[213]

Volunteers poured into Tōhoku to help after the disasters, and social welfare councils from cities and prefectures across the country sent in organized human resource support for volunteer councils in disaster-impacted areas.[214] Nevertheless, the most powerful social network effects came from friends, neighbors, and family nearby. Fear of losing new, stronger ties has kept some residents in remote temporary houses even as permanent homes have slowly become available. A strong sense of belonging and connection to their hometowns has pushed others, especially the elderly, to return to damaged coastal houses. As one observer argued, highly organized self-governance was rare, and strong recoveries and sites of mutual cooperation were found only where "residents had strong bonds with one another."[215]

At the same time, some decision makers and leaders have created strong governance systems that have cleared red tape and accelerated recovery. These leaders have demonstrated tremendous fortitude as they help residents work through mountains of paperwork, connect to mental health resources, and resume the rhythms of daily life despite their own personal tragedies. Other mayors and local leaders have shown less initiative and have been ineffective at moving through the labyrinthine formal procedures of recovery. This chapter has shown how residents and survivors in Tōhoku were embedded in networks and governance and how strongly those systems influenced the way they made it through 3/11. We turn now to the first level of political and administrative governance in which they were embedded—namely, the municipality.

THREE

Village, Town, and City Level: Vertical Ties Bringing Resources

The tsunami took more than 18,400 lives in Tōhoku and destroyed thousands of homes and businesses in the region. But mortality rates for Tōhoku municipalities—the lowest of the three levels of the Japanese government—varied tremendously across the region. A large number of towns in the area had no casualties from the tsunami. Others, such as Onagawa, Rikuzentakata, and Otsuchi, saw 10% (or more) of the population killed. Further, in the process of rebuilding, some towns have done quite well. Rifu and Fudai managed to achieve very rapid recoveries after the disaster, completely restoring their infrastructure and restarting businesses within two years of the event. Sendai, Rifu, and Natori have been among the very few municipalities that have seen populations increase since the disaster.

Almost all municipalities along the Tōhoku coast have rezoned their flat plains nearest the shore for commercial or nonresidential use only; they have relocated homes and apartments to higher ground. The city I am calling Coastal Town has used its connections to gain government support for a uniquely ambitious, large-scale construction project to raise its downtown by leveling mountains. Coastal Town's reconstruction plan has dwarfed that of other cities and towns in the area, which have relied instead on seawalls for mitigation of the impact of future tsunami. Many other communities have been slower to recover population and rebuild their schools, homes, and lives. Across the area, most towns have seen increasing depopulation, with an average decline of 15%.[1]

This chapter looks at Tōhoku municipalities through several lenses. First, I try to understand the variation in mortality rates during the tsunami; that is, why some cities, villages, and towns were decimated while others escaped major harm. Horizontal connections—the ties between neighbors—proved more important than demographics, seawall infrastructure, the height of the tsunami, or other factors typically considered important in driving mortality. Next, I investigate the degree to which politicians and other government officials changed their behavior as a result of the disaster. Council members from the most severely damaged municipalities began reaching out for assistance to regional and national authorities that they believed could help speed up rebuilding. Many municipalities showed evidence of responsive governance.

Finally, I look to understand what factors drove recovery outcomes. Governance mechanisms—the linking social ties between communities and decision makers in Tokyo—were critical. An area supported by more powerful politicians found itself recovering more quickly than similarly damaged and equipped areas with fewer champions. Alongside the quantitative analyses, I provide snapshots of communities in the region, along with a more detailed case study of Coastal Town, that illustrate these patterns of networks and governance.

Explaining Variation in Mortality

The tsunami traveled as far as 15 km (9 miles) inland in some locations (usually moving along a river), affecting coastal and inland cities alike with a typical inundation spread of 4–6 km (2.5–3.7 miles).[2] This meant that even cities not directly on the ocean faced a tremendous hazard from the black waves. The average proportion of the population missing or deceased in the inundated areas of each locality following the tsunami was .01, that is, some 1 in 100 residents. A number of municipalities experienced no casualties. However, the maximum was .11; that is, roughly 11% of the local population, which occurred in the city of Onagawa, where more than 600 people perished. Figure 3.1 lays out the tremendous skew in the distribution of mortality across municipalities. The vast majority of villages, towns, and cities in the Tōhoku

CHAPTER THREE

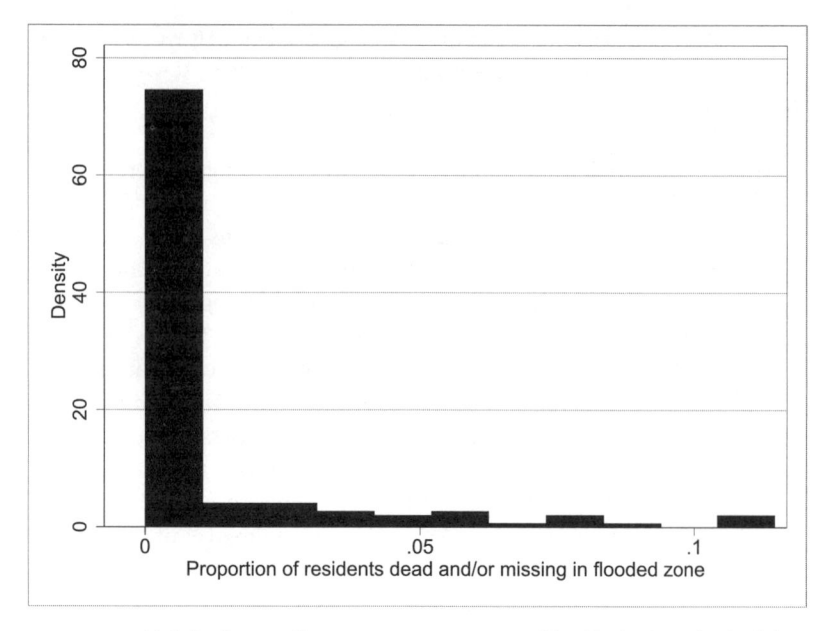

FIGURE 3.1. Variation in mortality outcomes across communities. The horizontal axis of the histogram captures the proportion of residents dead or missing in each town, village, and city in Tōhoku. Higher bars indicate more localities with that level of mortality.

region suffered no fatalities. The next cluster falls between 1% and 9%, with a number of towns in between, and the highest mortality rate cluster sits at 11%.

The most obvious factor that could influence mortality during a catastrophe would be the power of the event itself. An initial analysis of the height of the tsunami and mortality outcomes for 133 coastal and inland municipalities in Iwate, Miyagi, and Fukushima Prefectures illuminated a visible, but weak, connection.[3] I graphed the height of the tsunami against the mortality rate in each of these cities, labeling each point with the municipality name. As figure 3.2 illustrates, the general pattern involves areas struck by higher waves experiencing higher levels of mortality; higher waves seemed to create greater risks of death for residents. The empty, unlabeled circle at the point of 0 m in tsunami height and 0% killed stands in for the many Tōhoku cities, towns, and villages in our dataset without casualties or measurable waves. (Their names become illegible when they are all included.)

The pattern connecting wave height and mortality is far from perfect. Some cities—such as Tanohata and Miyako—with comparatively tall tsunami (greater than 19 m, roughly 60 feet) had comparatively low mortality rates. In other cities with relatively short tsunami (less than 7 m, roughly 21 feet)—such as Higashimatsushima and Yamamoto—the death toll was disproportionately higher. This variation in mortality rates—which do not vary exclusively with the strength of the tsunami—remains a critical puzzle for researchers to understand.

Determinants of Mortality

Past research has identified a number of factors that could influence disaster mortality.[4] These factors include disaster event and local environmental characteristics, demographic factors, the capacity of local social networks, and political as well as economic factors. It is intuitive that the *physical strength* of the tsunami—that is, its height and speed upon reaching the shore—strongly influenced mortality among affected communities. The chances of individual survival might have hinged on closeness to the ocean, the water's path, and geophysical land features.[5] Disaster experts regularly connect the amount of damage done by a disaster like a tsunami or earthquake to survival and recovery rates.[6]

Along with the height of the tsunami itself, topographic conditions may determine the actual impact of the wave when it reaches

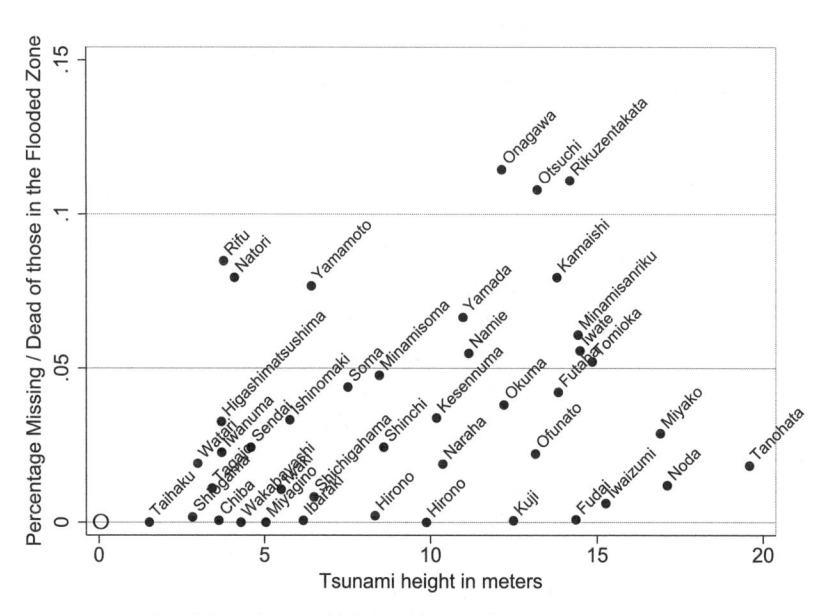

FIGURE 3.2. Correlation of tsunami height with mortality.

CHAPTER THREE

the shore. These *geographic conditions* include the length of the municipality's coastline, its height above sea level, its area, and the length of paved roads. The coastal length of the town, village, or city may determine its broader exposure to the wave itself; longer coastlines may create more victims than areas with a narrower set of beaches. Similarly, municipalities with larger areas may have more citizens vulnerable to the wave, or they may have easier escape paths from low-lying areas; the effect of these geographic features remains indeterminate. The length of paved roads provides a measure of the escape paths available to citizens fleeing from the disaster; such roads serve as the most likely evacuation routes. Finally, our data include a measure of the local population engaged in the fishing industry.

While the physical characteristics of the disaster event and the locations of potential victims may influence mortality, a great deal of work has focused on the role of *demography* in disaster situations. Characteristics such as age of the affected population strongly correlate with the individual capacity to evacuate and survive a disaster.[7] My colleague and I included a measure of the proportion of single-person households in each municipality; this variable captures the availability of immediate assistance to the vulnerable. One study of mortality in the 2004 Indian Ocean tsunami confirmed past research by finding that physical strength strongly predicted survival, with children and older adults least likely to survive the disaster.[8] In the Tōhoku region, many municipalities had large proportions of elderly residents, and their inability to flee, along with their relative physical vulnerability, may have increased mortality rates. To capture the presence of elderly community members, I include a baseline measure of pre-tsunami mortality (which correlates very highly—.91—with the proportion of the municipality above the age of 65).

Unlike coastal communities in the Indian Ocean, in which the 2004 earthquake and the retreating ocean water were not uniformly interpreted as a sign of tsunami danger (or acted upon by residents), communities in Tōhoku have been repeatedly exposed to tsunami or tsunami training in the past. As mentioned in previous chapters, residents in coastal regions of Japan have been trained to expect the arrival of a tsunami after an initial earthquake; children regularly take part in school evacuation drills, and a number of neighborhoods and towns practice communal evacuation as well. Furthermore, some towns and villages, such as Aneyoshi, have institutionalized collective memories of past tsunami (some which took place 1,000 years ago) through physical markers such as stones.[9]

As a result, the degree of community organization in the evacuation procedures may have played a powerful role in determining survival rate. Whether or not residents in Tōhoku and elsewhere actually leave a tsunami-vulnerable area to flee to higher ground depends not primarily on education, then, but rather on local norms and the behavior of one's family and geographically defined social network. Accordingly, a different approach to disaster mortality focuses on the ability of the community to self-organize and evacuate under extreme conditions.

Successful risk avoidance involves accurately receiving, interpreting, and passing along messages about hazards sent out by authorities and providing shared norms–based mutual support for evacuation.[10] Social networks in local communities can be seen as a preexisting informal insurance mechanism.[11] Where communities share norms and have deep reservoirs of trust in one another and in authorities, they are more likely to act on group information about risks. Therefore, pre-disaster levels of *bonding social capital*—the ties that bind residents to friends and neighbors—may matter because of their influence on information sharing, mutual help, and collective action. Localities with the ability to overcome barriers to collective action could better facilitate evacuation of the elderly and infirm; fragmented communities with less trust and less ability to work collectively may not be able to do so. As one study of the 1995 Chicago heat wave deaths argued, "Those at risk were isolated and lacked a concerned network of family and friends."[12] Linking social capital—the ability to connect quickly to decision makers and authorities to verify hazard warnings and to guide rescue efforts—may also have played a role in saving lives. Linking social capital ties strongly into political variables, as we explain below.

In order to test the roles of social capital in tsunami survival, my colleague Yasuyuki Sawada and I employed proxies that capture bonding (and linking) social capital in Tōhoku localities. While no single quantitative measure can perfectly capture the nuanced and rich social connections across more than a hundred coastal towns, we envision pre-tsunami proportional crime rates as a proxy for bonding social capital based on extensive sociological research.[13] Communities with fewer connections among individuals and lower expectations about future interactions have higher rates of major crimes than communities where neighbors feel tied to both one another and their homes.[14] In areas where people lack connections or envision themselves as outsiders, they are less likely to abide by local behavioral norms or worry about long-term social consequences of deviance.[15] Crimes such as robbery and assault become easier if you assume that no one will recognize you and that few bystanders will intervene. As Robert Putnam argued, "Higher levels of social capital, all else being equal, translate into lower levels of crime. . . . This inverse relationship is astonishingly strong—as close to perfect as one might find between any two social phenomena."[16]

In addition to social connections, some experts on Japan have emphasized that *political factors*—such as local support for the long-dominant Liberal Democratic Party (LDP) and whether or not a municipality has been merged with another locality—may have affected mortality. The first of these factors can be expected because stronger support for the LDP may translate to increased subsidies to local governments;[17] that money, in turn, may allow local government officials to expand disaster preparation measures. Towns supportive of, or at least cooperative with, the LDP may have received greater public investments in and experienced better availability of reliable infrastructure, such as seawalls, for tsunami protection.[18] The LDP itself may reward strongly supportive towns differently than those that have opposed it, or only weakly supported it, in past elections. That is, the LDP may provide fewer benefits to towns that have supported opposition parties yet larger benefits to communities that could "swing" toward the LDP.

Scholars have described *linking social capital* as composed of "norms of respect and networks of trusting relationships between people who are interacting across explicit, formal or institutionalized power or authority gradients in society."[19] Ties between municipalities and Japan's administrative center through party connections can be seen as a form of linking social capital. To incorporate measures of linking social capital and to capture the potential effect of political connections on mortality, we included several variables capturing each municipality's proportion of LDP support in the 2009 lower house election. We see this measure of electoral support for the LDP as a strong test of our hypotheses, as the LDP itself lost the 2009 election to the well-organized Democratic Party of Japan (DPJ). Communities in our sample strongly supporting the LDP displayed very deep loyalty to the party at a time when many of their fellow citizens supported the opposition.

Another political factor may decrease a municipality's survival rate during a catastrophe. Since the 1999 Law to Promote Municipal Mergers went into effect in Japan, the number of towns, villages, and cities has shrunk from more than 3,000 to fewer than 1,800. Local-level mergers can take place in two ways: existing municipalities can be merged so that a larger city subsumes a smaller municipality, or a new municipality can be created by the unification of localities. Villages, towns, and cities that have been merged may lack strong representation in local political arenas and/or lack strong identities. Social identity research on the mergers of organizations has underscored that the newly created institution (in this case, the town) may not meet the expectations of members who find themselves removed from their old environments and identities.[20] Further, strong identification with the newly merged (or created) municipality may take a long time to develop.[21] Some scholars have suggested that recently merged communities such as Minamisoma had "shallower" community identities than longer-established, independent communities;[22] this difference may result in uncoordinated disaster planning and less effective evacuation. Merged or "new" localities, therefore, may have faced higher mortality rates than more established communities. Our model includes variables for merged localities and new localities created through mergers.

Finally, I have included information on the heights of seawalls constructed to guard localities against tsunami to reflect the amount of public investment in tsunami protection (which may be unconnected to LDP support). The Japanese central government has long sponsored the construction of seawalls to diminish the physical strength of tsunami and therefore decrease mortality risk, as was the case in Fudai, in Iwate Prefecture, which was protected by its 15 m (49-foot) wall.[23] Yet such walls may weaken people's incentive to evacuate after an earthquake.[24] Hence, seawall height may have ambiguous, or even positive, effects on tsunami mortality.

Data for Mortality Analysis

Sawada and I used a dataset of all coastal municipalities, inland municipalities, and cities on the Pacific coast side of the Tōhoku region of Japan; this area includes the three most affected prefectures: Iwate, Miyagi, and Fukushima. Municipalities in these three prefectures sought assistance under the national Disaster Relief Act (Saigai kyūjo hō). The dataset includes coastal and inland localities alike because of the extent of the tsunami's inland inundation. The 133 communities in the dataset include the entire universe of localities that could have been affected by the 3/11 tsunami; table A.1 in appendix 2 describes the data used in this analysis. Note the variation in almost all of the factors captured here—tsunami height, for example, varied from 0 to nearly 20 m (65 feet), while demographic factors such as the proportion of those over the age of 65 were distributed between 12% and 55%.[25]

We carried out a regression analysis, which is essentially a way of controlling for potentially confounding factors while investigating the correlation between predictor or independent variables (e.g., tsunami height, height of seawalls, demographics, political support) and our dependent variable—that is, our outcome of interest (namely, mortality). A core factor proved robust across model types: proportional crime rate, which, as mentioned above, we interpret as a proxy for social capital. The variables that proved somewhat important across almost all of our models included the height of the tsunami and mid-range electoral support for the LDP. Rather than simply providing a list of coefficients from our regression analysis, I show marginal effects plots of major variables with simulated 95% confidence intervals based on the results reported in table A.2 in appendix 2.[26]

Figure 3.3 shows the relationship between the number of crimes per 1,000 people before 3/11 and the rate of mortality during the tsunami when all other factors are held constant. As mentioned above, we interpret the rate of major crime as a proxy for social capital. The graph has wider confidence intervals around the predicted values where we

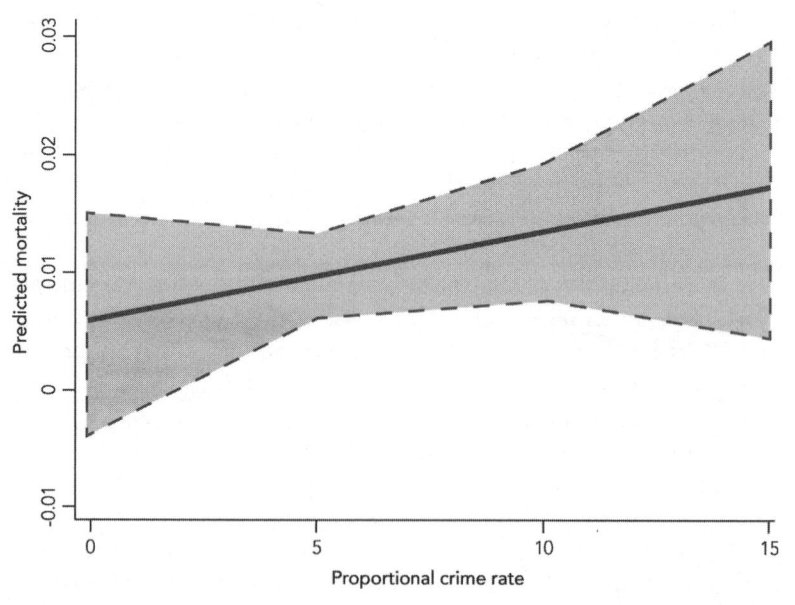

FIGURE 3.3. Relationship between pre-tsunami crime rate (per 1,000 people) and mortality. The shaded space represents the 95% confidence interval around the predicted mortality rate (the solid line) based on the crime rate before the disaster. $N = 133$; simulations = 1,000. The pre-tsunami crime rate was allowed to vary while all other factors (listed in table A.1) were set to their mean values.

are less certain of the outcomes due to scarcity of data. But there is a clear pattern: after controlling for potential confounding variables, including tsunami height, seawall height, demographic conditions, and the political environment, we found that communities that had higher crime rates before the tsunami are expected to experience greater rates of mortality during it. A municipality that had 15 crimes committed per 1,000 people would be expected to have a death rate some 30 times higher than one where there were only 1 or 2 crimes per 1,000 people.

While skeptics may think that crime rate is a poor proxy for social capital, there is, as mentioned, a rich sociological tradition based on this premise. Further, while casual observers may expect little variation in crime rates in Japan, they actually vary significantly across the many Tōhoku cities, villages, and towns in our dataset. Finally, there is no correlation between crime and wave height, meaning that we believe that we are capturing a specific relationship between social infrastructure and tsunami survival. Communities that had been plagued by low trust and high crime rates before the disaster experienced higher rates of mortality because of an inability to self-mobilize and provide mutual help during a critical period.

We also found that seawall height had no effect on mortality. Even for communities with tall seawalls, we found no evidence that residents in those areas survived at higher rates than those in communities with shorter or nonexistent seawalls. In contrast, similar communities with different levels of mobilization potential responded very differently to the same disaster. Interviews with survivors about their behavior and the behavior of family members who did not survive revealed that many did not evacuate upon hearing the initial tsunami warnings, as we saw in chapter 1.[27] Those who evacuated described being heavily influenced by neighbors and friends who urged them to do so or came directly to their homes to ensure their safety (as we also saw). Communities with lower evacuation rates were clearly at greater risk of mortality. Having focused on the role of networks in influencing mortality at the city, town, and village level, I now ask how governance in these communities was influenced by the disasters.

Changes in Governance

In the recovery process, local governments and council members can play an important role as local decision makers, as they have deep knowledge of the conditions in their communities and of the goals of their constituents. In contrast, politicians and bureaucrats located in Tokyo may have little working knowledge of the resources and practices that could improve quality of life in Tōhoku cities affected by the 3/11 disasters. Further, under Japan's unitary governance structure, in which Tokyo views local governments as extensions of the central government, cities, towns, and villages have comparatively few administrative and financial resources on which to draw during reconstruction. Japan's model contrasts with the federal systems of North America and Germany, for example, where local governments have some autonomy in policy making, taxation, and so forth. Japan's system comprises a vertical administrative control model[28] in which localities raise only one-third of their expenditures through local taxes.[29] As a result, cities, towns, and villages must make use of national and regional agencies to bring in disaster recovery money and new infrastructure development projects.

To accelerate recovery, and perhaps to claim credit for visible rebuilding outcomes, local political leaders in Tōhoku have reached out to a variety of groups, ranging from local constituents in their home districts to national agency bureaucrats, for advice, help, and resources. The types and frequency of consultation have varied across council members and localities. In some areas, decision makers on the municipal council have consulted primarily with local citizens as they have worked through challenging policy decisions, such as whether to relocate the entire community farther from the ocean. In other areas, council members have lobbied a variety of regional and national politicians for assistance and guidance through the complex bureaucratic process of securing grants and infrastructure assistance. Other council members may have reached out to highly visible but low-capacity agencies and institutions primarily to facilitate claiming credit in their home constituencies.

Using this variation in outreach to linking and bridging ties, my colleague Yoshikuni Ono and I investigated the factors that made it more likely that local politicians would expend their resources on consultation and meetings with other political actors. Our findings, after controlling for a number of potentially confounding factors, show that local decision makers from severely damaged areas were the most likely to reach out to political contacts at multiple levels. Moreover, the political incentives of local council members and partisan networks among political actors affected their outreach activities at the time of crisis as well.[30]

Governance Theories

Elected officials have strong incentives to seek reelection, and they attempt to respond to various demands and requests from their constituents to achieve that goal.[31] The members of municipal councils in Japan similarly try to keep their seats once elected; many of them have long careers in local politics. These council members are often strongly motivated to cultivate a personal vote due to the institutional framework of their elections: the single non-transferable vote (SNTV) system.[32] Under this system, candidates compete for multiple seats in a single electoral district, and voters are allowed to cast their votes for only a single candidate. As a result, individual candidates target narrow geographic constituencies to survive competition.[33] In addition, electoral politics at the municipal level works differently from that at the national level: political parties are less important in local council elections than in national ones.[34] Moreover, the turnout rates in local-level elections are often significantly lower than in national-level elections.

Candidates running for local council seats provide various services to their constituencies and publicize their activities by using electronic mail, websites, and newsletters, attempting to improve their name recognition. In their websites and newsletters, council members in the localities affected by the 2011 disaster presented information about their policy positions, their public discussions at the local council, and their meetings with various people. For example, Kikuchi Takayoshi, a member of the Sendai City Council, summarized his own speeches and statements made at the council meetings in his newsletters, explaining issues such as the importance of increasing the number of emergency and temporary shelters in his city. He also provided his constituents with information about navigating the bureaucratic procedures for receiving subsidies from the city office to repair damaged houses. Similarly, Ebihara Masato, a member of the Kamaishi City Council, reported on his website that he lobbied the minister for reconstruction and vice-minister for engineering affairs in the Ministry of Land, Infrastructure, Transport and Tourism (MLIT) to push for the creation of reconstruction projects in his municipality. Individual council members actively contact and meet with various people in the process of recovery from disaster in their attempts to accelerate rebuilding and show what they have done to improve the lives of their constituents.

A number of potential factors could explain both the targets of and the variation in consultation at the level of the individual council member and at the level of the municipality. Politicians may expend time and resources doing more than simply connecting with local residents in their home areas to shore up political support and guarantee reelection.[35] Council members may, for example, seek out material benefits for their home districts from governors, who either approve or propose prefecture-wide projects. Further, following a massive catastrophe, local council members will seek to claim credit for large-scale projects with which they may have had little to do (such as seawalls to prevent future tsunami damage) and may publicly seek out national politicians. The members of the National Diet (parliament of Japan) have the ability to pull levers of power and redirect disaster mitigation or pork barrel projects to their districts. Historically, Diet members such as Kakuei Tanaka were known for redirecting pork barrel projects to their home districts.[36] Council members have strong incentives to claim credit for large-scale infrastructure projects and other national benefits on behalf of their constituencies. Finally, council members may directly petition central government ministries, such as the MLIT, recognizing that these ministries can plan projects independently of politicians.[37]

Beyond the diversity of outreach, we are interested in factors, such as town-level attributes, that might also affect the intensity of local council outreach; namely, how often they connect with these individuals and institutions. These factors include the size (population) of the municipality, its financial capability, its merged status, the size of the town council, and the number of candidates running in council elections.

Financial capability varies tremendously among our sample of towns, villages, and cities; some have a high degree of autonomy through local property and payroll taxes while others, lacking in industry, rely more heavily on the central government for regional transfer tax payments and national treasury expenditures.[38] As stated earlier, cities, towns, and villages typically raise only one-third of their expenditures through local taxes.[39] We would assume that council members from more autonomous, financially independent areas would seek out less assistance than more dependent ones.

At the micro-level, it is important to consider the degree to which the personal characteristics of a politician may alter decisions about outreach targets and intensity. We control for length of career, party affiliation, and network width. Newer politicians who have served for shorter periods may have more naïve, ideologically driven political positions and feel less need to reach out to constituents and claim credit for their connections to powerful national politicians. Alternatively, senior politicians may have established connections and therefore feel less pressure to maintain these already strong and enduring ties. Many council members at the local level do not affiliate with any political party. These independent members may have a hard time accessing important political actors due to their lack of party-based political networks. Some of their targets, such as national-level politicians, are indeed constrained by party politics; party backbenchers and leaders may prefer that resources be spent on visible partisans and party supporters. Therefore, the gatekeepers may not provide access to independent council members.

Finally, given that our focus is on post-disaster political decisions, we seek to capture the effect of damage on outreach, here measured in both human damage (local resident deaths) and material damage (rubble and debris). I expect that greater levels of damage would increase outreach activities among council members because members in more affected areas would have more material demands and face more complex trade-offs in deciding on how to rebuild. In addition, many local governments have contingency plans that describe the actions to be taken by the administration during an emergency. For instance, in Iwate Prefecture, inland municipalities were supposed to help coastal areas at a time of emergency. However, such existing contingency plans did not work properly during the 3/11 disaster due to the massive scale of destruction. Moreover, local government administration in affected areas became dysfunctional after the disaster and failed to respond effectively to it; many municipalities lost a significant percentage of their civil servants to the tsunami along with their city halls and operations facilities. Under such circumstances, local political leaders can fill in the gaps and help their communities recover from disaster. Thus, I expect that council members would become very active in severely damaged cities, towns, and villages.

Governance Data

Ono and I used both qualitative and quantitative data to develop and test our theories of outreach targets. He spoke with local organizations and searched online to find examples of websites and newsletters from local council members to understand which targets would be appropriate to include in our survey (e.g., mayors, national politicians, bureaucrats). Further, these credit-claiming materials provided impressionistic evidence that council members varied in terms of their

CHAPTER THREE

targets of engagement (some targets for outreach were mentioned frequently, such as governors and ministerial officials, while others were not mentioned at all). While the information found in these websites and newsletters can be useful for developing theories, self-reports of such activities are neither comprehensive nor systematic. Moreover, not all council members equally engage in credit claiming in public, especially in rural areas such as the coastal municipalities affected by the 2011 disaster. Accordingly, we further employed data collected through a mail survey of local council members in the Tōhoku region to analyze the behavior of these local political leaders after the disaster. Moving from the qualitative investigation, our quantitative data allowed us to illuminate patterns in their political behavior.

For this investigation, we focused on 26 coastal municipalities in Iwate and Miyagi Prefectures, where the earthquake and tsunami hit the hardest and caused the most serious damage. Around 500 council members serve these villages, towns, and cities. Council members are elected political leaders at the local level and are closely connected to residents in their communities.[40] I provide an analysis of the vertical and horizontal linkages of these council members with various political actors after the disaster. Our primary outcome of interest is the change in the frequency of their meetings with local, prefectural, and national targets. We analyzed the frequency of meetings with these political actors to see how that frequency changed as a result of the disasters.

Our main independent variable in explaining the intensity of outreach is the degree of damage caused by the 2011 earthquake in the municipality served by a council member. We can measure the degree of damage in each municipality in two different ways: human damage and material damage. The first measure is the number of dead and missing persons per 100 people resulting from the earthquake and tsunami. This human damage varied significantly across municipalities. The second measure—material damage—is the amount of rubble and debris left behind by the earthquake and tsunami. After the disaster, rubble and debris were removed from residential areas and then piled up at temporary disposal depots in each municipality to be processed. The amount of material damage also differed significantly across municipalities.[41]

We employ two different measures of damage because some municipalities escaped significant human damage thanks to effective and organized evacuation of residents (e.g., Kamaishi). That is, there is a concern that the human damage variable might underestimate the degree of crisis caused by the earthquake and tsunami, which created the need for extended recovery after the disaster. However, even though the two measures are not identical, they are highly correlated; the correlation coefficient between the two measures is roughly 93 (out of 100). That is, municipalities that suffered higher amounts of human damage typically had more material damage, and vice versa.

We use other variables in our model to take local characteristics into account. These variables include town size, financial capability, merged status, council size, and the intensity of electoral competition. Town size is measured by (the natural log of) the population of the municipality in 2010 (before the disaster). Our financial capability index indicates the financial strength of a municipality calculated by the municipality's own revenue and expenditures. Merged status is a dichotomous variable that describes whether the municipality experienced any consolidation with other municipalities after 1995. Council size is the number of council members in the municipality. The intensity of electoral competition is measured by the number of candidates who ran for council seats in the previous election. I also included a dummy "no election" variable, which is 1 if there was no electoral competition and 0 otherwise.

The second group of independent variables controls for compounding factors at the level of the individual council member. Three variables describe differences across council members: length of political career, network width in the community, and party affiliation. The length of political career is the number of years that a member has served on the council. The network in the community is measured by (the natural log of) the number of acquaintances with whom the council members often met and communicated in their district. As a measure of partisan affiliation, we include a series of dummy variables on partisanship. These variables describe affiliation with any one of the major political parties at the national level: the Liberal Democratic Party (Jiyū Minshutō Jimintō, or LDP), the Clean Government Party (Komeitō, or CGP), the Democratic Party of Japan (Minshutō, or DPJ), the Social Democratic Party (SDP), and the Japan Communist Party (JCP).

Methods and Analyses

The logistic regression results presented in table A.3 in appendix 2 demonstrate that damage correlates strongly with the number of reported contacts between council members and political actors at various levels. Council members have established strong connections with local residents, as they serve as horizontal social capital in their communities. That is, they are connected to local citizens and residents in their communities along with civil society organizations, unions, and faith-based groups. At the time of the disaster, these council members also began to function as vertical ties between different levels of political actors. The results show that the degree of damage is highly correlated with the stated connection between council members and political actors at the national and prefectural levels. That is, council members in more severely damaged municipalities are more likely to self-report that they make frequent contact with political actors at higher levels and seek their help than are those in less damaged municipalities.

As interpreting the estimate coefficients in logistic regressions can be challenging, I visually present how the predicted probability changes in response to a shift of the damage level in order to better illuminate the relationship between severity of damage and reported outreach by local politicians to various political actors. Figure 3.4 shows the relationship between human damage and the likelihood that council members claimed they increased their outreach to a target group of lawmakers, namely, legislators in Japan's House of Representatives. The

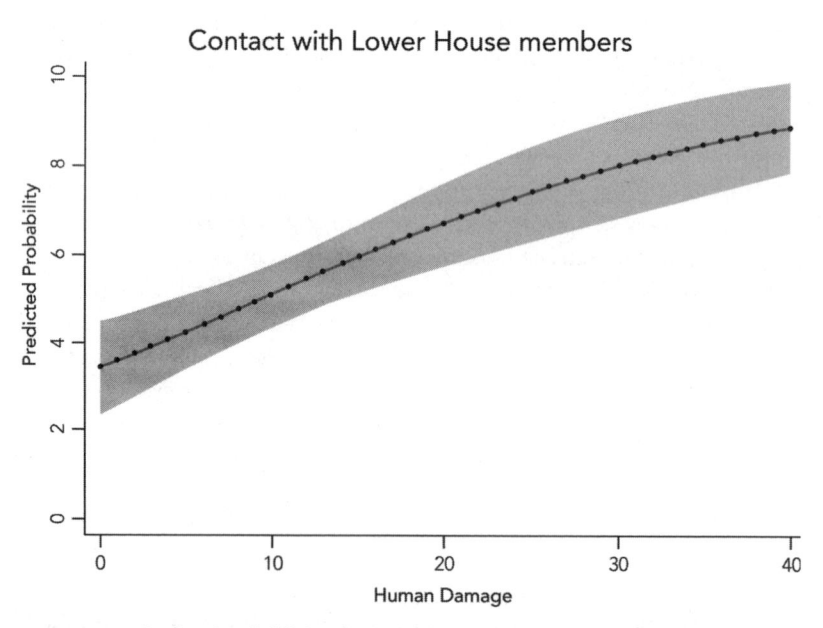

FIGURE 3.4. Predicted probabilities of municipal council members reaching out to members of the national House of Representatives.

predicted probability, which is based on the logistic regression results, has been shown with 95% confidence intervals. In this figure, we held all of the other variables (town size, experience of the politician, etc.) at their means and allowed only the amount of human damage to vary. As the damage to their towns and communities increased, local town council members reached out more regularly to lower house members. Damage levels—both human and material—greatly altered behaviors, pushing council members to invest more time and energy in reaching out to certain groups and less time in outreach to others.

Having looked at how governance itself changed after the disaster, I now look at how ties to powerful decision makers influenced the recovery process for towns, villages, and cities in Tōhoku.

Social Capital, Governance, and Recovery

More than seven years have passed since the disaster, yet visitors to some tsunami-struck communities might believe that the event had occurred yesterday. In some municipalities in coastal Tōhoku, homes sit abandoned near boarded-up businesses and empty parking lots, weeds have overgrown sidewalks and parks, and major highways into previously active towns are cracked. In others, bus service has resumed, electricity and gas services have been reestablished, schools are open and filled with pupils, and businesses have transitioned from temporary buildings into permanent structures. More than half a decade after the disaster, obvious differences in recovery speed remain visible. Why some communities have been able to bounce back more effectively than others is an important question for scholars of disaster and disaster managers to answer.

I gathered data on nearly 40 communities in the Tōhoku area to illuminate the factors—including governance networks through the relationships known as clientelism—that may have accelerated or retarded recovery.[42] *Clientelism* involves the deliberate redistribution of economic benefits to specific, politician-supporting groups[43] and meshes with the concept of linking social capital.[44] Holding constant a number of variables, including demographic, geographic, political, and social conditions, the data show that sociopolitical ties between the central government and the periphery served as the main drivers of the recovery process. The immediate conditions following the disaster—that is, how much of the capacity of these communities was lost due to the tsunami—were also significant in determining the pace of recovery.

More important than the financial capability of these municipalities, the height of the tsunami, or the local demographic conditions, however, were their vertical political connections to Tokyo—the administrative and financial center of Japan—which proved critical in accelerating rebuilding in Tōhoku.

Outcome of the Disaster

I first look at the intersection between the immediate post-disaster conditions following the March 11, 2011, tsunami and the conditions in the same communities two and three years later (in March 2013 and March 2014). I use Japan's National Institute for Research Advancement (NIRA) recovery index to parse precisely and objectively the conditions in each municipality. NIRA created a municipal capacity/recovery index modeled on the work of the Brookings Institution, which had captured the recovery process from Hurricane Katrina in New Orleans after August 2005.[45] The New Orleans Index (occasionally called the Katrina Index) used 28 measurements focusing on economic, social, and environmental metrics to capture that city's recovery trajectory following its flooding in the fall of 2005. Composite indices such as those used in New Orleans and Tōhoku allow us to better encapsulate the multifaceted, long-term processes of rebuilding and recovery and sum up infrastructure, market, and demographic conditions.

Among other factors, the NIRA recovery index captures a municipality's proportion of operating convenience stores; the proportion of people in evacuation shelters; the rate of temporary housing occupation among evacuees; the recovery rate of middle and junior high schools; the proportion of fully operational utility lines (electricity and gas); the functionality of transportation networks (railroads and roads); and debris disposal. The index scores sit on a scale from 0 to 100; a town or city is assigned 100 if all infrastructure and utility services are back to normal, debris is off the streets and fields, displaced people have found housing, and convenience stores have reopened. As discussed below, only two of the towns in the dataset received this "perfect recovery" score two years after the tsunami. A score of 50 would indicate that a municipality's businesses, transportation infrastructure, gas and electricity lines, and school attendance were at half of their initial, pre-disaster levels and that only half of the debris had been cleaned up. More of the municipalities in this study had scores centered near 50. Finally, the NIRA index score was set at 0 if none of those systems were functioning and none of the displaced residents had found permanent

VILLAGE, TOWN, AND CITY LEVEL

housing; this score applied to none of the municipalities two years after the tsunami.

Figure 3.5 illustrates core examples of municipalities in three categories. The communities studied had immediate post-disaster capacities ranging from 15% of their pre-disaster levels (the town of Yamada) to some 60% (the municipality of Iwaizumi). Two years later, a few towns had returned to full capacity; Rifu and Fudai, for example, had reopened stores, returned children to their schools, and removed all debris from their streets and residential areas (the fastest recoveries recorded here). Their NIRA recovery index scores of 99.90 and 100, respectively, indicate the strong—indeed, complete—recoveries in these two towns following the disaster. In contrast, other municipalities, such as Futaba and Naraha, hovered close to less than half of their pre-disaster capacity levels with NIRA scores at 46 and 51, respectively. Thus we see three groups of municipalities: those with slow (Namie, Futaba, Ōkuma), intermediate (Minamisoma, Shinchi, and Watari), and fast recovery speeds (Ofunato, Yamada, and Rikuzentakata). This strong variation in municipal capacity rebuilding two years after the disaster remains an important puzzle to solve.

CITY	IMMEDIATE CONDITIONS ON 3/2011	2 YEARS AFTER DISASTERS	3 YEARS AFTER DISASTERS	DIFFERENCE IN RECOVERY
SLOW RECOVERY TIME				
Namie	33	49	49	16
Futaba	29	46	48	18
Okuma	32	50	51	19
INTERMEDIATE RECOVERY TIME				
Minamisoma	35	74	75	40
Shinchi	41	75	82	41
Watari	52	94	96	47
FAST RECOVERY TIME				
Ofunato	29	89	99	70
Yamada	14	75	87	71
Rikuzentakata	23	92	96	73

Point Scale: 0 –100
0 – All Systems Offline
100 – Everything Operational

FIGURE 3.5. Conditions immediately after the disaster and two and three years later in various Tōhoku municipalities.

CHAPTER THREE

Theories of Recovery

Past research has identified a number of factors considered important in the recovery process. Broadly, these variables can be categorized into factors related to the disaster itself, geographic factors, political, economic, and demographic conditions, and levels of social cohesion. The first set of data revolves around *disaster* and *geographic factors*.[46] In this dataset, I capture the percentage of people in a municipality killed by the tsunami along with measurements of the area of the town.[47] Some communities lost only 2 in 100 residents while other populations were decimated, with 1 in 10 residents killed.

Beyond geographic and disaster-specific characteristics, however, a number of *financial factors* could alter the recovery trajectory. The ability of the local government to self-finance its recovery activities may be an important piece in the recovery; I therefore use a measure of each town's financial capability. Similarly, each town had money set aside for disaster mitigation before the tsunami, and this dataset captures the budget for disaster mitigation activities (such as training programs for children and adults, warning systems such as broadcast speakers, and search-and-rescue equipment) and then norms it by dividing by population.

I use three political variables: the town's support for the long-dominant Liberal Democratic Party (LDP); its support for the Democratic Party of Japan (DPJ) in the 2009 lower house election; and the number of powerful politicians elected from the municipality's electoral district. Given that the LDP has long ruled Japan, but the DPJ saw a victory in the 2009 election, support for either party may have generated additional benefits for the town. Separate from electoral outcomes, I define powerful politicians as those with long-term incumbent status; namely, politicians who have served six or more consecutive terms in the National Diet. Sending more powerful representatives to the Diet may provide municipalities with a stronger channel to the national government (and its resources) in Tokyo. Such politicians are chosen first to serve in Cabinet posts and have developed strong links to important resource holders and decision makers in the capital.

Next, *demographic factors* in the affected community, such as population density and the proportion of the population over the age of 65, may accelerate or slow the recovery process. In one study of disasters in developing countries, the authors argued that factors such as the percentage of the population that is undernourished, infant mortality, disease prevalence, and access to sanitation explained the majority of variation in the effects of disasters such as floods.[48] My dataset also captures the population density (people per square kilometer) and the proportion of the population over 65.[49] More densely populated towns with older residents may have a more difficult time achieving recovery.

The final factor that may retard or accelerate the recovery process is *social cohesion*; namely, the level of connections and trust among citizens inside a municipality. As before, this part of my investigation uses the proportional crime rate—the rate of major crimes (such as murder, rape, robbery, and assault) per 1,000 people—as a proxy for social capital, based on extensive sociological research.[50] Communities with fewer connections among individuals and lower expectations about future interactions have higher rates of crime than those where neighbors feel tied to one another and their neighborhood.

Data

I use a new sui generis dataset that captures all of the nearly 40 communities along the coast of the Tōhoku region in the three prefectures most affected by the disasters, namely, Fukushima, Miyagi, and Iwate. The municipalities in the dataset are the core communities struck by the tsunami and serve as a representative sample of the towns, villages, and cities critical for understanding; there is no need for reweighting. Table A.4 in appendix 2 provides descriptive statistics for the dataset, table A.5 provides the components of the NIRA recovery index, and table A.6 provides the source for each variable in the dataset. Municipalities along Tōhoku's coast faced different levels of damage from the disaster and then moved forward at differential rates as well. The two main outcomes of interest here (the dependent variables) are municipality capacity by March 2012 and capacity by March 2013, one and two years after the disaster, respectively, based on NIRA recovery index scores.

Results

Table A.7 in appendix 2 shows the estimated regression coefficients of the variables influencing recovery one year after the disaster (by March 2012). The immediate conditions after the 3/11 triple disasters, the area of the town, and the number of powerful politicians proved significant

CHAPTER THREE

across both models. Damage from the disaster, population density, spending on disaster mitigation beforehand, and demographic conditions were not significant. These findings are robust to the presence of all other demographic, social cohesion, political, economic, and disaster-related control variables. The estimated coefficients for the significant variables are positive, meaning that as the values of these variables increase, the outcome of interest—namely, the recovery index at one year—increases. Intuitively, the better the initial conditions (e.g., the fewer convenience stores damaged, the more schools remaining open, the better the condition of power and transportation infrastructure), the better conditions were one year later. Similarly, the larger the town, the faster its recovery, although this result was less significant statistically. Finally—and most significant statistically—the more politicians from the district in office for six continuous terms or longer, the better the recovery in the town one year after 3/11.

I now turn to the results two years after the disaster. Here again, two variables prove highly significant across both models: the immediate conditions after the earthquake and tsunami and the number of powerful politicians representing an area. In this model, an additional variable—support for the LDP—proved significant across both analyses, and its sign was negative. Table A.8 in appendix 2 provides the estimated coefficients for these models of recovery by March 2013. As with the recovery one year after 3/11, having more (or fewer) powerful politicians and better (or worse) initial conditions strongly drove town, village, and city recoveries two years later.

Figure 3.6 illustrates the predicted relationship between the number of powerful politicians and the recovery index, holding all other variables in the analysis constant. Based on this simulation, a typical municipality in Tōhoku struck by the disaster without any such representatives would—some two years later—find itself at roughly 65% capacity. This prediction for such a peripheral, isolated town involves controls for all of the other conditions investigated above, including demographic, political, social cohesion, and geographic factors. In contrast, a town with eight such powerful representatives—and several towns in the dataset have this many—is predicted be at 90% capacity, ceteris paribus. This difference is statistically significant and underscores the powerful channel served by these representatives in the central government through clientelism and strong linking social capital. Given these findings about the importance of vertical linking ties and connections to decision makers, I now turn to a case study to illustrate these outcomes.

VILLAGE, TOWN, AND CITY LEVEL

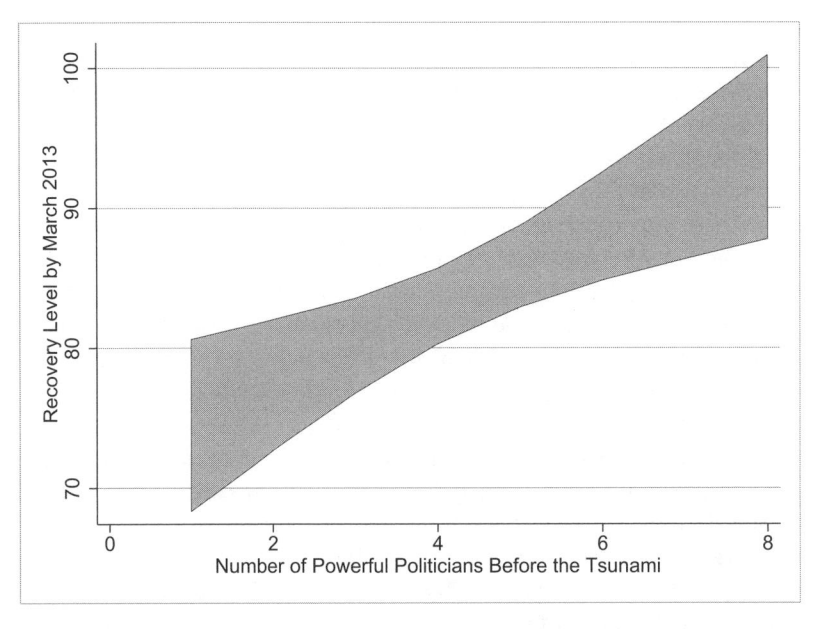

FIGURE 3.6. Relationship between number of powerful politicians representing a municipality and speed of recovery. For this simulation of 1,000 draws, all explanatory variables (demographic, economic, political, and disaster-related) have been set at their means except for the number of powerful politicians, which has been allowed to vary. The edges of the shaded area map the 95% confidence interval around the predicted outcome, which sits at the center. The figure is narrower when there are more data points and wider when there are fewer.

Case Study of Innovative and Networked Governance: Coastal Town

The community I refer to as Coastal Town, which faced an 18 m (nearly 60-foot) tsunami that devastated its population and physical infrastructure, sits squarely among the fastest-recovering municipalities in Tōhoku, as we saw earlier in this chapter. It was the first city in Tōhoku to start building temporary housing for its affected population, setting up 36 units within nine days of the event.[51] Beyond overall recovery, it has pursued a level of post-disaster terraforming seen nowhere else in Japan. It has literally leveled nearby mountains to provide the base for a raised downtown (some 11 m, or 36 feet, above the sea) and created new areas for businesses, factories, and the city hall. This city has been able to pursue an expensive and extensive set of reconstruction projects because of its vertical connections to decision makers in domestic and foreign positions of power.

CHAPTER THREE

Soon after the tsunami killed more than 10% of its population, wiped out 80% of its housing stock, and destroyed most of the 70,000 pine trees in its forests, the local government of Coastal Town recognized that it had to design the city from scratch. Setting up an advisory board, which included experts from Tokyo University and Tokyo Kokyo Daigaku (Tokyo Engineering University), was just the start. The city wanted to engage its citizens and bring them as active participants into the planning and recovery processes. The Coastal Town City Network drew in 40 nonprofit organizations, nongovernmental organizations, and other groups and worked alongside the Coastal Town Disaster Volunteer Center,[52] which continued operating for more than a year after the disaster. The city made sure to include feedback from citizens in the planning process.[53]

Coastal Town also reached out to mayors and decision makers from outside the city with whom it had strong social ties. Within a year of the disaster, for example, more than 60 personnel from other cities were working in Coastal Town City Hall, and personal connections with the cities of Nagoya and Takeo allowed additional workers to be dispatched to the community.[54] City officials also encouraged a well-connected "local son," a businessman who had developed an extensive network of domestic and international connections through work with the United Nations and in the financial sector, to help them with the process. "We were not just making a plan," this adviser told me. "We were building the city."[55]

From his initial contact with the mayor and other local politicians, this local businessman knew the potential power of his colleagues and acquaintances in the public and private sectors. When communities need resources, bridging ties can prove critical in creating channels to those outside the area.[56] "But we are thinking about the future. I also contacted the Cabinet Office and talked with Important Cabinet Member, the senior vice minister handling the Tōhoku emergency; he was a person whom I had known from before from my work with the United Nations. He asked me why I was involved in Coastal Town operations, and I explained that I was from the area. He said that we could have a direct hotline without interference from prefectural government; we wanted to become independent from Iwate Prefecture as they did not really assist us."[57]

It might seem logical for the city to turn to the regional government above it for assistance. But local residents in Coastal Town saw the prefectural government of Iwate, based in Morioka, as aloof from the realities of life in a destroyed town. As the next chapter shows,

Iwate prefectural authorities were not as adept at building connections as their neighbors in Miyagi. City authorities also believed that historical discrimination based on Edo period *han*-politics continued to show in prefectural policies, which ignored Coastal Town–focused interests. Instead of investing time and resources to connect with Iwate Prefecture, Coastal Town reached above it to the Cabinet and beyond Japan to nearby nations.

While prior to the tsunami, the city had coastal defenses in the form of pine trees and seawalls, neither had done anything to stop the tsunami. Accordingly, in discussions with MLIT representatives, Coastal Town pushed to create a city that could survive another once-in-a-millennium tsunami. The city spent two years formulating its plan for a massive undertaking: raising the downtown area some 11 m above sea level as well as constructing new seawalls and relocating homes in the mountains. The nearby mountains would be leveled to serve as the foundation for the elevated downtown. Local residents called it a "colossal experiment to create an artificial town."

To use the materials generated by razing the mountains, the city had to construct a conveyor belt to carry the crushed rock down into the center of the town. The conveyor belt system, created in 2014, itself cost more than ¥12 billion (more than $110 million). The conveyor belt, which was 3 km (1.8 miles) long and 1.8 m (6 feet) wide, was able to move the equivalent of 4,000 10-ton dump trucks of soil and rock. Elevating the city's business district cost some ¥118 billion ($1 billion).[58] Overall, restoration and recovery projects in the city have run more than ¥320 billion, or $3.2 billion.[59] Planners hope that two new residential neighborhoods, Takata District, with 1,650 homes, and Imazumi District, with 560 homes, will be settled soon.[60]

The amount of debris and material moved from the leveled mountains to raise the downtown area was unprecedented. The actual environmental effects of destroying whole ecosystems in this way have not been thoroughly discussed by the city. Further, the overall plan has not gone without hitches. Coastal Town city officials acknowledged that a minority of citizens were against the new seawalls, and that they had to gerrymander various aspects of the protection framework to exclude holdouts who did not want to relocate or sell their property. Overall, decision makers argued that the majority of citizens in the city wanted to protect their properties from future tsunami and hence signed on to the plan.

Other nearby Tōhoku communities have carried out smaller-scale changes to their landscape after the tsunami; the local government in

CHAPTER THREE

Onagawa, for example, cut down the trees on nearby mountains and began leveling them to make space for housing and material for raising the base elevation back in the town.[61] That project remains under way. Onagawa, with assistance from the prefectural and national governments, has only some $1 billion available for the reconstruction, although in interviews, city decision makers expressed the belief that they would be able to complete the project by 2020. Households from six tsunami-devastated communities in the city of Iwanuma relocated to a newly created inland town called Tamaura-Nishi, the first planned community with more than 100 households from municipalities affected by the disaster.[62] The new community, built on completely flat farmland some 3 km (1.8 miles) from the coast, includes a supermarket and parks and cost about ¥19.6 billion (about $158 million).[63] Minamisanriku, after elevating its fishing port area, hoped to elevate its downtown as well, but that city has to rely on its own funds to do so, and the project has stalled.[64] In short, Coastal Town's reconstruction on higher ground in its original location dwarfs other projects in similarly affected towns and villages.

Locals working with Coastal Town City Hall mentioned strong political connections with civil servants in the Tokyo office of MLIT and also with the MLIT office in the city of Sendai. The city's advocates reached out to central government agencies and politicians to make sure that the DPJ regime kept its ambitious plans in mind; lobbyists also reported talking to the CGP and the long-dominant LDP. Among the offshoots of the recovery plan have been a new paved road that will serve as an escape route for cars, an FM radio station (80.5 mHz), and a new city mascot, Yume-Chan. (Yume-Chan has small green wings to remind the audience of the pine forest that decorated the coast along with a yellow star on his head, which is said to represent a ray of hope.)

The city has not been content merely with a raised business district and a mountain-based residential area. It also has a memorial park with facilities for 3,000 in the works, along with a plan for a research museum on the tsunami. Coastal Town hopes to collect Japanese- and English-language materials for a library there. Further, officials are redeveloping one of the junior high school buildings to serve as a global campus for higher education focused on disaster management.

As central government funding is typically awarded for one-year periods, leaders in Coastal Town recognized that they would need more assistance than Tokyo could provide. They reached out to foreign governments—including Italy, the United States, and Singapore—to take action because they believed the Japanese government was moving too slowly.⁶⁵ In conversations with these governments, Coastal Town advocates focused on raising money through vertical ties abroad. As one told me, "We received ¥700 million [nearly $7 million] in support from the Singapore government beginning shortly after the disaster." That money has helped fund a new community center for the town. Italy has donated a mobile library, as the town's library was destroyed in the disasters, and the US-based Tomodachi Initiative's investment of $5 million has brought North American high school students in for a variety of programs focused on building an inclusive and open new city.⁶⁶ Coastal Town also reached out to private-sector firms, such as Itochu and Citibank, for financial assistance with public relations and outreach activities. The city even worked with Montblanc to sell more than 100 pens at $4,000 each, made from the wood of the sole tree, known as the "miracle pine," left standing after the tsunami. (Unfortunately, the tree eventually died and has been replaced by a sculpted replica.)

Other cities have attempted similar use of vertical networks to speed up recovery. Yoshiaki Suda, Onagawa's mayor since November 2011, tapped into local and external networks to move past bureaucratic impediments.⁶⁷ Suda brought in world-famous architect Shigeru Ban and pop group AKB48 producer Yasushi Akimoto as key supporters of the town. Onagawa also set up train service from the city of Ishinomaki in 2015 and runs day tours from Tokyo to increase tourism.⁶⁸ And while it has terraformed some nearby mountains to create new land, and plans were made to raise the waterfront and center by 5 m (16 feet), the new town center was initially prone to flooding during typhoons and heavy rainfall.⁶⁹

Of course, with Coastal Town's ambitious plans come unanswered questions: with residential neighborhoods separated from the raised downtown area, people may not be able to move easily between them, especially the elderly and those without cars.⁷⁰ Further, with this tremendous amount of investment in physical infrastructure, the ability of the town to spur actual business investment and a broader economic base remains unclear.

Conclusions

This chapter has looked at the role of networks and governance at the village, town, and city level. I began with an investigation into the factors that improved survival rates for towns hit by the tsunami and showed how tighter-bonding ties before the disaster helped people organize and save lives during it. I then analyzed how local politicians in disaster-affected areas changed their outreach behavior as a result of the event. Town council members in more heavily damaged towns reached out with greater frequency to activate their links to outside politicians and civil servants who could assist in the recovery. Then, I showed that communities with these vertical linking ties had faster recoveries than other damaged communities with fewer powerful allies. I ended my investigation with a discussion of one community—Coastal Town—that has activated its linking ties and created an ambitious (and expensive) plan for rebuilding the city on raised ground. Officials and advisers to the community have tapped Cabinet officials, colleagues in relevant ministries, and even foreign governments in an entrepreneurial rush to fund their expensive and expansive vision. Other communities have not shown this level of proactive outreach and governance.

Political intervention in markets and in disaster recovery processes has displayed remarkable resilience despite attempts at reform. Scholars have shown that Japan's long-ruling Liberal Democratic Party (LDP) continues to redistribute wealth to rural towns in the periphery to gain support despite major institutional changes to Japan's electoral system some two decades ago.[71] Even the arrival of Prime Minister Junichiro Koizumi with an explicitly anti-clientelist slogan ("change the LDP, change Japan") was counterbalanced by the Democratic Party of Japan's convergent policies, which redistributed projects and funds to disenfranchised groups in rural Japan.[72] In the very specific field of energy efficiency within Japan's transportation sector, clientelism has been similarly hard to erase, and the close ties involved make transparent and open politics a major challenge.[73]

In the field of disaster recovery, too, powerful incumbent politicians serve as important resources for damaged communities. By having more advocates and power brokers in the center of Japan, otherwise peripheral or potentially marginalized communities can receive money for rebuilding, support for large-scale infrastructure projects, and encouragement for firms to rebuild in the area. In contrast, communities without such powerful supporters in Tokyo may find themselves without political support for their local recovery efforts. This is especially true because many local governments remain financially and administratively dependent on the central government during standard operating times.

Many observers hoped to see evidence of major, non-incremental change in Japan after the Great East Japan Earthquake; despite these expectations, most evidence points to continuity, not innovation, in the fields of politics and administration.[74] Notwithstanding clear signs of high dependency and a lack of autonomy at the local government level, Tokyo undertook few, if any, attempts to rebalance financial and logistic power between center and periphery. The patterns unearthed in this analysis of recovery resonate with earlier research, which has long stressed the importance of political and social ties between center and periphery in Japan.[75] This chapter has brought strong evidence that precisely because of their ties to the center, Tōhoku municipalities with more powerful politicians did better than similar communities without such ties.

Horizontal and vertical ties proved critical for individuals and for cities, towns, and villages throughout Tōhoku during and after the disaster. These municipalities sit at the bottom level of Japan's three-tiered government system and are embedded within larger regional governments, known as prefectures, to which we will turn next.

FOUR

Prefectural Level: Networks Making a Difference

Three Tōhoku prefectures felt the effects of the 3/11 disasters most strongly: Iwate, Miyagi, and Fukushima. They faced high numbers of casualties, destruction of homes and businesses, disruptions in energy, transportation, and delivery networks, and challenges in managing evacuees. Of the three, Miyagi had the largest number of casualties, damaged buildings, and evacuees. Table 4.1 details some of the outcomes of the triple disasters in the three prefectures.

This chapter looks into the 3/11 disasters at the prefectural level with a focus on governance and connections, beginning with pre-disaster preparation, moving through the first days after 3/11, and then examining the intermediate and long-term recovery periods. While Miyagi and Iwate Prefectures focused their recovery efforts on the destruction caused by the Great East Japan Earthquake and the tsunami, Fukushima bore the additional burden of responding to the Fukushima Dai-ichi nuclear reactor meltdowns. Surveys of government personnel show that Fukushima bureaucrats faced more challenges than their colleagues in Iwate and Miyagi. For example, when asked about their work post-disaster, Fukushima civil servants reported the largest burden of handling tasks completely unrelated to their normal, pre-disaster work routines.[1]

Fukushima's radiation challenges have brought admittedly small-scale benefits. The ongoing *josen*, or radioac-

Table 4.1. Comparative Damage across Prefectures

	Iwate Prefecture	Miyagi Prefecture	Fukushima Prefecture
Dead/missing	5,989	11,250	1,989
Indirect deaths	446	900	1,793
Buildings damaged	24,739	222,081	83,557
Damage to agriculture, forestry, and fishery (millions of yen)	449,391	1,227,342	275,360
Inundated area/building + infrastructure land use	58 km^2 (37%)	327 km^2 (23%)	112 km^2 (13%)
Coastal area capital loss rate	47.3%	21.1%	11.9%
Maximum evacuees	51,553	320,885	131,665
Evacuees in March 2012	42,771	127,952	98,221

Sources: Data from Geospatial Authority of Japan, Iwate Reconstruction Plan, Miyagi Reconstruction Plan, Development Bank of Japan, Reconstruction Agency, and Mimura (2015a, 2015b).

tive decontamination of the soil, in Fukushima Prefecture has proved a short-term boon for some Fukushima communities, employing many in low-skill, stable jobs. Cities where nuclear power plant workers have established a base for the plant decommissioning process have seen an increase in tax revenues; Hirono's revenue, for example, rose 61.7% in fiscal 2014 thanks to hotel and restaurant sales. But the long-term consequences of radiation leakage, and the outcome of efforts to regain the trust of the local population in order to promote childbearing, education, and local infrastructure, are much harder to measure and anticipate. Communities close to the Fukushima Daiichi plant, such as Namie, saw a 73% decrease in tax revenues for fiscal 2014.[2] Many residents have yet to return to the areas of Fukushima closer to the plant, and those who have come back have been elderly.

Further, prefectural officials and organizations across Tōhoku have not shown the same level of active, broad outreach and good governance. Of the three prefectures, Miyagi has proved the most adept at building and maintaining horizontal and vertical connections between residents and local, regional, and national decision makers. Thanks to this strong governance, its deliberate creation of network ties to relevant organizations in the public and private sectors, and its lack of radioactive contamination, Miyagi has also demonstrated the fastest overall recovery. I show qualitatively and quantitatively that Miyagi's social ties and governance have been stronger than Iwate's and Fukushima's.

CHAPTER FOUR

Pre-Disaster/Preparation

These three coastal prefectures in the northeastern part of Japan's main island were no strangers to risk. As one Fukushima prefectural official told me, "We did have a disaster response plan in place for earthquakes and tsunamis, which are quite common in the region, as well as strategies for supplies and evacuations in case of a bigger hit to the city."[3] Iwate Prefecture, for example, faced multiple tsunami over the past two centuries, including the 1896 Sanriku tsunami, which killed 22,000, and it recognized these risks during its preparation efforts. It had organized disaster drills, set up evacuation plans and designated shelter locations, and coordinated with schools across the prefecture to teach disaster preparedness.

Miyagi prefectural authorities, too, had long sought to prepare the prefecture for major disasters. After the magnitude 7.7 Miyagi-Oki Earthquake killed 28 and injured more than 1,300 in 1978, they designated June 12 as an annual Citizens' Disaster Prevention Day in Miyagi, featuring comprehensive emergency drills. By the early 1980s, Miyagi had created seismic hazard maps of the prefecture. In the late 1990s, Miyagi published research showing that there was nearly a 100% chance of another major earthquake within the next 30 years. The prefecture continued to update its earthquake countermeasures plan after smaller earthquakes, such as the 2003 Northern Miyagi Earthquake and the 2008 Iwate-Miyagi Nairiku Earthquake. Less than a year before the 3/11 disasters, Miyagi Prefecture budgeted roughly ¥34 billion ($300 million) for 38 initiatives to minimize the impact of future quakes.

Fukushima Prefecture also had extensive emergency response plans in place for disasters such as earthquakes, tsunami, and flooding before March 11. It held disaster drills to practice responses to these natural catastrophes. Prior to 3/11, however, prefectural government officials had been told that the nuclear plants at locations like Fukushima Dai-ichi's were completely safe in the event of disaster and required no special plans. One municipal official told me in 2015, "As for the nuclear power plant failure, city offices had been reassured time and time again by the national government and TEPCO that the plant was 'completely safe and risk free.' This meant that even municipalities like Minamisoma, which was within 20 km [12 miles] from the plant, did not know of or attempt to implement any disaster intervention plans."[4]

Because of the widespread safety myth pushed by TEPCO and other nuclear power utilities, there had been no prefecture-wide emergency drills, evacuation plans, or response plans for a nuclear disaster in recent memory.[5] Indeed, Japanese nuclear engineers and private utilities had long argued that their facilities were not subject to the same risks that other countries' nuclear plants faced. They continued to say so despite the creation of smaller-scale nuclear evacuation plans in Japan after the 1979 Three Mile Island nuclear disaster in the United States.[6] (That incident, rated a level 5 event on the 7-point INES, involved the release of reactor coolant into the atmosphere.) In 2008, Japanese authorities had planned on setting up detailed evacuation plans for zones with a radius of 2.5 km (1.5 miles) around troubled atomic reactors,[7] but those abstract plans did not translate into on-the-ground planning in Fukushima itself.

All three prefectures had released hazard maps of their jurisdictions, outlining areas at high and low risk from events such as earthquakes and tsunami. These maps proved not just useless, but dangerous. Many of the tsunami- and flood-inundated businesses, schools, and hospitals—some of which served as emergency evacuation shelters—had been in areas marked as safe by the experts.[8] As other experts have argued, these maps give the public a false sense of safety.[9] Previous chapters discussed how many of the places designated as evacuation sites were themselves flooded by the tsunami, turning evacuees who followed government guidance into victims.

Search and Rescue/First Days

The first days after 3/11 were chaotic for all of Tōhoku, including prefectural authorities. An evacuee who had lived through World War II said the situation reminded him of past crises: "This was like wartime."[10] Without needing guidance, local residents and, where possible, official first responders such as volunteer and professional firefighters, police officers, and the Japan Self Defense Forces carried out ground search and rescue in Tōhoku. Disaster Medical Assistance Teams (DMATs) and hospitals set up field hospitals or used existing hospital and health-care structures, if they were still operable. These trained medical professionals—doctors, nurses, and logistics experts among them—filled the gaps for the first days after the crisis until regular operations could resume at local hospitals.[11] Government bureaucracy soon reduced the efficiency of these ad hoc measures. The DMATs ran into problems when the government prioritized reopened hospitals in the evacuation zone and local municipalities refused to provide support to mobile DMAT members in the field.[12]

Hazardous conditions impeded access to many homes and facilities in the area. Most roads into coastal areas were impassable due to debris for the first week;[13] instead of trucks, rescue personnel relied on public and private helicopters to deliver supplies and pick up victims. Where possible, the SDF flew wounded victims from locations such as Hanamaki Airport in Iwate Prefecture to hospitals in other prefectures,[14] as discussed in chapter 2. Victims and evacuees went to meeting spots such as the airport or nearby medical centers, and together they evacuated from coastal communities to safer, more stable areas inland where they could rest in shelters or with family.

In the midst of the unprecedented destruction, prefectures sought to coordinate actions with national and local governments. But prefectural officials said that communication with those governments typically relied almost exclusively on landline-based telephones and the internet, which were not operational after the tsunami. Prefectural civil servants were effectively cut off following the disaster. Many bureaucrats ended up learning about the status of their municipalities and evacuees through broadcast media coverage, and in turn used television and radio reporters to relay information about their needs for specific aid and supplies to other parts of the country. In Fukushima, even TEPCO's command center for handling potential nuclear disasters had to be evacuated due to a lack of radiation protection. Public-sector responders were even less prepared for simultaneous nuclear, earthquake, and tsunami disasters.[15]

As Fukushima Prefecture had no functioning headquarters to handle the disaster, the central government in Tokyo initially stepped in to assist with time-sensitive needs. Tokyo, not Fukushima Prefecture, for example, made deals with fuel companies in the area in order to provide fuel to hospitals and shelters.[16] Elsewhere, disaster managers and hospital and shelter directors used television news to make appeals and bring in needed supplies.[17] All three prefectures initially sent out available supplies from headquarters and depots to cities, towns, and villages via trucks without knowing whether the food and water were necessary or even being delivered to their intended targets.

Despite years of planning and various programs designed to mitigate the effects of disasters, staff of the Miyagi prefectural government's disaster recovery policy division admitted that they were not prepared for the grim realities of 3/11. As Miyagi Prefecture described its response in a report, "The original plan for disaster response was not effective, and it became difficult for the staff of the Prefectural Disaster Task Force to respond to the disaster."[18] Altering its institutional structure on the fly, the prefecture quickly set up a broader disaster task force that included staff from each department of the prefectural government. While innovative, Miyagi's task force suffered from a lack of working communications equipment, insufficient shift rotations for staff, and an inability to coordinate between groups within the prefectural government office.

Disaster officials in all three prefectures were short on food, drinkable water, and medical supplies for survivors. As one Fukushima official remarked, "Before 3/11, we had created plans with local stores and convenience stores to provide emergency food and water, but there were no means of distribution available due to the evacuation notice following the nuclear plant disaster which left us unable to fully support our citizens."[19] Disaster planners across the region believed that most evacuees would return to their own homes within 24 hours, and many localities prepared sufficient food supplies for three meals for their residents.[20] But, as mentioned in chapter 2, in most cases Tōhoku evacuees did not return home within a short time, and food supplies ran out quickly at institutions across the area.

While first responders and medical care providers initially tried to continue standard provision of three daily meals, meals at locations such as hospitals and shelters were cut to two or even one a day. At one hospital, many nurses gave up their meals to support the dining hall staff and local volunteers who had chosen to stay in the facilities for safety. Food was scarce. One evacuee reported, "I remember eating only half of a *manjū* [steamed bun with red beans] because there were too many people for everyone to have one."[21] Medical supplies were also in short supply. As a director at a hospital said, "What we also desperately needed were things like bandages and diapers for our elderly; by the end of the week we were inserting catheters into patients to conserve diapers, which were washed and reused."[22]

Recognizing that it was not communicating well with critical partners in the response phase, Miyagi Prefecture took a step beyond its neighboring prefectures and invited relevant organizations to set up shop inside its main prefectural headquarters. There it was "possible to immediately hold meetings to share information and coordinate rescue efforts, medical relief efforts, and the acceptance and delivery of relief supplies, which proved to be highly effective."[23] As a result, the Miyagi police, fire, and rescue squads, the SDF, and the Second Regional Japan Coast Guard could stay informed about ongoing operations and work to share resources and avoid duplication. A search-and-rescue liaison committee, made up of representatives from these various disaster-related agencies, met daily after the events to share information. Their previous experience with yearly evacuation drills allowed a smooth exchange of critical data thanks to the trust already in place.

The Miyagi prefectural task force was flooded by rescue and information requests from citizens who could not contact first responders because coastal telecommunications and power systems were gone. Someone leaked the unpublished phone number of the task force to the public, and affected citizens with working cell phones began sending text and Twitter messages to its members asking for help. The Miyagi Prefecture report admitted that "an enormous amount of unreliable and overlapping information and rumors flooded in. It became a huge burden for the task force to confirm and organize all the inquiries and information."[24] Many local residents throughout the disaster-affected area appealed to the task force to undertake rescues of friends and family by helicopter, but it could not respond to most requests for aid.

At 6:00 a.m. on March 12, on the 11th floor of the Miyagi Prefectural Government Building, the national government set up an Emergency Response Disaster Management Headquarters, led by the vice minister, in Miyagi Prefecture. This move, which was based on the Disaster Basic Countermeasures Act, marked the first time that a headquarters had been set up since the creation of the law. Iwate and Fukushima Prefectures similarly set up headquarters for coordinating with national bureaucrats during this initial period.

The Miyagi response headquarters had a broad mandate. It coordinated applicable information from relevant organizations, assessed requests coming from disaster-affected areas, and transmitted those requests to relevant parties. The headquarters liaised with and coordinated personnel from central government agencies in areas focused on the transportation of goods and supplies. The location of the headquarters within the prefectural government building allowed for face-to-face exchanges, which cut down on the red tape and ensured coordination.

In addition to connecting with the central government after the disaster, the Miyagi prefectural government had previously set up institutional and personnel ties with the SDF, which has five bases in the prefecture. As the prefecture's report stated, "Before the disaster, an exclusive line was installed between the Japan Ground Self-Defense Force Northeastern Army Commandant and the prefectural governor, so that requests could be promptly made to dispatch the Japan Ground Self-Defense Forces for disaster relief."[25] Further, the SDF had participated in years of map exercises and hands-on training with prefectural authorities. Well before 3/11, the SDF and prefectural authorities had reviewed disaster relief details to improve response times and efficacy. The Ministry of Defense and SDF established the Ministry of Defense Disaster Management Headquarters on March 11 at 2:50 p.m. and soon began conducting large-scale disaster relief operations with 8,400 troops across the area at the request of the governor. After roughly six months of assistance and cooperation, SDF joint rescue, recovery, and relief operations were terminated on August 1, 2011.

Miyagi Prefecture also sought to coordinate its relief efforts with the nongovernmental and nonprofit organizations active in Miyagi. The prefecture had no formal system of interaction or coordination with these organizations, however. As prefectural officials reported in a self-evaluation, "There were no arrangements made to coordinate and cooperate with NPOs before the disaster. Therefore, time and effort were needed to coordinate their activities, and it took time until the NPOs' abilities could be fully utilized."[26] Miyagi's Victim Support 4-Way Liaison Council, made up of the Government Local Response Headquarters, Miyagi prefectural authorities, the SDF, and NGOs and NPOs was a model of cooperation.[27] Further, the prefecture invited the Miyagi branch of the Japan Red Cross Society to set up disaster relief and emergency management headquarters in the lecture hall on the second floor of the Miyagi Prefectural Government Building after the Red Cross had its building damaged. The Red Cross first worked with various DMATs that offered care across the area. Then, as outside assistance arrived, the organizations worked with the SDF to transport relief supplies between municipalities, establish and manage disaster relief volunteer centers, coordinate psychological care, and accept relief donations.

Beyond coordinating with domestic government and nonprofit organizations, Miyagi Prefecture worked with foreign countries and their representatives. Search-and-rescue teams and medical support teams from 17 countries and regions joined in support operations, and 23 countries sent in relief supplies.[28] More than 15 years earlier, miscommunication and a lack of preparedness during the 1995 Great Hanshin-Awaji Earthquake had pushed the national government to clarify contact points for rescue teams from overseas. During the post-3/11 influx of offers of aid, there were far fewer major disruptions because Japan sent requests to overseas rescue teams specifying which experts and what materials and supplies it needed.

Rescue squads from Australia, New Zealand, South Korea, and the United States came to Japan after 3/11 as self-sufficient system groups, where they found simplified procedures for medical inspections and customs clearance when entering.[29] Foreign countries sent some $700 million in donations.[30] Israel sent a full field hospital to Miyagi Prefecture and treated victims on the ground, making headlines as it was the first time foreign doctors without a Japanese license had done so.[31] In Iwate, strong connections to the German state of Rhineland-Palatinate and to Taiwan brought in medical supplies and financial donations. Iwate also received 5 million barrels of crude oil from Kuwait along with ¥8.4 billion (some $70 million) in aid money through the Japanese Red Cross Society, both of which were used to cover the high costs of restarting Iwate's Sanriku Railway in 2014.

Fukushima prefectural officials described having fewer connections to the nonprofit sector. One said bluntly, "We don't work with NPOs and NGOs, or track their efforts in the community. I'm sure they are still around and helping individual hospitals and temporary housing facilities, but that is a relationship formed between the NPO or NGO and the locals and is not facilitated by the local government."[32] Further, when Fukushima set up a disaster response headquarters to handle the ongoing crisis, there were no members of the medical profession included, despite the obvious radiological and health hazards for residents and disaster teams alike.[33] Without institutionalized ties to the nonprofit sector, Fukushima, and to a lesser extent, Iwate, lost a chance to coordinate and improve their recovery efforts.

Recognizing that many of the municipalities had lost civil servants during the disaster, the Fukushima prefectural government added local staff members to towns, villages, and cities in the disaster zone by transferring them temporarily to those municipalities. In some cases, the prefecture tripled the budget of local communities for revitalization.[34] Iwate Prefecture brought in more than 7,000 emergency fire and rescue teams, along with 171 government workers to fill the roles of those killed in the disaster. By 2014, more than 1,000 bureaucrats and workers had been transferred from other prefectures to assist Iwate local governments. Iwate also set up the Center for Research and Training on Community Health Services during Disaster, which was staffed by more than 4,400 medical personnel from other prefectures.

First Years

After the immediate period of rescue and relief, the prefectural governments worked with private and public actors to undertake recovery.

Private firms such as NTT East, a massive telecommunications company, enabled the rapid reconstruction of infrastructure lifelines, such as roads and communication. Beyond repairing critical telecommunications infrastructure, NTT East donated thousands of mobile phones to temporary housing facilities, established telephone lines in shelter areas, and provided free internet service to disaster zones within the first week of the crisis.[35] Phones and internet helped Tōhoku residents maintain their social ties during the crisis itself, a mechanism that has proved critical in facilitating community resilience in disaster-hit areas around the world.[36]

Other firms, such as Yamato Transport, provided shipping services to hard-hit coastal areas and helped to coordinate the provision of supplies from private and public donors.[37] Yamato, like other private-sector firms, also undertook philanthropic giving, donating ¥10 (roughly 8 cents) for every parcel it shipped for the first year after the triple disasters. Yamato also collected donations from customers, eventually providing ¥14 billion ($120 million) for Tōhoku reconstruction projects.[38] The Japan Trucking Association provided transport for 26 million meals, 8 million bottled beverages, and some 160,000 kiloliters of fuel.[39] In addition, an industry of contractors focused on infrastructure analysis and repair emerged to help analyze cracks in roads and pipes caused by earthquakes and subsidence.[40] Mitsubishi and Softbank provided funds for NGOs along with technical assistance.[41]

But while the private sector was an important actor in the recovery process, prefectures played a broader role in rebuilding. Prefectures in Tōhoku took on middleman-like roles in the recovery processes. Money for most activities, including housing leases or construction, business restarts, and decontamination efforts, comes from the national government. Tokyo's control over the purse strings and the majority of tax revenue results from the unitary structure of Japan's government. Municipal governments—cities, villages, and towns—initiate requests, which the prefectural governments compile and process and then, once the central government has sent funds, distribute as needed. As the middle tier in the three levels of government, prefectural officials receive annual aid from the central government to build new public housing options for cities. The central government provides the funding, but major planning and construction are done independently by each prefecture. After the 3/11 disasters, the procedures remained the same, with the prefectures sending requests up to Tokyo from municipalities. As one prefectural official said, "In order to receive national funding our department must gather data in a yearly report with statistics on number of houses needed and timeline which we then submit to the government. From there, Fukushima prefectural office determines land, construction contracts, distribution of funds across cities."[42]

In Miyagi Prefecture, municipal governments coordinated the provision of emergency temporary housing, selecting sites according to the guidelines set by the regional and national governments. While the money for housing came from the central government via the prefecture, local cities, towns, and villages still needed logistic and administrative assistance from prefectural authorities. "The municipalities in coastal areas could not secure enough sites as most flat and usable areas were flooded and the necessary number of temporary houses that needed to be built was overwhelming."[43] With many of their own civil servants affected by the events, and with multiple disasters requiring prefectural government officials to work well outside their areas of expertise, some sought creative ways to handle the chaos.

Because of the inherent administrative challenges and the poor quality of much of the prefabricated housing, Miyagi and the other affected prefectures changed the system for delivering temporary housing to evacuees. Rather than relying solely on prefabricated FEMA trailer–like boxes, prefectural governments allowed evacuees and residents from damaged or destroyed houses to rent privately owned homes and apartments to speed up the relocation process. Despite this innovation, the extensive paperwork involved in selecting occupants and making contracts with private firms delayed the process of moving evacuees into more permanent homes. The number of applications exceeded initial predictions, and wrangling over the interpretation of the Disaster Relief Act also caused delays. The central government continued to pay for the maintenance of temporary homes that housed evacuees until 2018; these units had been designed to last two years, not to serve as long-term housing.

Similarly, in Fukushima Prefecture, the nearly 1,400 temporary homes set up by the national government were insufficient, so prefectural officials made up the difference through leased corporate housing and public housing.[44] As the temporary homes were constructed relatively quickly, they had design and implementation flaws. As a prefectural official said, "A major concern about temporary shelters is that these houses were built with the goal of speed, not quality, so the buildings have a weak foundation and are becoming higher-risk homes for inhabitants past their original contracted term."[45] As mentioned in previous chapters, these trailer-like modules lacked insulation, provided no privacy, and were regularly placed in isolated areas.

The central government has shown a strong commitment to supporting prefectures financially for certain types of investments. Funding for non-construction projects has been less generous. Between 2011 and 2015, the central government spent roughly ¥26 trillion ($225 billion) on construction and reconstruction efforts.[46] Of that money, some ¥25 trillion has gone solely into construction work.[47] Miyagi Prefecture itself spent ¥5.423 trillion ($48 billion) on recovery and reconstruction projects, and local municipal governments within the prefecture have contributed another ¥3.545 trillion ($31 billion). Miyagi Prefecture has also provided funding and loans for city planning efforts such as "Comprehensive Support for Administrative Functional Recovery of Towns and Cities" and the "City/Urban Planning Support Project," as most municipalities within the prefecture lack the resources and personnel to carry out effective planning.

During the same period, Iwate Prefecture sought to guide its municipalities through consultation and scheduling for disaster-related public housing and coastal development projects such as seawalls, which are funded primarily by the central government.[48] The prefecture has insisted that local coastal communities follow its lead and set up 14.5 m seawalls[49] even when residents have pushed back against this large-scale infrastructure plan. Iwate Prefecture estimated damage to its public works (parks, harbors, rivers) at ¥273 billion and damage to industry (including agriculture, fishing, and tourism) at ¥829.4 billion. The prefecture spent some ¥2.1 trillion between April 2011 and March 2016 on reconstruction.[50]

Prefectural governments also worked to help restart businesses. In Fukushima Prefecture, for example, businesses seeking to restart received funding from the prefecture's branch of the Reconstruction Agency (Fukkōchō), which in turn sends their requests in to the central government for reimbursement. In 2015, a Fukushima prefectural official told me that "they have about 8,000 businesses they are examining right now to determine distribution."[51] In Iwate Prefecture, the government can provide up to ¥2 million ($17,800) in assistance to firms interested in starting businesses along the coast. Demand for this assistance has overwhelmed available funds. In the first year after the disaster, Iwate Prefecture received applications worth ¥25.5 billion ($226 million) from firms looking to rebuild, but had only ¥15 billion ($133 million) to distribute.[52]

CHAPTER FOUR

Fukushima Prefecture's Unique Challenges

Beyond rebuilding infrastructure and restarting businesses, Fukushima Prefecture has been burdened with the challenges of the nuclear meltdowns, and its recovery process has diverged from those of Iwate and Miyagi. The mayor of one village located just outside the nuclear power plant described how the "invisible enemy" of radiation continued to cause anxiety and uncertainty among residents and to alter public policy decisions in the prefecture. The social impact of disaster has been severe in Fukushima, with suicide, divorce, alcoholism, and gambling on the rise.[53] While the prefectural government is aware of these mental health issues (discussed previously in chapter 2), it has not been able to hire sufficient counselors, therapists, and staff to monitor mental health cases. The prefecture intended to hire 400 mental health workers in 2015, but it could bring in only 274 due to the lack of job security. Central government subsidies are offered as one-year contracts, which keep the psychosocial support programs going but provide no long-term employment guarantees. A prefectural bureaucrat said in 2015 that prefectural officials have asked the government to revise the subsidy program to allow for more, longer contracts, but they remain pessimistic.[54]

Along with the mental health issues they face, Fukushima residents and evacuees have also suffered physical health complications from the 3/11 disasters. In fact, the number of locals killed directly by the tsunami is smaller than the number killed by stress and evacuation. Within two years of the 3/11 disasters, for example, more than 1,656 people in Fukushima had died from stress- and evacuation-related illnesses, including suicide, while only 1,607 were killed directly by the tsunami.[55]

The lack of medical personnel and support from the central government has made addressing these challenges to mental and physical health in Fukushima difficult. Roughly a third of nurses in the Minamisoma hospital, located just outside the 20 km ring around Fukushima Dai-ichi, are temporary volunteers from other regions in Japan who join for year-long stints. In interviews, medical directors and government officials acknowledged the difficulties in retaining personnel. Observers have urged hospitals to deploy mobile clinics and community life support centers to reach a broader proportion of the elderly and sick in the Tōhoku area at a time when few medical personnel are available.[56]

Personnel shortages in the medical fields and elsewhere are no doubt exacerbated by concerns over radiation. Roles in decontamination efforts near the nuclear power plant are split between the national government and the Fukushima prefectural government, which then oversees the progress in individual municipalities. The central government has set up Josen Tokubetsu Chiiki, or Special-Case Decontamination Zones, within a 20 km (12.5-mile) radius of Fukushima Dai-ichi and in any zone with particularly high levels of radiation (including Minamisoma and Iitate).[57] These are the areas in Fukushima where crews have been washing down buildings, stripping topsoil, and placing it in black garbage bags for storage within the prefecture itself. Ministry of Environment officials have argued that decontamination efforts have reduced air dose exposure levels by up to 60% in residential areas, although experts have contested these claims. Despite these signs of progress in the reduction of potential harm, a variety of challenges remain in the prefecture.

In addition to personnel shortages, another problem has plagued Fukushima's business restart process: despite attempts to synchronize the two, national agencies funding reconstruction and local banks are not working in tandem. Local banks tend to work on a two-year cycle for loan applications and disbursements, while the national approval process is standardized to five years. In several cases, a business's loan contract with a Fukushima bank expired while it was waiting for a national grant, forcing bank employees to work with prefectural officials to begin the application process again. As one decision maker argued passionately, "It should not have taken 4 years to rebuild a hospital that provided the sole source of care for an entire city after it was exposed to dire health conditions."[58] Hospitals are among the businesses seeking to rebuild both their facilities and their client base.

In a survey of business establishments in 12 municipalities across Fukushima in 2015, 627 businesses, or 45% of the 1,388 that responded, expressed hope about reopening or continuing their operations in their hometowns. Among those surveyed, 19% (270 establishments) had either returned to their hometowns and wished to continue business there, or had returned and resumed operations. Another 12% (161 establishments) had resumed business in other locations as a result of evacuation but wished to reopen in their hometowns in the future. And 14% (196 establishments) had suspended operations but hoped to return and reopen in their hometowns. Local entrepreneurs in Fukushima continue to state that they want to revitalize their communities.[59]

The private sector's efforts were complemented by the work carried out by NPOs and NGOs. Prefectural authorities in Miyagi, Iwate, and Fukushima reached out to these organizations even if they had not established strong connections before the disaster. Most cities and towns across Tōhoku already had social welfare councils, which operated under local government supervision.[60] Fukushima Prefecture's volunteer center, under its Council of Social Welfare, continues to assist those living in temporary housing. The nonprofit organization Cash for Work (CFW)-Japan, set up in December 2011, sought to connect unemployed Fukushima evacuees and residents with paying reconstruction-focused jobs in the prefecture. Participants, many of whom reported that they were the main earners in their households, carried out office work, community support, and radiation monitoring, among other tasks, through a program known as Kizuna (connections or social bonds).[61] These emergency cash-for-work projects hired some 31,700 jobless people, yet struggled to transition participants into full-time jobs in the local economy. Other NGOs, such as the organization @Rias in Kamaishi, set up emergency job creation programs for recovery projects.[62] Some NGOs provided startup grants, reemployment funds, and loan interest subsidies to both brand-new and established businesses in the Tōhoku area through the Shinkin Bank.[63]

Other prefectural NGOs sought to improve the quality of life for evacuees not through economic or job-focused programs, but rather through psychosocial support programs. Many social workers in Fukushima recognize the magnitude of the work to be done.[64] Psychosocial support activities include group discussions about and with at-risk communities, family tracing and reunification, supportive parenting programs, communal healing practices, structured activities for children and youth, and organized access to shelter and basic services.[65] Many have reported that "there was little in the way of formal counseling or mental health care" for survivors and evacuees.[66] To counter this, various NGOs and NPOs have stepped up. Fukushima librarians, for example, sought to build safe spaces where children and adults alike could feel relaxed after the tragedies.[67] They raised money and advocated for facilities where evacuees and returnees could browse in comfort. Some 280 Fukushima University students moved into temporary housing facilities in 2015 for three-month intervals to provide emotional support for those still in the shelters.[68] The SocialHearts NGO, based in Otsuchi in Iwate Prefecture, reaches out to support seniors through adult education and cooperative learning programs.

What has saved some residents, especially mothers, from the tremendous uncertainty and stress created by 3/11 are peer support groups

—organizations specifically created for women to share information and give one another mutual support. Among them is Beteran Mama no Kai (Veteran Moms' Group), which formed branches in both Fukushima and Tokyo in the year after the triple disasters. The group's main goal is to encourage mothers who were victims of 3/11 to speak to other women in a similar situation and make connections. Monthly events are held to check up on one another and to relieve stress.[69] Iwate Prefecture began supporting NPOs after the disaster, recognizing the strong contributions that they have made to the recovery process. Twenty-one groups in the prefecture have received financial support since 2013.[70] Iwate Prefecture also set up the Iwate Disaster Relief Welfare Support Team in 2013 as a public-private-academic partnership to assist the elderly and those with special needs. The connections fostered by such groups played an important role in helping to improve the quality of life for evacuees across the three most affected prefectures.

Into the Future

Until the middle of the first decade of the twentieth century, Tōhoku held 5% of Japan's population but produced only 4% of its GDP. Even before the 3/11 disasters, the region was not an economic powerhouse, nor did it possess major attractions for young people. One indoor farm manager in Tōhoku pointed out that "young people don't seem to want to work here."[71] All three prefectures hit by the triple disasters faced and continue to experience serious depopulation challenges. Well before the crises, cities across Tōhoku saw dropping populations, with some losing more than 15% of their population between 1970 and 2010.[72] The National Institute of Population and Social Security Research argues that "the Tōhoku area's population is falling faster than other areas in Japan. Maintaining vacant apartments in the future will become a huge burden on these governments."[73] The overall population of these three prefectures has decreased by 6.7% (some 90,000 people) as a result of the tsunami and out-migration. Of those who have remained, many are concentrating in the metropolis of Sendai.[74] Iwate Prefecture faced rapid depopulation after the tsunami, with some cities and towns showing 8% declines. Otsuchi lost 23%, and Rikuzentakata and Yamada lost 15%, due to tsunami deaths and migration.[75]

Fukushima, Iwate, and Miyagi Prefectures have used a variety of tools to fight this depopulation problem, many of which center on disaster mitigation efforts to bolster the confidence of residents. If citizens feel that they will be able to survive future earthquakes and tsunami, the reasoning goes, they will want to live along the Tōhoku coast. As a result, the prefectures have supported infrastructure reconstruction and tsunami protection efforts along the ocean. Every community along the coast has banned residents from living in old neighborhoods on flat plains close to the ocean, replacing those tracts of housing with commercial districts, parks, or open space.

Bureaucrats have recommended tsunami preparation strategies including coastal dikes (*bōchō tsutsumi* or *bōchōtei*), disaster prevention green space, disaster prevention forests (*bōsai ryokuchi* and *bōsairin*), relocation of residential areas to high ground, and separation of business and residential spaces. The disaster prevention forests are intended to slow down future tsunami, although the previously extant pine forests were destroyed by the 3/11 tsunami, and observers have found little evidence that they saved lives. These large-scale, public works–based mitigation approaches rely on central government funding and continue Japan's reputation as a "construction state."[76] Some prefectures, however, have tried to think outside the box. Miyagi Prefecture bureaucrats spoke of a creative recovery that incorporates the strength of NPOs and citizens through expansion and industrialization of marine products and agriculture. Miyagi has also proposed privatizing the Sendai airport, advancing university-level medical facilities, and creating "smart cities" and "eco-towns" that showcase advances in energy conservation and zero carbon outcomes.[77] Whether these policies will be sufficiently interesting to draw in new residents and businesses remains an open question.

Financial incentives serve as a policy instrument for municipalities desperate to keep their populations from dropping further. Some towns in Fukushima Prefecture offer extensive, layered incentives to young families willing to move to the prefecture. One public servant described an extensive set of incentives for would-be residents: young couples seeking to purchase homes in the prefecture can receive up to ¥4 million ($36,000), and those who have children receive child support beyond that already provided by the central government. The prefecture provides ¥100,000 ($890) for the first child, ¥200,000 for the second child, ¥300,000 for the third child, and ¥500,000 for the fourth child onward. Families with high schoolers are eligible for ¥30,000 a month for transportation and ¥30,000 a month for rent to stay in a dorm should they seek schooling elsewhere. Newly married couples receive ¥200,000 as a wedding present.[78] While generous, these incentives cannot replace broader needs, such as sustainable jobs and a feeling of safety. In contrast to Iwate's revitalization plans, which set an eight-year timeline for recovery, Fukushima's plans currently have a ten-year timeline, reflecting the longer-term nature of the problems posed by decontamination.

Other incentives in Fukushima Prefecture center on children and education. One city provides free access to *juku*, or cram schools, which are additional education programs provided to students who wish to do well on the exams that determine their college placement. Another city provides college exam tutors and has made preschool and kindergarten free for parents. In explaining why they believe enhancing education will be a key to attracting residents, one city employee explained, "It is difficult, especially when families move out to the city and realize the different caliber of education available. This city was never really strong academically and now there is more competition than ever."[79] Private fundraising has provided authorities in the three prefectures with larger than expected budgets for children's scholarships: ¥9 billion ($73 million) for Miyagi, some ¥7.74 billion for Iwate, and ¥4.25 billion for Fukushima.[80] Much of the money is directed at kids who lost one or both of their parents.

Incentives and better educational opportunities may not be enough to bring residents into Fukushima because of the seriousness of concerns about radiation in the area. To allay concerns about the health and environmental impacts of the meltdowns, Fukushima Prefecture has been offering regular, free thyroid examinations for its residents. The new, broader annual thyroid screenings of all residents under the age of 18 resulted in the discovery of an excess number of thyroid cancers among children. Some sought to explain the rate of 20 to 50 times the number of thyroid abnormalities found elsewhere as "more likely to be the result of screening using highly sophisticated ultrasound techniques."[81] Here, the argument is that because more people are being screened more thoroughly, the tests are picking up relatively normal levels of illness. Other scientists have stated that these anomalous findings were not "explained by the screening surge" but instead should be linked to the Fukushima Dai-ichi meltdowns.[82] Observers have pointed out that any broader health effects and risks may take decades to unfold.[83]

Discussion of Fukushima Dai-ichi's influence on the health of children and adults will continue to be contentious. Disagreement about health outcomes after a nuclear disaster is unfortunately not new. Health experts and epidemiologists continue to spar over the long-term health impact of the April 26, 1986, Chernobyl nuclear disaster in Ukraine. Radiation specialists and scientists who had direct experiences in managing the long-term consequences of Chernobyl held a series of workshops under the Fukushima Dialogue Initiative from November 2011 through late 2015 with Fukushima farmers, housewives, residents, and government officials. Participants expressed anger and frustration, asked questions of the experts, and sought to understand the health and livelihood implications of the disaster along with ways to manage risk in the area.[84] As we have seen in this book so far, however, the measurable health impact from the disasters has come in terms of mental health, risk-taking behavior, and divorce. Even if scientists support government claims about the relatively low impact of radiation, residents still encounter stigma, anxiety, and PTSD because of the events.

Recognizing these obstacles to return, the national government has set up various institutional roadblocks and behavioral nudges in an attempt to push voluntary evacuees from Fukushima to return to their home prefecture. As discussed earlier, Fukushima residents who left without a mandate are considered to be voluntary evacuees and receive fewer benefits than those ordered to depart by the government.[85] Some domestic critics have argued that using the term "domestic refugee" would remove some of the stigma from these displaced people and create more trust in the government agencies responsible for their social welfare.[86]

Fukushima prefectural government employees said that they would create their own measures to support some tens of thousands of voluntary evacuees across the country. Yet as the six-year anniversary of the meltdowns arrived, the central government ended housing subsidies for these voluntary evacuees.[87] Some families continue to pay for two homes: one where the husband lives and works in Fukushima, and the other where the wife and children live outside the prefecture. Estimates in the fall of 2018 place the number of voluntary evacuees over 50,000, while the number of mandatory evacuees is more than 100,000.

At the same time, the government of Fukushima Prefecture has made controversial choices to improve its economic standing that may delay its ability to retain population. While the prefecture and residents have made it clear that they will not allow TEPCO to restart the undamaged Fukushima Dai-ichi reactors, communities in Fukushima will continue to depend on the nuclear power industry even if no reactors are producing power. Fukushima Prefecture will host a privately run disposal center known as Fukushima Ecotech Clean Center, which will process highly radioactive waste produced by the 2011 nuclear disaster. Local residents and officials initially opposed the proposal, arguing it would discourage evacuees from returning. In response, the central government promised safeguards for the center while the prefectural government offered ¥10 billion ($81 million) to advance the project.[88]

Beyond serving as a dump for nuclear waste generated by the accident, another economic revival plan for Fukushima centers on a giant ¥85 billion ($700 million) facility that hopes to research, develop, and test specialized radiation-proof robots and other nuclear industry technology.[89] Such facilities usually draw their staff from among well-educated professionals in major cities and do not provide the training necessary for locals to join the organization. Even for communities in Fukushima without such facilities dedicated to cleanup or waste storage, the four-decade-plus timetable for decommissioning the Fukushima Dai-ichi reactors will continue to bring nuclear engineers and technicians to local hotels and businesses. Decommissioning, nuclear waste management, and other nuclear industries dominate industry in the prefecture and suggest that a broader, more sustainable financial base made up of diverse businesses is unlikely for Fukushima.

While the 3/11 disasters may have intensified preexisting conditions such as dependence on the nuclear industry and depopulation, it has also provided a policy window in which prefectures can improve their disaster preparedness.[90] The Fukushima prefectural office, for example, created satellite phone connections between central and regional government offices that will always be functional in case landlines or electricity are down. They are working on securing three days of living supplies for 10,000 people, specifically including milk and diapers for babies and the elderly.[91]

As prefectures plan for the future, they fight to rebuild from the past. While Miyagi had the greatest life and property losses in the earthquake and tsunami, and Fukushima the least, Fukushima Prefecture has struggled to recover since 3/11. Even in the first few months after the disasters, as people were living in evacuation shelters, Iwate moved fastest to set up temporary housing, with Miyagi close behind and Fukushima a distant third.[92] Miyagi Prefecture's tourism industry was slowly recovering by mid-2015; it had risen some 3% from 2014 but still hovered at less than 94% of its pre-disaster levels.[93] Figure 4.1 uses data on recovery—with 100% recovery indicating pre-3/11 levels of economic and infrastructure activity—to compare progress in the three prefectures over the first two years after the disaster. Iwate and Miyagi moved most quickly to regain their pre-disaster business, infrastructure, and housing levels, while Fukushima lagged behind.

CHAPTER FOUR

FIGURE 4.1. Recovery after 3/11 in Iwate, Miyagi, and Fukushima.

The Future of Fukushima Prefecture

Fukushima's trailing recovery requires additional investigation. Fukushima Prefecture seeks to decontaminate its towns, bring evacuees back through jobs and education, and provide temporary and permanent housing. Interviews with experts in Fukushima showed that the recovery is lagging for a number of reasons, described earlier in this chapter. Decision makers believe that disaster mitigation infrastructure, such as seawalls, may help give residents a sense of safety. Yet the rebuilding of roads (there is heavy traffic around the few streets that remain open) and the reopening of major railroad stations (which would allow travel from rural areas to the cities) remain incomplete. Fukushima residents are fully aware of their lagging recovery status. In a winter 2016 poll, half of Fukushima residents expressed the belief that recovery was not progressing, whereas fewer than 20% of those living in the neighboring prefectures of Iwate and Miyagi shared this belief.[94]

Fukushima prefectural officials expressed anger at the burden that the nuclear accident has placed on them. "As a prefectural office, we requested that the central government take full responsibility for problems inflicted by the nuclear plant. We want them to not only support evacuation and relocation of the affected families, but also aid in the regeneration of farming and the economy in those places long-term by supporting employment fees, recovery projects, additional money for radiation measurements and safety precautions for commercial products made in that area."[95] For example, the prefecture has sought to reassure potential consumers of Fukushima agricultural products about the safety of those products. Therefore, each batch of rice from Fukushima sold domestically or internationally is screened thoroughly, and all other agricultural and aquaculture products are routinely checked and tested. As the 2020 Summer Olympics approaches, Fukushima prefectural officials have advocated that they be allowed to provide the vegetables for athletes competing in the games.

While prefectural authorities and TEPCO promoters alike have sought to project an image of safety, recovery, and revitalization, concerns and fears have altered residents' behaviors. Children in Fukushima, for example, have changed their play activities because of the accident. Parents have kept children inside rather than allowing them to play on playgrounds and school grounds that may still present a health danger. As a result, by 2012, Fukushima had the highest percentage of obesity in the country among young and middle-school-aged children.[96] Older students have also changed their behavior, in some cases dropping out of colleges and universities across Fukushima because of concerns about radiation. In 2013, for example, 18.7% fewer children enrolled in Fukushima schools, a much higher decrease than in neighboring Iwate (4.7%) and Miyagi Prefectures (2.2%).[97]

While upset at their predicament, Fukushima officials have sought to direct businesses and residents toward a more positive future. The prefecture has installed a "Decontamination Information Plaza" to educate the public on radiation, decontamination, and the timeline for recovery. The prefecture and various towns promote the "Alternative Energy for Fukushima" exhibit, an interactive display that demonstrates alternative forms of energy and provides details on the complete conversion of nuclear power to other safer, more sustainable sources of energy. Soon after the disaster, Fukushima set up a renewable energy pact with Germany to work together on technologies and best practices in the field.[98] Fukushima Prefecture has a goal of generating 100% of its power from green sources by 2040, using solar power, wind power, geothermal power, and hydropower.[99] Municipal centers and schools will receive solar power collection and energy storage systems to make them more resilient to power losses during future disasters. Further, the prefecture has pushed the installation of solar-powered lighting in temporary housing projects and fire escapes as well. These efforts come together in the Sanriku Eco-Town Project, which claims it is creating an "independent, decentralized energy supply system that can provide the area with power even during a disaster."

Networks and Governance across Prefectures

This chapter has so far used qualitative data to understand disaster response and recovery efforts at the prefectural level. Miyagi Prefecture did the most to ensure that it had connections not only to the central government, which provides the core funding for recovery, but also to NGOs, NPOs, the SDF, and even foreign rescue teams. It actively reached out to other disaster-related organizations such as the Red Cross and moved them into a space where regular contact and daily coordination were possible. I now move to a quantitative analysis of the connections in the three affected prefectures to confirm this intuition, drawing on a 2016 study of their networks.[100] Social network analysis of the contacts between prefectural governments, foreign governments, the SDF, and domestic nongovernmental organizations showed measurable differences among the prefectures in terms of their outreach and contacts. By analyzing nearly 1,000 activities after the Tōhoku disaster, such as food distribution, search and rescue, shelter, debris removal, and logistic assistance, one scholar illuminated the degree to which prefectural governments in Tōhoku connected to local, regional, national, and international groups.

Social scientists seek to understand how many direct connections, or edges, an organization or person has to others, and they label this attribute *degree centrality*. Miyagi Prefecture had a far higher degree of normalized degree centrality, at 0.434, than Iwate Prefecture, at only 0.094. In context, the only other organization in the study with higher degree centrality was the NGO known as Japan Platform, at 0.501, which had a massive network of volunteers and professional members across the area. Experts list Japan Platform among the top five humanitarian relief organizations in Japan in terms of its budget.

The study also looked at *betweenness centrality*, the degree to which an organization or person connects others who are not directly connected. Imagine this measurement as the number of people that would have to pass through you to get to another contact in your network. Should a friend of yours want to contact someone at a certain company, betweenness centrality would capture the ease of reaching them through your other friends and acquaintances. A high score for this social network attribute indicates that a person or organization is highly influential. Miyagi Prefecture showed a far higher rate of betweenness, at 34, than Iwate Prefecture, which measured only 1.69. Even the American Red Cross operating in Japan was ranked as more influential than Iwate, with a score of 1.7.

In short, a quantitative social network analysis of the activities of Miyagi and Iwate Prefectures showed that Miyagi measurably outperformed its neighbor in terms of connecting more often with and serving as a bridge between organizations such as NPOs and foreign groups. While Fukushima data were not available for the quantitative study, various civil servants working on the disaster reported that Fukushima Prefecture had relatively little contact with external organizations, including NPOs, NGOs, and even the national government. Most of its connections were to local governments from outside the region.[101] I interpret these social network analysis measures as showing very strong governance in Miyagi and weaker governance in Iwate and Fukushima.

The second factor of interest throughout this book has been social connections; that is, the ties between residents and neighbors. I have collected 20 years of various measurements of social capital at the prefectural level, including levels of trust, norms, tolerance, and network density, which I display in table 4.2. These quantitative measures of social connections—how much people trust one another and their neighbors, how similar their worldviews are, how able they are to handle different perspectives, and the reach of their connections, respectively—provide little conclusive evidence about levels of connectedness across residents of the three prefectures. In some years, and with some measures of social capital, Miyagi Prefecture leads (e.g., 2000 homogeneity measures), while in other years with other measures (e.g., 1996 trust, 2016 social time), it falls to third place. The similarity across the three prefectures in the 2000 and 2008 measurements shows that there is not much observable difference between them. In short, at the prefectural level, connections between residents may be similar, and they matter less than governance for public policy and disaster outcomes. This conclusion is logical, as there is no reason why one prefecture's citizens would be more (or less) connected than another's. Most social networks tend to be geographically constrained and emerge from daily physical interactions with neighbors, businesses, and coworkers. Social networks thus vary at the neighborhood or town level, but not necessarily at the prefectural level. As such, there are few theoretical reasons to believe in prefectural level variation in social capital and networks.

One more set of quantitative measurements reinforces the importance of governance styles over social connections at the prefectural

CHAPTER FOUR

Table 4.2. Social Connections in the Three Prefectures

	1996 Trust	1996 Norms	2000 Trust	2000 Tolerance	2000 Homogeneity	2005 Networks	2008 Social capital index	2016 Social time (ranking)
Miyagi	−1.038	0.227	48%	46%	13.06%	−0.44	15.1	13th of 47
Iwate	0.403	0.662	51%	63%	13%	n.d.	14.9	6th of 47
Fukushima	0.989	0.155	43%	43%	12.8%	0.63	16.2	5th of 47

Sources: 1996 trust and norm data from MLIT (2005); 2000 trust, tolerance, and homogeneity data from Westlund and Calidoni-Lundberg (2006); 2005 networks measure from Sakai (2012); 2008 social capital index from Pekkanen, Tsujinaka, and Yamamoto (2014); 2016 social time data from *Shakai seikatsu kihon chōsa* (Sōmushō 2016).
Note: Across all measurements, higher scores or rankings indicate deeper levels of social capital. The phrase "n.d." indicates no data are available.

level. A mail survey of some 1,600 people across Tōhoku in summer 2014 showed differences in perceptions of governance among residents of the three prefectures. People in Fukushima were most likely to see themselves as victims after the disaster, with 72% of them seeing themselves this way compared with 48% in Miyagi and 30% in Iwate. No doubt the meltdowns at Fukushima Dai-ichi and the inadequate responses from the government and TEPCO contributed to that sense of victimhood. When asked about their confidence in the local government (*chihō no seiji*), fewer than 35% of Fukushima residents saw it as reliable or mostly reliable. In contrast, more than 59% of Miyagi respondents saw local government as reliable or mostly reliable, while in Iwate that number was around 47%.[102] Here, too, we see quantitative evidence supporting the qualitative descriptions of the different ways that these prefectures reached out to relevant parties and displayed strong (or weak) governance.

A major challenge for prefectures stems from their role as middlemen between the well-resourced, but often heavy-handed, central government and the needs and visions of local residents. Under pressure, prefectures have often passed along central government recommendations not as recommendations, but as mandates. Many Tōhoku municipalities, lacking their own planning departments and not wishing to push back against these suggestions, have taken the central government's recommendations transmitted to them via prefectures as gospel. As one observer stated, "As always, the lower-ranking governments are simply working in line with standards that have been imposed."[103] One example is the standardization of seawall height, which has triggered contentious political movements across the area, as I will discuss in the next chapter.

The three hardest-hit prefectures faced varying challenges; in response, some engaged in self-driven improvement in outreach and governance. Where Miyagi sought to connect with other groups and coordinate its activities, Iwate and Fukushima created fewer channels for resources and new ideas. The data on social connections are ambiguous and indicate that vertical, more than horizontal, connections mattered at this level in the disaster response and recovery. Where prefectural officials could build coalitions across sectors, integrate NGOs and residents into the recovery, and ensure communication, the recovery moved more efficiently.

So far, we have seen the bottom two tiers of Japan's government system. Miyagi, Iwate, and Fukushima Prefectures are themselves embedded within the national government structures of Japan, and I will now turn to this level.

FIVE

National Level: Governance Challenged

This chapter focuses on the decisions made by the Japanese central government before, during, and after the triple disasters. While Tokyo had invested in a variety of mitigation and preventive measures to reduce the impact of an earthquake or tsunami, it was not prepared for a nuclear disaster. The central government lacked administrative resources such as legal frameworks and personnel to respond quickly and effectively to the meltdowns at Fukushima Dai-ichi. Despite the presence of 54 nuclear power plants across the nation, dating back over 40 years, it had a "practically insufficient, prevalently ambiguous nuclear liability law."[1] The lack of a legal framework for handling responsibility muddied the waters as citizens sought to rebuild their lives.

Further, beyond legal ambiguity, choices made by government agencies, including the decision to withhold information about radiation exposure during the crisis[2] and the use of top-down, cookie-cutter rebuilding frameworks, showed poor national-level governance.[3] Central government officials yo-yoed the radiation levels it considered acceptable for residents without clear empirical evidence guiding their decisions. Further, the government continues to focus on investing in structural coastal protection facilities, land-use regulation, and emergency management[4] rather than putting more effort into social infrastructure.

I trace the Japanese central government's struggle to build trust with its people even before the disasters and the further widening of this trust deficit after 3/11. Despite a strong and creative start after the 3/11 disasters—including the creation of several new institutions, flexibility in handling small-scale deviations from the norm, and pledges to use innovative rebuilding frameworks—the national government reverted to standard operating procedures. While it successfully handled large-scale construction and reconstruction projects, such as the removal of debris and the building of seawalls, it has faltered on issues of societal trust and permanent housing, failing to act in ways that cement civil society's faith in its policies and moving slowly to rehouse residents.[5] In short, while the national government initially demonstrated strong governance in areas where it had some expertise, it soon reverted to its standard practices of conformity and top-down authority, struggling to move beyond poor governance in areas where it lacked experience.

Progress to Date

The central government and its infrastructure-focused policies have achieved some significant milestones in the recovery process. For example, almost all utility infrastructure in Tōhoku—including electricity, gas, and water pipelines and services—was restored by June 2011, just three months after the triple disasters.[6] The government also made brisk progress in rebuilding transportation infrastructure such as highways and railroads and in restoring and reopening schools. Tokyo prioritized creating a physical environment where recovery would be more likely. Within three years of the disaster, the government had cleared a tremendous amount of debris and rubble. Some 5.84 million tons sat in Iwate Prefecture, 19.3 million in Miyagi Prefecture, and 4.22 million in Fukushima Prefecture after the tsunami receded.[7] Despite this tremendous amount of debris, all of it was consigned to standard landfills, incinerated at temporary or permanent incineration facilities, recycled, or moved to special dump areas for radioactive materials in a relatively short period. Clearing the streets and fields of Tōhoku communities served as a clear and obvious symbol of the status of the recovery process, and the media and academics kept close track of debris removal. The central government also briskly rebuilt schools and medical facilities.

Other areas of recovery lagged far behind, especially the bottom-

CHAPTER FIVE

up procedures that rely on social networks, trust, and the market: private home reconstruction, repopulation, and construction of permanent housing for displaced residents. Acquiring land for development requires strong relationships between residents and decision makers, and in many areas, locating and then getting agreement from landowners and relevant organizations for new housing developments has been slow. Along with constructing new housing in coastal areas, it is a struggle to carry out plans driven by national government support in areas many residents are leaving.

Out-migration to higher ground (*takadai*) will make future residents less vulnerable to tsunami, but may speed up population outflow and the long-term trend of coastal depopulation. While the government may envision moving neighborhoods a short distance from sea-level residential areas to nearby hills and mountains as a chance for the community to remain in the same town while becoming safer, many residents have taken the opportunity to relocate out of the area completely. In one hamlet in a town in Miyagi Prefecture, only ten households—fewer than one-third of the original neighborhood—have agreed to move to a relocated hamlet farther from the water. In another *shūraku* (settlement) outside Ishinomaki, only five households have moved together, the bare minimum for government assistance during group relocation. Those who are moving are between the ages of 50 and 86; in some areas, more than two-thirds of the remaining residents are over 65. Other, younger members of the community have left the area to build in urban areas.[8] Communities that do move locally will certainly be older and have weaker economic and social bases.

The government's weakest outcome comes in the field of permanent housing. Of some 200,000 people still living as evacuees, tens

Table 5.1. National Reconstruction Progress

	2014	2015	2016	2018
Public housing for evacuees	2%	15%	49%	96%
Plots for private homes	6%	11%	32%	89%
Schools	94%	96%	98%	98%
Seawalls	14%	21%	25%	50%
National highways	99%	99%	99%	100%
Railway	89%	91%	93%	98%
Farmland	63%	70%	74%	89%
Fishing ports	37%	56%	73%	No data
Aquaculture	82%	89%	90%	No data

Source: Personal communication with Reconstruction Agency officials (2015, 2017, 2018).

of thousands are housed in prefabricated units built to last only two years.[9] Local authorities in cities, including Kesennuma, have admitted that life in temporary homes may continue for another 15 years.[10] Of the 174,000 evacuees still in temporary accommodations, more than half—98,000—are from Fukushima Prefecture. Table 5.1 displays the central government's progress over time on all of these areas of recovery (with 100% indicating completion of the task).

Trust in Government Before and After 3/11

While many observers see Japan's relative ethnic homogeneity as a guarantee of nationwide cohesion and trustworthiness, Japan has in fact long struggled to build trust between citizens and the central government.[11] Scholars have described Japan as a cooperative, vertically integrated society where citizens work easily with one another and their government.[12] Well before the March 11, 2011, disasters, however, Japanese citizens had little taste for their elected officials. For example, World Value Survey data showed that only 28% of respondents expressed confidence in Japan's National Diet in the 1980s. Their confidence hovered around this same low level over time, at 29% in the 1990s and 27% in the mid-1990s.[13]

Early in the first decade of the twenty-first century, only 14% of respondents in Japan stated that they trusted their Diet representative a great deal or a lot. Only 25% of respondents said that they moderately or strongly trusted their national government—bureaucrats included.[14] In comparative terms, Japan sat closer to Spain, Italy, and Belgium, at the low end of the spectrum of generalized trust in government, than to other, more trusting advanced industrialized democracies such as Finland, Norway, Sweden, and Canada.

The triple disasters accelerated the overall trend of declining trust in government, which was paralleled by an increase of trust in fellow citizens. Like past disasters,[15] 3/11 increased trust among citizens, especially survivors directly affected by the earthquake, tsunami, and nuclear meltdowns.[16] Happiness and altruism measurably increased after the disasters.[17] People in Tōhoku rallied together to save and support one another in the short term after the crises. As the weeks turned into months and years, survivors worked cooperatively and shared resources, as we have seen in chapters 2 and 3.[18] Quantitative studies found that trust in family and trust among survivors remained high or increased after the event.[19] A number of Japan-wide phenomena,

CHAPTER FIVE

including volunteers traveling to Tōhoku to assist, an upsurge in donations of money to Tōhoku-focused NGOs and philanthropic causes, an increase in various slogans (such as *Ganbapesshi*, "Go for it!" in the vernacular of Tōhoku dialect), and the popularity of Japanese *kanji* (pictographs) such as *kizuna* (connections), confirm that overall civil society responded collectively and positively to the disaster.[20] Going through a shock together strengthened citizen-to-citizen bonds.

But citizen-to-state bonds weakened. Government authorities in Japan deliberately withheld information that they thought would create anxiety among the public and pursued top-down strategies that ignored the interests and wishes of local residents. These choices resulted in Tōhoku residents and citizens nationwide pulling further away from their government bureaucrats and representatives. Following the Fukushima Dai-ichi disaster, only 16% of respondents to a survey expressed trust in government institutions.[21] Beyond these attitudinal changes, civil society altered its behavior in a number of areas, creating new outlets for citizen science,[22] protesting government support for continuing the use of nuclear energy, and resisting cookie-cutter rebuilding plans that would put identically sized public works projects in each coastal town.[23] While citizens may have found increased trust in one another following the disasters, they have yet to place that faith in authorities.

Among the factors that widened the gap between civil society and the state was the government's lack of any legal or administrative framework for responding to the nuclear disaster. For example, it had no radiation-related food safety standards, wide-scale contingency plans for nuclear accidents, or laws for handling radioactive materials in the environment.[24] These are serious gaps in the legal and administrative procedures for handling what has been a major energy source for Japan since the 1970s. Further, nuclear power plant regulations had not considered the possibility of total, long-term power loss to a reactor, and authorities scrambled to come up with administrative and emergency responses to the triple disasters.[25] Local governments and residents received contradictory information, if they received any guidance at all. Then Prime Minister Naoto Kan had few advisers with any real knowledge of nuclear power or radioactivity and had to act during the crisis in an information vacuum.[26] As the breadth of the nuclear disaster became apparent, regulators set acceptable radiation exposure levels without extensive consultation with experts. With no plans, laws, or approaches in place, the central government had to improvise responses on the fly rather than building a consistent, evidence-based set of comprehensive disaster policies.

Creative First Responses

Initially, the central government showed signs of shifting away from the standard operating procedures that had undermined its ability to respond effectively to past disasters. After the 1995 Great Hanshin-Awaji Earthquake that devastated Kobe, for example, the central government lacked the information and political will to respond quickly. It took several hours for then–prime minister Murayama Tomiichi to receive information about the event and then to dispatch a small SDF team of 170 people to the area. Critics saw Tokyo as reacting slowly and capriciously, especially when it began turning away offers of international aid. Finally, in responding to the Kobe disaster, the government had no structures for engaging with the NPOs and NGOs that were already on the scene and deeply knowledgeable about the actual conditions there.[27]

In contrast, following 3/11, the central government moved rapidly and decisively. By 3:15 p.m. on March 11, 29 minutes after the earthquake hit, the Ministry of Land, Infrastructure, Transportation and Tourism (MLIT) had set up its emergency headquarters in the crisis management center located in the basement of the prime minister's compound. The central government had established an Emergency Response Team and Extreme Disaster Management Headquarters at the prime minister's office by 3:37 p.m. Within three hours, Tokyo sent national stocks of oil to evacuation shelters, which needed the fuel for electricity generators and heaters. The prime minister had declared a nuclear emergency by 7:00 p.m. that evening and had set up the Nuclear Disaster Management Headquarters near his office. Tokyo also sent out over 700 medical teams in the first 72 hours and reached out to NGOs and volunteers in an innovative way. This rapid response was followed by a deliberate move to integrate civil society and nonprofit organizations into the recovery process.

Next, Prime Minister Naoto Kan appointed Tsujimoto Kiyomi as his aide in charge of disaster volunteering and activist Yuasa Makoto as director of the Cabinet Secretariat Volunteer Coordination Office.[28] In contrast to previous disaster-period leaders, Kan—who himself had entered politics from an earlier career as an activist—embraced NGOs. He also called on outside experts to guide him as he envisioned handling, in his words, "a scenario involving the evacuation of 50 million people within several weeks."[29] This worst-case scenario, involving spent fuel rods in Fukushima Dai-ichi storage pools being exposed to the air,

CHAPTER FIVE

resulting in a catastrophic release of radioactivity that could force residents as far away as Tokyo to flee, fortunately did not come to pass.

Whereas the government had previously struggled to integrate the nonprofit sector into disaster response, after 3/11 it became more comfortable incorporating NPOs into its structures.[30] The number of volunteers traveling to the Tōhoku area was lower than those who went to Kobe after its disaster some 15 years before, but this was due to several challenges, among which were problems entering the Tōhoku area (with most road and rail infrastructure destroyed) and concerns about radiation.[31] After 3/11, the government openly recognized the role of these civil society organizations in the recovery process and sought to work alongside them.

In 2013, the central government also updated the 1961 Disaster Countermeasures Basic Act, explicitly calling for cooperation between the government and NGOs/NPOs.[32] The Reconstruction Agency itself set up a number of hotlines so that NPOs, volunteers, and other civil society organizations could connect on projects and avoid duplication in their rebuilding efforts. NPOs and NGOs often seek funding from the government for their work in Tōhoku, whether for psychosocial support for children in schools or assistance for the elderly in temporary shelters. For their part, local civil society organizations such as the Sanaburi Foundation have helped bridge the gap between national responses, government agencies, and local needs.[33]

The central government used the resources available to it domestically and also collaborated with its allies in the recovery process. Tokyo sent in the Self Defense Forces to augment local search and recovery efforts, and local residents regularly praised the SDF for quickly providing food, water, and medical assistance.[34] Some 100,000 SDF personnel participated in recovery and cleanup efforts. The largest force of government personnel dispatched actually came from the National Police Agency, which sent out more than 307,000 officers across Tōhoku to help with rescue operations, assist with traffic, and help capture data on fatalities and injuries. The government also reached out to US military forces in a plan labeled Operation Tomodachi (friend), which used some 18,000 troops (of the more than 50,000 US personnel based in Japan) to assist.

Along with this vertical cooperation, Tokyo recommended that local governments work with cities and villages outside the disaster area to bring in new civil servants and receive materials and information.[35] As discussed in chapter 3, a number of towns, villages, and cities in Tōhoku received aid from sister cities based far from the disasters. Some

57,000 local government officials from across Japan traveled to Tōhoku towns and communities to take the places of those killed during the disaster and to bolster the cadre of civil servants in city halls as they struggled to deal with immense personal and communal loss.[36] This meant that roughly 3% of local government officials across the disaster area had been seconded to the area.[37] Firefighters also streamed into the region from towns and villages across Japan; more than 30,000 firefighters joined search-and-rescue operations during the first three months after the disasters.

The Japanese central government also recognized and sought to change the moral hazard it had created in the field of nuclear regulation. Since the 1970s, the Ministry of the Economy, Trade, and Industry (METI) had regulated nuclear energy through the Agency for Natural Resources and Energy (Shigen enerugi chō, or ANRE) while simultaneously promoting it through various programs.[38] On the one hand, bureaucrats had to keep a tight rein on private electric utilities to ensure that they were not skimping on safety spending and management oversight. Market-based forces in the volatile energy business had the potential to push TEPCO and other Japanese firms to reduce spending on safety, as had happened in various cases in North America.[39] As regional monopolies, the electric power companies in Japan, such as TEPCO, have strong incentives to increase profits by decreasing spending on safety-focused systems.

On the other hand, the same central government agency used a redistributive tax to provide financial incentives to local communities to host nuclear facilities and developed a variety of policy instruments to persuade them to do so. The central government also used a variety of hard and soft social control tools alongside these incentives to bring civil society's opinions in line with its nuclear power goals.[40] That is, the Japanese government clearly supported the expansion of the nuclear industry and supplemented the financial and administrative resources of the private firms in the field. The United States had a similar conflict of interest in the field of offshore oil and gas drilling, in which the Minerals Management Service within the Department of the Interior generated tremendous revenue through leasing federal lands and waters to drillers, but also regulated them to keep them safe.[41] The weak regulations resulting from this moral hazard came to a head with the massive *Deepwater Horizon* oil spill under BP's control in April 2010. Soon after, the MMS was dissolved and its responsibilities split among three new agencies.

The Fukushima Dai-ichi nuclear disaster confirmed the views of many critics who saw the state as a weak or captured regulator that had not pushed hard enough for safety procedures in the field of nuclear energy. They had long argued that regulators moved too easily into "lucrative jobs in the industries they police, and vice versa."[42] Large-scale antinuclear protests across Japan in summer 2011 showed a major swing in public opinion against the technology. In a shallow attempt at allowing public participation in the decision-making process on energy, the government held eleven public hearings over that summer about nuclear power. Most attendees (70%) supported ending its use, but the government limited the number of people allowed to speak at the hearings. Though more than 90,000 comments were submitted to the government on the issue, it was difficult to see whether bureaucrats actually read them or how this massive amount of citizen input actually altered post-3/11 policy.

In September 2011, after tremendous criticism of its weak regulation of the industry, the Cabinet proposed creating a new government body that would "separate regulation from utilization" of nuclear power.[43] In September 2012, almost a year and a half after the disasters, the central government established the Nuclear Regulation Authority (NRA) under the Ministry of Environment. The NRA replaced a piecemeal network of regulators, including the Nuclear and Industrial Safety Agency (NISA), which had been located within METI; the Nuclear Safety Commission (NSC) under the Cabinet Office; the Japan Atomic Energy Agency (JAEA); and nuclear-related agencies affiliated with MEXT. With a staff of some 500 and physically removed from Tokyo's bureaucratic beltway, the NRA displayed backbone early in its tenure. NRA scientists carried out their own geological surveys, and the agency decided not to grant restart licenses to nuclear plants located over seismic faults active within the past 100,000 years.

In the field of recovery, the government set up new councils in 2011 to guide its efforts, such as the Reconstruction Design Council and the Reconstruction Promotion Committee, which stressed bottom-up, social infrastructure–based approaches to the challenge.[44] For example, the council stated that "all of us living now shall view the disaster as affecting our own lives, and shall pursue reconstruction with a spirit of solidarity and mutual understanding that permeates the entire nation."[45] The council pushed the use of the term *kizuna*, or social bonds, as a critical part of the disaster prevention framework.[46] The council also argued against constructing seawalls as the primary infrastructure for mitigating future tsunami.[47] For the first time, the central government set up national-level field offices in the three worst-affected prefectures to serve as centers for coordination and information sharing.[48]

Political divisions within the Diet slowed down the creation of other disaster-relevant institutions but not, interestingly, disaster-related legislation. In May 2011, Prime Minister Kan, drawing on the nation's experience in the 1995 Kobe earthquake, proposed the idea for a reconstruction agency, that would center the government's powers and logistic mechanisms within a single headquarters.[49] Within a month, the Diet began to set up a reconstruction law framework to guide both the design of that institution and financial instruments for recovery.[50] This large-scale change, similar to the creation of the Department of Homeland Security (DHS) in the United States after the 9/11 terror attacks, would build a one-stop agency, the Fukkōchō, or Reconstruction Agency. It took until February 2012, nearly a full year after the disasters, before this new agency was reporting directly to the prime minister with its own Reconstruction Minister.

The delay in creating a functional Reconstruction Agency came from the political environment in the year of the 3/11 disasters; namely, a divided Diet and a series of prime ministers who lasted only a brief time in office. The long-ruling Liberal Democratic Party (LDP) lost control of the upper house to the Democratic Party of Japan (DPJ), which had almost no experience governing the nation. Prime Minister Naoto Kan faced a series of challenges after taking office and sought to build a coalition. After March 11, 2011, Kan reached out to the LDP and the Clean Government Party (CGP, a smaller party connected to the religious group Soka Gakkai) for assistance in forming a stable government, but both refused, perhaps to avoid blame for any failures in handling the ongoing nuclear disaster.[51]

While the three parties—LDP, DPJ, and CGP—all pushed for legislation to create an agency that would coordinate disaster recovery, their versions of the bill differed. Kan suffered a no-confidence vote in June 2011 and eventually stepped down in August 2011. Toward the end of his term, Kan still sought to negotiate the conditions for the Reconstruction Agency.[52] Yoshihiko Noda of the DPJ took over as prime minister in September 2011, but while reports suggested a more positive relationship with the LDP and CGP, he, too, failed to form a coalition. Though the delay in setting up the agency angered many survivors in Tōhoku, bills related to disasters and disaster funding actually sped through the divided Diet at three times the pace of non-disaster-related bills, suggesting that the parties recognized some need for speed during the crisis.[53] Noda and the DPJ lost the election of December 2012 to the LDP, which installed Shinzō Abe as prime minister; by that time, the Diet had passed a law establishing the Reconstruction Agency.

Politicians in Tokyo hoped that the Reconstruction Agency would help speed up the rebuilding process by coordinating, streamlining, and unifying procedures that were typically fragmented among multiple ministries. As mentioned in chapter 2, leveling mountains and clearing forests to build new homes, for example, required a tortuous series of interagency meetings and documents. The Reconstruction Agency did not recruit new bureaucrats, instead bringing in a rotating staff of 190, made up of personnel from other agencies. It established branches in Morioka, in Iwate; Sendai, in Miyagi; and Fukushima City, in Fukushima Prefecture.[54] The Diet provided some ¥19 trillion ($220 billion) to be spent over five years with four additional budgets supplementing that allocation. The Reconstruction Agency sought to rebuild homes and communities, support health and daily life, revive industries, and revitalize Fukushima. While the central government saw the Reconstruction Agency as a sign of its new responsiveness, Tōhoku residents criticized the length of time it took to create it and get it running.

The central government's recovery efforts after 3/11 benefited from changes made following the 1995 Kobe earthquake, which had made clear that there were no real financial supports in place for individuals and families. By 1999, the Diet had passed the Act on Support for Reconstructing Livelihoods of Disaster Victims, which allowed prefectures to issue grants of up to ¥3 million to individuals. Many Kobe victims and evacuees had to rely on private insurance, NGOs, or friends and family during the period of unemployment that often follows disasters. In contrast, 3/11 evacuees and Tōhoku residents had a framework of government financial support in place.

The Kobe earthquake also triggered broad-scale changes in the NPO registration law, which had been quite restrictive before and during that disaster.[55] After the disaster, the central government made it easier for civil society organizations to register as NPOs and receive benefits, such as the ability to hold a lease and to send mail at a reduced rate.[56] By removing obstacles to interaction and coordination and by helping structure civil society growth, legislative changes made after 1995 Kobe earthquake allowed for stronger civil society organization and NGO work during and after 3/11.[57]

Like the 1995 Kobe earthquake and 9/11 in the United States, the wide-scale destruction wrought by the Great East Japan Earthquake could have served as a focusing event for the Japanese government. Crisis can serve as a moment when politicians and bureaucrats step back from traditional approaches and innovate or experiment.[58] Decision makers in Tokyo could have used the crisis to redistribute financial and administrative power between localities and the central government, revise the Bilateral Coordination Mechanism between the United States and Japan, and rethink Japan's approach to commercial nuclear power.[59] More specifically, a shift in reconstruction policy might have allowed each disaster-affected community more administrative and financial flexibility in designing its own rebuilding and recovery process. This flexibility eluded Kobe after its 1995 earthquake,[60] and its lack continues to plague local authorities post-3/11. New government agencies such as the NRA, the explicit inclusion of NPOs in recovery efforts, and the promise to engage in bottom-up approaches seemed to signal a new era in good recovery governance, but soon the government reverted to more conservative approaches.

A Return to Standard Operating Procedures

Rather than investing in change or continuing the initial innovative streak it showed immediately following 3/11, however, the central government defaulted to business as usual. Tokyo regularly ignored creative approaches from Tōhoku residents and experts when engaging in top-down planning.[61] As a scholar pointed out soon after the disaster, "Normal politics prevailed . . . and 'staying the course'" emerged as the government's safe position.[62] Japan's continuation of past policies may have resulted from the lack of a powerful political entrepreneur, strong pressure from the power utilities and the broader business community, and path dependence (that is, the challenges institutions such as government agencies and firms face in altering behavior that has become routine). Some past political leaders, such as Prime Minister Junichiro Koizumi, had demonstrated an ability to buck the status quo and ignore criticism. But the list of charismatic and politically independent prime ministers remains short.

Strong ties between the business community, central government bureaucrats, and politicians—a network known as the "Iron Triangle"—may explain why central government decision makers seemed "out of step with the times" when initiating the recovery.[63] Many of its choices favored large-scale businesses and filled the coffers of construction firms, which long served as the backers of the traditionally minded LDP. Additionally, following the criticisms of its responses to the 1995

Kobe earthquake, the national government had further centralized its disaster response framework, strengthening the command and control mechanisms to make them similar to those used by the military and first responders. This change limited the degree to which local residents and NPOs could truly participate in the recovery. Government ministries often defined revitalization and recovery as policies that could be plugged into existing plans for large-scale public works projects, rather than locally conceived and supported goals. Further, at the local level, rural cities and towns rely heavily on construction jobs and infrastructure spending for economic stimulus; they had little leverage to build their own spaces.

When reconstruction began in earnest after 3/11, Japan's central government emphasized homogeneity in planning requirements and demonstrated top-down, bureaucratic inflexibility.[64] Other major disasters—such as Hurricane Katrina in the United States—have similarly failed to drastically alter major national policies.[65] In recent history, only the 9/11 attacks were able to push decision makers out of typical, incremental responses to overhaul the intelligence and defense communities into the conglomeration of the DHS.[66] Japanese law further reinforces the government's path dependence in its focus on large-scale construction projects, requiring that damaged or ruined public facilities such as ports, dams, and seawalls "must be rebuilt as before."[67] That is, even if seawalls or other large-scale concrete projects served little or no purpose, or saved no lives, the regulations push governments at all levels to spend to rebuild them.

In response to the earthquake, tsunami, and nuclear meltdowns, the government set up a framework to spend more than $200 billion, primarily on concrete-based rebuilding projects. For example, in mid-2011, the Diet passed a law laying out the need to create tsunami-resilient cities, primarily through seawall reinforcement and pine forests. As we shall see, these pushes for "resilience" merely continued government support of massive projects, often boondoggles that offered dubious value to locals. Further, the law contained no provisions for environmental assessment of these large-scale building projects. Many of these concrete-based works will impact the habitat of river-spawning fishes along with brackish-water ecosystems, which are home to species sensitive to changes in their environment.[68] Yet regulations allow developers and construction firms to move these projects forward without even paper studies of their potential influence on ecosystems.

Despite the government's official commitment to rebuilding Tōhoku, investigations revealed that, by the end of the first year after 3/11, up to 25% of the money set aside for Tōhoku reconstruction had gone to unrelated projects. These projects included the building of seawalls in Okinawa (the island chain on Japan's southeastern coast, far from the site of the disasters), prisoner training in Hokkaido (the large island far to the north), and atomic fusion projects carried out far from the affected areas in Miyagi, Fukushima, and Iwate.[69] One Tokyo governor hoped to use the Tōhoku reconstruction budget to cover the costs of holding the 2020 Tokyo Summer Olympics.[70] An audit board found 513 cases of government organizations wasting money meant for disaster recovery, totaling some ¥529.6 billion ($4.5 billion). Redirecting spending toward projects that had nothing to do with disaster recovery undermined citizens' faith in the central government to carry out the public will. Many residents saw the central government decision makers' willingness to spend money on unrelated projects as a sign of "construction state" thinking, which would forward the interests of the state, but not its citizens.[71] Under this framework, Japan's central government often spends money on concrete, rather than on projects citizens want or need, to bolster political connections and lower unemployment rates.

Even when money has been available for relevant projects in Tōhoku, Tokyo's bureaucratic inflexibility and personnel shortages have dragged the process out and slowed the use of available money at a local scale. The mayor of Ishinomaki complained that it took six months for the Ministry of Agriculture, Forestry, and Fishing (MAFF) to allow rice paddies to be rezoned into housing areas in his community.[72] By mid-2015, only a few hundred families, out of the more than 12,000 evacuees, had moved into permanent housing in Ishinomaki. Local officials in another town in Tōhoku reported that attempts to consolidate the local schools into a single building because of shrinking numbers of students were stymied by MEXT.[73]

During the first year after the disaster, Tōhoku coastal communities used, on average, less than half of the money distributed to them due to personnel shortages and lack of land acquisition.[74] Some three years after the disaster, due to a combination of red tape, labor shortages, and rising construction costs,[75] only 40% of the funds budgeted for local communities had been accessed.[76] As a result, the three worst-affected prefectures have yet to complete construction of their planned permanent housing stock.[77] Observers have pointed out that while the central government offered to fund locally proposed reconstruction projects,

CHAPTER FIVE

those "projects must fall into one of 40 predetermined categories; the funds are doled out in tranches over time; [and the] reconstruction agency's policy and guidance manuals run to 130 pages."[78]

Inflexibility in existing laws governing disaster situations has also handicapped recovery efforts. The Act on Support for Reconstructing Livelihoods of Disaster Victims provides up to ¥3 million (some $30,000) to victims whose homes were completely destroyed. With rising construction costs, this sum was insufficient to support the full costs of rebuilding. But more importantly, the law did not cover partially damaged homes.[79] Two families side by side struggling to rebuild their lives received very different amounts of aid if one house was not judged to be completely destroyed.

The central government has further strained its relationships with Tōhoku municipalities by asking that they bear some of the cost for certain projects, such as road improvements in inland areas.[80] The central government's push to have disaster-affected cities and towns pay more of the reconstruction costs has not gone over well with local authorities. While the municipalities' contributions are only between 1% and 3% of the total cost, they have argued that doing so will empty their already-depleted treasuries.[81]

Continuing the Construction State

The construction of large-scale seawalls along Tōhoku's coast is the most visible sign of the central government's involvement in rebuilding. Tokyo continues to pour money into seawall construction (and reconstruction) and replanting of coastal forests even though the science shows that these barriers may have little real mitigation effect on future tsunami.[82] Before the tsunami, some 300 km (186 miles) of concrete seawalls, constructed at a cost of $10 billion, guarded Tōhoku's coasts.[83] Of that concrete protection, about 190 km (118 miles) collapsed under the onslaught of the tsunami. Since 3/11, the central government has been working on a 46 km (28.5-mile) long, 10 m (32-foot) high seawall in Iwate and Miyagi Prefectures at the cost of approximately ¥1 trillion ($8.3 billion). Government agencies have hinted at plans for the construction of mega-levees and other concrete barriers along rivers that swelled when the tsunami traveled upstream and inundated inland communities.[84] Engineers looking to pour more concrete no doubt took these floods as a chance to build additional walls, dikes, and levees.

Local citizens have argued that these massive concrete structures will negatively affect the fishing and tourism industries and divert money from alternative mitigation approaches, such as evacuation roads, railroad tracks that serve as natural barriers, and smaller-scale reconstruction projects.[85] Without a required environmental impact statement, it is difficult to assess how these projects will affect fish and wildlife, which create recreational opportunities and serve as draws to tourists. Further, residents in a variety of municipalities have argued that these projects are not in the public interest. Locals have criticized plans to construct seawalls as tall as 14.5 m (47 feet), like the one built in Ofunato, in their towns. That wall, constructed directly next to the shoreline[86] at a cost of ¥2.865 billion ($24 million), extends out 1.5 km (nearly 1 mile) and blocks the ocean view for locals and sightseers alike.[87] Experts have regularly suggested moving the concrete walls inland to create more natural beaches and allow ecosystems to remain undisturbed, but authorities have ignored this advice.[88]

Similarly, locals argued that the 7.5 m (24-foot) high, 1.61 km (1-mile) long walls built in in Yamada, in Iwate Prefecture, blocked their view of the ocean. "The scenery I used to know was taken away completely when the barriers were installed," said one resident.[89] Locals in Taro District near Miyako (also in Iwate) called their 10 m (32-foot) tall, 2.4 km (1.5-mile) long seawall the "Great Wall of Japan" when it was completed nearly 50 years ago. Town planners hoped that the seawall—built in multiple sections over time—would save lives. While it seemed an ideal form of protection against tsunami, this wall, too, blocked residents' view of the sea. After the 3/11 earthquake, most could not see the tsunami coming, and few fled the area. Nor did the seawalls in towns such as Taro reduce all risk from inundation, as water could flow in from rivers or entrances behind the wall and then be trapped inside the concrete sections. "Hence, the highest amount of casualties was among the people living in the shelter of the first seawall."[90] Our own research, discussed in chapter 2, showed that seawalls had no measurable impact on mortality rates at the municipal level.[91] We believe this outcome was a combination of the power and height of the tsunami itself and the moral hazard that supposedly impregnable protective barriers posed for local residents.[92]

Japanese observers have demonstrated that the central government issued guidelines for seawall heights that were then passed down to prefectures as commands, rather than as recommendations.[93] The prefectures have good reason to defer to the central government, as it covers two-thirds of the cost of dike and wall construction[94] (the pre-

CHAPTER FIVE

fectures cover any additional costs). Even though building and determining the heights of seawalls is voluntary and under the control of local governments, prefectural authorities saw the plans as mandated from above because they feared liability should the walls not be built.[95] Further, the central government pays some 80% of the cost of hiring engineers to plan the walls, and therefore regional and local governments often accept this expert-guided approach without deeper reflection or consulting their own counter-experts.[96]

Local government officials, lacking their own planning teams and recovery data, have turned to the prefectures and contractors for guidance and have adopted suggestions from the prefectural authorities as gospel. As one observer of the Tōhoku recovery process commented, "Some municipal personnel feel the temptation to mechanically make budgets flow to models, formats, and standard designs prepared by consultants and general contractors."[97] In short, for some villages and towns, the easy availability and funding of central government planners and plans alters local preferences to match what is offered from above.

There have been some exceptions to the cargo cult of seawalls, Kerobe, a village near Kamaishi in Iwate, and Onagawa, in Miyagi Prefecture, among them.[98] Those two communities have mustered residents, fishermen's unions, and town council members to push back on top-down plans for local seawalls. Onagawa has only a single main industry—fishing—and local leaders believed that a standard seawall would wreck the possibility of reviving their only livelihood by blocking access to the sea.[99] In Ishinomaki, authorities have not sought to build a massive Great Wall or to raise the level of the downtown. Rather, they have used a series of breakwaters, parkland, and levees with roads on top to deflect smaller waves and slow future tsunami to allow residents time to escape.[100] But these towns are the exceptions, not the norm.

Central government planners rarely listen to or consider local opinion, and the law does not require them to do so. Attempts by local residents to challenge tall tsunami walls have rarely been successful, especially when local communities have not been unified in their opposition.[101] Similarly, many of the plans for permanent housing in rural coastal communities merely mimic the large-scale, impersonal high-rise apartments found in urban centers, often known as *danchi*.[102] These soulless, Soviet-style blocks have little character or individuality and few spaces for social interactions. Elderly evacuees placed in such locations may face the same lonely deaths (*kodokushi*) that Kobe saw after similar attempts at relocation following its 1995 earthquake. Visits to Watari and Rikuzentakata showed that many of the elderly and poor have indeed moved into large-scale public apartment buildings, where rents are low and are often based on income. Overall, Tōhoku residents have seen few positive results from central government efforts on which to pin their faith.

Business as Usual: Japan's Energy Policy

Beyond the effects of the central government's infrastructure-focused spending choices, citizen trust in the government has been damaged by its choices in the field of energy policy. The Japanese government has long supported its commercial nuclear power program through a number of policy instruments beyond the standard policies of risk amortization (such as North America's Price-Anderson Act) and financial assistance with research and design found in many advanced industrial democracies.[103] The central government, through ANRE and connected quasi-government agencies (such as the Center for the Development of Power Supply Regions and the Japan Atomic Energy Relations Organization), promoted the "safety myth" of Japan's nuclear power plants. These agencies sent state-employed scientists to lecture local residents on the need for nuclear power. When these scientists came to communities to talk about safety and Japan's obligation to reduce its carbon dioxide output, they were represented as neutral third-party authorities despite their strong ties to national government plans. These pro-nuclear central government organizations also set up junkets for government officials and town council members to sites that already had atomic reactors in a "habituation" strategy. Further, communities hosting nuclear power–related industries in Fukushima, Fukui, Niigata, and other prefectures received subsidies from the central government via the Dengen Sanpō (three laws that provide assistance to communities and organizations that further the government's energy production goals).[104] In one case, a city involved in the nuclear fuel cycle received ¥100 million ($885,000), composed of a ¥30 million power source grant and ¥70 million from a nuclear fuel tax.[105]

While we might imagine that well-publicized nuclear accidents around the world would have turned Japanese residents against the use of nuclear power, this was not the case. Despite Chernobyl and Three Mile Island, the Japanese public broadly supported Japan's nuclear power program for decades. Regular surveys until the March 11, 2011, disasters showed that two-thirds of respondents supported expanding the use of nuclear power in the country.[106] Engineers, politicians, and bureaucrats alike regularly spoke of Japan's nuclear sector as 100% safe and said a meltdown was impossible. This narrative became known as the "safety myth" after the Fukushima Dai-ichi accident.

But that accident, and the central government's poor response to it, caused a massive change in public opinion: less than one-third of the public now supports the use of nuclear energy. Japanese citizens lost trust in the central government agencies responsible for nuclear power because the accident clearly showed nuclear energy's costs to livelihoods and mental health. Many residents who lived far away from nuclear power plant host communities had envisioned nuclear power solely in terms of its promise of energy security and baseload power without carbon emissions. Host communities—those rural coastal towns where the reactors were located—had always seen nuclear power as an economic lifeline that could sustain their depopulating municipalities.[107] This was true even though for many host communities, the actual economic benefits were at best mixed.[108] The highly publicized Fukushima Dai-ichi accident, the mandatory evacuations of more than 100,000 residents, and the long-term concerns over livelihoods and health effects of radiation exposure[109] served as a focusing event for the Japanese public. Yet beyond these concerns, the central government's policy choices weakened the public's trust.

First, public officials failed to communicate accurately and clearly.[110] The chief cabinet secretary at the time, Yukio Edano, for example, made a number of public statements about radioactive exposure and risk that had little scientific backing. Beyond misleading the public, these false claims broke existing laws mandating accountability and information during disasters. In interviews, local officials pointed out that the 1999 Genshiryoku Saigai Taisaku Tokubetsu Sochi Hō (Special Law for Preparedness for a Nuclear Power Accident) required utilities such as TEPCO to provide the central government with information on the nature and extent of nuclear accidents. Yet local chief executives received information neither from TEPCO nor the central government during the meltdowns at Fukushima Dai-ichi, as we saw in previous chapters.

Second, Tokyo provided inconsistent advice, or none at all, to residents and communities during the nuclear catastrophe. For example, the central government told residents from the Fukushima Prefecture towns of Namie and Tomioka to evacuate, but gave them no guidance on what to do. Local decision makers had to figure out where to go, where to stay, and how to get there. At the same time, the central government helped coordinate the provision of buses to the communities of Futaba and Ōkuma. As mentioned in chapter 2, many residents of Namie and Tomioka, lacking guidance from those with knowledge of the ongoing risk, went to Iitate. Yet winds blew radioactive particles precisely to that area, and people were outside, exposed to radiation, for several days before being encouraged to evacuate again. The Japanese government refused to release forecasts and data from SPEEDI—provided to US embassy personnel and military forces by March 14, 2011—to the Japanese public until March 23.[111] For many Japanese, the failure to provide the same critical forecast data and guidance to residents that had been released to allies was a sign of incompetence at the least or of a lack of concern about the health of the nation at the worst.[112] Other ambiguous public announcements, added to the lack of clear information, increased anxiety levels among Fukushima residents.[113]

Third, central government decision makers failed to carry out standard emergency plans, such as the distribution of potassium iodide pills to local children exposed to high levels of radiation. Poland, in contrast, distributed millions of the pills to children soon after the Chernobyl accident. Even though some—but not all—local towns near Fukushima Dai-ichi had stockpiles of the pills, some local governments waited until the central government gave the go-ahead before distributing them. It took some five days for the order to arrive from Tokyo, by which point some 100,000 residents had already been exposed to radiation and evacuated to other areas. Local officials in several communities, such as Kawauchi, claimed that they did not receive the pills until March 16.[114] Some towns, such as Futaba and Tomioka, gave out the pills without waiting for the order from Tokyo. To understand how these decisions influenced local feelings about the disaster, one scholar surveyed the broader population two years afterward, in 2013. She concluded that "instead of creating stability and helping disaster victims to cope, the governmental conduct seems to have resulted in increasing anxiety, uncertainty and distrust, especially among those who need support most urgently."[115]

The most notable lack of clarity surrounded the acceptable levels of radiation exposure set by the central government. Before the disaster, ordinary citizens were told that 1 millisievert (mSv) per year was the maximum acceptable level of exposure. Soon after the 3/11 meltdowns, the government raised that annual acceptable dose to 20 mSv. That higher level has been the nuclear industry standard for its professionally trained personnel who work in hospitals with X-ray machines or in facilities with radioactive materials, such as uranium mines. When measurements at schools in the area dropped beneath 4 microsieverts (μSv) per hour, MEXT lowered the acceptable level to 1 μSv per hour.[116] The opaque and top-down nature of the central government's decision making on the issue of radiation exposure standards dramatically increased public distrust. The government also sought to raise the limit for reusing radioactive soil to 8,000 becquerels per kilogram, even though in other fields where workers are exposed to radioactivity, such as the iron industry, the maximum is 100 becquerels.[117] Many people were angered by these changes, which were made without clear explanation at a time of emergency, without consultation with the public, and were maintained long after the emergency.

Fourth, the government and TEPCO withheld information about the extent of the disaster, not admitting publicly that there had been fuel meltdowns at the Fukushima Dai-ichi reactors until nearly three months after 3/11.[118] As citizen scientists worked independently of the government and TEPCO to map the levels of radiation exposure across Fukushima and the nation, they faced threats of prosecution from civil authorities. On April 6, 2011, less than a month after the meltdowns, central government officials in the Ministry of Health, Labor, and Welfare hinted to citizen scientist groups that they would fine them or sue them for publishing "false rumors on the internet," which many interpreted as referring to unofficial radiation data. As one mentioned, "I don't think they ever did [prosecute violators], but it likely had a chilling effect on many people."[119] Threats of punishment for those who sought transparency about a major public health risk showed the government's focus on controlling information rather than promoting recovery.

Other government decisions about nuclear power have also sapped public trust. The Japanese central government stepped in to keep TEPCO from collapsing under the costs of compensation for Fukushima evacuees and the 40-year project of decommissioning the Fukushima Dai-ichi nuclear power plant.[120] The government's bailout of TEPCO had run to more than ¥2 trillion (some $22 billion) by March 2013 and resulted in its essentially nationalizing the firm.[121] Yet the government no longer gives financial support to voluntary evacuees, has been unable to construct sufficient quantities of permanent housing for evacuees, and has pushed reconstruction costs back onto prefectural authorities.

Further, the administration of Prime Minister Shinzō Abe, who came to power in 2012, has insisted it intends to restart Japan's nuclear power program and restore its role in providing up to 20% of Japan's electricity.[122] As of summer 2018, eight reactors in five nuclear power plants had been restarted since the Fukushima Dai-ichi meltdowns. This push comes despite broad societal opposition to the restarts.[123] More specifically, polls continue to show that more than two-thirds of respondents want to end the use of nuclear power in Japan.[124] And while pro-nuclear organizations regularly argue that Japan's already high electricity bills will rise further if nuclear plants are not restarted, more than 60% of the public has argued that they will accept higher electricity prices as a consequence of taking nuclear power plants offline.[125]

More than seven years after the Fukushima Dai-ichi disaster, it is not clear that the central government has learned critical lessons from the event. For example, roughly half of medical institutes, nursing homes, and care facilities within 30 km (18 miles) of nuclear plants still lack mandatory evacuation plans, despite new laws that require those institutions to provide evacuation destinations for patients along with detailing routes and modes of transport. Further, nearby cities must create lists of the elderly, infirm, and those unable to evacuate on their own in the case of an emergency; only roughly 70% have done so.[126] A lack of trust in authorities slows down the process of providing information to government agencies and cripples the ability of the government to construct evacuation plans.

Measurable Consequences of Poor Governance

The Tōhoku disaster undermined what little trust citizens had in their elected officials and in their bureaucracy.[127] Japan's trust in government institutions plummeted after 3/11, putting it close to the bottom in a ranking of 27 countries.[128] One survey completed in 2013 showed that individuals affected by the disaster had even less confidence in the trustworthiness of the government than other citizens did. "This discrepancy," argued the author, "between affected and not affected was most explicit amongst the over-64-year-olds, whose trust in governmental institutions is usually comparatively high."[129] A MEXT survey in 2012 showed that, because of their role in perpetuating the safety myth and working for private, as opposed to public, interests, the public also lost trust in scientists and engineers. One observer argued that "this loss of trust is the most serious challenge that nuclear policy makers and the nuclear industry now face in Japan."[130]

Another challenge for civil society–state relations in Japan has been the central government's paradoxical stance on TEPCO. Citizens' anger against the company and its managers can be seen in the 1,300+ criminal complaints filed against it by Fukushima citizens for neglecting to take sufficient precautions against a disaster.[131] While the government continues to push TEPCO to take responsibility for the accident by paying extensive compensation claims, it has propped up the company with massive financial support. The government purchased some ¥1 trillion worth of TEPCO stock and took over management of the firm, as it holds the majority of the company's voting rights.[132] The central government's bailout of TEPCO and its push for nuclear restarts reinforce the belief of many Japanese that the government has its own, and not its citizens', interests in mind. That scholars have connected the operations of the nuclear industry with the Japanese mafia, also known as the *yakuza*, cannot help matters.[133]

The governor of Fukushima Prefecture, Masao Uchibori, told one media outlet that because the government was "unable to take sufficient measures in such issues . . . the residents developed a sense of mistrust."[134] While "trust levels in many other hazards remained stable or even increased . . . the Japanese people's trust in risk managing organizations for earthquakes and nuclear accidents was damaged."[135] This loss of trust in government agencies makes it more challenging for Tokyo to issue orders that will be followed smoothly and to be seen as a source of reliable information during future crises.

Another, albeit positive, change in civil society resulting from the 3/11 disasters has been a surge in the practice of citizen science.[136] Rather than relying on radiation exposure data from Tokyo or from corporations such as TEPCO, Japanese residents have formed nonprofit and civil society organizations that collect, analyze, and publish relevant information. Citizens in the village of Date, 60 km (37 miles) from the Fukushima Dai-ichi complex, used personal dosimeters to measure actual radiation exposure levels.[137] The NGO Minna no Data (Everyone's Data) brings together around 30 groups to talk about shared findings and challenges in the citizen science of radiation measurement.

One of the best and largest-scale examples of this kind of citizen science has been the Safecast platform and website, which holds more than 100 million pieces of data uploaded by volunteers.[138] In a transparent way, Safecast allows anyone with a radiation detector or Geiger counter to measure, upload, and map radiation observations using an open-source Google map-based platform.[139] The Safecast site, in fact, provides do-it-yourself information on how to build radiation detectors and lends them to those who cannot afford to purchase a premade device. Safecast holds regular workshops and symposia throughout Japan on constructing radiation measuring devices and has given away its technology for free to encourage others to build their own Geiger counters ("bGeigies") and begin measuring radiation levels.

In an interesting twist, Safecast has partnered with local post offices near Fukushima Dai-ichi to provide mobile radiation counters for small delivery vehicles such as motorcycles. In this way, civil servants who continue to deliver mail can better understand their radiation exposure over extended periods, and Safecast gains additional observations of areas with relatively few residents. Fukushima City, like other local governments, has made its own efforts to provide up-to-date and understandable information to citizens through its Decontamination Information Plaza, set up in January 2012. The space holds public lectures on nuclear decontamination, explains the process to those who drop into the facility, and dispatches experts to other communities that want to know more about it.[140]

A third change in civil society behavior has been an increase in lawsuits against the central government and TEPCO. The government set up the Dispute Reconciliation Committee for Nuclear Damage Compensation on April 11, 2012, along with the Nuclear Damage Compensation Dispute Resolution Center (NDCDRC), to handle the myriad of claims for compensation from residents and businesses alike. Despite these new institutions, lawsuits have proliferated. For example, nearly half of the village of Iitate—some 2,800 residents—filed a petition in winter 2014. These former Iitate residents asked TEPCO to admit legal responsibility for the Fukushima Dai-ichi meltdowns, raise compensation levels, and pay for psychological damage that resulted from the accident.[141] Many of these residents were angered when government prosecutors dropped charges against TEPCO managers rather than seeking to hold them legally responsible.[142] Beyond Iitate's petition, some 30 class action lawsuits with more than 12,000 participants are seeking damages from the central government and TEPCO.[143] Some 370 US Navy sailors have sued TEPCO over their supposed exposure to radiation while serving on the USS *Ronald Reagan* in March 2011 off Fukushima's coast.[144]

While Japanese courts have a history of ruling against citizen activists, some, including Otsu District Court in Shiga Prefecture, have supported residents and plaintiffs seeking to stop nuclear restarts. In March

CHAPTER FIVE

2017, the Maebashi District Court in Gunma ruled in favor of evacuees who argued that the central government and TEPCO were responsible for preventable infrastructure damage and psychological distress.[145] Its ruling cited studies showing that TEPCO had been aware of the threat to Fukushima Dai-ichi from a tsunami 15 m or higher, but had taken no measures to prepare for one. Whatever the outcomes of these many lawsuits, which will probably continue, the drop in trust has resulted in local residents, and even foreign visitors, relying on lawsuits and third-party enforcement to create a sense of justice and fairness.

A fourth outcome has been wide resistance to government-led plans to restart nuclear power plants. The Abe administration's insistence[146] on returning to a pre-3/11 energy policy is a political decision that flows against the general will.[147] The large-scale demonstrations, some with over 120,000 participants, that began after the meltdowns have petered out over time, but smaller, more sporadic protests continue, including weekly protests on Friday evenings at the residence of the prime minister and in nuclear power plant host communities that have attempted restarts. Many local communities slated for nuclear power plants, such as Kaminoseki, Yamaguchi Prefecture, have found renewed enthusiasm for antinuclear protests following the Fukushima Dai-ichi disaster. A number of activist groups have started petitions to allow local residents to select nuclear-free electricity sources for their use. NGOs and NPOs have started various funds to promote renewable energy sources.[148] The Fukushima Renewable Future Fund set up in 2016, for example, funnels money into solar, wind, and geothermal projects in the prefecture, which has pledged a non-nuclear future for its energy sources.

A final consequence of the drop in trust has been that, despite the enormous amount of spending on physical infrastructure, large-scale public works projects, and decontamination, repopulation of permitted areas of Fukushima has been slow.[149] In fact, it may be precisely because of these large-scale expenditures that few citizens have returned. One scholar who reviewed 27 cities in Tōhoku between 2009 and 2015 found that, for cities that had large numbers of casualties from 3/11, higher levels of government spending on large-scale projects correlated with fewer returns. He dubbed this phenomenon the "reconstruction paradox."[150] With authorities seeking to undertake complicated and expensive projects, the process of moving into relocated or new homes may take longer as citizens wait for the often-delayed infrastructure to be complete. Further, ex-residents have said that they do not believe government claims about successful decontamination or reduced health risks in the area despite the expenditures. As one resident of Naraha said, "We don't believe that the government and TEPCO can be trusted. Although the graves of my ancestors are in the town and I go back in order to watch over them, I don't want my children or grandchildren to go back to Naraha."[151]

The government continues to excavate topsoil from residential and business areas and bag it for indefinite storage in Fukushima Prefecture, arguing that this procedure has reduced exposure to radiation by as much as 60%. But few evacuees—especially mothers with young children—are confident that these localized, experimental approaches to decontamination will lower risks to themselves and future generations. Particles such as cesium 134 and cesium 137 have half-lives of 4 and 30 years, respectively. Because it takes years for these radioactive isotopes to disintegrate naturally, they will continue to exist and be a hazard in the environment for decades unless actively contained. Further, football field–sized stacks of black plastic garbage bags filled with radioactive debris in the prefecture are not encouraging sights for potential returnees. Authorities have used areas such as fields and deserted valleys in the no-entry zones near the nuclear power plant itself to store some 9 million bags of waste, and additional materials are being sent across the country. As residents return to the area, many have expressed their discomfort with massive stacks of plastic and burlap bags filled with radioactive materials within sight of their railroad stations, homes, and schools. The government has sought more creative ways to use or reuse the soil. The Ministry of the Environment recently announced a plan to begin using radioactive soil—emitting some 1,000 becquerels of radiation per kilogram of dirt—as road materials, a decision angering residents of the city of Nihonmatsu, which will serve as the pilot site for the experiment.[152]

Alongside radiation concerns, rising construction costs and uncertainty about future occupancy have led to a 30% reduction in the number of homes to be built on higher ground, from 28,060 planned in 2012 to fewer than 19,707 by 2016. Reports indicate that overall, less than 80% of the planned housing had been completed by the spring of 2017.[153] Some 40% of Fukushima evacuees remain in prefabricated temporary housing; 36,000 evacuees are still in such low-quality homes across the three prefectures. After waiting nearly seven years for the government to prepare new home sites, many homeowners have left the area to build on their own. Among the elderly, concerns about rising costs have reduced interest in purchasing land in decontaminated or raised areas. Instead, senior evacuees have stayed in temporary shel-

CHAPTER FIVE

ters when allowed to or have moved into rental properties instead.[154] A lack of trust makes it challenging for government expenditures to raise confidence and bring back evacuees.

Ways to Shrink the Gap in Trust between Citizens and State

Nearly 20 years ago, scholars identified a lack of trust in the Japanese government as a major issue threatening that nation's future.[155] The choices made by central government decision makers and TEPCO managers after the 3/11 disasters caused many residents to doubt state claims, to collect and analyze their own data about radiation, and to file suit against decision makers over risks to their homes, health, and livelihoods. Japan's central government missed a chance immediately following the Great East Japan Earthquake to move out of its standard operating procedures and adopt new approaches based on two-way communication and bottom-up planning.

Rather than embracing transparency and allowing citizens to make their own choices, the government chose to filter the information it released to the public. As one scholar said, "Overall, the sense was that the government was holding back information or intentionally keeping low their estimates when no data was available."[156] Radiation expert Tatsuhiko Kodama argued that there was no excuse for the false promises made by the government about risks to health, which he described as "censorship."[157] The government's initial refusal to call the accident a meltdown, its implicit threats to prosecute those who provided independent information about radiation levels, and its optimistic claims about radiation exposure depleted trust levels.

Now, more than seven years into recovery efforts, the central government can still rethink its top-down, centralized, homogeneous approach to better engage with the factors that actually improve the chances of revitalization and mitigate against future disasters. There are several areas in which the government could seek to improve its approaches. First, many NGOs in the field of health and environment have asked the central government to permit them to verify the status of decontamination efforts in Fukushima, but the government has yet to agree to allow this oversight.[158] Allowing third-party verification of decontamination might decrease the distance between citizens and state on this important topic. Further, some 30,000 workers, many in their 50s and 60s, and others from foreign countries have served as "decontamination troops," under short-term contracts paying only some ¥8,000 ($73) per day, to clean up contaminated topsoil and bag it.[159] These workers operate with little oversight or radiation monitoring and without proper gear. Stronger government oversight over this extensive and expensive attempt to decontaminate the ground would also reassure residents that the government takes the health of workers and citizens seriously.

Next, the government could seek to truly integrate citizen feedback into the nuclear restart process. Nuclear restarts have relied for some 40 years on informal gentlemen's agreements between mayors, governors, and private utilities. When mayors and governors give approval for a new plant or the restart of an existing one, utilities move ahead, although some post-3/11 cases of nuclear restarts have cast doubt on the actual veto powers held by mayors and governors.[160] But future interactions could involve not just political elites, but also locals living within 30 km (18 miles) of the plants—the evacuation radius should there be an accident. Those individuals should have a direct say in projects that may affect their health and livelihoods. The government should also acknowledge that for many years it did not serve as a neutral umpire in the field of energy policy; instead, it had a strong interest in promoting nuclear power that continues to this day.[161] It should back away from its promotion efforts and allow the market and civil society, not top-down incentives, to drive energy decisions. In North America, despite earlier claims about an upcoming nuclear renaissance, the realities of the market, regulatory uncertainty following the Fukushima Dai-ichi meltdowns, and the discovery of new technologies such as hydraulic fracturing have made the future of nuclear plants quite uncertain. Observers have argued that nuclear power's role in a post-3/11 world will "never be more than marginal."[162]

The Japanese central government actually sought to capture—but not incorporate—the views of the broader public on the issue of nuclear power beginning in 2012. Its National Policy Unit carried out public hearings, sought comments, and undertook a Deliberative Poll on Energy and Environmental Policy Options. Deliberative polls are similar to public opinion polls in that they randomly sample residents, rather than waiting for volunteers to attend an event like a hearing. But they provide information and the chance to hear specifics about an issue in a way that a standard poll cannot.[163] In the poll, carried out by telephone, more than 6,800 citizens from across the country rated various nuclear restart plans. The majority supported a mix of energy with no nuclear plants operating.[164] In addition, more than 89,000 people submitted comments on the plans, with massive support (close to 88%) for a no-nuclear-energy mix. Again in December 2013, the government opened up a website for public comment, and more than 18,000 people sent in their opinions. While the government did not release an analysis of the results, a journalist found that more than 94% of the submissions were antinuclear.[165] As in the past, the central government asked for input from civil society on the topic of nuclear power, but then did nothing with the voice of the people.[166]

Finally, the central government could allow individual cities, towns, and villages to pursue their own infrastructure reconstruction plans. Currently, suggestions from central ministries become mandates at the prefectural and local levels, resulting in homogeneity in seawall heights and public housing designs, which many residents have opposed.[167] The central government could push the prefectural governments to allow municipalities to design their own specialized city plans with selected, not mandated, tsunami wall heights. Local governments should be encouraged to try out housing approaches that do not hark back to Soviet-style apartment-block *danchi*. And the government could put more bite into the various Special Zones for Reconstruction where it promises "non-uniform tax rates . . . as well as relaxation of regulations for medical staff to maintain medical care service."[168] As mentioned in chapter 4, many local medical providers face personnel shortages due to population outflow and challenging working conditions. Should the government seek to close the trust gap, it could seriously embrace these reforms and move to shore up its shaky relationship with its people.

The consequences of widening the trust deficit in Japan may be among the most severe that the central government faces in the long run. After the Soviet government restricted information about the Chernobyl disasters in the 1980s, researchers observed more than a decade of increased mistrust and suspicion toward that government, even among people who had almost no exposure to the radioactive contamination.[169] Some have argued that the accident and the state's handling of it "triggered the rapid acceleration of the breakup of the Soviet society beyond the expectations and intent of Gorbachev himself."[170] Even Soviets who were not directly affected by the meltdown saw that the government was withholding or altering information about the nuclear catastrophe and lost faith in the authorities.

Japanese residents across the country, and especially those in Tōhoku, see their government as acting in its own interests, not theirs. Societies run on trust, and the central government has depleted much of the trust and goodwill of the people toward it. The Japanese government's choices have made its citizens less likely to trust any future information it provides and unlikely to engage enthusiastically in plans that could benefit them. Yet Japan's national-level institutions, whatever their governance failings after the 3/11 disasters, compare favorably with those of other nations that have experienced similar disasters. It is to the international level that I now turn.

SIX

International Level: How Institutions Save Lives

A brief look away from Japan provides insights into why a close, comparative understanding of the levels of governance in countries facing disasters is critical. On August 26, 2008, Hurricane Gustav barreled through the Caribbean, causing more than $8 billion in damage to the area. Authorities in some nations labeled it the worst in 50 years. After passing through the Caribbean, its storm track took it over the US mainland, causing Mayor Ray Nagin to order a mandatory evacuation of New Orleans, the first since Hurricane Katrina devastated the city in 2005. With winds ranging from 75 to 155 mph as it made landfall, Gustav knocked over buildings, downed power lines, and flooded businesses and homes. When the storm subsided, it was clear that its effects on the nations in the Caribbean had varied tremendously. The same storm that killed 8 people in the Dominican Republic—primarily in a mudslide that killed an entire extended family—slew 77 in Haiti, whose fourth largest city, Gonaives, was completely flooded. The UN special representative to Haiti told the *New York Times*, "What I saw in this city today is close to hell on earth."[1]

Further, the nearby nation of Cuba—which evacuated more than 300,000 people in the path of the 155 mph winds—suffered no fatalities whatsoever, despite an increase in wind speeds as the hurricane passed over that island. Given that the same storm system pounded all three nations, the difference in the number of casualties is striking. Observers pointed out that different governance structures across the Caribbean resulted in different outcomes from an identical threat. While each nation had set up institutions and procedures to keep their inhabitants safe from harm, some had done a better job than others.

This chapter puts Japan's 3/11 disasters and government responses in context at the international level. Yearly, countries around the world face a variety of hazards and crises, with extreme weather events, flooding, and typhoons among the most common. As we saw with Hurricane Gustav, while damage does not stop at national borders, individual nations have varying levels of civil defense structures and procedures, infrastructure resilience, and preparedness. Those characteristics can magnify or diminish the impact of a hazard. Japan's institutional structures and high-capacity government, despite governance challenges such as the top-down and cookie-cutter responses described in chapter 5,[2] allowed it to minimize mortality during its triple disasters in 2011. Other countries facing similar or lesser-scale earthquakes in recent years have seen far more causalities and slower responses. At the country level, an obvious question is the degree to which factors such as governance, as we have stressed throughout the book, influence disaster outcomes.

International Comparison of Disaster Outcomes

As I have argued at the individual, municipal, and prefectural levels, neither the intensity of a disaster nor the aid provided afterward is strongly connected with outcomes such as survival and recovery. Instead, the strength of a nation's governance, especially in terms of rule of law and regulatory quality,[3] serve as better predictors for overall disaster outcomes. Countries with more stable governments have lower death tolls and economic losses.[4] More developed countries—those with higher incomes, for example—also demonstrate lower vulnerability to disaster.[5] These more resilient countries create better mitigation and preventive measures—such as stronger building codes, early warning systems, disaster preparedness training, well-equipped hospitals, better transportation infrastructure, and better-trained doctors—along with more active civil society organizations such as volunteer firefighters, faith-based organizations, and philanthropic and outreach groups that seek to assist others during crises. These well-governed countries encourage innovation, but also welcome feedback on policies and allow watchdogs outside the government to push them toward better policies.

CHAPTER SIX

To better understand the relationship between governance and disaster outcomes, I tracked the standardized number of fatalities per year over more than a decade, from 1995 until 2005, in 160 countries, using figures available from the disaster data repository known as EM-DAT, known more formally as the International Disaster Database. EM-DAT has compiled information on thousands of disasters around the world, using government agencies and NGOs along with insurance companies, to learn about the types of disasters that have occurred, the numbers of lives they have claimed, and their economic impacts. While no dataset is perfect, EM-DAT is the gold standard when experts want to understand large-scale patterns among disasters over time and across countries.

Precisely what to measure in terms of disaster impact, though, remains somewhat unclear. Rather than simply measuring the number of dead after a major storm, mudslide, earthquake, or other disaster, I normalized the score by controlling for the size of the country's population. Two hundred dead in a nation of hundreds of millions holds a different significance than the same number of fatalities in a small island nation. More specifically, I took the natural log of the number of disaster deaths divided by population. I used this standardized mortality rate and sought to connect it to one measure of governance: how much each government spent on services such as health care and education. Richer countries tend to spend more on public goods, services, and social protections than poorer ones, but not always. Even poorer countries can decide to invest in safety nets for their citizens.

Figure 6.1 isolates a few countries in a single calendar year and puts their data in the broader context of all the countries in EM-DAT. The downward-sloping line shows the general relationship between governance—here measured as government spending on social protections as a proportion of a country's GDP—and standardized mortality rate in disasters. The shaded area around the line is the 95% confidence interval into which we believe most real-life observations would fall. The higher the country on the *y*-axis, the more people have passed away due to disasters (controlling for the size of the country). The farther the country lies along the *x*-axis, the more it has spent on social protections. While I've deleted a number (actually, most) of the available individual country observations for readability—otherwise the graph becomes an unreadable blob—it is quite clear that there is a relationship between these two factors.[6] Countries that spend more money on policies such as education and health care can reduce their vulnerability to disaster. For example, Haiti has extremely high disas-

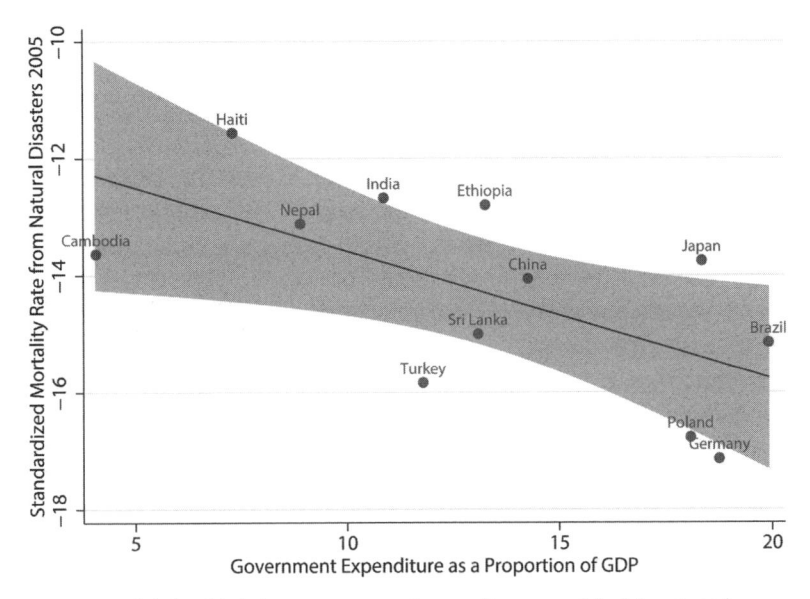

FIGURE 6.1. Relationship between government expenditure on social safety nets and disaster mortality.

ter mortality rates compared with other countries and very low levels of spending on social protections. In contrast, countries such as Poland, Brazil, and Germany have invested more in their citizens and can keep them relatively safe from harm. Japan spends an average of 17% of its GDP on these kinds of expenditures. In this way, governance has a clear effect on disaster mortality.

To make sure that these results are not a function of this one measure of governance, which may be linked to country wealth, I bring in another figure, which displays how mortality in disasters connects with a more direct measure of governance; namely, the Polity IV Democracy Score. This score is actually an index that captures components such as political competition, constraints on the executive branch, and processes of executive recruitment. Countries that have hereditary monarchies, such as Saudi Arabia, would receive the lowest possible score, –10, while countries with democracies, such as Poland and Japan, would receive a 10, the highest.

Figure 6.2 uses the same handful of nations to illustrate the connection between governance and mortality rate in disasters: nations that are more democratic have fewer casualties from disasters. In fact, Haiti was so far to the left of the other countries in terms of its democracy

CHAPTER SIX

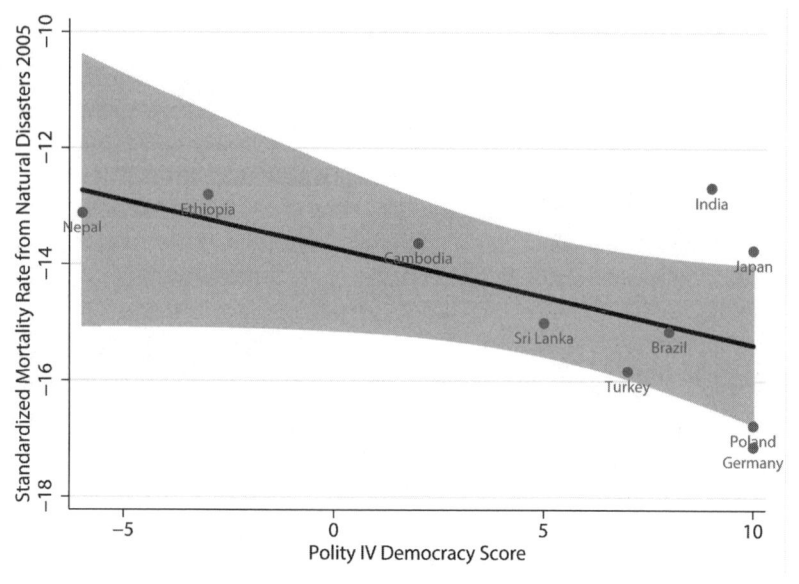

FIGURE 6.2. Relationship between Polity IV Democracy Score and disaster mortality.

score that I had to drop it from the figure for the sake of readability. These results confirm past research that has linked higher institutional quality in government to fewer consequences from disasters.[7]

Japan scored high on both measures of governance: government expenditure on social protections (around 17%) and democracy (10 on a −10 to +10 scale). As we have seen in previous chapters, following the 3/11 triple disasters, the Japanese government's responses were rapid and measured despite the destruction of much critical infrastructure, the deaths of nearly 19,000 residents, and anxiety about radiation. Early warning systems, disaster training, and strong building codes saved lives in Tōhoku and across the nation. The Japanese government sent in more than 100,000 Self Defense Force troops alongside hundreds of thousands of police officers, foreign troops, and domestic and international medical teams to respond to the event. Rapid provision of medical care meant that many individuals who might have died from treatable ailments, such as hypothermia, survived the event. Along with a strong and focused emergency policy response from authorities, local citizens in places such as Rikuzentakata, Watari, and Kesennuma worked to save one another and move the recovery forward. Further, Tōhoku residents ensured that societal stability remained: there were no reports of looting, increased crime, or other socially damaging behaviors.

Japan's government response to disaster stands in sharp contrast with those of some other disaster-affected nations. The government of Haiti struggled to respond to the January 2010 earthquake, and its poor governance did little to alleviate the looting, food riots, and public mob justice meted out following the quake. After the Great Sichuan Earthquake in 2008, the Chinese government ignored citizen cries for stronger building codes in schools while speeding up physical infrastructure recovery and ignoring social infrastructure. The differences in disaster outcomes, such as mortality rates, and in post-disaster social coordination and mobilization speak to the importance of additional factors beyond the strength of the catastrophe and the robustness of physical infrastructure. Through case studies of three nations with regular exposure to disasters—China, India, and Haiti—and with different combinations of governance and state capacity, this chapter illustrates how these national-level government characteristics influence disaster outcomes and responses.

Governance and Civil Society

Scholarship on governance has emphasized that the structure of a government and its quality of governance are often functions of the interaction between the state and civil society. Societies with better governance—that is, where civil society groups, NPOs, and other nonstate actors work independently and in collaboration or competition with the state—show higher potential for economic growth and for better policy management.[8] One study of French government policies in the 1970s and 1980s illustrated the need for feedback from civil society in achieving good governance.[9] Where groups in civil society could push back against poorly designed plans or work collectively to support nascent ones, the French government developed better policies. Similarly, research on the siting of controversial facilities such as garbage dumps and airports showed how negative feedback from affected communities halted what would have been less effective plans and forced developers to rethink their assumptions.[10] Broadly, nations with higher spending on social safety nets and more democratic governance encourage the flourishing of civil society, which in turn cultivates more responsive governance.

This chapter, which builds on such research, emphasizes the relationship between the government and civil society as critical to good governance. In the same way that direct measures of spending on social protections, political competition, and democracy can capture elements of governance, so too can measures of the *capacity* of the central government and its *openness to civil society*. Societies where citizens can access decision makers, have their opinions heard, and alter state policies to a significant degree are classified as having open input structures. In such countries, citizens and politicians engage in constructive disagreement, and civil servants and government officials remain embedded in positive and negative feedback loops. Residents' feedback may alter plans set in place, and popular support for new policies can result in their enlargement. The head of the Safecast citizen science organization observed that Fukushima communities with more active civil society groups had more radiation monitoring stations installed by local authorities. Local governments had to demonstrate to residents who regularly asked about their safety and pressed them for information that they were taking their concerns seriously. That is, pressure from an active and engaged citizenry altered public policy and made the decision makers more responsive to local concerns.

In contrast, nations where decision makers are more insulated from the public, where only certain interests are heard (if any), and where inputs from citizens are ignored or overlooked have closed input structures. In such states, residents may respond angrily to plans for unwanted facilities such as chemical factories or large-scale developments that uproot them from long-established neighborhoods, but have little chance of altering the proposals. In states with closed input structures, decision makers may feel threatened by negative responses and can use censorship or coercive force to end criticism of their policies. Such states may be able to collect less in taxes (as citizens distrust their intentions) and may spend less on social protections as well.

Scholarship has shown a tight link between the ability of citizens to have their voices heard and broader trust in the government. In societies where citizens have low efficacy and believe their ideas and desires will not permeate into actual policy, they tend to have lower trust in government. In turn, lower trust creates less desire to monitor and police decision makers, who may then do even less to enact the general will. A negative spiral can arise in which citizens disengage from their own government and lose trust in authorities, thereby making government itself more insular and aloof. In Italy, for example, northern authorities interacted positively with civil society groups over hundreds of years, beginning more than a millennium ago, creating an environment that facilitated trade, economic growth, and innovation. By drawing citizens into the governance sphere and encouraging their participation, medieval authorities created long-lasting norms for horizontal ties and vertical trust. In contrast, southern government authorities did little to encourage the public's faith in their activities and became less responsive to their needs over time, setting the stage for stunted growth.[11]

Alongside its interaction with civil society, we can judge a government by its capacity.[12] The most basic form of capacity relates to a government's monopoly over legitimate force, based on Weber's definition: "The state is a human community that (successfully) claims the monopoly of the legitimate use of force within a given territory."[13] Pragmatically, states need to be able to control events within their borders and prevent rival groups—whether terrorists, political opponents, or other domestic interest groups willing to use violence—from effectively challenging their rule. Somalia, for example, serves as a core example of a failed or low-capacity state because of the government's inability to keep warlords from controlling trade, exchange, and police functions.[14]

Beyond coercive force, scholarship has further characterized state capacity in terms of administrative and extractive strength.[15] Administrative capacity refers to the ability of the state to gather, organize, and analyze relevant information that informs its decision making and its policies. A well-trained elite cadre of civil servants drawn from specialized academies (such as those in Japan trained at the Law Faculty of Tokyo University or in France at the École Nationale d'Administration) furthers the state's interest more than inexperienced political cronies filling critical positions across the bureaucracy. Nation-states with a productive, transparent, and honest bureaucracy can better achieve effective policy. Finally, extractive capacity refers to the ability of the state to extract revenues—often through taxes—from the population to fund its programs, military expansion, and so forth. States with higher extractive capacity can leverage natural resource endowments, such as oil and mineral wealth, into long-term development funds, while nations with lower extractive capacity often struggle to ensure that the citizens—and not kleptocrats or warlords—benefit from such endowments. Norway and Nigeria both have extensive oil resources, but Norway has managed to secure its endowments to provide long-term subsidies to residents and extensive educational opportunities, while Nigeria has suffered from its "resource curse" and has struggled to keep from disintegrating due to civil war.

Development specialists, bureaucrats, and scholars have worked to assess levels of state capacity by considering provision of goods and services, use of repressive force, and the administration of democratic processes.[16] A number of indicators compiled by organizations such as the World Bank and Transparency International provide quantitative ways of classifying the capacity of states along these lines. Further research has argued that states with high levels of democracy and high-quality bureaucracies have higher GDP and better health and economic outcomes for their citizens, while those without these characteristics have lower GDP and worse outcomes.

India and Japan have relatively open input structures, in that citizens have a number of avenues through which their voices can be heard. These include not only institutionalized channels such as responsive political parties and public hearings, but also informal channels such as protests, lawsuits, riots, and hunger strikes. In contrast, Haiti and China allow fewer avenues for citizen voices to be heard. Citizens in Haiti find it difficult to access their very weak state, while China has deliberately repressed dissent and attempts at broader consensual decision making. In China, for example, the state regularly activates armies of state-sponsored internet users who, when contentious political issues arise, write dozens if not hundreds of posts on positive, irrelevant subjects on social media sites such as WeChat and Weibo.[17] Rather than shutting down dissent, the state seeks to distract those who would otherwise challenge state policy or foment opposition to its plans. China and Japan, though, both have far higher capacities than Haiti and India, which are hamstrung in their ability to gather information, collect revenue, and enforce state mandates.

Previous chapters, especially 4 and 5, have provided details about of Japanese prefectural and central government responses during and after the 3/11 triple disasters. I now describe three disasters that occurred in China, India, and Haiti in the decade preceding 3/11, compare them with the Tōhoku disaster, and investigate how the intersection of capacity and input structure affected each country's response.

China

On May 12, 2008, at 2:28 p.m., a magnitude 8.0 earthquake struck Sichuan Province in western China. The impact of this disaster on China was a function of its governance systems. China has a Polity IV Democracy Score of −10; that is, experts believe that China has the same quality of governance as Bahrain and North Korea, countries known for poor records on human rights and little space for civil society organizations. In terms of its citizen safety nets, China spends around 14% of its GDP on social protections, the highest percentage among the three countries in these case studies.

The quake, known as the Great Sichuan or Wenchuan Earthquake, took place about 50 miles (80 km) west of the provincial capital of Chengdu, with the epicenter in Yingxiu Township in Wenchuan County of Sichuan Province. Roughly 88,000 people died—among them thousands of children—when numerous public buildings, including schools and hospitals, collapsed.[18] Nearly 8 million homes also collapsed, and more than 24 million were damaged. Businesses and factories across the region were destroyed. Estimates show that some 115 million people were affected by the disaster, with direct economic costs around $123 billion.[19] Approximately 370,000 people were injured and 5 million left homeless; the affected area covered more than 38,000 square miles (98,400 km²). Some 18,600 miles (30,000 km) of water pipes and other infrastructure were destroyed. Later, cascading failures complicated the recovery process as floodwaters spilled out of new lakes formed by local mudslides. China formally requested assistance from the international community and received more than $500 million in aid, along with loans from international organizations such as the World Bank.[20]

China's top-down, authoritarian structure brought rapid, but often controversial, responses to the disaster. China's Ministry of Housing and Urban-Rural Development ordered 1 million temporary residences to be completed within three months. These camps housed internally displaced people until the government arranged new, permanent housing for them, a process it expected to take two to three years. For many citizens, this meant relocation to new cities, as the government labeled certain earthquake-hit areas as "relic parks" that were designated as areas only for tourists to visit, not for living.[21] Several disaster-affected towns were informed that they would promote the culture of a local indigenous group, the Qiang, for tourists.[22] In others, such as Yingxiu, residents were told that they would have a new town where "every household has a shop, and everyone can work in tourism."[23] Over time, though, tourism to these disaster-affected areas has waned, making livelihoods challenging.

In November 2008, the central government announced that it

would spend more than $150 billion to rebuild local homes and economies. It announced a three-year target for the completion of permanent housing for all families that lost residences to the earthquake, much of it far from their original homes. Some entire villages were moved up to 35 km (21 miles) away from their initial locations to less vulnerable sites. To assist the reconstruction, the government provided each household with some RMB 20,000 (roughly $2,800).[24]

The strong capacity of the Chinese government allowed it to quickly direct necessary resources to the rebuilding process after the crisis. Whereas the Chinese government set out new legislation and mobilized economic and administrative resources within a month of the earthquake, it took Japan more than a year to bring the Reconstruction Agency on line, as we saw in the previous chapter.[25] Yet a lack of regulation of pre-quake construction projects multiplied the effects of the Sichuan quake. Parents protested the low-quality construction of schools that had resulted in the deaths of many of their children. During the quake, some 12,000 schools in Sichuan and 6,500 in Gansu were destroyed.[26] More than 1,000 of the Beichuan High School's 2,790 students passed away during the quake.[27] Locals called the school buildings "tofu dregs" or "tofu skins" due to their weakness. Following the collapse of the schools, "grieving parents accused local officials of corruption and cutting corners, setting off a storm of criticism of the government."[28] Several reports pointed out that schools in the region that had been funded by donations from Hong Kong—and whose construction had evidently been of a higher quality—did not collapse during the subsequent 2013 earthquake, which struck the same area.[29]

After the Sichuan earthquake, Chinese state security forces suppressed protests against school collapse and construction corruption, often detaining or arresting those local parents or activists who spoke to the media on the issue. The exact number of children killed in the 2008 earthquake is not known; some have estimated that as many as 10,000 may have perished in their schools due to shoddy engineering and lack of effective regulation of construction. Within two months of the quake, some reported that local governments offered bereaved parents up to $9,000 on condition that they not raise their voices in protest. Volunteers and concerned outsiders could donate money and provide physical assistance, but pressure from the state kept them, too, from openly discussing issues like the collapse of schools.[30] Chinese authorities blocked attempts some 10 years later to hold a memorial service for the victims.[31] Artists such as Ai Weiwei took up the cause through their work, creating art that drew attention to the school collapses and the government's silence on the issue.[32]

Despite attempts from activists to raise the issue of building regulations in place before the quake, Chinese state authorities influenced media coverage of the disaster and the recovery process. China regularly ranks at the bottom of the world in terms of media openness, as it uses coercion and co-optation to guide its domestic media to produce positive views of the government. One comparative study of US and Chinese newspaper coverage of disasters showed the very different frames and approaches used by newspapers. In China, "the media played the role of a 'guard dog' for the Party, upholding the government and the dominant ideology."[33] Rather than pushing Chinese authorities to alter future responses to disasters or chastising them for regulatory failures, the Chinese media supported their decisions and lashed out at those who criticized the Communist Party. They argued, for example, that the reconstruction was a "miracle" that showed how "hard work for two to three years can leap across twenty years of monumental change."[34] This contrasted with the coverage of disasters such as Hurricane Katrina by US newspapers, which used a variety of frames, including human mortality and damage, in their approach. Scholars showed that either direct government control over the media or the media's own concern about state intervention drove coverage by Chinese newspapers, which took seriously the constitutional claim that Chinese citizens must defend "the security, honor, and interests of the motherland."[35] No such norms or restrictions govern the press in the United States, where news coverage of past disaster responses—such as for Hurricane Katrina—criticized the government directly and suggested alternative ways of responding to future disasters. Following the 1995 Kobe earthquake and the 2011 triple disasters, Japanese media outlets—often known for their weak watchdog role—criticized decisions made by the central government.

China's nondemocratic system and culture of corruption have made it harder for civil society to create and enforce building codes that could save lives during disasters. Parents could not push local governments and politicians to check on the structural integrity of school buildings, and the media did not support protests against what many saw as corruption in the state and in the construction industry. Further, while volunteers and unregistered civil society organizations stepped up to assist after the earthquake, there was no mechanism in place to integrate them into the rescue, response, and recovery processes. Finally,

CHAPTER SIX

as one group of researchers points out, "the top-down institutional framework has limited the autonomy of township governments from ensuring disaster related policy to be executed effectively."[36] As in Japan, where localities cannot pursue their own plans and visions for either mitigation or recovery, disaster-affected communities in China lack effective and satisfactory rebuilding processes.

Whereas China has strong state capacity but poor governance, India faces a different set of challenges when it meets crisis.

India

On the morning of January 26, 2001, a magnitude 6.9 earthquake struck India some 19 km (12 miles) northeast of Bhuj, in the state of Gujarat in the northwestern part of India. What governance systems were in place to handle the event? India has held steady in terms of spending on citizen safety nets, putting about 11% of its GDP into such expenditures (coming in third behind Japan and China), and it is a highly ranked democracy, earning a Polity IV Democracy Score of 9. After Japan, it is the highest-scoring democracy in our sample, far above China and Haiti.

In the 2001 earthquake, some 20,000 people died and 170,000 were injured. Almost 600,000 homes were destroyed by the quake, leaving more than 1.7 million residents homeless across the area. Estimates of the cost of the damage ranged as high as $5 billion. It remains the deadliest earthquake in India to date. The government immediately activated the National Disaster Management Control Room and sent in army troops to assist with the search-and-rescue efforts; within days, more than 25,000 rescue teams and personnel were deployed to the area. But due to damage to roads and other transportation infrastructure, many teams could not reach survivors in remote village areas. As the Indian government was still handling the lasting effects of floods in 1999, it sought assistance from the international donor community and organizations such as the Asian Development Bank.[37]

Along with the official response from the Indian government, private aid organizations and NGOs sought to assist the survivors with medical assistance, housing construction, and food and water. Some 14 NGOs worked together under a grouping known as Kutch Navnirman Abhiyan. The government of Gujarat set up the Gujarat State Disaster Management Authority to manage the recovery process and soon planned $1 billion in reconstruction projects.[38] Some observers labeled the authority's approach "systematic and scientific" because it used strategies such as public-private partnerships to create high-quality infrastructure.[39] Rather than relying solely on public funds, the new approach brought in investment from the private sector. Indian government officials argued that the quake had changed the way future disasters will be handled. In a retrospective conference paper, one Indian civil servant argued that "the Gujarat earthquake resulted in a paradigm shift in the policy of the Government from relief and humanitarian assistance oriented post-disaster intervention to a proactive prevention, mitigation and pre-disaster preparedness."[40]

Despite such praise for the Gujarat-focused policies and hope for future responses, scholars underscored that the recovery process was not as participatory as it could have been, and that a number of obstacles undermined the process, including the government's excessive bureaucracy, an underdeveloped disaster response policy, and irrelevant relief provision.[41] Other experts showed that many of the recovery plans put in place in areas such as housing ignored local citizen input and neglected to include bottom-up participation.[42] Some observers argued that the state focused its aid delivery and assistance on rural areas such as Bachau, Rapar, and Anjar, overlooking the needs of middle-class residents in more urban areas. Others illuminated the weak regulation of construction codes in the area; a few were hopeful that local authorities could tighten enforcement. Still others pointed out that while there is no national law enforcing building codes, individual cities have enacted such laws.[43]

The lack of financial and, in some cases, administrative and technical capacity weakened the Indian government's response to the disaster. However, its open input structure allowed the participation of NGOs, and decision makers at least claimed that they hoped to incorporate bottom-up participation into the recovery process. Civil society organizations and the private sector played key roles in the process. In these ways, India was far ahead of Haiti when that nation faced an earthquake.

Haiti

On January 12, 2010, a magnitude 7.0 earthquake struck some 25 km (16 miles) from Haiti's capital, Port-au-Prince. Haiti typically spends around 8% of its GDP on its citizen safety nets (with a low of 6% and a high of 9%, the smallest expenditure in our sample), and its Polity IV Democracy Score has whiplashed between a –10 (completely autocratic) until the late 1980s and up to 5 in 2010, when the earthquake arrived (political scientists would label it an *anocracy*, a country neither fully autocratic nor democratic). Such rankings place it as more democratic than China, but less democratic than India and Japan.

The 2010 quake killed at least 220,000 people and injured 300,000, causing the collapse of 250,000 homes and some 30,000 office and factory buildings. The lack of strong building codes and government capacity to enforce them meant that many concrete structures were vulnerable to seismic shocks. More than a million people across Haiti were left homeless. Critical government infrastructure was destroyed, including the Presidential Palace, the National Assembly, and the headquarters of the United Nations Stabilization Mission, and many of the civil servants and specialists at these agencies perished. One-quarter of the civil servants employed by the Haitian government were killed. Additionally, transportation, communication, and other infrastructure networks were destroyed by the quake.

Because of Haiti's status as a failed state and the fact that it "has endured political instability, chronic challenges in governance and the highest levels of poverty in the Western Hemisphere,"[44] many residents of the nation suffered from extreme vulnerability well before the earthquake. The United Nations Stabilization Mission in Haiti (MINUSTAH) had been established in 2004 as a caretaker authority, assisting the government with issues such as security, elections, and human rights protection. MINUSTAH itself lost a number of its personnel in the quake, with at least 36 dead and more than 300 missing or unaccounted for.[45] WHO reports stated that roughly half of Haitians lacked access to clean drinking water, and a similar percentage lacked access to health care, before the quake. Because of inadequate space, malnutrition, and overcrowding, sanitation and vector-borne diseases were serious challenges for responders to the disaster.[46] The nation also suffered from tremendous underemployment (roughly three-quarters of the population lived on $2 a day or less) and widespread slum conditions.

Following the collapse of many structures and the damage done to those remaining, some 1.5 million people moved into overcrowded, unsanitary temporary camps. Because of difficulties in distributing sufficient food to the huge number of survivors, violence and looting broke out a number of times. When aid workers went to distribute food in the camps, they often required military escorts due to concerns over security.[47] Further, cholera and other infectious diseases brought by the aid workers themselves claimed the lives of close to 6,000 and sickened more than 200,000 well after the earthquake. Later studies showed that Nepalese UN workers had introduced cholera to Haiti when they

INTERNATIONAL LEVEL

camped upstream from water sources, despite initial attempts to cover up its origin. Three years after the earthquake, despite more than $7.5 billion in aid, 500 camps remained in place, providing shelter to 360,000 displaced Haitians.

When donors sought to assist the state in rebuilding, they often had to work around the weak and volatile national government.[48] Few ministries had sufficient funds, organization, or personnel to carry out their administrative responsibilities. According to one report, "a governance review of the health sector carried out by the Ministry of Health in 2007 shows that leadership and regulatory functions in Haiti were 'weak or very weak' at the central, departmental, and periphery levels."[49] Overall, Haiti's government had a very low capacity before the earthquake, and the disaster reduced that capacity even more. Further, with a caretaker authority in place, few financial resources, and a "brain drain" of talented Haitians abroad to countries such as the United States and Canada, the country had a structure that was relatively closed to input from average citizens. In Haiti, the combination of a lack of government capacity and a lack of civil society input created an environment in which the earthquake, and then the consequences of a pandemic, were devastating.

The four nations in our sample—India, Haiti, China, and Japan—have all suffered earthquakes over the past two decades, but the impact of those disasters has been a function of the state, not of the magnitude of the quake. Table 6.1 summarizes the four earthquakes used here as case studies, in order from weakest to strongest. It is worth remembering that the magnitude scale is logarithmic, so that a magnitude 9.0 earthquake is 10 times greater than a magnitude 8.0 earthquake and

Table 6.1. Four Disasters and Their Outcomes

Disaster	Earthquake magnitude	Number killed	Impact
January 26, 2001, Gujarat earthquake	6.9	20,000	400,000 homes destroyed
January 12, 2010, Haiti earthquake	7.0	220,000	250,000 homes destroyed
May 12, 2008, Great Sichuan Earthquake	8.0	88,000	5 million made homeless
March 11, 2011, Great East Japan Earthquake	9.0	18,400 (dead and missing from tsunami, almost none in quake)	470,000 evacuated

CHAPTER SIX

100 times greater than a magnitude 7.0 one. Japan's 3/11 earthquake, 100 times more powerful than those in Haiti and India, killed roughly the same number of residents (as in India) or far fewer (than in Haiti).

Discussion

This chapter has used brief case studies of disasters over the last 20 years to illustrate the interaction between governance, survival, and recovery. Perhaps the most obvious lesson is that poorly responsive governments, failed states, and social and infrastructure vulnerabilities multiplied the impact of a disaster. Weak political institutions in nations such as Haiti and India meant that decision makers were often unable to create or enforce building codes, so that even relatively weak seismic events created large numbers of casualties. Chinese local residents lacked the political voice to force changes in shoddy construction of schools. The Chinese government controlled the media and prevented open discussion of the conditions that led to thousands of student deaths. In contrast, Japanese authorities had long ago upgraded building standards so that almost no buildings collapsed, even in the areas closest to the epicenter of the quake. Around the world, strong building codes, rule of law, and state legitimacy have proved critical in effective and rapid rebuilds.[50]

Even though the Haiti earthquake was far less powerful than its counterparts in China and Japan, it claimed far more lives because of weak building regulation. Then the conditions of poverty and lack of access to medical care meant that a disease brought in by those sent to assist with the quake ended up spreading and killing thousands. Similarly, more people died in the relatively weak Gujarat quake than in Japan's earthquake and tsunami combined. China, despite its financial and coercive capacity, had not invested sufficiently in building codes pre-disaster, and therefore the lives of many children and other residents were lost. Broadly speaking, countries with low government capacity and little bottom-up input had lower regulatory standards for built structures, which then collapsed quickly, raising the casualty count and creating tremendous suffering.

More responsive governments invested in early warning systems and raised engineering standards to meet international expectations. Japanese authorities had tsunami warning measures in place and had made significant investments in tsunami and earthquake countermeasures, including enforced building codes, tsunami shelters, evacuation drills, seawalls, and disaster response plans. Despite failures in its physical infrastructure, Japan's social infrastructure, education, and government capacity helped reduce the overall death toll from the 3/11 disaster. Poorer countries are unable to invest in risk reduction measures to this degree and therefore faced significantly more damage from disasters of the same size.

Japan and India had the most open input structures of the four countries in our case studies, meaning that post-disaster, authorities at least recognized the need to demonstrate that they listened closely to the demands of the public. Following the meltdowns at the three Fukushima Dai-ichi reactors, regulators moved to separate the overseers of the atomic energy industry from the organizations responsible for promoting it over the last half of the twentieth century (see chap. 5). Local citizens had the latitude and lack of censorship to collect, publish, and analyze their own data on radiation exposure levels through NGOs such as Safecast, despite grumblings from the central government. Indian authorities spoke openly of the need to incorporate the desires of local citizens and to seek to keep their needs in mind when building Gujarat back. In contrast, the Chinese government suppressed and then co-opted those who criticized the school collapses as a function of bribery or incompetence. Only outsiders and artists could criticize the state and attempt to raise the issues of corruption and lack of regulation. The Haitian government had little need to respond at all to citizen demands because most citizens felt disconnected from their state and uninterested in engaging it through protest or collaboration.

Earlier chapters that focused on resilience to disaster at the communal level demonstrated the role of local-level societal characteristics—such as social capital and social networks—in helping affected areas bounce back from adversity. Strong social bonds provide assistance during and after disaster through several mechanisms: strengthening survivors' voices, increasing their capacity for collective action, limiting out-migration, and creating networks of mutual aid.[51] In the same way that at the community level, social characteristics matter for disaster resilience and recovery, on the national level, relationships between the state and society strongly predict the effectiveness of recovery efforts along with likely mortality from disasters.

A combination of low government capacity and lack of access points for citizens created a situation in which Haitians were incredibly vulnerable to the 2010 earthquake. Japan's strong rule of law, high government capacity, and democratic governance allowed for an effective response to the triple disasters along with movement toward reform of poorly performing institutions (such as governance of the nuclear industry). Much of the disaster response industry is a reactive one, driven by the most recent disaster or crisis abroad. But these results indicate the need to create transparent governance, trust between citizen and state, and state legitimacy in nations across the world. It is precisely the weakest states in which citizens feel the most distance from their decision makers, and it is in these countries that outside agencies—whether state organizations such as the UK's Department for International Development (DFID), the Japan International Cooperation Agency (JICA), or the US Agency for International Development (USAID), or nonstate actors such as Amnesty International, MercyCorps, Transparency International, and WorldVision—should push the hardest to improve governance.

The increasing numbers of disasters worldwide and the rising economic costs of these disasters should focus our attention on improving the ways in which states listen to and interact with their citizens. Increasing state legitimacy and capacity will improve disaster responses and survival around the world. Having covered the 3/11 disasters at the individual, city, prefectural, national, and international levels, I now turn to policy suggestions and concrete recommendations for residents, NGOs, and decision makers.

SEVEN

Conclusions and Recommendations: Building Trust and Tying Us Together

In this book I have argued that two factors—networks and governance—drove the processes of survival and recovery after the 3/11 earthquake, tsunami, and nuclear meltdowns. At the individual level, social ties were activated as soon as the quake ended. Many Tōhoku residents—especially the elderly and infirm—survived because family members, neighbors, and neighborhood association (*chōnaikai*) members came to warn them to evacuate. In some cases, kin and friends carried the most vulnerable to safety in the 40 minutes between the earthquake and the tsunami. In handling the stresses of evacuation and worries about jobs, homes, and health, evacuees' horizontal ties again came into play. Evacuees from communities near the Fukushima Dai-ichi nuclear power plant had far better mental health outcomes when they remained in contact with neighbors from their old towns as they moved from place to place seeking safety and shelter. Social connections lessened anxiety, depression, and fears over radiation more significantly than obvious factors such as health and wealth. Similarly, communities where residents trusted and interacted with one another before the tsunami had lower rates of mortality from the tsunami.

While pre-disaster networks influenced disaster outcomes, the crisis itself affected governance structures. In the hardest-hit towns across Tōhoku, politicians invested more in networking after the events than in areas that suffered less damage and fewer fatalities. Town council members reached out to prefectural and national authorities not only to claim credit and boost their election chances, but also to bring in resources. Many towns benefited from sister cities that provided personnel and aid rapidly. Further, communities that were fortunate enough to have powerful politicians representing their interests to the central government showed stronger and faster recoveries. One coastal community undertook a massive redevelopment program, leveling nearby mountains to raise its downtown for protection against future tsunami. Coastal Town used connections to domestic and international authorities to bring in money and support its ambitious vision of the future. Whether safer physical infrastructure can bring back its citizens and attract new residents from other depopulating coastal towns remains a critical question.

At the prefectural level, social ties among citizens were less important than ties between prefectural authorities, NGOs, central government agencies, and international aid groups. Prefectural authorities in Japan undertaking good governance set up flexible communication and control structures that reached beyond the standard government silos. Miyagi Prefecture stood out with its broad and deep network of connections, and it recovered more rapidly than the other two prefectures under study. Fukushima and Iwate lagged behind in maintaining or establishing links to those with the resources, information, and assistance they needed. A social network analysis and data on social cohesion over time confirmed these trends across the three most affected prefectures.

At the national level, Japan's governance record post-disaster is mixed. The central government's response started with rapid deployment of domestic and international first responders and new institutions such as the Nuclear Regulation Authority (NRA) and the Reconstruction Agency. Additionally, claims of a recovery centered on social networks rather than physical infrastructure. The central government immediately created a new position—the Deputy Chief Cabinet Secretary for Crisis Management—to handle the tremendous logistic and administrative burden of responding to the disasters.[1] Ministries showed flexibility in granting licenses to emergency radio stations that sprang up to serve the population right after the disasters.[2] In some cases, community and emergency FM stations received licenses from the Ministry of Internal Affairs and Communications within an hour of applying.[3] Experts pushed a citizen-centered recovery plan that used social, not physical, infrastructure to save lives.

Yet the central government soon reverted to standard operating procedures, withholding critical information from residents of Fukushima, insisting on uniform mitigation infrastructure, and widening the trust gap between itself and its people. While local and prefectural governments held the most knowledge of local conditions and actual needs, a lack of autonomy hindered their responses to the disaster and their implementation of mitigation policies.[4] The Kobe government faced similar problems in accessing resources and regaining financial autonomy more than two decades ago after its earthquake due to bureaucratic red tape and an insistence on conformity.[5]

The biggest objective failure of government policy after 3/11 remains evacuee displacement and lack of permanent housing; following the 1995 Kobe disaster, citizens moved into new or refurbished homes far more quickly than they did following 3/11.[6] Attempts at relocation have scattered previously tightly integrated communities across Tōhoku and Japan, and too many people remain in temporary housing long after the triple disasters.[7] Less than 80% of overall planned replacement housing has been completed to date.[8] Nearly 40,000 evacuees remain in prefabricated temporary shelters more than seven years after the disasters, the majority of them elderly.

Despite these governance challenges, the high capacity of the Japanese government and its willingness to learn, at least to a limited degree, put it head and shoulders above other nations dealing with lesser disasters. Haiti, India, and China all suffered more casualties when faced with earthquakes of lesser magnitude. Citizens in those nations had fewer points of access to their governments where they could suggest alternative approaches to recovery, and their governments lacked the personnel and resources to assist them. Watchdogs and consumer groups in high-capacity nations with open input structures could push their governance systems to enforce building code regulations or create stricter standards to mitigate future disasters. In Japan, pressure from citizens altered government structures and influenced some decision makers to look to NGOs for data on radiation exposure, and civil society served as a watchdog when recovery funds were diverted or misappropriated. Further, before the 3/11 disasters, Japan had mitigation measures in place, such as well-trained and well-equipped fire and rescue personnel, along with sister-city agreements and civil service assistance plans.[9]

Given these findings based on qualitative and quantitative data, I now look to provide concrete recommendations and lessons from the 3/11 triple disasters. Other nations have much to learn from Japan's experiences and frameworks. To benefit from these lessons, however, we must move beyond claims that Japan's resilience in the face of disaster is solely a function of its national culture. We have seen variation in how individuals, cities, and prefectures across the country responded to the crises. There was no single culture of Japanese response, and despite claims about passive acceptance in the face of mismanagement and poor governance, we have seen a range of contentious political behaviors. People have marched en masse, taken up petitions, sued public and private institutions, and sought to change their own energy consumption and production patterns. While observers have pointed out that much has stayed the same as before the quake, we also see that it has opened up policy windows with the potential for change in several fields.[10]

As one researcher has pointed out, disasters like the 3/11 events occur during a period of crisis;[11] no catastrophe happens without a series of mishaps and misses well before the main trigger. On the surface, Japan had been doing well before the triple disasters: its unemployment levels were the envy of many, its citizens continued to save money at higher rates than those of most other countries, and its education levels and math scores placed it near the top among the OECD countries. But underneath the surface were the makings of a crisis: residents and developers had ignored ancient warnings against coastal development, TEPCO had pushed the myth of nuclear safety, a gap in trust had formed between civil society and the state, and few disaster managers had thought through what a nuclear accident would mean for residents and neighbors. TEPCO had no plans to handle a total station blackout, its managers and employees had not trained with local firefighters or other external agencies, and the regulators in Tokyo had not pushed stronger tsunami countermeasures. In many senses, the earthquake, tsunami, and nuclear meltdowns have served as a kind of accelerator or time machine, bringing into focus issues that Japan and other nations will have to struggle with in the future.[12]

I next look for lessons in the following policy areas: depopulation, sagging peripheral economies, physical infrastructure investment, and energy diversification and democratization. I also return to the broader themes of networks and governance to illuminate best practices and policy instruments that can prepare societies for disaster.

Depopulation, Aging, and Peripheral Economies

The earthquake, tsunami, and nuclear meltdowns have highlighted and accelerated the long-term trends of rural depopulation and a lack of economic innovation and development in Japan's periphery. While not all scholars have adopted the "catastrophic demography" perspective, and some have encouraged us instead to see what Japan has been doing right to manage population aging,[13] many observers are pessimistic about likely outcomes. "If residents won't return," an official in Naraha, in Fukushima, said, "we have to find ways to make Naraha attractive to a new group of families and workers."[14] But enticing newcomers to Tōhoku remains a serious challenge. One NGO has created a program to bring in volunteers to help fishermen in coastal communities with the hope that they will stay on—or at least stay connected—after their experiences.[15] The communities themselves have pushed local produce, fruits, and alcohol to rebrand themselves. Despite these efforts, predictions for population trends in the region are quite grim. In Naraha, barely 1 in 10 of the 7,400 former residents expressed an interest in returning. Most of the few hundred who have returned to date are senior citizens;[16] rather than coming home, young families from the area have moved inland to larger communities. Regular surveys of thousands of displaced Fukushima residents indicate that, as time has gone on, the number interested in returning has dropped.[17] By 2040, the coastal population of Tōhoku will probably fall some 50% from 2005 levels.[18]

As communities struggle with reduced populations, they must simultaneously come to grips with the reality that Tōhoku lacked strong economic bases before the disaster, with most jobs in fishing, farming, and agriculture. Cities, towns, and villages across Tōhoku were already losing tens of thousands of residents as they left for jobs in larger cities or for education in Osaka, Sendai, or Tokyo. Communities such as Watari, Rikuzentakata, and Naraha lacked strong economic infrastructure, high-quality educational institutions, and points of interest. The best-known educational institution in the region remains Tōhoku University (Tōhokudai), located far from disaster-struck areas, such as Tagajo, in the metropolitan city of Sendai. These challenges are amplified in Fukushima, where the core industries remaining after the nuclear power plant meltdowns are in the field of nuclear power, dealing with waste, reprocessing, and decommissioning. Residents there commute in trains that run past massive outdoor dumps for radioactive topsoil, distinguished by large black garbage bags piled one atop the other.

As local communities struggle to rebuild, the central government remains wedded to its post–World War II approach of overspending on physical infrastructure and recovery in depopulating areas.[19] Tokyo's price tag of more than ¥1.83 trillion ($16.5 billion) for radioactive decontamination in Fukushima means that it would be cheaper to purchase each household a new home than to clean up the area.[20] As one scholar mourned, "The Sanriku disaster area shows how resources have been squandered due to the path dependency of an approach that took root during the epoch of economic growth. Reconstruction cannot escape this path dependency because no leeway has been allotted for reflection and reconsideration."[21] Without serious consideration of the social consequences of spending money primarily on infrastructure and concrete projects, Japan is unlikely to be diverted from its well-traveled path. The central government will build roads, ports, dams, and seawalls without considering whether they truly benefit residents in the long run.

The central government has long attempted to redistribute economic activity away from major population centers such as Tokyo and Osaka to the rural periphery. One scholar listed more than eight development strategy laws, which began in the 1960s with the Mountain Village Promotion Act in 1965, progressed through a variety of Emergency Acts that sought to Improve Depopulated Areas (1970s), and ended with various laws promoting Revitalization or Repopulation of Depopulated Areas (1980s through the first decade of the twenty-first century).[22] The incentive systems for nuclear power plant host communities known as the Dengen Sanpō, discussed in chapter 5, can be seen as an extension of these programs.[23] Providing funds for rural, depopulating communities willing to host nuclear power plants did not build robust economies in the periphery.

Disasters only worsen the position of such poor, vulnerable areas. Despite top-down spending and occasionally innovative bottom-up development programs, scholars have demonstrated that towns and communities struggle for decades to recover financially from big disasters. Kobe, for instance, hit by a devastating earthquake in 1995, still suffers from a significantly lower GDP than in other nearby areas in Japan. Kobe's lower wages and depressed economy persisted even after the central government spent a huge amount of money to reconstruct its physical infrastructure.[24] Whereas before the 1995 earthquake Kobe's port facilities were among the top five in the world, some 15 years later it was barely 46th.[25] Clients and firms moved their business to other ports in East Asia. Putting more money into ports, roads, and seawalls may create jobs in the short term, but they are blue-collar, low-skill jobs that neither move the lower classes out of poverty nor create diverse economic bases.

Some experts have proposed a variety of policy responses to Tōhoku's anemic economic conditions, including *relocalization* (encouraging locals to eat local produce), *multifunctionality* (connecting industries such as agriculture to energy, preservation, leisure, and tourism), and *promotion of unique characteristics*.[26] Others have taken a more radical approach to depopulation and failing economies: encouraging local communities in peripheral, rural areas to embrace the loss of population and foster greening by allowing nature to take its course.[27] This "green retreat" approach is certainly controversial. But repeatedly investing in the shrinking periphery has done, and will do, little to alter the economic and political dominance of the Kanto region, where Tokyo sits, or to convince local youth and entrepreneurs to stay in Tōhoku. As Japan's overall population shrinks, Tokyo's grows.

By ending attempts at maintaining current town sizes and stepping back to allow trees and nature to return to previously inhabited areas, rural areas in Japan can increase habitat for local flora and fauna and create potential spots for wildlife tourism. In short, rather than fighting the ocean with concrete structures, Tōhoku communities could recognize that population maintenance and growth are unlikely and move to embrace a smaller footprint. The past 60 years of the central government's plans, though, leave little room for optimism that it will radically depart from its standard spending approach.[28]

Energy

Before the triple disasters, Japan's energy future seemed stable and predictable. The majority of the population supported the expansion and continued use of nuclear power. Despite scandals, cover-ups of accidents such as the sodium leak at the Monju fast breeder reactor in 1995, and the deaths of two workers at the Tokai reprocessing plant in September 1999,[29] the public saw the industry as safe and well managed. The central government envisioned building a fleet of new reactors and increasing Japan's use of nuclear power.

The meltdowns at three reactors in the Fukushima Dai-ichi nuclear power plant broke the safety myth of the industry, exposed mismanagement at TEPCO, and pushed many people in Japan and abroad to oppose nuclear energy.[30] The accident also illuminated unresolved challenges in the nuclear energy field, including the use of pools for interim storage of spent fuel and the lack of a clear plan for long-term disposal of radioactive waste.[31] Other challenges for Japan's nuclear energy field include the lack of safe and effective evacuation routes for nuclear power plant host communities across the nation.[32] As scholars have pointed out, 3/11 seemed like a moment for a "major transition in the domestic energy system."[33] The central government bailed out TEPCO, allowing the company to pay compensation to evacuees, manage radioactive water at the Fukushima Dai-ichi plant, and begin what will be at least a four-decade-long process of decommissioning its reactors. What will become of Japan's extensive fleet of existing nuclear reactors remains to be seen.

As I completed the writing of this book in October 2018, the struggle between nuclear energy advocates (such as TEPCO, business groups, and the LDP) and antinuclear groups (environmentalists and local residents) continues in courts and in street demonstrations. Japanese energy companies envision that Japan will restart many of its shuttered reactors to generate more than 20% of its power from nuclear sources by 2030.[34] Local actors such as antinuclear mayors and governors, along with sympathetic judges and a strict new energy regulator, the Nuclear Regulation Authority (NRA), have slowed down central government plans for these restarts.[35] The NRA has showed considerable backbone for a nascent organization, sacking senior officials for leaking a draft report to the Japan Atomic Power Company,[36] a private firm in the industry, and refusing to license plants on seismic faults. In March 2015, the NRA refused to allow the restart of Tsuruga reactor 2 due to its position over a fault, and it may shut down the Higashidori plant in Aomori Prefecture due to seismic risk.

While Japanese judges had traditionally sided with the state against civil society, the post-3/11 period has seen a number of more populist rulings against the nuclear energy industry. Several local courts, including those in Fukui and Takahama, have supported blocking of reactor restarts and indicted senior TEPCO officials in August 2015 for liability in the accident. Analyses of the public debates about nuclear power reveal that nuclear energy proponents have taken on a "technological nationalistic" stance, while its opponents have instead have adopted a "democratic values" perspective.[37] The Maebashi District Court ruling in March 2017, which held the government and TEPCO responsible for their actions before the accident, reinforced this pattern of increasing sympathy in the courts for antinuclear groups.

Whatever the outcome of those contentious debates, Japan has undergone a type of *Energiewende* (energy transition) parallel to that ongoing in Germany.[38] Soon after the Fukushima Dai-ichi accident, the German government decided to phase out the use of nuclear power and undertake a shift to renewable energy, focusing on solar, thermal, and wind sources.[39] Chancellor Angela Merkel's decision, which resonated with a large antinuclear social movement, encouraged local communities to democratize the generation of electricity through cooperatives and communes.[40] The impact of Japan's 2011 nuclear accident around the world has in fact become known as the "Fukushima effect."[41]

While Japan was the site of the Fukushima Dai-ichi accident, Germany was the first to move away from nuclear energy and toward energy democratization and decentralization. Japan has followed suit by pursuing energy efficiency and conservation. Japan's *setsuden*, or energy savings, movement pushed people to increase the temperatures in their homes and offices to 80°F to decrease air conditioner use, shut down appliances, and reduce exterior lighting. Public and private institutions across the country took on its "Cool Biz" recommendations; for example, men who traditionally dressed in suits wore short-sleeved shirts instead. During some parts of Japan's hot summer, these voluntary measures reduced energy use in Tokyo by as much as one-third compared with the previous year.

Beyond reducing energy use, local communities have started installing solar panels on roofs, building 100 m (328-foot) wind turbines, and doing exploratory drilling for geothermal energy plants. Fukushima Prefecture itself has indicated that it will no longer allow the use of nuclear energy and is constructing solar, wind, and geothermal power stations.[42] Miyako, in Iwate Prefecture, has also started diversifying its energy sources, including mega-solar, biomass, and hydroelectric power plants in its plans. Typically, Japan has relied on large-scale power plants generating electricity at a few concentrated sites, whether the six nuclear reactors at Fukushima Dai-ichi or the seven at Kashiwazaki-Kariwa in Niigata Prefecture. But after the disaster, more individual homeowners, businesses, and NGOs have decided to install solar panels, to join energy cooperatives, and to create and consume their own energy rather than relying on the regional energy monopolies.

Finally, the envisioned global nuclear renaissance now faces economic challenges, such as dropping prices for liquid natural gas (LNG) and other fossil fuels, increasing investments in renewable energy, and the bankruptcy of Westinghouse, Toshiba's nuclear arm in the United States. The Japanese firm Toshiba had purchased US-based Westinghouse, which sold nuclear products and services internationally, back in 2006. But massive losses due to attempts at constructing nuclear power plants in South Carolina and Georgia led to its bankruptcy in 2017.

The accident at Fukushima Dai-ichi has had consequences well beyond the boundaries of Japan, with nations such as Belgium, Switzerland, and Italy, as well as Germany, rethinking their involvement with nuclear technology. While some countries continue to pursue nuclear power plants, they tend to be autocratic societies with little input from their citizens, such as Russia and China.[43] The Japanese government may be intent on restarting its commercial nuclear power program after the Fukushima Dai-ichi meltdowns, but its own citizens and other countries have taken the opposite lesson.

Physical Infrastructure

Japan has faced earthquakes and tsunami for millennia, and individuals and communities have sought to pass on lessons to their descendants through physical symbols and markers. Coastal communities throughout Japan have built stone monuments and shrines to mark safe high ground, warning future residents not to build beneath that area. One of the stones in the village of Aneyoshi reads, "High dwellings are the peace and harmony of our descendants. Remember the calamity of the great tsunamis. Do not build any homes below this point."[44] And in the town of Onagawa, stone tablets erected in 1933 were built "to warn future residents to build no closer to the port, marking the boundary between safety and danger."[45] One scholar who surveyed some 84 shrine locations across Tōhoku showed that the vast majority were above even the highest reach of the tsunami on March 11, 2011. These religious spaces provided safe haven during the most extreme inundations[46] and showed the sensible limits of urban growth.

These structures physically embedded historical memory in the landscape and served as a paradigm of physical infrastructure that has the potential to save lives. Clearly, recent generations overlooked these warnings. Rather than giving nature its due and building only in less vulnerable areas, communities have moved closer and closer to risk. More problematically, Japanese authorities, believing that seawalls above a certain height did save lives,[47] continue to expend vast sums of money to restore damaged seawalls and construct new ones.[48] But our research on mortality in Tōhoku communities, highlighted in chapter 2, found that levees and seawalls had no measurable impact on mortality rates. Further, experts such as those on the Reconstruction Design Council argued soon after the disaster that the nation should not pursue seawalls and breakwaters as primary mitigation systems against tsunami.[49] Analysts have pointed out that the Japanese government often defaults to a focus on "hardware" (such as seawalls in this case) rather than "software" (such as evacuation plans, expectations about safety, and collective action that saves lives).[50]

Despite these analyses and recommendations, a tremendous amount of the budget (nearly $200 billion) set aside for disaster mitigation pre-3/11 and for recovery post-disaster has gone into physical infrastructure, especially the construction of seawalls. Visits to Watari, for example, found a "defense in depth" approach under way, with a 9 m (29-foot) seawall, a 10 m (32-foot) wide forest, and a 5 m (16-foot) elevated highway serving as barriers against future tsunami.[51] These expensive investments may, as discussed, slow down evacuations from future tsunami by providing a false sense of security to residents. Whether they can actually protect locals from future massive waves also remains an open question, as most seawalls in the area crumbled under the 2011 tsunami.

Even if these massive new investments raise the seawalls to heights effective in protecting against future tsunami, the existence of such a seawall may create a moral hazard, as local community members may believe themselves to be safe because of its existence. If seawalls encourage residents to remain in place after an earthquake, they set up a dangerous precedent. As noted in previous chapters, many fishing- and tourism-dependent communities oppose the creation of extended seawalls, fearing that these barriers may reduce the efficiency of fishing and cut down on the number of tourists interested in coming to the community. Further, it may be that the very construction of large-scale, contentious projects such as seawalls actually damages social cohesion. Fights between pro- and anti-seawall groups have serious consequences at a time when coastal towns are already struggling to retain population. Should local decision makers ignore local sentiment and follow central government guidance, they may be dividing and reducing their own populations.

Such investments in large-scale physical infrastructure projects regrettably have no influence on the real long-term social problems that

Japan and especially Tōhoku face: depopulation, graying cities, and movement from rural areas to urban ones. Scholars like Shingo Nagamatsu have shown that Tōhoku communities with higher levels of government spending demonstrate lower rates of population return.[52] As the central government pours money into concrete and continues to tinker with large-scale projects, residents have seen brighter lives and more viable futures elsewhere. Communities in Iwate, Miyagi, and Fukushima struggle with increased levels of gambling, smoking, alcoholism, prostitution, and divorce. Obesity rates and diabetes diagnoses have increased at all ages across the region. Top-down investment in public works projects will not mitigate these serious challenges.

Japanese decision makers continue to prioritize investment in physical infrastructure for a number of reasons, most of them political. First, large-scale public works projects provide income for construction firms, which have long been LDP supporters. Cutting off or reducing their benefits could have election consequences. Next, concrete-pouring jobs and other employment within the construction industry works as a kind of shock absorber for the Japanese economy. Many men and women in rural coastal areas such as Tōhoku find work in the field and may think kindly of politicians who claim credit for their employment. Finally, politicians under pressure to show that they have made their communities safer find it easier to point to tangible outputs such as seawalls than to long-term, slow-moving investments such as strengthening social cohesion.

Social Capital

This book has shown repeatedly that social capital—the ties between people—serves as a critical factor in resilience to disaster. Importantly, social capital—like other forms of capital, such as financial and human—can be created and maintained through policy interventions, whether by social welfare councils, NGOs, faith-based organizations, or local governments.[53] Randomized field experiments—the gold standard for social science—have demonstrated the possibility of increasing generalized and specific trust through various policies in undereducated, underserved areas of South Africa and Nicaragua.[54] A number of organizations around the world, including the Wellington Region Emergency Management Office (WREMO), Greening the Rubble in New Zealand, San Francisco's Neighborhood Empowerment Network (NEN), and the NGO BoCo Strong (Boulder, Colorado) have built on this evidence to invest heavily in building social ties and enhancing governance.[55] Locally tailored, bottom-up policies can create more trust among neighbors, build more intense interactions between residents and their decision makers, and help overcome barriers to collective action.

Japan and other nations regularly facing disasters should reallocate their budgets toward community-friendly physical and social infrastructure to reconstruct and strengthen social ties. Local and national decision makers should also do all they can to provide psychosocial support[56] during and after the emergency. These interventions facilitate the accumulation of bonding, bridging, and linking social capital among residents. Several Tōhoku communities, including Onagawa, are experimenting with community currency and time-banking programs, which have been shown to have strong positive influences on local levels of bonding and bridging social capital.[57] More than 2,000 people have participated in the community currency program in Onagawa[58] by volunteering and assisting others. In exchange, they receive currency that can be exchanged for services such as food from local farmers' markets or access to town facilities such as hot baths. Community currency and time banking increase volunteering rates and create a virtuous cycle in which effort and currency flow through local businesses.

A number of other social interventions in Tōhoku have demonstrated measurable increases in social cohesion and improved mental and physical health. These interventions include the Hamarassen Farm urban farming project, run by a municipal hospital to provide *ikigai* (purpose in life) for elderly evacuees who otherwise might have retreated to their temporary shelters. Participants have shown more social interactions as well as better health, as measured by improvement in bone density.[59] Programs such as Ochakko (Tea salon) and Hamatte-kerain kadatta-kerain (Gather up and let's talk), along with rotating credit associations (RCAs), similarly build social networks for evacuees.[60]

My colleague Emi Kiyota and I studied the impact of her bottom-up intervention known as Ibasho (literally, "one's place" in Japanese), which embeds elderly residents in vulnerable areas within larger social networks and encourages them to participate in leadership activities.[61] Based in a physical structure with flexible space that can be used as a library, cafe, and meeting spot, among other things, Ibasho brings together people who may otherwise have limited social contact. We found empirical evidence through our surveys of more than 1,000 residents that Ibasho enhanced feelings of efficacy, broadened social networks, and deepened the sense of belonging among frequent participants.

The Ibasho project builds on the belief that elder-led, community-centered projects not only empower the elderly but simultaneously build bonding social capital and develop community resilience to future crises. By placing decision-making power in the hands of those with the most experience, and by encouraging the elderly to play active, rather than passive, roles in the community, Ibasho helps to change narratives about aging and to better prepare communities for future shocks. The pilot Ibasho project in Japan, in the town of Ofunato in Iwate Prefecture, is based in a repurposed wooden farmhouse placed close to a field of temporary houses occupied by survivors of the earthquake and tsunami.

Many of those in Tōhoku whose homes were destroyed were forced to move into cramped, FEMA trailer–like spaces with limited privacy, described previously in chapter 2. In this environment, Ibasho was created to serve as a "third space," beyond home life and the workplace, where people can socialize freely.[62] The Ibasho building provides a meeting space for local residents of all ages and regularly hosts programming focused on engaging children, adults, and the elderly. While Ibasho holds regular operational meetings among the community elders, it also emphasizes that it serves as an "ordinary place where everyone can come and go as they please, where they can be themselves, and can interact with other people."[63]

The commonly held vision of Ibasho's community space revolved around informality—a place the participants could enter and leave at their whim. In that space, they would be able to undertake meaningful activities, such as cooking, volunteering, storytelling for children, and teaching skills such as fire starting, that would allow them to take on the active roles of educators. The elderly also wanted to engage the younger members by creating a multigenerational learning community from which both sides would benefit. The design that emerged from community meetings embodied these goals and allowed for the community to personalize the physical space as they saw fit. For example, rather than seeking to complete a perfectly finished building, Ibasho planners deliberately allowed many details to remain unfinished so that participants could add doors, space for children to play, and so forth.

The simplicity of the Ibasho approach and its relatively low cost (compared with technology-driven interventions or ones relying on

CONCLUSIONS AND RECOMMENDATIONS

massive infrastructure investment) suggest that it may be ideal for transport into other cultures and settings. Every society has a growing population of elderly whose experience and wisdom could be of use to younger generations. The elderly are typically less likely to be engaged in full-time employment and are also likely to be at risk for senility, dementia, and social withdrawal. Encouraging them to engage with a community-building project can draw them out from this potential isolation and help enhance the overall community's resilience. Further, while the Ibasho project requires an extended time commitment, its small-scale nature means that the costs for its implementation are far lower than those for other comparable projects. The Ibasho team is currently working with local elders on satellite projects in the Philippines and Nepal, which run on the same principles. We hope that, as our world enters an era of increased vulnerability to extreme weather and growing numbers of elderly, programs such as Ibasho can serve as a vanguard of a new way to mitigate risks and enhance resilience.[64]

At the most basic level, if policy makers refuse to invest in new community-building programs, residents should at least have a strong voice in determining the future of their towns and villages. For example, the *machizukuri* (town-strengthening) plans of municipalities—which consider locations of and access to public services such as government offices, hospitals, elderly and infant/child care centers, and schools—should be carefully guided by community-participatory decisions. Communities should also increase the number of shared and communal or third spaces, whether libraries, parks, or sacred spaces. Much research has shown that neighborhood-level factors strongly influence social network continuity or breakage.[65] Several residents of Ogatsu, in Miyagi Prefecture, spoke about the Shinto shrine that served as a focal point for festivals in their town, saying, "The *matsuri* [yearly festival] is a lot of work, but we're all together. We share a meal and sake, and talk with each other. We'd share stories, memories, sometimes a bit of work talk too. It really was a place of community."[66]

Governance Challenges

Japan's longest-term and most severe challenge—beyond resolving inherent tensions in the field of nuclear energy, managing the Fukushima Dai-ichi disaster, and permanently housing tens of thousands of evacuees—rests in the area of governance. This is especially unfortunate because a number of formal government structures—the dispersion of assistance through sister-city agreements, the flexibility shown by local bureaucrats in allowing unregistered evacuees to receive benefits from their host municipalities,[67] and the coordination of search-and-rescue personnel—proved indispensable in the days and weeks after the crises.

Government expectation of public participation is low, and Japanese citizens have little sense of efficacy or trust in their government. This may be because the government continues to handle reconstruction as a technical problem as opposed to one involving social infrastructure as well.[68] One observer, who subtitled the 3/11 events as the "Death of trust," said that the triple disasters "shattered Japanese faith in many of the country's institutions."[69] This outcome created a deleterious cycle in which politicians do not feel constrained by citizens, who in turn feel ignored by those who are supposed to represent them.[70] Many Japanese citizens have disengaged from the political sphere and expect that the government will do little to listen to them or their concerns. As we saw in our discussion of Chernobyl, the societal consequences of poor governance in Russia in the 1980s resonated over time, even across those who were not directly affected by either evacuation or radiation exposure. Similarly, even Japanese citizens far from Tōhoku who already felt disenfranchised saw more evidence supporting their negative perception of the state.

Tōhoku evacuees see little progress in their own lives in critical areas such as housing and employment and continue to doubt promises made by the government.[71] Choices made by the central government and TEPCO during the "elite panic" following the meltdowns, such as suppressing information about the spread of radioactive materials and threatening to prosecute those who provided independent data on the subject, undermined their trust in the system, as we saw in chapter 3. Decision makers have compounded this distrust by taking on policies that clearly go against public opinion, such as restarting Japan's mostly idle reactor fleet.[72]

Regular opinion polls have shown that while many Japanese distrusted the National Diet and their representatives before the 3/11 disasters, even fewer of them now have confidence in their political system. Rather than engaging in formal political activities such as voting in national elections, many young Japanese prefer to ignore them completely or instead participate in creating comics,[73] attending protest movements and rallies, and putting on antinuclear concerts and art exhibits.[74] Without strong, formal citizen participation, it is challenging for the government to receive the negative (and positive) feedback that it needs to adjust its policies. Rebuilding citizens' trust and the belief that the government is working for their good will take time.

In the planning process, experts and authorities have a variety of frameworks to choose from, including consensus-based, fair, and top-down approaches. The consensus-based approach requires considerable time for hashing out a plan acceptable to parties who may hold very different visions of their collective future. Under the fair approach, local residents draw lots or receive benefits such as early placement in housing randomly. No group, not even the elderly or disabled, has priority. In the top-down approach, the regional or national government sets standards based on technocratic expertise specifying where locals can build or how high seawalls and embankments must be.[75] A regular and accurate critique of the Tōhoku rebuilding process focuses on the lack of originality in plans; many local governments adopt proposals from the central government and consultants about apartment block styles and the heights of seawalls.[76] While the Japanese system tends to default to top-down approaches, local and regional authorities have been able to create pockets of autonomy and bottom-up innovation. Around the world, consensus-based and fair planning approaches are growing in popularity.

Much work on disaster management remains centered on the belief that the "government is required to act, for it is the only means by which the necessary resources can be mustered, organized, and deployed."[77] Certainly many disaster-affected cities and towns in Japan and elsewhere will need financial and logistic assistance from the central government. But scholars have observed that the friction between internal actors—those impacted by the event—and external ones—those providing resources and assistance—requires smooth information flow along with a reduction of uncertainty about policy outcomes.[78] As a result, long-term successful disaster management in Japan and around the world will require strong public-sector coordination with firms and corporations in the private sector, which scholars have shown control much critical infrastructure.[79] Japan and other nations will also need to better engage with residents and local entrepreneurs to create a climate in which small and medium-sized business owners feel empowered to experiment and occasionally fail.[80]

This book has sought to understand how Tōhoku residents and communities faced the unimaginable personal and regional challenges that came with the 3/11 disasters. Successes at all levels—from personal through national—have come when denser, tighter connections and good governance have worked hand in hand. Japan and other nations

CHAPTER SEVEN

need to develop both a strong disaster culture and strong disaster institutions;[81] that is, "simultaneous top down and bottom up initiatives."[82] Residents need to connect to one another and their decision makers in a bottom-up, organic way that builds cohesive and inclusive networks of social ties. At the same time, decision makers, from mayors to national politicians, need to provide resources and respond to local needs in a top-down, organized way. When societies have deep and broad horizontal connections alongside strong governance, people like the Shimizutanis and cities like Coastal Town will stand prepared for the next black wave.

Appendix 1: Interviewees and Surveyed Residents

For this research, I met with residents, NPOs, NGOs, and business owners in disaster-affected areas in Tōhoku along with local, regional, and national government agencies and elected officials. Over a period of almost two years in the field, I—and sometimes my colleagues—conducted face-to-face interviews at institutions, sometimes speaking with multiple people at the same agency, for a total of 100 or more interviews between May 2011 and August 2018. Where necessary, I have used pseudonyms for both individuals and locations to protect their privacy.

BUREAUCRACIES AND AGENCIES

Fire and Disaster Management Agency
Fukushima Prefecture, Comprehensive Recovery Planning Committee
Fukushima Prefecture, Disaster Prevention Implementation Department
Fukushima Prefecture, Disaster Recovery Planning Department
Fukushima Prefecture, Environmental Regeneration Department
Fukushima Prefecture, Nuclear Decontamination Department
Fukushima Prefecture, Temporary Housing Department
Ishinomaki City Hall, Office of the Mayor
Ishinomaki City Hall, Recovery Division
Iwanuma City Hall
Iwate Prefecture, Bureau of Reconstruction

APPENDIX ONE

Iwate Prefecture, Disaster Countermeasures Headquarters
Minamisanriku City Hall
Minamisoma, Mayor
Minamisoma City Office, Disaster Recovery Planning Department
Minamisoma Municipal General Hospital
Miyagi Prefecture, Crisis Management Section
Miyagi Prefecture, Earthquake Disaster Recovery Policy Division
Ofunato, Vice Mayor
Ofunato City Hall
Omachi Hospital
Omaezaki City Hall
Reconstruction Agency, Headquarters (Tokyo)
Rikuzentakata, Mayor Futoshi Toba
Rikuzentakata City Hall employee
Rikuzentakata group home manager
Rokkasho, Vice Mayor
Sendai City Hall
Soma, Mayor
Tamauranishi Recovery Committee
Taro City Hall
Watari City Hall

CORPORATIONS AND PRIVATE SECTOR

Chubu Electric Company
FEPC
Lawyers for antinuclear plaintiffs
Takamasa & Co. Ltd
TEPCO

NONGOVERNMENTAL ORGANIZATIONS

AidTakata
Care Miyagi
Chabad Japan
CWS [Church World Service] Japan
Habitat for Humanity Japan
Heart Net Project
Hospital in Fukushima Prefecture
Ibasho

INTERVIEWEES AND SURVEYED RESIDENTS

Ishinomaki Future Support Association
Japan Disability Forum
Morioka Fukkou Shien Senta
Onagawa Community Currency Program
Peace Boat
Plan Japan
RCF (Revalue as Coordinator for the Future)
Safecast
SAVE IWATE
Sendaishi Shōgaisha Fukushi Kyokai
Shizuoka 2.0
Soka Gakkai, Tōhoku Bunka Kaikan
Soka Gakkai International
Soma Follower Team (Soma FT)
Soma-Haragama Charity Morning Market in Fukushima
Tenjinkai Shakai Fukushi Hōjin
Tomodachi
Yellow Line Coalition

RESIDENTS

Ishinomaki

Otsuchi
Rikuzentakata
Sendai
Watari

JOURNALISTS

Asahi Shinbun
Freelance (various)
Seikyo Shinbun
TBS

SOCIAL ENTREPRENEURS

Makoto Kawakami
m table

APPENDIX ONE

ACADEMICS

Taiwan

Academica Sinica

China

Beijing Normal University
Beijing University
Fudan University

Japan

International Christian University
Ishinomaki Senshu University
Kansai University
Keio Business School
Kobe University
Kyoto University
Miyagi Gakuin Women's University
Nagasaki University
Taisho University
Teikyo University
Tōhoku University
Tokyo University
Yamagata Daigaku

Appendix 2:
Statistical Tables

APPENDIX TWO

Table A.1. Descriptive Statistics for Mortality Dataset

Variable (city/town/village level)	N	Mean	Standard deviation	Min	Max
Mortality					
Proportion of dead/missing from inundated area	132	0.010	0.024	0.000	0.115
Geographic/tsunami characteristics					
Tsunami height (m)	132	2.760	5.031	0.000	19.592
Area of municipality (km^2)	132	275.359	277.787	13.270	1259.890
Seawall height (m)	132	2.086	3.835	0.000	15.500
Coastline length (km)	132	4.505	10.281	0.000	64.870
Length of paved roads (km)	127	104.102	104.113	11.000	649.000
Demographic factors					
Population density (people/km^2)	132	287.030	563.064	1.629	3278.365
Pre-tsunami mortality rate	132	0.013	0.004	0.005	0.026
Percentage of population in fishing industry	65	0.003	0.005	0.000	0.025
Percentage of single-person households	132	0.219	0.068	0.109	0.533
Social capital proxies					
Crimes per 1,000 residents	132	0.007	0.003	0.000	0.016
Political factors					
Below 25% LDP support in 2009 LH election (default category)	134	0.224	n/a	0	1
25%–30% LDP support in 2009 LH election	134	0.507	n/a	0	1
30%–35% LDP support in 2009 LH election	134	0.194	n/a	0	1
Above 35% LDP support in 2009 LH election	134	0.0746	n/a	0	1
Merged locality (0/1)	132	0.053	n/a	0	1
New locality created through merger (0/1)	132	0.219	n/a	0	1
Firefighting expenditure per capita (¥)	34	23.072	9.074	10.120	48.280
Interaction term					
Tsunami height × crimes per 1,000 residents	132	0.017	0.030	0.000	0.136

STATISTICAL TABLES

Table A.2. Mortality Regression Analysis Results

Model	OLS regression (robust standard errors)	Negative binomial regression (robust SEs)	GLM logit family (robust standard errors)	Zero inflated beta distribution	Tobit (lower limit at zero, robust SEs)
Tsunami height (m)	0.00390***	0.223*	0.230*	0.0913*	0.00691***
	(3.07)	(1.85)	(1.90)	(1.69)	(3.09)
Area of municipality (km²)	−0.00000837	−0.000325	−0.000300	0.000397	−0.00000683
	(0.77)	(0.24)	(0.22)	(0.35)	(0.26)
Seawall height (m)	−0.000475	0.243	0.245	−0.0189	0.00704**
	(0.26)	(1.10)	(1.12)	(−0.23)	(2.51)
Coastline length (km)	0.000479	0.00869	0.00919	−0.00477	0.000497
	(1.65)	(0.35)	(0.37)	(−0.26)	(0.89)
Length of paved roads (km)	−0.00000011	−0.00104	−0.00116	−0.00318	−0.0000367
	(0.0000261)	(0.38)	(0.42)	(1.08)	(0.60)
Population density (people/km²)	−0.00000183	0.000313	0.000312	−0.000357	0.0000104**
	(0.73)	(1.13)	(1.12)	(1.47)	(2.35)
Pre-tsunami mortality rate	0.601	−10.48	−11.44	99.62	−0.948
	(1.08)	(0.11)	(0.12)	(1.39)	(0.43)
Percentage of population in fishing industry	−0.564	−18.51	−20.17	−10.06	−0.234
	(0.89)	(0.27)	(0.29)	(0.24)	(0.19)
Percentage of population in fishing industry missing	−0.000585	−0.619*	−0.625*	−1.048**	−0.00652
	(0.14)	(1.68)	(1.67)	(2.50)	(0.79)
Percentage of single-person households	−0.00268	−3.782	−3.861	−0.818	−0.0592
	(0.06)	(0.65)	(0.66)	(0.30)	(0.47)
Crimes per 1,000 residents	0.957	174.7*	180.0**	170.4*	4.257*
	(1.26)	(1.93)	(1.96)	(1.87)	(1.91)
25%–30% LDP support in 2009 LH election	−0.0117*	−1.136*	−1.179*	−1.903***	−0.0409***
	(1.88)	(1.72)	(1.80)	(3.47)	(3.84)
30%–35% LDP support in 2009 LH election	−0.00746	−0.223	−0.240	−1.226**	−0.0124
	(1.03)	(0.26)	(0.28)	(2.28)	(0.71)
Above 35% LDP support in 2009 LH election	−0.0212**	−0.862	−0.903	−1.475*	−0.0328
	(2.09)	(0.33)	(0.35)	(1.72)	(0.93)
Merged locality (0/1)	−0.00774	0.559	0.547	1.144	0.000518
	(1.32)	(0.65)	(0.64)	(1.38)	(0.03)
New locality created through merger (0/1)	−0.00315	−0.747	−0.770	−0.266	−0.0266*
	(0.74)	(1.40)	(1.42)	(0.54)	(1.93)
Firefighting expenditure per capita (¥)	−0.000751	−0.0959	−0.0996	−0.0301	−0.00340
	(1.43)	(0.57)	(0.60)	(0.48)	(1.55)
Firefighting expenditure per capita missing (¥)	−0.0137	−0.385	−0.456	0.412	−0.0344
	(1.00)	(0.13)	(0.15)	(0.35)	(0.87)
Constant	0.0139	−5.706***	−5.633***	−4.298***	−0.00354
	(1.12)	(2.87)	(2.78)	(2.64)	(0.09)

(continued)

APPENDIX TWO

Table A.2. (*continued*)

Model	OLS regression (robust standard errors)	Negative binomial regression (robust SEs)	GLM logit family (robust standard errors)	Zero inflated beta distribution	Tobit (lower limit at zero, robust SEs)
Log α	−29.42				
Tsunami height (zero-inflated)				−1.254***	
Constant				3.674***	
Log φ				4.391***	
σ					0.0235***
N	127	127	127	127	127

Note: Robust standard errors in parentheses.
*$p < .10$; **$p < .05$; ***$p < .01$.

Table A.3. Logistic Regression Coefficients for Council Member Outreach

	Lower house member	Upper house member	National civil servant
Human damage	0.0675***	0.0291*	0.0530**
	(0.02)	(0.02)	(0.02)
Area of municipality	0.178	0.485	−0.435
	(0.28)	(0.34)	(0.70)
Financial capability index	0.503*	0.862*	0.0515
	(0.28)	(0.44)	(0.86)
Merged status	−0.0737	−0.851**	−0.838
	(0.49)	(0.40)	(0.95)
Council size	−0.104	0.0786	0.105
	(0.10)	(0.12)	(0.27)
Number of candidates	0.0595	−0.0810	−0.0528
	(0.07)	(0.08)	(0.18)
No election dummy	1.125*	0.400	−0.0177
	(0.59)	(0.69)	(0.76)
Length of political career	−0.00376	0.0100	0.0596**
	(0.02)	(0.02)	(0.03)
Network width	0.114	−0.00843	0.102
	(0.12)	(0.18)	(0.20)
LDP	1.025***	1.343***	0.799
	(0.33)	(0.40)	(0.51)
CGP	2.389***	1.655**	0.922
	(0.71)	(0.79)	(1.12)
DPJ	1.313	1.089	2.245*
	(0.99)	(0.83)	(1.24)
SDP	−1.371	−0.750	0.137
	(1.38)	(1.63)	(0.80)
JCP	1.460*	1.514**	0.618
	(0.76)	(0.73)	(0.68)
Constant	−3.087	−6.853**	0.407
	(2.30)	(2.99)	(5.50)
N	167	168	162

Note: *$p < .1$; **$p < .05$; ***$p < .01$.

STATISTICAL TABLES

Table A.4. Descriptive Statistics for Recovery Study

Variable	N	Mean	Standard deviation	Minimum	Maximum
Outcomes					
Immediate post-tsunami capacity	37	38.01	10.64	13.80	60.40
Capacity by March 2012	37	75.14	12.96	45.00	91.20
Capacity by March 2013	37	84.65	15.20	46.10	100.00
Proportion of dead and missing	37	0.02	0.02	0.00	0.09
Geographic factors					
Area of municipality (km^2)	37	266.39	325.95	13.27	1259.89
Economic factors					
Financial capability index	37	0.59	0.34	0.14	1.50
Normed budget for disaster mitigation	37	1.15	2.023	0	10.67
Political factors					
Percentage supporting LDP	36	0.31	0.05	0.22	0.45
Percentage supporting DPJ	36	0.47	0.05	0.33	0.57
Number of powerful politicians	35	4.29	2.46	1.00	8.00
Demographic factors					
Population density (people/km^2)	37	433.35	749.35	10.88	3209.16
Percentage of population over 65	37	0.27	0.05	0.16	0.38
Social cohesion					
Crimes per 1,000 residents	37	0.01	0.00	0.00	0.01

Table A.5. Components of NIRA Recovery Index

Convenience store presence
Number of people in evacuation shelters
Number of evacuees from outside the prefecture
Rate of temporary housing occupation
Recovery rate of middle and junior high schools
Electricity restoration level
Gas line restoration level
Railroad restoration
Road restoration
Emergency medical service restoration
Restoration of medical testing
Debris pickup levels
Support from other municipal governments
Private and public insurance rates

APPENDIX TWO

Table A.6. Sources for Recovery Data

Variable	Source
Immediate post-tsunami conditions and 2012/2013 recovery conditions	NIRA recovery index
Tsunami height (m)	The 2011 Tōhoku Earthquake Tsunami Joint Survey (TTJS) Group (http://www.coastal.jp/ttjt/index.php)
Area of municipality (km^2)	Ministry of Internal Affairs and Communications, Statistics Bureau (http://www.stat.go.jp/data)
Seawall height (m)	Ministry of Land, Infrastructure, Transport and Tourism (http://www.thr.mlit.go.jp/)
Percentage of population over 65	Ministry of Internal Affairs and Communications (MIAC), Statistics Bureau (http://www.stat.go.jp/info/shinsai/)
Population density (people/km^2)	Author's calculation (people per square kilometer, data from MIAC)
Crimes per 1,000 residents	Ministry of Internal Affairs and Communications, Statistics Bureau (http://www.stat.go.jp/data)
LDP support in 2009 LH election (proportion)	Calculations from Steven Reed electoral database
Proportion of dead/missing in locality	National Police Agency
Financial capability index	Ministry of Internal Affairs and Communications (MIAC), Statistics Bureau (http://www.stat.go.jp/data/ssds/5b.htm)
Budget for disaster mitigation	Data from each municipality's home page
Voter turnout	Calculations from Steven Reed electoral database
Number of powerful politicians	Calculations from Steven Reed electoral database

Table A.7. Estimated Regression Coefficients for Recovery by 2012

Outcome: Recovery level by 2012	Ordinary least squares (robust SE)	Tobit (upper bound at 100)
Immediate conditions	0.512***	0.512***
	0.18	0.14
Proportion of dead/missing	98.18	98.18
	55.78	66.88
Area of municipality (km²)	0.008*	0.009*
	0.00	0.00
Financial capability Index	−3.44	−3.44
	6.27	5.01
Normed budget for disaster mitigation	0.77	0.77
	0.76	0.72
Percentage supporting LDP	−69.89	−69.89
	50.08	45.19
Percentage supporting DPJ	−12.41	−12.41
	34.12	36.96
Number of powerful politicians	3.41***	3.41***
	0.92	0.76
Population density (people/km²)	0.00	0.00
	0.00	0.00
Percentage of population over 65	2.88	2.88
	56.73	46.28
Crimes per 1,000 residents	1220.45	1220.45
	762.22	651.25
Constant	55.24	55.24
	45.59	40.13
σ		6.27
		0.76

*.05 < p < .01; **.01 < p < .005; ***p < .005.

APPENDIX TWO

Table A.8. Estimated Regression Coefficients for Recovery by 2013

Outcome: Recovery level by 2013	Ordinary least squares (robust SE)	Tobit (upper bound at 100)
Immediate conditions	0.587***	0.584***
	0.18	0.17
Proportion of dead/missing	158.85	148.73
	82.98	80.20
Area of municipality (km²)	0.01	0.01
	0.00	0.01
Financial capability index	−2.80	−2.01
	8.17	6.01
Normed budget for disaster mitigation	1.72	2.25*
	0.82	0.98
Percentage supporting LDP	−139.5**	−141.8*
	48.89	53.89
Percentage supporting DPJ	−64.00	−65.51
	39.70	44.07
Number of powerful politicians	4.67***	4.855***
	1.11	0.92
Population density (people/km²)	0.00	0.00
	0.00	0.00
Percentage of population over 65	−2.28	0.21
	63.13	55.20
Crimes per 1,000 residents	1713.82	1790.4*
	936.66	779.07
Constant	99.24	98.08
	48.26	47.84
Σ		7.48
		0.92

*.05 < p < .01; **.01 < p < .005; ***p < .005.

Notes

PREFACE

1. While casual observers may use the phrase "natural disaster," scholars of the field point out that the phrase is nonsensical. Hazards such as hurricanes, tsunami, and floods are natural. Hazards become disasters because of the choices made by societies (see Oliver-Smith 1999).
2. See National Police Agency of Japan 2018. More than 90% of the deaths were due to the tsunami.
3. All amounts preceded by a dollar sign are in US dollars unless otherwise noted.
4. Ranghieri and Ishiwatari 2014.
5. *Nikkei Asian Review*, December 9, 2016.
6. See Feldman 2015 for a detailed analysis of the complex requirements and "arbitrary distinctions" for victims to access a comparatively large compensation pool for the Fukushima Dai-ichi disaster.
7. United Nations University (UNU) 2016.
8. Mimura 2015a.
9. Interview, Rikuzentakata, April 3, 2016.
10. The games are to be played in the city of Kamaishi in Iwate Prefecture in the Tōhoku region. See Takezawa 2013 [2016], 54.
11. The central government has argued that the budget for the disaster-affected area will end by March 2021. Various observers have pointed out that the government is unlikely to simply cut off funding for projects, such as massive seawalls, that have yet to be completed by that date.
12. Ishiguro and Yano 2015; Suppasri et al. 2016.
13. Otani 2012; Tatsuki 2013; Yun and Hamada 2015.

14. Useem, Kunreuther, and Michel-Karjan 2015. Given the relatively short tenure of most Japanese prime ministers, long-term guidance from a singular charismatic figure is relatively rare in Japan.
15. *Mainichi Shinbun*, January 7, 2017; Isabel Reynolds and Emi Nobuhiro 2016, Residents Who Fled Fukushima Fear Return to Ghost Town, Bloomberg, October 20; Jiji Press, March 31, 2017.
16. Y. Itō 2018, 377.
17. Kubo and Miwa 2011, 76.
18. *Wall Street Journal*, June 18, 2012, A5.
19. Some have argued that Japan's national population in fact peaked in 2004. See Siembieda and Hayashi 2015.
20. Phelan 2016. One community in Fukushima Prefecture recently named its new sake Kizuna-mai, based on the words for "social bonds" and "dance"; the proceeds from its sale will go as donations to disaster-affected areas (Kyodo News, May 27, 2018).
21. Interview with TEPCO officials, May 2, 2017.
22. Japan's calm group behavior in the face of adversity may seem peculiar or unique. But many disaster experts have pointed out that, rather than panicking, people around the world tend to be "controlled, rational, and adaptive" (Goltz and Mileti 2011, 491).
23. *Time*, March 28, 2011, 44; see Bestor 2013 for a discussion of these tropes.
24. Gusterson 2000.
25. Manabe 2015; Kariya and Hanasaki 2014.
26. *Yomiuri Shinbun*, September 6, 2011; Kyodo News, March 10, 2014; *South China Morning Post* October 26, 2016. Unfortunately, that school closed in the spring of 2018 due to low enrollment after the disaster.
27. For a review of the tremendous amount of work that lawyers are carrying out in Tōhoku, see Leflar et al. 2012.
28. *Asahi Shinbun* September 9, 2011.
29. CNIC 2015.
30. RJIF 2015, 82–83. See also Gerald Curtis 2012, If Culture Explains Behavior, Then No One Has to Take Responsibility, Writes Gerald Curtis, *Financial Times*, July 10; and Winchester 2017 for critiques of observers who have used culture as their main framework for approaching the disaster.
31. Funabashi and Takenaka 2011, 7.
32. Samuels 2013, 183.
33. Aldrich 2012.
34. Aldrich 2008.
35. Aldrich 2013.
36. Takezawa 2013 [2016]. But see Birmingham and McNeill 2012 for an exception.
37. Asad 2015.
38. See coverage of one town's slow recovery in *Japan Times*, March 6, 2014, A1.

39. Funabashi and Takenaka 2011; Samuels 2013; Tsunekawa 2015; Feldman 2015.
40. Hiyama et al. 2012.
41. Y. Itō 2018, 335.
42. Yamashita et al. 2018.
43. *Economist*, October 8, 2011, 54.
44. This has been true because parents have kept children indoors out of fear of radioactive contamination and because of the destruction of many public places for play. See Kinoshita and Woolley 2015.
45. Lieberman 2005.
46. For most in-depth interviews with individuals and extended case studies of localities, I have used pseudonyms to protect the identities of those people and places. I use real names only for public figures speaking on the record or with permission.

CHAPTER ONE

1. Morris 2012, 34. Modern apartments have early warning systems built into intercoms and lighting controls, and many residents have earthquake apps on their smartphones that count down to forthcoming quakes.
2. *Akita Sakigake Shimpo*, July 28, 2011.
3. *Asahi Shinbun*, July 28, 2011.
4. Yamashita 2008.
5. Wood 2016, 12.
6. Among the better-known stories aimed at children is *Inamura no Hi* (Fires among the Rice Sheaves), based on a true story of a man who set crops on fire during the 1854 Ansei-Nankai tsunami to get the attention of his neighbors and draw them to higher ground. See http://www.town.hirogawa.wakayama.jp/inamuranohi/english/siryo_inamura.html for details.
7. Parry 2017, 5.
8. Morris 2012, 35.
9. *Mainichi Shinbun*, July 18, 2012.
10. Slater, Nishimura, and Kindstrand 2012, 98.
11. Birmingham 2011.
12. Tatsuki 2013, S407.
13. *Mainichi Shinbun*, August 29, 2012.
14. *Sankei Shinbun*, January 3, 2016.
15. Ishiwatari 2012, 20; Takezawa 2013 [2016], 162.
16. *Shūkan Asahi*, April 29, 2011.
17. The *Kahoku Shimpo* has details on this tragedy. See https://www.kahoku.co.jp/special/spe1114/20130103_01.html.
18. *Yomiuri Shinbun*, September 1, 2011.
19. Kyodo News, April 14, 2011.

NOTES TO PAGES 5–10

20. *Economist*, March 10, 2012.
21. The actual term's origin and content remain unknown, but some have claimed it stands for the words "safety control rod axe man" based on experiences at the University of Chicago's experimental nuclear plant. See *Economist*, March 10, 2012, 6.
22. Bricker 2014, 5.
23. NAIIC 2012.
24. Bricker 2014, 12.
25. RJIF 2015.
26. Aldrich 2008.
27. Hasegawa 2011, 9.
28. Bricker 2014, 9.
29. RJIF 2105, 18.
30. Osnos 2011.
31. Hasegawa 2011, 10. See also *Wall Street Journal*, December 27, 2011. One nuclear regulator in France said, "If you had asked me a year ago about an incident in which multiple units were left without power and cooling I would have said it was not possible" (*Economist*, March 10, 2012, 11).
32. See *Economist*, January 7, 2012, 38.
33. *Wall Street Journal*, December 3–4, 2011, A10.
34. *Wall Street Journal*, April 11, 2013. TEPCO has sought to replace some 100 leaky, bolted-together steel storage tanks with newer welded-together versions (site visit, July 12, 2018).
35. *Japan Times*, August 21, 2014, A1.
36. Tsunekawa 2018, 400. The tritium contamination seems impossible to resolve.
37. Abe 2016, 151.
38. Bricker 2014, 13.
39. Birmingham and McNeill 2012, 113. Some Japanese observers drily argued that with the outflow of foreigners, they should be known as *flyjin*, a pun on the name for foreigners (*gaijin*).
40. Sasakawa Peace Foundation 2012, 48.
41. Greenpeace 2014.
42. Tsujiuchi 2015.
43. Tamba and Yokemoto 2013, 90.
44. These contractors often have little or no training in handling radioactive materials. "One, who earns ¥15,000 ($190) a day clearing radioactive rubble at the plant, says he was given just half an hour of safety training. Almost everything he has learned about radiation risks, he says, came from television" (*Economist*, November 5, 2011, 49).
45. Y. Itō 2018, 360.
46. Kyodo News, May 12, 2018.
47. Edgington 2017.
48. Hasegawa 2011, 3.

49. Samuels 2013, 158. Samuels's perspective matches that of the empirical research done by Kawamura and Bohacs (2015).
50. Wein, Johnson, and Bernknopf 2011, 523.
51. *Economist*, November 5, 2011, 49.
52. I focused on these issues in a previous book (Aldrich 2012).
53. Ritchie and Gill 2006.
54. See Aida et al. 2017 for a look at how social ties helped the elderly recover after the 3/11 disasters.
55. Varshney 2001.
56. Granovetter 1973.
57. Chen, Kang, and Tjosvold 2017.
58. Shimada 2014.
59. See Arai, Kobayashi, and Nakajo n.d. for an interesting quantitative investigation of this phenomenon.
60. Scholars have mapped out how digital networks through social media platforms and online websites provide information and support during a crisis. See Hoshikawa 2014.
61. Kondo 2016.
62. Aldrich 2012, 43–44. While some have sought to position social capital and resilience as concepts undergirding neoliberal attempts to move government functions to the less accountable private sector, I see them instead as placing the agency of local residents front and center. Ideally, strong governance would result in local, regional, and national institutions supporting the bottom-up vision and drive of residents seeking to recover and resume their lives after disaster. Despite this hope, as this book and many other studies illustrate, governments at all levels may hope to reduce their own service provision to residents by outsourcing, rather than making residents the focus of their programs. See Johnson 2011 and Gotham 2012 for discussions of privatization in one post-disaster city.
63. Social ties have been critical in developed and developing nations alike during crises. For a study of how social ties helped save lives and speed up recovery in Bangkok, see Roasa 2013.
64. There has been a tremendous amount of research connecting social capital and health. See, among other works, Kawachi, Subramanian, and Kim 2008, Fujisawa, Hamano, and Takegawa 2009, and Hamano et al. 2010.
65. Takahashi et al. 2015.
66. Kawawaki, Osaka, and Yamauchi 2014.
67. See Nakao 2014.
68. Geiger, Kawauchi, and Bellamy 2015.
69. Takahashi et al. 2015.
70. For a great study of how governance and social capital interact—especially after disasters—see Carlin, Love, and Zechmeister 2014.
71. Japan's government structure contrasts with the North American and German federalist systems, in which the central government devolves some power to the periphery.

NOTES TO PAGES 19–37

72. See Edgington 2014 for a primer on how the three levels of Japan's government work (or don't work) together during disaster.
73. Fukuyama 2013, 3.
74. Waltz (1999, 696) talks about the pattern in which "states that adapt easily have considerable advantages."
75. See Rose-Ackerman 2004 for a discussion of (poor) governance and corruption.
76. International Fund for Agricultural Development 1999.
77. Tsujinaka and Inatsugu 2018, 16.
78. Fukushima Booklet Publication Committee 2015, 24.
79. Wada 2018, 265.
80. Tsunekawa 2016, 16.
81. Samuels 2013, 171.
82. Inatsugu 2018, 254.
83. Nakajima 2012; Morioka 2015; Shimizu 2015.
84. LeBlanc 1999.
85. Fukushima Booklet Publication Committee 2015, 30.
86. See their website at https://blog.safecast.org/.
87. Chamlee-Wright 2010.
88. Shifleen 2015.
89. One newspaper found that the average population decline was 15.6% in 36 of the 42 cities, towns, and villages in the prefectures of Iwate, Miyagi, and Fukushima, with 13 towns and villages (many in Fukushima) reporting a decline of more than 20% (*Asahi Shinbun*, February 11, 2016).
90. Tsunekawa 2016, 11.
91. M. Itō 2018, 237.
92. Tsujinaka and Inatsugu 2018, 21.
93. Wood 2016.

CHAPTER TWO

1. Unless otherwise noted, I will be using pseudonyms to protect the identities of informants and their locations.
2. Radio provided information to many survivors in temporary shelters as well; see Ikeda 2015.
3. *Mainichi Shinbun*, April 14, 2011.
4. Birmingham and McNeill 2012, 8, 25.
5. Interview, May 24, 2016.
6. Interview 1, Watari, July 9, 2011.
7. Michishita and Pressello 2015, 43.
8. Interview 15, July 17, 2011.
9. Interview 21, July 24, 2011.
10. Hasegawa 2013.
11. Sagara 2011.

12. *Mainichi Shinbun*, June 13, 2013.
13. Tatsuki 2013, S428.
14. *Asahi Shinbun*, April 18, 2012.
15. Takezawa 2013 [2016], 37.
16. *Asahi Shinbun*, April 27, 2011.
17. Birmingham and McNeill 2012, 145.
18. Ranghieri and Ishiwatari 2014, 67.
19. Ishikawa 2012; Hasegawa 2013; UNU 2016.
20. Reconstruction Agency 2013.
21. Kondo and Shoji 2016, 6.
22. Yahoo Japan News, September 18, 2013.
23. Visit to Tōhoku branch of the Soka Gakkai organization, July 10, 2018.
24. Ranghieri and Ishiwatari 2014, 14.
25. Nakajima 2012.
26. Otani 2012, 244.
27. Interview, Ishinomaki City Hall, June 22, 2014.
28. Tamba and Yokemoto 2013, 94.
29. Wada 2018, 264.
30. Brannigan 2015, 17.
31. Ueda and Shaw 2015, 132.
32. Birmingham and McNeill 2012, 164.
33. *Mainichi Shinbun*, March 8, 2018.
34. Hikichi et al. 2017.
35. Tamba and Yokemoto 2013, 94.
36. Y. Itō 2018, 363.
37. Ueda and Shaw 2015, 140.
38. UNU 2016, 18.
39. Tsuchiya, Sugawara, and Taniguchi 2015, 120–122.
40. *Sankei Shinbun*, March 28, 2011; *Shizuoka Shinbun*, March 15, 2011.
41. Hibino and Shaw 2015.
42. UNU 2016, 17.
43. The three zones became "difficult to return," "area where living is prohibited," and "area preparing to lift evacuation."
44. MEXT shared radiation monitoring duties with foreign partners through the Ministry of Foreign Affairs.
45. Kyodo News, June 19, 2011.
46. Yoshida 2013, 26.
47. RJIF 2015, 80.
48. Birmingham and McNeil 2012, 67.
49. *Tokyo Shinbun*, March 22, 2012.
50. *Asahi Shinbun*, June 28, 2012.
51. Tsunekawa 2016, 22.
52. RJIF 2015, 78.
53. Osnos 2011; Hasegawa 2013.

54. Solnit 2009.
55. Bricker 2014, viii.
56. Associated Press, June 21, 2016.
57. Birmingham and McNeill 2012, 92.
58. *Wall Street Journal*, December 1, 2011, A8.
59. Birmingham and McNeill 2012, 83.
60. Hasegawa 2013, 26.
61. Miska (2016) and many others have argued that the rushed evacuation of hospital patients and the elderly cost, rather than saved, lives.
62. Tsujiuchi 2015.
63. Fujino 2016, 20.
64. UNU 2016, 15.
65. *Asahi Shinbun*, April 26, 2011.
66. Tanigawa et al. 2012.
67. *Asahi Shinbun*, August 22, 2012.
68. *Japan Times*, September 12, 2015.
69. Murakami et al. 2015.
70. Some have argued that the relocation of more than 160,000 people out of concern for the radiological effects of the Fukushima Dai-ichi meltdowns was not justifiable (Waddington et al. 2017).
71. *Newsweek*, April 13, 2011.
72. Jacobs 2011.
73. Jiji Press, November 16, 2016.
74. *Mainichi Shinbun*, January 12, 2017.
75. Kyodo News, June 12, 2012.
76. Manabe 2015, 84.
77. Ash 2013.
78. Tamba and Yokemoto 2013, 100.
79. *Mainichi Shinbun*, February 28, 2018.
80. UNU 2016, 17.
81. Maly, Matsushita, and Suzuki 2015, 3.
82. Megan Green 2015, Reluctant to Speak, Fukushima Moms Admit Fear of Radiation, Pressure from Families, *Japan Times*, September 29.
83. Mimura 2015b.
84. Green, *Japan Times*, 2015.
85. Asia News documentary, March 2018.
86. *Fukushima Minpo*, March 26, 2015.
87. Abe 2016, 163.
88. Otake and Sakata 2014, 22.
89. Takezawa 2013 [2016].
90. Takezawa 2013 [2016].
91. Birmingham and McNeill 2012, 107.
92. Takezawa 2013 [2016].
93. Hasegawa 2013, 21.

94. Takezawa 2013 [2016].
95. *Fukushima Minpo*, February 16, 2013.
96. *Japan Times*, March 3, 2014.
97. Interviews, Summer 2015.
98. Snider, Chehil, and Walker 2012.
99. *Aljazeera*, March 12, 2013.
100. Jennifer Percy 2016, I Have No Choice but to Keep Looking, *New York Times*, August 2.
101. Hommerich 2012.
102. Tsujiuchi 2015, 4.
103. Interview with mayor of city in Fukushima, July 23, 2015.
104. *Asahi Shinbun*, March 11, 2016.
105. Konishi 2013, 77. Post-traumatic stress disorder can manifest in a myriad of ways, including insomnia, short attention spans, and self-harm. In severe cases, survivors with PTSD may be unable to hold down a job or engage in healthy relationships.
106. Tsujiuchi 2015, 5.
107. Kamiyama, Nakatani, and Sato 2014.
108. This section draws on Iwasaki, Sawada, and Aldrich 2017. Material used with permission.
109. For a discussion of the consequences of the compensation, see *Asahi Shinbun*, March 5, 2014, A13.
110. Phelan 2016.
111. Philip Brasor and Masako Tsubuku 2016, Tohoku Is Literally Still Waiting to Move On, *Japan Times*, March 5.
112. Tsuboya et al. 2016, 54.
113. See Lien, Peng, and Zheng 2016.
114. Sawada and Kuroishi 2015.
115. Hanaoka, Shigeoka, and Watanabe 2014.
116. *Aljazeera*, March 12, 2013.
117. Birmingham and McNeil 2012, 201.
118. *Wall Street Journal*, March 11, 2012.
119. *Asahi Shinbun*, September 11, 2014.
120. *Japan Times*, December 11, 2015.
121. Kyodo News, March 7. 2016.
122. Maly and Matsushita 2014.
123. Hirai et al. 2015.
124. Ishii et al. 2015.
125. Contreras, Blaschke, and Hodgson 2017.
126. *Tokyo Shinbun*, October 4, 2016.
127. Inoue et al. 2014.
128. *Wall Street Journal*, March 11, 2012, A1.
129. Personal communication, Kondo Naoki, March 29, 2016.
130. Quoted in *Asahi Shinbun*, July 20, 2015.

NOTES TO PAGES 56-63

131. Birmingham and McNeill 2012, 157.
132. *Asahi Shinbun*, March 29, 2011.
133. *Japan Times*, June 23, 2011. During the months after the meltdowns, the government struggled to manage contaminated straw, which was unknowingly fed to hundreds of cows, whose products were then sent to consumers and restaurants (Kyodo News, July 19, 2011).
134. Agence France-Presse, February 24, 2014.
135. Shigemura et al. 2016, 121.
136. Interview with TEPCO official, May 2017.
137. Iwasaki, Sawada, and Aldrich 2017.
138. Kondo and Shoji 2016.
139. Otake and Sakata 2014, 55–56.
140. Leng 2015.
141. See Daimon and Atsumi 2018 for a look at this "pay it forward" phenomenon.
142. Daisuke Wakabayashi 2011, Making Home Sweet Again: After Tsunami, a Baker Finds Purpose, *Wall Street Journal*, November 12–13.
143. Patrick Barta, Daisuke Wakabayashi, and Gordon Fairclough 2011, After Tsunami, a Mayor Plants Seeds of Renewal, *Wall Street Journal*, December 10.
144. Tamba and Yokemoto 2013, 96.
145. Quoted in Martin Fackler 2013, Japan's Nuclear Refugees, Still Stuck in Limbo, *New York Times*, October 1.
146. Bruch 2016.
147. Brasor and Tsubuku, *Japan Times*, 2016.
148. See *Japan Times*, April 13, 2018, for a discussion of TEPCO's compensation and how it has occasionally made matters worse.
149. *Japan Times*, September 6, 2016.
150. Wakabayashi 2011.
151. Aldrich 2012.
152. Interview, Ishinomaki, October 2015.
153. Toko Sekiguchi 2014, Fukushima Evacuees Reject a Return, *Wall Street Journal*, October 25–26, A7.
154. *Wall Street Journal*, March 5, 2012, A12.
155. Interview, Ishinomaki, June 17, 2014.
156. Interview, Ishinomaki, October 2015.
157. *Asahi Shinbun*, February 18, 2016.
158. *Japan Times*, December 11, 2015.
159. Daniel P. Aldrich and Mika Shimizu 2011, Smaller Is Better: Private and Individual Philanthropy after the 3/11 Disaster, *Asahi Shinbun*, August 10.
160. Geiger, Kawauchi, and Bellamy 2015.
161. Kimura 2016.
162. *Wall Street Journal*, March 11, 2012.
163. Aldrich 2011.
164. Midford 2014.

165. Fujimori et al. 2014.
166. Birmingham and McNeill 2012, 193.
167. Sugimoto et al. 2014; Akiyama et al. 2015.
168. NHK, March 8, 2018.
169. Naito 2016, 64.
170. *Japan Times*, May 12, 2016.
171. Ash 2013.
172. Interviews with survivors, 2017.
173. *Mainichi Shinbun*, February 28, 2018.
174. Kyodo News, March 1, 2018.
175. Normile 2016.
176. Interview with mayor of city in Fukushima, July 23, 2015.
177. *Japan Times*, November 6, 2016.
178. Marui and Gallardo 2015.
179. UNU 2016.
180. Quoted in Reynolds and Nobuhiro, Bloomberg, 2016.
181. Jiji Press, June 5, 2015.
182. *Asahi Shinbun*, October 19, 2015.
183. *New York Times*, October 1, 2013.
184. Reynolds and Nobuhiro, Bloomberg, 2016.
185. Reuters, March 8, 2017.
186. "Japan Struggles to Revive Tsunami Zone," *Wall Street Journal*, March 30, 2016, A8.
187. UNU 2016, 17.
188. Eiichiro Ishiyama 2016, Tainted Fukushima Towns Stuck in Time as Decon Crews Plug Away. Kyodo News, April 1.
189. Sandi Doughton 2014, Recovery Isn't in Sight 3 Years after Japan's Tsunami, *Seattle Times*, March 8. The red tape ensnared even first responders carrying out vital duties in devastated communities. In the aftermath of the tsunami, the Self Defense Forces had been transporting and burying victims as they found them, which raised the ire of local police officers, who wanted to enforce an ordinance of the Family Registration Act that requires police officers to write up death certificates before burial. Local police confronted SDF to say they were being "arrested red handed" because of their activities. It took a face-to-face confrontation followed by behind-the-scenes legal wrangling to allow critical emergency practices such as timely burial of dead bodies. RJIF 2015, 49.
190. Brannigan 2015, 18.
191. *Nikkei Asian Review*, February 10, 2012.
192. Interview with Sendai City Hall official, May 10, 2013.
193. See Toba 2013.
194. Quoted in Jeff Bayliss 2013, Rikuzentakata, Part One: An Interview with Mayor Toba Futoshi, *Where Does It All Go? An Aftermath Travelogue* (blog), August 21, http://commons.trincoll.edu/jbaylis3/.

195. *Economist*, March 10, 2012.
196. Interview, March 29, 2017.
197. *Straits Times*, March 11, 2014.
198. Brasor and Tsubuku, *Japan Times*, 2016.
199. Interview, Ishinomaki, September 13, 2014.
200. Brasor and Tsubuku, *Japan Times*, 2016.
201. Brannigan 2015, 66–68.
202. *Wall Street Journal*, April 9, 2011.
203. Interview, July 2018.
204. Birmingham and McNeill 2012, 177, 219.
205. Weitzdorfer 2014, 124.
206. Hoshino 2016.
207. Maly and Matsushita 2014.
208. For an excellent historical overview of the environmental catastrophe at Minamata, see George 2002.
209. Jeff Kingston 2016, Onagawa Is On the Rebound from Devastation, *Japan Times*, February 13.
210. Masanori 2015.
211. Phelan 2016.
212. *Economist*, August 6, 2011.
213. Inagaki 2012, 2013.
214. Nishide 2018, 310.
215. Takezawa 2013 [2016], 98–99.

CHAPTER THREE

1. *Asahi Shinbun*, February 11, 2016.
2. Lovholt et al. 2012.
3. Much of this section draws on Aldrich and Sawada 2015. Material used with permission.
4. Kahn 2005.
5. Frankenberg et al. 2011.
6. Dacy and Kunreuther 1969; Kates and Pijawka 1977.
7. Guha-Sapir et al. 2006; Nishikiori et al. 2006.
8. Frankenberg et al. 2011; Rofi, Doocy, and Robinson 2006.
9. Martin Fackler and Norimitsu Onishi 2011, Utility Reform Eluding Japan after Nuclear Plant Disaster. *New York Times*, May 31; Ranghieri and Ishiwatari 2014, 100.
10. Elinder and Erixson 2012.
11. Beggs, Haines, and Hurlbert 1996; Sawada and Shimizutani 2008.
12. See also Klinenberg 2002.
13. See, among many other studies of the connection between social ties and crime, Akçomak and Weel 2008; Buonanno, Montolio, and Vanin 2009; Ramseyer 2015.

14. Newman 1996.
15. Deller and Deller 2010.
16. Putnam 2000, 308.
17. Saito 2010.
18. Kerr 2002.
19. Szreter and Woolcock 2004, 655.
20. Gleibs et al. 2013.
21. Gleibs, Mummendey, and Noack 2008.
22. Samuels 2013, 40.
23. *Daily Mail*, May 14, 2011.
24. Murao 2015b, 102.
25. To handle the issue of missing data for two of our quantities of interest (i.e., percentage of the population in the fishing industry and firefighting expenditures per capita) we substituted zeroes for missing values and then employed a dummy variable in the model to capture any potential effects from doing so.
26. King, Tomz, and Wittenberg 2000.
27. Ando et al. 2013.
28. Muramatsu 1997, 31.
29. Ikawa 2008.
30. This section draws on Aldrich and Ono 2016. Material used with permission.
31. Mayhew 1974.
32. Horiuchi, Saito, and Yamada 2015.
33. See Hirano 2006.
34. Oliver, Ha, and Callen 2012.
35. Fenno 1978; Muramatsu 1997.
36. Johnson 1995; Krauss and Pekkanen 2011.
37. Muramatsu 1997, 50.
38. Muramatsu 1997, 118.
39. Ikawa 2008.
40. Specifically, there were 492 incumbent council members across those municipalities at the time of our survey; 247 of them responded to the survey (a response rate of 50.2%).
41. The average value is about 5,890 tons, and the range is between 0.17 and 32,560 tons.
42. This section is based on Aldrich 2015. Material used with permission.
43. Cf. Lipscy 2012, 410; Scheiner 2005.
44. Hawkins and Maurer 2009.
45. Cf. Liu and Plyer 2010.
46. Bolin 1994.
47. See Dacy and Kunreuther 1969; Kates and Pijawka 1977; Frankenberg et al. 2011; Chang and Rose 2012.
48. ESCAP 2010, 36.

NOTES TO PAGES 93-104

49. Cf. Guha-Sapir et al. 2006.
50. Plenty of scholars, as mentioned previously, have used crime as a proxy for social capital. See, among others, Fukuyama 1995; Newman 1996; Akcomak and Weel 2008; Buonanno, Montolio, and Vanin 2009; Deller and Deller 2010; Putnam 2000, 308; and Ramseyer 2015.
51. Kubo and Miwa 2011, 62.
52. Bisri 2016.
53. Kubo and Miwa 2011, 65.
54. Inatsugu 2018, 257.
55. Interview with Coastal Town adviser, April 3, 2016.
56. Elliott, Haney, and Sams-Abiodun 2010.
57. Interview with Coastal Town adviser, April 3, 2016. I have substituted a pseudonym into his statement.
58. *Japan Times*, March 7, 2017.
59. Personal communication, Coastal Town adviser, November 10, 2016.
60. Strusińska-Correia 2017; site visit, 2017.
61. Phelan 2016.
62. *Asahi Shinbun*, July 20, 2015.
63. Site visit, July 2015.
64. See Edgington 2019 for a discussion of artificially elevated towns in Tōhoku.
65. Barta, Wakabayashi, and Fairclough, *Wall Street Journal*, 2011.
66. Tomodachi Initiative 2014.
67. Cf. Tolan 2015.
68. Kingston, *Japan Times*, 2016.
69. Masanori 2015.
70. Matthew Gillam 2015, On the Fourth Anniversary of the Great Eastern Japan Earthquake and Tsunami, JLGC Blogs, Japan Local Government Center, http://www.jlgc.org/on-the-fourth-anniversary-of-the-great-eastern-japan-earthquake-and-tsunami/.
71. Horiuchi and Saito 2003.
72. Reed, Scheiner, and Thies 2012.
73. Lipscy 2012.
74. Samuels 2013.
75. Samuels 1983; Muramatsu 1986.

CHAPTER FOUR

1. Matsui 2018, 280.
2. *Asahi Shinbun*, November 24, 2015.
3. Interview with Fukushima Prefecture Disaster Recovery Planning Department official, August 2015.
4. Interview with Minamisoma City Office Disaster Recovery Planning Department official, August 2015.

5. Interview with Fukushima Prefecture Comprehensive Recovery Planning Committee member, August 2015.
6. The Chernobyl accident in Ukraine garnered less attention from the Japanese media than Three Mile Island and triggered fewer policy changes. See Aldrich 2008.
7. Fujino 2016, 19.
8. Koresawa 2011.
9. Ranghieri and Ishiwatari 2014, 7.
10. Quoted in Tamba and Yokemoto 2013, 102.
11. See Edgington 2014 for a historical overview of the DMAT structure.
12. Fortun and Morgan 2016, 59.
13. *Iwate Nippō*, May 16, 2011.
14. *Sankei Shinbun*, March 21, 2011.
15. Interview with Fukushima Prefecture Environmental Regeneration Department employee, August 2015.
16. Interview with Fukushima Prefecture Comprehensive Recovery Planning Committee member, August 2015.
17. *AERA*, May 2, 2011; interview with hospital director, August 2015.
18. Miyagi Prefecture n.d.
19. Interview with Fukushima Disaster Prevention Implementation Department official, August 2015.
20. Interview with Sendai City Hall official, May 10, 2013.
21. JFS 2016.
22. Interview with nursing director at a hospital in Fukushima Prefecture, July 2015.
23. Miyagi Prefecture n.d.
24. Miyagi Prefecture n.d.
25. Miyagi Prefecture n.d.
26. Miyagi Prefecture n.d.
27. Honjo and Tatsuki 2014, 1.
28. Miyagi Prefecture n.d.
29. *Reuters News*, March 12, 2011.
30. Gannon 2016.
31. *Jerusalem Post*, March 21, 2011.
32. Interview with Fukushima Prefecture Disaster Recovery Planning Department official, August 2015.
33. Yoshida 2013, 44.
34. Interview with local government official in Fukushima, summer 2015.
35. NTT East 2012.
36. For discussion of how maintaining social ties helped the Vietnamese and Vietnamese American community in New Orleans East after Hurricane Katrina, see Leong et al. 2007, Aldrich 2012, and Truitt 2012.
37. UNISDR 2013, 77.
38. Yamato 2012.

39. Soga 2016, 45.
40. Tomita 2015.
41. See Siembieda and Hayashi 2015, 154.
42. Interview with Fukushima Prefecture Temporary Housing Department official, July 2015.
43. Miyagi Prefecture n.d.
44. Interview with Fukushima Prefecture Disaster Prevention Implementation Department manager, August 2015.
45. Interview with Fukushima Prefecture Temporary Housing Department official, July 2015.
46. *Mainichi Shinbun*, March 11, 2016.
47. *Japan Times*, March 7, 2017.
48. Reconstruction Promotion Committee 2012, 13.
49. Takezawa 2013 [2016], 124.
50. Personal communication, Iwate prefectural government official, January 23, 2017.
51. Interview with Fukushima Prefecture Comprehensive Recovery Planning Committee member, August 2015.
52. Karan 2016, 36.
53. *Japan Times*, June 23, 2011, 3; Mimura 2015a.
54. Quoted in *Japan Times*, December 11, 2015.
55. Agence France-Presse, February 24, 2014.
56. Harvard University Graduate School of Design n.d.
57. Interview with Fukushima Prefecture Environmental Regeneration Department employee, August 2015.
58. Interview with Fukushima Prefecture liaison for rebuilding of geriatric care facility, July 2015.
59. Kyodo News, November 18, 2015.
60. Takezawa 2013 [2016], 109.
61. Nagamatsu 2014.
62. Kawahara 2014.
63. MercyCorps 2014.
64. Yoshida 2012.
65. IASC 2007, 102–103.
66. Parry 2017, 122.
67. Suzuki and Miura 2014.
68. *Fukushima Minpo News*, May 6, 2015.
69. Green, *Japan Times*, 2015.
70. Iwate Prefecture 2014, 10.
71. Sekiguchi, *Wall Street Journal*, 2014.
72. Ueda and Shaw 2015, 136.
73. Brasor and Tsubuku, *Japan Times*, 2016.
74. Brasor and Tsubuku, *Japan Times*, 2016.
75. *Asahi Shinbun*, December 29, 2015.

76. Kerr 2002.
77. Interview with Miyagi Prefecture Earthquake Disaster Recovery Policy Division civil servant, July 2015.
78. Interview with mayor of city in Fukushima, July 23, 2015.
79. Interview with Minamisoma City Office Disaster Recovery Planning Department official, August 2015.
80. *Asahi Shinbun*, November 11, 2015.
81. Suzuki 2016.
82. Tsuda et al. 2016.
83. Nadesan 2013. For people interested in the relationship between identity, citizenship, and radiation measurement, please see Lindee 2016.
84. See Clement and Ogino 2016 for reports about the dialogue and its outcome among residents.
85. Maly, Matsushita, and Suzuki 2015.
86. *Japan Times*, March 7, 2017.
87. *Japan Times*, March 7, 2017.
88. *Asahi Shinbun*, December 3, 2015.
89. *AP News*, September 8, 2015.
90. Kingdon 1995.
91. Interview with Fukushima Disaster Prevention Implementation Department official, August 2015.
92. Murao 2015a, 45.
93. *Kahoku Shinbun*, July 6, 2015.
94. UNU 2016,18.
95. Interview with Fukushima Prefecture Comprehensive Recovery Planning Committee member, August 2015.
96. *Asahi Shinbun*, December 26, 2012.
97. *Japan Times*, December 24, 2013.
98. *Japan Times*, February 11, 2014.
99. *Wall Street Journal*, September 13, 2016.
100. This section draws heavily on Bisri 2016.
101. Interviews with Fukushima Prefecture civil servants, August 2015.
102. Kawamura and Bohacs 2015.
103. Hideo Nakazawa 2013; Reconstruction Stuck at the Recovery Level, *Yomiuri Shinbun*, July 22.

CHAPTER FIVE

1. Weitzdorfer 2014, 136.
2. Bricker 2014.
3. Takezawa 2013 [2016], 122.
4. Strusińska-Correia 2017.
5. Cf. Gillam, JLGC Blogs, 2015.
6. Tsunekawa 2016, 13.

7. Reconstruction Agency 2015.
8. *Kahoku Shinbun*, May 25, 2015.
9. *Asahi Shinbun*, September 12, 2015; site visits, March 2017.
10. *Kahoku Shinbun*, September 3, 2015.
11. Pharr and Putnam 2000. This section draws on Aldrich 2017: Trust Deficit: Japanese Communities and the Challenge of Rebuilding Tohoku, Japan Forum 29 (1): 39–52, copyright © BAJS, reprinted by permission of Taylor & Francis Ltd., http://www.tandfonline.com on behalf of BAJS.
12. Doi 1974; Nakane 1978.
13. Newton and Norris 1999, 18.
14. Diamond 2007.
15. Sweet 1998; Solnit 2009; Takeda, Tamura, and Tatsuki 2003.
16. Veszteg, Funaki, and Tanaka 2014.
17. Ishino et al. 2012.
18. See Okuyama and Inaba 2017 for a study of how residents more affected by the disasters participated more actively in groups and volunteer activities.
19. Hommerich 2012, 59.
20. Inagaki 2012, 2013.
21. Hommerich 2012, 52.
22. Aldrich 2012b.
23. Takezawa 2013 [2016].
24. Fujino 2016.
25. Suzuki 2011.
26. Kan 2017.
27. Edgington 2010, 51–52.
28. Avenell 2012, 62.
29. Kan 2017, 9.
30. Cf. Leng 2015.
31. Akasaka and Oguma 2012.
32. Honjo and Tatsuki 2014, 1.
33. Geiger, Kawauchi, and Bellamy 2015.
34. Cf. Michishita and Pressello 2015.
35. Bisri 2016.
36. Samuels 2013, 170.
37. Inatsugu 2018, 239.
38. Hasegawa 2004; Aldrich 2008; Fackler and Onishi, *New York Times*, 2011; *Nikkei Shinbun*, August 18, 2011; Ando 2015.
39. MacAvoy and Rosenthal 2005.
40. Aldrich 2008.
41. Fortun and Morgan 2016.
42. Osnos 2011. This practice, called *amakudari* (or descent from heaven), has been studied by Colignon and Usui (2003).
43. Suzuki 2011.

44. Dimmer 2014.
45. Cabinet Office 2011, 2.
46. Inagaki 2013, 2.
47. Kubo and Miwa 2011, 73.
48. Iuchi, Johnson, and Olshansky 2013.
49. M. Itō 2018, 221.
50. *Asahi Shinbun*, June 21, 2011.
51. Hamamoto 2018, 41.
52. As Kan came closer to the end of his time in office, he began publicly announcing his opposition to nuclear power; official government spokespeople declared that his statements were personal rather than representing the official government position (*Japan Times*, July 15, 2011).
53. Hamamoto 2018, 53.
54. M. Itō 2018, 229.
55. Burgess 2015.
56. Pekkanen 2000.
57. Leng 2015.
58. Birkland 1997.
59. Samuels 2013.
60. Aldrich 1999.
61. See Shiozaki, Nishikawa, and Deguchi 2012.
62. Samuels 2013, 200.
63. Fackler and Onishi, *New York Times*, 2011.
64. Oguma 2013.
65. Farley et al. 2007.
66. Boin, McConnell, and Hart 2008.
67. Tomita 2012, 244.
68. Akemi Yamauchi 2016, Environmental Consciousness Needed in Japan's Reconstruction, *Tokyo Shinbun*, September 6.
69. Philip Brasor 2012, Scrutiny of Tohoku Reconstruction Funds Needed, *Japan Times*, September 23.
70. *Mainichi Shinbun*, February 13, 2015.
71. Interviews with Tōhoku residents, July 2015.
72. *Economist*, February 7, 2015.
73. Interviews with Tōhoku officials, 2014.
74. *Japan Times*, November 19, 2012.
75. *Mainichi Shinbun*, September 12, 2016.
76. Kyodo News, March 3, 2015.
77. Shusuke Murai 2015, Some Tohoku Disaster Areas on Fast Track to Rebuilding While Others Stuck in Slow Lane. *Japan Times*, March 9.
78. *Economist*, March 10, 2012.
79. *Mainichi Shinbun*, September 12, 2016.
80. *Japan Times*, April 24, 2015.
81. *Mainichi Shinbun*, June 4, 2015.

82. Cyranoski 2012, 142.
83. Strusińska-Correia 2017.
84. Yamauchi, *Tokyo Shinbun*, 2016.
85. *Sankei Shinbun*, January 3, 2016.
86. Takezawa 2013 [2016], 139.
87. *Iwate Nippō*, December 7, 2015.
88. Normile 2012, 1165.
89. Quoted in *Asahi Shinbun*, September 21, 2015.
90. Shifleen 2015.
91. Cf. Aldrich and Sawada 2015.
92. Murao 2015b, 102.
93. Cf. Hein 2014; Takezawa 2013 [2016].
94. Ranghieri and Ishiwatari 2014, 26.
95. Interviews in Tōhoku, February 2014.
96. Murakami and Wood 2014, 238.
97. Nakazawa, *Yomiuri Shinbun*, 2013.
98. Takezawa 2013 [2016], 158.
99. Interview, Ishinomaki, July 2018.
100. Gillam, JLGC Blogs, 2015.
101. See Edgington 2019 for a discussion of how this aspect of "building back better" may not have been ideal.
102. Nakazawa, *Yomiuri Shinbun*, 2013.
103. Aldrich 2005.
104. Hasegawa 2011, 27.
105. Interview with mayor of city in Fukushima, July 23, 2015.
106. Aldrich 2010.
107. Aldrich 2012b.
108. Ando 2015.
109. Reiher 2016.
110. Yilmaz 2011, 2.
111. Kyodo News, January 18, 2012.
112. Cleveland 2014.
113. Ishikawa 2011.
114. *Wall Street Journal*, September 29, 2011.
115. Hommerich 2012, 53.
116. Higuchi 2016, 119.
117. *Mainichi Shinbun*, April 1, 2017.
118. *New York Times*, August 8, 2011.
119. Interview with citizen scientist, May 12, 2016.
120. Birmingham and McNeill 2012, 179.
121. Weitzdorfer 2014, 134.
122. *Japan Times*, December 22, 2014.
123. See *Asahi Shinbun*, April 3, 2012, A1.
124. *NBC News*, May 25, 2015; *Globe and Mail*, May 27, 2015.
125. *Nikkei Shinbun*, August 24, 2014.

126. *Asahi Shinbun*, August 3, 2015.
127. Yamashita and Kainuma 2012.
128. 2016 Edelman Trust Barometer, https://www.edelman.com/2016-edelman-trust-barometer.
129. Hommerich 2012, 59.
130. Suzuki 2015.
131. Kyodo News, June 12, 2012.
132. Tagawa 2016, 103.
133. Ramseyer 2015.
134. Quoted in Erik Slavin 2016, Fukushima Radiation Poses Little Risk, but Lack of Trust Lingers, *Stars and Stripes*, March 7.
135. Nakayachi 2015.
136. Reiher 2016.
137. Kornei 2017.
138. Site visit, Safecast office, July 23, 2018.
139. Safecast 2016.
140. Site visit, Summer 2016.
141. Yoshioka 2015.
142. *Japan Times*, March 3, 2014, A1.
143. *New York Times*, August 8, 2015.
144. *Stars and Stripes*, March 13, 2016.
145. *Japan Times*, March 22, 2017.
146. Some have argued that "as long as Abe is prime minister, there is little hope of a paradigm shift on energy" (Gurtov 2014, 101).
147. *Asahi Shinbun*, May 31, 2013.
148. Hasegawa 2011, 121.
149. *Asahi Shinbun*, March 11, 2015.
150. Nagamatsu 2018.
151. Quoted in Nakazawa, *Yomiuri Shinbun*, 2013.
152. *Newsweek*, April 30, 2018.
153. Thompson 2017.
154. *Asahi Shinbun*, February 16, 2016.
155. Pharr and Putnam 2000.
156. Yilmaz 2011, 2.
157. *Economist*, March 10, 2012.
158. Interview, May 12, 2016.
159. *Japan Times*, March 12, 2016.
160. Aldrich and Fraser 2017.
161. Aldrich 2008.
162. *Economist*, March 10, 2012, 3. For an analysis of the conditions that make post-disaster nuclear power investments more (or less) likely, see Aldrich, Forester, and Horhager 2019.
163. Sone 2012.
164. Kamikawa 2018, 111.
165. Kamikawa 2018, 127.

166. Aldrich 2008.
167. Takezawa 2013 [2016].
168. Reconstruction Promotion Committee 2012.
169. Koscheyev et al. 1997.
170. Hasegawa 2011, 4.

CHAPTER SIX

1. *New York Times*, September 7, 2008.
2. Edgington 2019.
3. Kahn 2005.
4. Raschky 2008.
5. Strömberg 2007.
6. Including all of the countries over all of the years available produces a similar, but unreadable, graph. I selected these countries for the figure because they include the four under study in this chapter (Japan, Haiti, China, and India) and provide some familiar countries with different levels of mortality and government expenditure (e.g., Nepal, Cambodia, Turkey, Poland, etc.).
7. Ahlbom and Povitkina 2016.
8. Brinkerhoff 1999.
9. Levy 1999.
10. McAvoy 1999.
11. Putnam 1995.
12. Linz and Stepan 1996.
13. Weber, Politics as a Vocation, 1919 [1958], 212.
14. Cf. Tilly 1992.
15. Hendrix 2010; Hanson and Sigman 2011; Young 2013.
16. Cf. Carbonetti 2012.
17. King, Pan, and Roberts 2017.
18. This is probably an undercount, as China has been criticized repeatedly for covering up and not reporting deaths during disasters. See *South China Morning Post*, March 30, 2017.
19. World Bank 2017, 15.
20. Wei, Zhao, and Marinova 2013.
21. Hsu 2017.
22. The Chinese government has promoted ethnic tourism whether locals actually belonged to or participated in these cultures.
23. Li 2018.
24. Tse, Wei, and Wang 2013.
25. Siembieda and Hayashi 2015.
26. UNICEF 2010.
27. Hsu 2017, 379.
28. Benjamin Carlson 2013, Sichuan Earthquake: China's Government Praised for Swifter Reaction Than 2008 Quake, GlobalPost, April 22.

29. Keith Zhai and Joyce Ng 2013, Hong Kong–Funded Schools Survive Sichuan Earthquake, *South China Morning Post*, April 26.
30. Xu 2017.
31. *New York Times*, May 12, 2018.
32. *Guardian*, February 11, 2018.
33. Liu 2010, 58.
34. Sorace 2017, 54.
35. Sorace 2017, 62.
36. Zhang et al. 2015.
37. Duenas 2011.
38. Sinha n.d.
39. Mahurkar 2004.
40. Thiruppugazh 2007.
41. Bremer 2003.
42. Sanderson and Sharma 2008.
43. Vatsa 2001, 23.
44. Rencoret et al. 2010, 8.
45. Taft-Morales and Margesson 2010.
46. WHO 2010.
47. Rencoret et al. 2010, 22.
48. Deborah Sontag 2012, Rebuilding in Haiti Lags after Billions in Post-Quake Aid, *New York Times*, December 23.
49. de Ville de Goyet, Sarmiento, and Grunewald 2011, 4.
50. Useem, Kunreuther, and Michel-Kerjan 2015, 156, 163.
51. Aldrich 2012a.

CHAPTER SEVEN

1. Nishikawa 2011, 35.
2. Hibino and Shaw 2015, 153.
3. Ideta, Shaw, and Takeuchi 2012, 97.
4. Hein 2014.
5. Aldrich 1999.
6. Gillam, JLGC Blogs, 2015.
7. Thanks to Liz Maly for pointing out that the problem is less about the delay in providing housing than the displacement and relocation, which are perhaps bigger, longer-term problems.
8. Thompson 2017.
9. Inatsugu 2018, 245.
10. Samuels 2013.
11. Singleton 2016.
12. Aldrich 1999.
13. Campbell 2008.
14. *Wall Street Journal*, March 30, 2016, A8.

NOTES TO PAGES 181-186

15. See Peace Boat Annual Report 2013–2014.
16. Associated Press, September 8, 2015.
17. Abe 2016, 163.
18. Dimmer 2017.
19. McCormack 1996; Strusińska-Correia 2017.
20. Y. Itō 2018, 377.
21. Oguma 2013.
22. Feldhoff 2013, 103.
23. Aldrich 2008.
24. duPont et al. 2015.
25. Takenaka 2011, 137.
26. Feldhoff 2013.
27. Matanle 2011; Matanle and Rausch 2011.
28. Kerr 2002.
29. See Aldrich 2008 for details on these accidents.
30. After 3/11, antinuclear protestors used a variety of channels to express their displeasure with government policy, including large-scale rallies, citizens' referenda on energy, and disruption of closed government meetings (*Wall Street Journal*, January 19, 2012). Popular manga (comic) creators have brought out topics such as radiation exposure and health in their works (Kariya and Hanasaki 2014). Culture-based activism, including antinuclear music (cf. Manabe 2015) and humorous antinuclear Twitter characters such as Monju-kun, round out the repertoires of resistance (cf. Manabe 2017).
31. Macfarlane 2011.
32. Chester Dawson 2012, Japan's Nuclear Crisis Plan Still Lags, *Wall Street Journal*, March 19.
33. Samuels 2013, 118.
34. See FEPC 2016, http://www.fepc.or.jp/english/.
35. Aldrich and Fraser 2017.
36. *Asahi Shinbun*, February 2, 2013.
37. Abe 2015.
38. Hasegawa 2011.
39. Aldrich 2011.
40. Daniel P. Aldrich and Jennie Stephens 2017, The Fukushima Effect: Decentralization and Diversification. *Asahi Shinbun*, April 8; Aldrich, Forester, and Horhager 2019.
41. Hindmarsh and Priestly 2016. North Americans living near nuclear power plants also used the Fukushima Dai-ichi accident as a moment to rethink their nuclear neighbors (*Wall Street Journal*, April 6, 2013).
42. *Wall Street Journal*, September 13, 2016.
43. Fuhrmann 2012.
44. Quoted in Lewis 2015.

45. Kingston, *Japan Times*, 2016.
46. Kumagai 2012.
47. Nateghi et al. 2016.
48. Ben Dooley 2014, Community Bonds, Not Seawalls, Key to Minimizing Deaths: 3/11 Study, *Japan Times*, April 16.
49. Kubo and Miwa 2011, 67.
50. Littlejohn 2018.
51. Site visits, March 8, 2014; March 29, 2017.
52. Nagamatsu 2018.
53. An interview with a leader of the organization Peace Boat (August 4, 2015) drove home the variety of ways in which these civil society organizations work to fill the gaps between formal government institutions and on-the-ground needs. One example: While the Self Defense Forces had jurisdiction over providing hot meals in official disaster shelters to evacuees, they could not do so in unofficial gathering areas such as the second floor of a home where neighbors stayed together for comfort and mutual assistance.
54. Pronyk et al. 2008; Brune and Bossert 2009.
55. See WREMO n.d., WREMO 2012, and Montgomery 2013 along with BoCo Strong's website at http://bocostrong.org/.
56. See IASC 2007, 100–109 and Nakao 2014.
57. Aldrich 2012a.
58. Onagawa cho kassei ka shien dantai, 2012.
59. Takahashi et al. 2015.
60. Kondo et al. 2012.
61. This section draws on Aldrich and Kiyota 2017: Creating Community Resilience through Elder-Led Physical and Social Infrastructure, *Disaster Medicine and Public Health Preparedness* 11 (1): 120–126, © 2017, published by Cambridge University Press, reproduced with permission.
62. Oldenburg 1999.
63. Ibasho n.d., Ibasho Cafe Brochure.
64. Kiyota et al. 2015.
65. Mollenhorst, Volker, and Flap 2014.
66. Lahournat 2016, 194.
67. Tsunekawa 2016, 16; Wada 2018, 265.
68. Littlejohn 2018.
69. *Economist*, March 10, 2012, 35.
70. Cf. Putnam 2000.
71. Matsushita 2013.
72. *Japan Times*, July 3, 2014, 3.
73. Kariya and Hanasaki 2014.
74. Manabe 2015.
75. Delaney 2015, 71.
76. Nakazawa, *Yomiuri Shinbun*, 2013.

77. Quoted in Thaler and Sunstein 2008, 13.
78. Siembieda 2012.
79. Abou-Bakr 2013; Roberts 2013.
80. Storr, Haefelle-Balch, and Grube 2015.
81. Wood 2016.
82. Useem, Kunreuther, and Michel-Kerjan 2015, 99.

Sources

Abe, Masaki. 2016. Local Autonomy and the Complete Resident Evacuation in Fukushima. In Keichi Tsunekawa, ed., *Five Years After: Reassessing Japan's Responses to the Earthquake, Tsunami, and the Nuclear Disaster*, 151–167. Tokyo: University of Tokyo Press.

Abe, Yuki. 2015. The Nuclear Power Debate after Fukushima: A Text Mining Analysis of Japanese Newspapers. *Contemporary Japan* 27 (2). https://doi.org/10.1515/cj-2015-0006.

Abou-Bakr, Ami. 2013. *Managing Disasters through Public-Private Partnerships*. Washington, DC: Georgetown University Press.

Ahlbom, Tove, and Marina Povitkina. 2016. Gimme Shelter: On the Political Determinants of Vulnerability. Paper presented at the Southern Political Science Association Conference, San Juan, Puerto Rico, January 7–9.

Aida, Jun, Hiroyuki Hikichi, Yusuke Matsuyama, Yukihiro Sato, Toru Tsuboya, Takahiro Tabuchi, Shihoko Koyama, S. V. Subramanian, Katsunori Kondo, Ken Osaka, and Ichiro Kawachi. 2017. Risk of Mortality During and After the 2011 Great East Japan Earthquake and Tsunami among Older Coastal Residents. *Scientific Reports* 7:1–11.

Akasaka, Norio, and Eiji Oguma, eds. 2012. *Henkyō kara hajimaru Tokyo/Tōhoku Ron*. Tokyo: Akashi Publishers.

Akçomak, I. Semih, and Bas Ter Weel. 2008. The Impact of Social Capital on Crime: Evidence from the Netherlands. IZA Discussion Paper no. 3603.

Akiyama, Junichi, Shigeaki Kato, Masaharu Tsubokura, Jinichi Mori, Tetsuya Tanimoto, Koichiro Abe, Shuji Sakai, Ryugo Hayano, Michio Tokiwa, and Hiroaki Shimmura. 2015. Minimal Internal Radiation Exposure in Residents Living South of the Fukushima Daiichi Nuclear Power Plant Disaster. *PLOS One*, October 20. doi: 10.1371/journal.pone.0140482.

SOURCES

Aldrich, Daniel P. 1999. Localities That Can Say No? Autonomy and Dependence in Japanese Local Government. *Asian Journal of Political Science* 7 (1): 60–76.

———. 2005. Limits of Flexible and Adaptive Institutions. In S. Hayden Lesbirel and Daigee Shaw, eds., *Managing Conflict in Facility Siting: An International Comparison*, 109–134. Cheltenham, UK: Edward Elgar.

———. 2008. *Site Fights: Divisive Facilities and Civil Society in Japan and the West.* Ithaca, NY: Cornell University Press.

———. 2010. Fixing Recovery: Social Capital in Post-crisis Resilience. *Journal of Homeland Security* 6:1–10.

———. 2011. Nuclear Power's Future in Japan and Abroad. *ParisTech Review*, August 25.

———. 2012a. *Building Resilience: Social Capital in Post-Disaster Recovery.* Chicago: University of Chicago Press.

———. 2012b. Post-Crisis Japanese Nuclear Policy. *Asia Pacific Issues* 103:1–12.

———. 2013. A Normal Accident or Sea-Change? Nuclear Host Communities Respond to the 3/11 Disasters. *Japanese Journal of Political Science* 14 (2): 261–276.

———. 2015. It's Who You Know: Factors Driving Recovery from Japan's 11 March 2011 Disaster. *Public Administration* 94 (2): 399–413.

———. 2017. Trust Deficit: Japanese Communities and the Challenge of Rebuilding Tohoku. *Japan Forum* 29 (1): 39–52.

Aldrich, Daniel P., Summer Forester, and Elisa Horhager. 2018. Triggers for Policy Change: The 3.11 Fukushima Meltdowns and Nuclear Policy Continuity. *Environmental Politics*, https://doi.org/10.1080/09644016.2018.1510216.

Aldrich, Daniel P., and Tim Fraser. 2017. All Politics Is Local: Judicial and Electoral Institutions' Role in Japan's Nuclear Restarts. *Pacific Affairs* 90 (3): 433–457. https://doi.org/10.5509/2017903433.

Aldrich, Daniel P., and Emi Kiyota. 2017. Creating Community Resilience through Elder-Led Physical and Social Infrastructure. *Disaster Medicine and Public Health Preparedness* 11 (1): 120–126.

Aldrich, Daniel P., and Yoshikuni Ono. 2016. Local Politicians as Linking Social Capital: An Empirical Test of Political Behavior After Japan's 3/11 Disasters. *Natural Hazards* 84 (3): 1637–1659.

Aldrich, Daniel P., and Yasuyuki Sawada. 2015. The Physical and Social Determinants of Mortality in the 3/11 Tsunami. *Social Science & Medicine* 124:66–75.

Ando, M. 2015. Dreams of Urbanization: Quantitative Case Studies on the Local Impacts of Nuclear Power Facilities Using the Synthetic Control Method. *Journal of Urban Economics* 85:68–85.

Ando, M., M. Ishida, Y. Hayashi, C. Mizuki, Y. Nishikawa, and Y. Tu. 2013. Interviewing Insights Regarding the Fatalities Inflicted by the 2011 Great East Japan Earthquake. *Natural Hazards and Earth System Sciences* 13:2173–2187.

SOURCES

Arai, Kiichio, Yoshiharu Kobayashi, and Miwa Nakajo. n.d. Voters Punish Local Governments for Natural Disasters: Evidence from the 2015 Kinu River Flood in Japan. Working paper. https://ijrdp.org/paper/jaes2017.pdf.

Asad, Asad. 2015. Contexts of Reception, Post-disaster Migration, and Socioeconomic Mobility. *Population and Environment* 36:279–310.

Ash, Ian. 2013. *A2-B-C*. http://www.a2documentary.com/.

Avenell, Simon. 2012. From Kobe to Tohoku: The Potential and the Peril of a Volunteer Infrastructure. In Jeff Kingston, ed., *Natural Disaster and Nuclear Crisis in Japan*, 53–77. New York: Routledge.

Beggs, John, Valerie Haines, and Jeanne Hurlbert. 1996. The Effects of Personal Networks and Local Community Contexts on the Receipt of Formal Aid during Disaster Recovery. *International Journal of Mass Emergencies and Disasters* 14 (1): 57–78.

Bestor, Theodore. 2013. Disasters, Natural and Unnatural: Reflections on March 11, 2011 and Its Aftermath. *Journal of Asian Studies* 72 (4): 763–782.

Birkland, Thomas A. 1997. *After Disaster: Agenda Setting, Public Policy, and Focusing Events*. Washington, DC: Georgetown University Press.

Birmingham, Lucy. 2011. Japan's Earthquake and Tsunami Warning System Explained. *Time*, March 18.

Birmingham, Lucy, and David McNeill. 2012. *Strong in the Rain: Surviving Japan's Earthquake, Tsunami, and Fukushima Nuclear Disaster*. New York: Palgrave Macmillan.

Bisri, Mizan. 2016. Observing Partnership Innovation through Inter-organizational Network Analysis on Emergency Response of the Great East Japan Earthquake and Tsunami 2011. *Japan Social Innovation Journal* 6 (1): 27–41.

Boin, Arjen, Allan McConnell, and Paul 't. Hart, eds. 2008. *Governing after Crisis: The Politics of Investigation, Accountability, and Learning*. New York: Cambridge University Press.

Bolin, Robert C. 1994. *Household and Community Recovery after Earthquakes*. Boulder, CO: Institute of Behavioral Science.

Brannigan, Michael. 2015. *Japan's March 11 Disaster and Moral Grit*. Lanham, MD: Lexington Books.

Bremer, Rannveig. 2003. Policy Development in Disaster Preparedness and Management: Lessons Learned from the January 2001 Earthquake in Gujarat, India. *Prehospital Disaster Medicine* 18 (4): 372–384.

Bricker, Mindy, ed. 2014. *The Fukushima Daiichi Nuclear Power Station Disaster*. New York: Routledge.

Brinkerhoff, Derick. 1999. Exploring State–Civil Society Collaboration: Policy Partnerships in Developing Countries. *Nonprofit and Voluntary Sector Quarterly*, December 1, 59–86.

Bruch, Carl. 2016. Refugees Unwilling to Return to Tohoku. Presentation at US-Japan Research Institute, February 24. https://www.youtube.com/watch?v=yC7EBDxz9Z4.

SOURCES

Brune, Nancy, and Thomas Bossert. 2009. Building Social Capital in Post-conflict Communities: Evidence from Nicaragua. *Social Science & Medicine* 68:885–893.

Buonanno, Paolo, Daniel Montolio, and Paolo Vanin. 2009. Does Social Capital Reduce Crime? *Journal of Law and Economics* 52:145–170.

Burgess, Chris. 2015. Silencing the Voices in Tokyo's First Ever Local Referendum. *Electronic Journal of Contemporary Japanese Studies* (15): 1.

Cabinet Office, Government of Japan. 2011. *Report to the Prime Minister of the Reconstruction Design Council in Response to the Great East Japan Earthquake.*

Campbell, John. 2008. Japan's Aging Population: Perspectives of "Catastrophic Demography." *Journal of Asian Studies* 67 (4): 1401–1406.

Carbonetti, Benjamin C. 2012. The Cards Dealt Matter: Rethinking Conceptions of State Capacity. Prepared for the Annual Meeting of the Western Political Science Association, Portland, Oregon, March 22–24.

Carlin, Ryan, Gregory Love, and Elizabeth Zechmeister. 2014. Trust Shaken: Earthquake Damage, State Capacity and Interpersonal Trust in Comparative Perspective. *Comparative Politics* 46 (4): 419–435.

Chamlee-Wright, Emily. 2010. *The Cultural and Political Economy of Recovery: Social Learning in a Post-disaster Environment.* London and New York: Routledge.

Chang, Stephanie E., and Adam Rose. 2012. Towards a Theory of Economic Recovery from Disasters. *International Journal of Mass Emergencies and Disasters* 32 (2): 171–181.

Chen, Yi-Feng, Yi Kang, and Dean Tjosvold. 2017. Constructive Controversy and *guanxi* Relationships for Disaster Recovery. *International Journal of Conflict Management* 28 (4): 410–436.

Clement, C. H., and H. Ogino, eds. 2016. Proceedings of the International Workshop on the Fukushima Dialogue Initiative. *International Commission on Radiological Protection* 45 (2S).

Cleveland, Kyle. 2014. Mobilizing Nuclear Bias: The Fukushima Nuclear Crisis and the Politics of Uncertainty. *Asia-Pacific Journal* 12 (7) no. 1, May 19.

CNIC (Citizens' Nuclear Information Center). 2015. Residents of Fukushima's Iitate Village File Petition for Nuclear Damage Compensation to Restore Home Village. *Nuke Info Tokyo* 164 (January 30). http://www.cnic.jp/english/?p=3002.

Colignon, Richard, and Chikako Usui. 2003. *Amakudari.* Ithaca, NY: Cornell University Press.

Contreras, Diana, Thomas Blaschke, and Michael Hodgson. 2017. Lack of Spatial Resilience in a Recovery Process: Case L'Aquila, Italy. *Technological Forecasting and Social Change* 121 (August): 76–88.

Cyranoski, David. 2012. After the Deluge. *Nature* 482:141–143.

Dacy, Douglas, and Howard Kunreuther. 1969. *The Economics of Natural Disasters: Implications for Federal Policy.* New York: Free Press.

SOURCES

Daimon, Hiroaki, and Tomohide Atsumi. 2018. "Pay It Forward" and Altruistic Responses to Disasters in Japan: Latent Class Analysis of Support following the 2011 Tohoku Earthquake. *Voluntas* 29 (1): 119–132.

Delaney, Alyne E. 2015. Taking the High Ground: The Impact of Public Policy on Rebuilding Neighborhoods in Coastal Japan after the 2011 Great East Japan Earthquake and Tsunami. In Michèle Companion, ed., *Disaster's Impact on Livelihood and Cultural Survival: Losses, Opportunities, and Mitigation*, 63–74. Boca Raton, FL: CRC Press.

Deller, Steven, and Melissa Deller. 2010. Rural Crime and Social Capital. *Growth and Change: A Journal of Urban and Regional Policy* 41(2): 221–275.

De Ville de Goyet, Claude, Juan Pablo Sarmiento, and Francois Grunewald. 2011. *Health Response to the Earthquake in Haiti January 2010: Lessons to Be Learned for the Next Massive Sudden-Onset Disaster*. Pan American Health Organization. http://new.paho.org/disasters/dmdocuments/HealthResponseHaitiEarthq.pdf.

Diamond, Larry. 2007. Building Trust in Government by Improving Governance. Paper presented to the 7th Global Forum on Reinventing Government: "Building Trust in Government," sponsored by the United Nations, Vienna, June 27, 2007.

Dimmer, Christian. 2014. Evolving Place Governance Innovations and Pluralizing Reconstruction Practices in Post-disaster Japan. *Planning Theory and Practice* 15 (2): 260–265.

———. 2017. Japan after March 11th 2011: Between Swift Reconstruction and Sustainable Restructuring. In W. Yan and W. Galloway, eds., *Rethinking Resilience: Adaptation and Transformation in a Time of Change*. New York: Springer.

Doi, Takeo. 1974. *Amae no Kōzō* [Anatomy of dependence]. Tokyo: Kobundo.

Duenas, Maria Christina. 2011. Rising from the Rubble: Reconstruction and Rehabilitation after the 2001 Gujarat Earthquake. ADB Knowledge Showcases, July, 35–36.

duPont, William, Ilan Noy, Yoko Okuyama, and Yasuyui Sawada. 2015. The Long Run Socio-Economic Consequences of a Large Disaster: The 1995 Earthquake in Kobe. *PLOS One*, October 1. https://doi.org/10.1371/journal.pone.0138714.

Edgington, David. 2010. *Reconstructing Kobe: The Geography of Crisis and Opportunity*. Vancouver: UBC Press.

———. 2014. Local Government Emergency Response Following the Great East Japan Earthquake. In *Japan: Facing Major Natural and Political Challenges in the 21st Century: Proceedings of the 25th and 26th Annual Conferences of the Japan Studies Association of Canada*. http://www.jsac.ca/jsac_web_pub/jsac2012-13_pub.pdf.

———. 2017. How Safe Is Safe Enough? The Politics of Decontamination in Fukushima. In Mitsuo Yamakawa and Daisaku Yamamoto, *Unravelling the Fukushima Disaster*, 79–105. New York: Routledge.

SOURCES

———. 2019. Building Back Better along the Sanriku Coast of Tohoku, Japan. *Town Planning Review*, forthcoming.

Elinder, Mikael, and Oscar Erixson. 2012. Gender, Social Norms, and Survival in Maritime Disasters. *PNAS* 109 (33): 13220–13224.

Elliott, James R., Timothy J. Haney, and Petrice Sams-Abiodun. 2010. Limits to Social Capital: Comparing Network Assistance in Two New Orleans Neighborhoods Devastated by Hurricane Katrina. *Sociological Quarterly* 51 (4): 624–648.

EM-DAT (The International Disaster Database). http://www.emdat.be/.

ESCAP [United Nations Economic and Social Commission for Asia and the Pacific]. 2010. *Protecting Development Gains*. Bangkok, Thailand: UNISDR.

Farley, Joshua, Daniel Baker, David Batker, Christopher Koliba, Richard Matteson, Russell Mills, and James Pittman. 2007. Opening the Policy Window for Ecological Economics: Katrina as a Focusing Event. *Ecological Economics* 344–354.

Feldhoff, Thomas. 2013. Shrinking Communities in Japan: Community Ownership of Assets as a Development Potential for Rural Japan? *Urban Design International* 18 (1): 99–109.

Feldman, Eric. 2015. Compensating the Victims of Japan's 3-11 Fukushima Disaster. *Asian-Pacific Law and Policy Journal* 16 (2): 127–158.

Fenno, Richard. 1978. *Home Style: House Members and Their Districts*. Boston: Little Brown.

Fortun, Kim, and Alli Morgan. 2016. Thinking across Disaster. In Jun Shigemura and Rethy Chhem, eds., *Mental Health and Social Issues Following a Nuclear Accident*, 55–67. New York: Springer.

Frankenberg, Elizabeth, Thomas Gillespie, Samuel Preston, Bondan Sikoki, and Duncan Thomas. 2011. Mortality, the Family and the Indian Ocean Tsunami. *Economic Journal*. https://doi.org/10.1111/j.1468-0297.2011.02446.x.

Fuhrmann, Matthew. 2012. Splitting Atoms: Why Do Countries Build Nuclear Power Plants? *International Interactions* 38 (1): 29–57.

Fujimori, Keiya, Hyo Kyozuka, Aya Goto, Seiji Yasumura, Misao Ota, Akira Ohtsuru, Yasuhisa Nomura, Kenichi Hata, Kouta Suzuki, Akihito Nakai, Mieko Sato, Shiro Matsui, Kyoko Nakano, and Masufumi Abe. 2014. Pregnancy and Birth Survey after the Great East Japan Earthquake and Fukushima Dai-ichi Nuclear Power Plant Accident in Fukushima Prefecture. *Fukushima Journal of Medical Science* 60 (1): 1–7.

Fujino, Mitsuko. 2016. Unforeseeable Accidents from the Point of View of the Legal System. In Jun Shigemura and Rethy Chhem, eds., *Mental Health and Social Issues Following a Nuclear Accident*, 15–27. New York: Springer.

Fujisawa, Yoshizaku, Tsuyoshi Hamano, and Shogo Takegawa. 2009. Social Capital and Perceived Health in Japan: An Ecological and Multilevel Analysis. *Social Science & Medicine* 69:500–505.

Fukushima Booklet Committee. 2015. *10 Lessons from Fukushima: Reducing Risks and Protecting Communities from Nuclear Disasters.* http://fukushimalessons.jp/assets/content/doc/Fukushima10Lessons_ENG.pdf.

Fukuyama, Francis. 1995. *Trust: The Social Virtues and the Creation of Prosperity.* London: Hamish Hamilton.

———. 2013. What Is Governance? Center for Global Development Working Paper 314. https://www.cgdev.org/files/1426906_file_Fukuyama_What_Is_Governance.pdf.

Funabashi, Yoichi, and Heizo Takenaka, eds. 2011. *Lessons from the Disaster: Risk Management and the Compound Crisis Presented by the Great East Japan Earthquake.* Tokyo: Japan Times.

Gannon, James. 2016. Getting International Disaster Philanthropy Right: Lessons from Japan's 2011 Tsunami. Tokyo and Washington: Japan Center for International Exchange.

Geiger, Atsuko, Kaede Kawauchi, and Serina Bellamy. 2015. *Innovative Disaster Responses: Model Approaches from Japan's 3/11 Disaster.* Tokyo: Japan Center for International Exchange.

George, Timothy. 2002. *Minamata: Pollution and the Struggle for Democracy in Postwar Japan.* Cambridge, MA: Harvard University Press.

Gleibs, Ilka, Amelie Mummendey, and Peter Noack. 2008. Predictors of Change in Postmerger Identification during a Merger Process: A Longitudinal Study. *Journal of Personality and Social Psychology* 95 (5): 1095–1112.

Gleibs, Ilka, Susanne Tauber, Viki Tendayi, and Steffen Giessner. 2013. When What We Get Is Not What We Want. *Social Psychology* 44:177–190.

Goltz, James, and Dennis Mileti. 2011. Public Response to a Catastrophic Southern California Earthquake: A Sociological Perspective. *Earthquake Spectra* 27 (2): 484–504.

Granovetter, Mark. 1973. The Strength of Weak Ties. *American Journal of Sociology* 78 (6): 1360–1380.

Greenpeace. 2014. Fukushima Nuclear Crisis Timeline. Amsterdam.

Gotham, Kevin. 2012. Disaster Inc.: Privatization and Post-Katrina Rebuilding in New Orleans. *Perspectives on Politics* 10 (3): 633–646.

Guha-Sapir, D., L. V. Parry, O. Degomme, P. C. Joshi, and J. P. Saulina Arnold. 2006. *Risk Factors for Mortality and Injury: Post-Tsunami Epidemiological Findings from Tamil Nadu.* Brussels, Belgium: Centre for Research on the Epidemiology of Disasters.

Gurtov, Mel. 2014. Rotting at the Core: Why There Is No End to Japan's Nuclear Crisis. *Global Asia* 9 (1): 98–101.

Gusterson, Hugh. 2000. How Not to Construct a Radioactive Waste Incinerator. *Science, Technology and Human Values* 25 (3): 332–351.

Hamamoto, Shinsuke. 2018. Coalition Formation and the Legislative Process in a Divided Diet. In Yutaka Tsujinaka and Hiroaki Inatsugu, eds., *Aftermath: Fukushima and the 3.11 Earthquake*, 25–57. Australia: TransPacific Press.

SOURCES

Hamano, Tsuyoshi, Yoshizaku Fujisawa, Yu Ishida, S. V. Subramanian, Ichiro Kawachi, and Kuninori Shiwaku. 2010. Social Capital and Mental Health in Japan: A Multilevel Analysis. *PLoS One* 5 (10): 1–6.

Hanaoka, Chie, Hitoshi Shigeoka, and Yasutora Watanabe. 2018. Do Risk Preferences Change? Evidence from the Great East Japan Earthquake. *American Economic Journal: Applied Economics* 10 (2): 298–330.

Hanson, Jonathan, and Rachel Sigman. 2011. Measuring State Capacity: Assessing and Testing the Options. Paper prepared for the Annual Meeting of the American Political Science Association, Seattle, WA, September.

Harvard University Graduate School of Design. n.d. *Here Today. Here Tomorrow: Sustainable Revitalization for the Tohoku Region.*

Hasegawa, Koichi. 2004. *Constructing Civil Society in Japan.* Melbourne, Australia: TransPacific Press.

———. 2011. *Beyond Fukushima: Toward a Post-Nuclear Society.* Melbourne, Australia: TransPacific Press.

Hasegawa, Reiko. 2013. Disaster Evacuation from Japan's 2011 Tsunami Disaster and the Fukushima Nuclear Accident. Studies no. 05/13. IDDRI, Paris, France.

Hawkins, Robert, and Katherine Maurer. 2009. Bonding, Bridging, and Linking: How Social Capital Operated in New Orleans following Hurricane Katrina. *British Journal of Social Work* 40 (6): 1777–1793.

Hein, Patrick. 2014. Expecting the Unexpected: A Case Study on Tsunami Mitigation in Fujisawa. *Environmental Hazards* 13 (1): 1–20.

Hendrix, Cullen. 2010. Measuring State Capacity: Theoretical and Empirical Implications for the Study of Civil Conflict. *Journal of Peace Research* 47 (3): 273–285.

Hibino, Junichi, and Rajib Shaw. 2015. Establishment and Sustainability of Emergency Radio in Tohoku. In Rajib Shaw, ed., *Tohoku Recovery: Challenges, Potentials, and Future*, 147–164. New York: Springer.

Higuchi, Toshihiro. 2016. Radiation Protection by Numbers: Another "Man Made" Disaster. In Edward Blanford and Scott Sagan, eds., *Learning from a Disaster: Improving Nuclear Safety and Security after Fukushima*, 109–135. Stanford, CA: Stanford University Press.

Hikichi, Hiroyuki, Yasuyuki Sawada, Toru Tsuboya, Jun Aida, Katsunori Kondo, Shihoko Koyama, and Ichiro Kawachi. 2017. Residential Relocation and Change in Social Capital: A Natural Experiment from the 2011 Great East Japan Earthquake and Tsunami. *Science Advances* 3:1–9.

Hindmarsh, Richard, and Rebecca Priestly. 2016. *The Fukushima Effect: A New Geopolitical Terrain.* New York: Routledge.

Hirai, Hiroshi, Naoki Kondo, Ryohei Sasaki, Shinya Iwamuro, Kanko Masuno, Rika Ohtsuka, Hisayuki Miura, and Kiyomi Sakata. 2015. Distance to Retail Stores and Risk of Being Homebound among Older Adults in a City Severely Affected by the 2011 Great East Japan Earthquake. *Age and Aging* 44 (3): 478–484.

Hirano, Shigeo. 2006. Electoral Institutions, Hometowns, and Favored Minorities: Evidence from Japanese Electoral Reforms. *World Politics* 59 (1): 51–82.
Hiyama, Atsuki, Chiyo Nohara, Seira Kinjo, Wataru Taira, Shinichi Gima, Akira Tanahara, and Joji Otaki. 2012. The Biological Impacts of the Fukushima Nuclear Accident on the Pale Grass Blue Butterfly. *Scientific Reports* 2 (570).
Hommerich, Carola. 2012. Trust and Subjective Well-Being after the Great East Japan Earthquake, Tsunami, and Nuclear Meltdown: Preliminary Results. *International Journal of Japanese Sociology* 21:46–64.
Honjo, Yuichi, and Shigeo Tatsuki. 2014. A Study on the Disaster Response Network Organizations for Promoting Cooperation with Governments and NGOs/NPOs in the Cities, Towns, Villages after the Great East Japan Earthquake. Paper prepared for the 2nd Asia Conference on Urban Disaster Reduction, November 20–21.
Horiuchi, Yusaku, and Jun Saito. 2003. Reapportionment and Redistribution: Consequences of Electoral Reform in Japan. *American Journal of Political Science* 47 (4): 669–682.
Horiuchi, Yusaku, Jun Saito, and K. Yamada. 2015. Removing Boundaries, Losing Connections: Electoral Consequences of Local Government Reform in Japan. *Journal of East Asian Studies* 15:99–125.
Hoshikawa, Tsuyoshi. 2014. *Digitaru netto wokingu no tenkai* [The evolution of digital networking]. Tokyo: Kōyōshobō.
Hoshino, Yusuku. 2016. *From Mayor to Scrivener, The Man Who Won't Stop Serving Tsunami-Hit Town.* Sanriku Fukkōu, February 20.
Hsu, Da-Wei. 2017. Vulnerability and Resilience during Disasters. *China Information* 31 (3): 371–390.
IASC (Inter-Agency Standing Committee). 2007. *IASC Guidelines on Mental Health and Psychosocial Support in Emergency Settings.*
Ideta, Ai, Rajib Shaw, and Yukiko Takeuchi. 2012. Post Disaster Communication and Role of FM Radio: Case of Natori. In Rajib Shaw and Yukiko Takeuchi, eds., *East Japan Earthquake and Tsunami: Evacuation, Communication, Education and Volunteerism*, 73–108. Singapore: Research Publishing.
Ikawa, Hiroshi. 2008. *15 Years of Decentralization Reform in Japan.* Tokyo: Council of Local Authorities for International Relations (CLAIR).
Ikeda, Kenichi. 2015. *Shinsai kara mieru jōhō media to netto woku* [Information networks and media through the lens of disaster]. Tokyo: Tōyō Kezai.
Inagaki, Yusuke. 2012. Kizuna wa fukkyū wo sokushin sit aka: Higashi Nihon Daishinsai no chiiku fukkyū ato no sosharu Kapitaru no kankei [Did the Bonds Facilitate Post-disaster Recovery?: The Relationship between Social Capital and Local Area Recovery from the Great East Japan Earthquake]. *Bunka* 76:39–59.
———. 2013. The Power of Kizuna: Did Social Capital Promote Recovery from the Great East Japan Earthquake? Center for the Study of Social Stratification and Inequality (CSSI) Working Paper Series no.4.

Inatsugu, Hiroaki. 2018. Deployment of Local Government Personnel: Autonomy and Cooperation. In Yutaka Tsujinaka and Hiroaki Inatsugu, eds., *Aftermath: Fukushima and the 3.11 Earthquake*, 239–261. Australia: TransPacific Press.

Inoue, Machiko, Shoko Matsumoto, Kazue Yamaoka, and Shinsuke Muto. 2014. Risk of Social Isolation among Great East Japan Earthquake Survivors Living in Tsunami Affected Ishinomaki, Japan. *Disaster Medicine and Public Health Preparedness* 8 (4): 333–340.

International Fund for Agricultural Development. 1999. Good Governance: An Overview. Prepared for International Fund for Agricultural Development Executive Board, 67th Session, Rome, September 8–9.

Ishiguro, A., and E. Yano. 2015. Tsunami Inundation after the Great East Japan Earthquake and Mortality of Affected Communities. *Public Health* 129 (10): 1390–1397.

Ishii, Takeaki, Sae Ochi, Masaharu Tsubokura, Shigeaki Kato, Takahiro Tetsuda, Junpei Kato, Yoshitaka Nishikawa, Tomohiro Morita, Masahiro Kami, Yukihide Iwamoto, and Hidekiyo Tachiya. 2015. Physical Performance Deterioration of Temporary Housing Residents after the Great East Japan Earthquake. *Prevention Medicine Reports* 2:916–919.

Ishikawa, Kiyomu. 2011. What Has Been Brought to Residents and Communities by the Nuclear Power Plant Accident? Special and Serious Disaster Relief Procedure Modification after the 2011 Tohoku Earthquake and Tsunami in Fukushima. *Nihon Ronen Igakkai Zasshi [Japanese Journal of Geriatrics]* 48 (5): 489–493.

Ishikawa, Yoshitaka. 2012. Displaced Human Mobility due to March 11 Disaster. *Bulletin of the Tohoku Geographical Association*, April 1.

Ishino, Takuya, Akiko Kamesaka, Toshiya Murai, and Masao Ogaki. 2012. Effects of the Great East Japan Earthquake on Subjective Well Being. Paper prepared for the 4th OECD World Forum on Statistics, Knowledge, and Policy, New Delhi, India, October 19.

Ishiwatari, Mikio. 2012. Review of Countermeasures in the East Japan Earthquake and Tsunami. In Rajib Shaw and Yukiko Takeuchi, eds., *East Japan Earthquake and Tsunami: Evacuation, Communication, Education and Volunteerism*, 15–24. Singapore: Research Publishing.

Itō, Masatugu. 2018. Design and Development of the Recovery Agencies. In Yutaka Tsujinaka and Hiroaki Inatsugu, eds., *Aftermath: Fukushima and the 3.11 Earthquake*, 217–238. Australia: TransPacific Press.

Itō, Yasushi. 2018. The Cost Effectiveness of Radioactive Decontamination. In Yutaka Tsujinaka and Hiroaki Inatsugu, eds., *Aftermath: Fukushima and the 3.11 Earthquake*, 346–381. Australia: TransPacific Press.

Iuchi, Kanako, Laurie A. Johnson, and Robert Olshansky. 2013. Securing Tohoku's Future: Planning for Rebuilding in the First Year Following the Tohoku-Oki Earthquake and Tsunami. *Earthquake Spectra* 29 (S1): S479–S499.

Iwasaki, Keiko, Yasuyuki Sawada, and Daniel P. Aldrich. 2017. Social Capital as a Shield against Unusually Low Mental Health among Displaced Residents from Fukushima. *Natural Hazards* 89 (1): 405–421.

Iwate Prefecture. 2014. *Iwate Moving toward Reconstruction: A Record of the Reconstruction from 2011 to 2014 after the Great East Japan Earthquake and Tsunami.*

Jacobs, Robert. 2011. Social Fallout: Marginalization after the Fukushima Nuclear Meltdown. *Asia-Pacific Journal* 9 (28), no. 4, July 11.

JFS (Japan for Sustainability). 2016. Disaster Affected Ishinomaki—Present Status. Newsletter no. 171, November.

Johnson, Cedric, ed. 2011. *The Neoliberal Deluge: Hurricane Katrina, Late Capitalism, and the Remaking of New Orleans.* Minneapolis: University of Minnesota Press.

Johnson, Chalmers. 1995. *Japan: Who Governs? The Rise of the Developmental State.* New York: W. W. Norton.

Kahn, Matthew. 2005. The Death Toll from Natural Disasters: The Role of Income, Geography, and Institutions. *Review of Economics and Statistics* 87 (2): 271–284.

Kamikawa, Runoshin. 2018. Nuclear Policy after 3.11. In Yutaka Tsujinaka and Hiroaki Inatsugu, eds., *Aftermath: Fukushima and the 3.11 Earthquake*, 95–149. Australia: TransPacific Press.

Kamiyama, Machiko, Kyoto Nakatani, and Masae Sato. 2014. A Study of Changes in the Impressions of Yogo Teachers about the Condition of School Children over a Three Year Period in a Prefecture Severely Affected by the Tsunami of March 2011 in Japan. Paper prepared for the Second World Congress on Resilience: From Person To Society, Timisoara, Romania, May 8–10.

Kan, Naoto. 2017. *My Nuclear Nightmare: Leading Japan through the Fukushima Disaster to a Nuclear-Free Future.* Ithaca, NY: Cornell University Press.

Karan, Pradyumna. 2016. After the Triple Disasters: Landscape of Devastation, Despair, Hope, and Resilience. In Pradyuma Karan and Unryu Suganuma, eds., *Japan after 3/11*, 1–44. Kentucky: University of Kentucky Press.

Kariya, Tetsu, and Akira Hanasaki. 2014. *Oishinbo* [Gourmet], vol. 22/23: Fukushima no shinjitsu [Fukushima Truth]. Tokyo: Shogakukan.

Kates, Robert, and David Pijawka. 1977. From Rubble to Monument: The Pace of Reconstruction. In J. E. Haas, R. W. Kates, and M. J. Bowden, eds., *Reconstruction Following Disaster*, 1–23. Cambridge, MA: MIT Press.

Kawachi, Ichiro, S. V. Subramanian, and Daniel Kim, eds. 2008. *Social Capital and Health.* New York: Springer.

Kawahara, Yasunobu. 2014. "Turing 15 Management Capabilities into Organizational Capabilities." In *Rebuilding Community after the Great East Japan Earthquake*, 12–18. Tokyo: Japan NPO Center.

Kawamura, Kazunori, and David Bohacs. 2015. Confidence in Japanese Administration in Areas Affected by the Great East Japan Earthquake. Presentation for Nineteenth Asian Studies Conference Japan (ASCJ), Meiji Gakuin University, June 20–21.

Kawawaki, Yasuo, Yukari Osaka, and Naoto Yamauchi. 2014. Residents' Sense of Recovery and Relationship between Giving Aid and Receiving Aid: The Analysis of Local Residents' Survey in the Areas Affected by the Great East Japan Earthquake. Japan NPO Research Association Discussion Paper 2014-002-J.

Kerr, Alex. 2002. *Dogs and Demons*. New York: Penguin.

Kimura, Toshiaki. 2016. Revival of Local Festivals and Religion after the Great East Japan Earthquake. *Journal of Religion in Japan* 5:227–245.

King, Gary, Jennifer Pan, and Margaret Roberts. 2017. How the Chinese Government Fabricates Social Media Posts for Strategic Distraction, not Engaged Argument. *American Political Science Review* 111 (3):484–501.

King, Gary, Michael Tomz, and Jason Wittenberg. 2000. Making the Most of Statistical Analyses: Improving Interpretation and Presentation. *American Journal of Political Science*, 44 (2): 341–355.

Kingdon, John. 1995. *Agendas, Alternatives, and Public Policies*. New York: HarperCollins.

Kinoshita, Isami, and Helen Woolley. 2015. Children's Play Environment after a Disaster: The Great East Japan Earthquake. *Children* 2 (1): 39–62.

Kiyota, Emi, Yasuhiro Tanaka, Margaret Arnold, and Daniel P. Aldrich. 2015. Elders Leading the Way to Resilience. World Bank Conference Paper Series. http://works.bepress.com/daniel_aldrich/28/.

Klinenberg, Eric. 2002. *Heat Wave: A Social Autopsy of Disaster in Chicago*. Chicago: University of Chicago Press.

Kondo, Ayako, and Masahiro Shoji. 2016. Peer Effects in Employment Status: Evidence from Housing Lotteries for Forced Evacuees in Fukushima. IZA Discussion Paper no. 9708.

Kondo, Naoki. 2016. Disasters, Economic Crisis, and Social Capital: Evidence from Social Epidemiology. Paper prepared for Mini-Conference on Disasters and Recovery, University of Tokyo, December 19.

Kondo, Naoki, Kohta Suzuki, Junko Minai, and Zentaro Yamagata. 2012. Positive and Negative Effects of Finance Based Social Capital on Incident Disability and Mortality. *Journal of Epidemiology* 22 (6): 543–550.

Konishi, Mariko. 2013. What Is Enabling? A Study of Support Groups of the Tōhoku Earthquake. *Ritsumeikan gengo bunka kenkyū* 24 (4): 73–86.

Koresawa, Atsushi. 2011. March 11 Great East Japan Earthquake and Tsunami in Japan's Tohoku Region: Rapid Damage Assessment and Need Survey. Presentation at Asian Disaster Reduction Center, March 21–24.

Kornei, Katherine. 2017. Fukushima Residents Exposed to Far Less Radiation Than Thought. *Science*, January 23. doi:10.1126/science.aal0641.

Koscheyev, V. S., G. R. Leon, A. V. Gourine, and V. N. Gourine. 1997. The Psychosocial Aftermath of the Chernobyl Disaster in an Area of Relatively Low Contamination. *Prehospital Disaster Medicine* 12:41–46.

Krauss, Ellis, and Robert Pekkanen. 2011. *The Rise and Fall of Japan's LDP: Political Party Organizations as Historical Institutions*. Ithaca, NY: Cornell University Press.

Kubo, Takayuki, and Yasuyuki Miwa. 2011. A Community Wiped Off the Map and a Shattered Community. In Yoichi Funabashi and Heizo Takenaka, eds., *Lessons from the Disaster: Risk Management and the Compound Crisis Presented by the Great East Japan Earthquake*, 49–80. Tokyo: Japan Times.

Kumagai, Wataru. 2012. Hachiju yon sha no chōsa kekka [Results of a survey of 84 shrines]. In Hōshi Takase, Kazushi Yoshida, and Wataru Kumagai, eds., *Jinja wa keikokusuru-kodai kara tsutawaru tsunami no messeji* [Shrines as warnings: The tsunami message sent from our past]. Tokyo: Kodansha.

Lahournat, Florence. 2016. Reviving Tradition in Disaster-Affected Communities: Adaptation and Continuity in the Kagura of Ogatsu, Miyagi Prefecture. *Contemporary Japan* 28 (2): 185–207.

LeBlanc, Robin. 1999. *Bicycle Citizens*. Berkeley: University of California Press.

Leflar, Robert, Ayako Hirata, Masayuki Murayama, and Shozo Ota. 2012. Human Flotsam, Legal Fallout: Japan's Tsunami and Nuclear Meltdown. *Journal of Environmental Law and Litigation* 27 (1): 107–124.

Leng, Rachel. 2015. Japan's Civil Society from Kobe to Tohoku. *Electronic Journal of Contemporary Japanese Studies* 15 (1).

Leong, Karen, Christopher Airriess, Wei Li, Angela Chia Chen Chen, and Verna Keith. 2007. Resilient History and the Rebuilding of a Community. *Journal of American History* 94:770–770.

Levy, Jonah. 1999. *Tocqueville's Revenge: State, Society, and Economy in Contemporary France*. Cambridge, MA: Harvard University Press.

Lewis, Danny. 2015. These Century-Old Stone "Tsunami Stones" Dot Japan's Coastline. *Smithsonian*, August 31.

Li, Quixi. 2018. A Return to the Epicentre: The Qiang Communities in the Post-Restructured Sichuan. Paper prepared for the annual meeting of the Association for Asian Studies, March 25.

Lieberman, Evan. 2005. Nested Analysis as a Mixed-Method Strategy for Comparative Research. *American Political Science Review* 99 (3): 435–452.

Lien, Jaimie W., Qingqing Peng, and Jie Zheng. 2016. Major Earthquake Experience and Present-Focused Expenditures. Paper prepared for Workshop on Disasters and Recovery, University of Tokyo, December 9.

Lindee, Susan. 2016. Survivors and Scientists: Hiroshima, Fukushima, and the Radiation Effects Research Foundation, 1975–2014. *Social Studies of Science* 46 (2): 184–209.

Linz, Juan, and Alfred Stepan. 1996. *Problems of Democratic Transition and Consolidation: Southern Europe, South America and Post-Communist Europe*. Baltimore, MD: Johns Hopkins University Press.

Lipscy, Phillip. 2012. A Casualty of Political Transformation? The Politics of Energy Efficiency in the Japanese Transportation Sector. *Journal of East Asian Studies* 12:409–439.

SOURCES

Littlejohn, Andrew. 2018. Recovering Agency: The Politics of Reconstruction in Post-Tsunami Tohoku. Presentation at Weatherhead Center for International Affairs, Harvard University, February 13.

Liu, Amy, and Allison Plyer. 2010. *The New Orleans Index at Five*. Washington, DC: Brookings Institution. https://www.brookings.edu/wp-content/uploads/2016/06/08neworleansindex.pdf.

Liu, Daqi. 2010. A Comparative Look at the Coverage of the Sichuan Earthquake in Chinese and American Newspapers. Master's thesis, Iowa State University.

Løvholt, F., G. Kaiser, S. Glimsdal, L. Scheele, C. B. Harbitz, and G. Pedersen. 2012. Modeling Propagation and Inundation of the 11 March 2011 Tohoku Tsunami. *Natural Hazards and Earth System Sciences* 12:1017–1028. https://doi.org/10.5194/nhess-12-1017-2012.

MacAvoy, Paul, and Jean Rosenthal. 2005. *Corporate Profit and Nuclear Safety*. Princeton, NJ: Princeton University Press.

Macfarlane, Allison. 2011. The Overlooked Back End of the Nuclear Fuel Cycle. *Science* 333 (6047): 1225–1226.

Mahurkar, Uday. 2004. The High Road to Recovery. *India Today*, September 27.

Maly, Elizabeth, and Tomoko Matsushita. 2014. Temporary Housing Innovation within the Post Disaster Housing Recovery Process. Paper prepared for the 3rd International Conference on Urban Disaster Reduction, Boulder, Colorado.

Maly, Elizabeth, Tomoko Matsushita, and Hiroshi Suzuki. 2015. Fukushima: The Housing Situation and Condition of Evacuees of the Triple Disaster Four Years after the 2011 Great East Japan Earthquake. Paper prepared for 7th i-Rec Conference: Reconstruction and Recovery in Urban Contexts.

Manabe, Noriko. 2015. *The Revolution Will Not Be Televised: Protest Music after Fukushima*. New York: Oxford University Press.

———. 2017. Monju-kun: Children's Culture as Protest. In S. Fruhstuck and A. Walthall, eds., *Childs' Play: Multi-Sensory Histories of Children and Childhood in Japan*, 264–285. Oakland, CA: University of California Press.

Marui, Atsunao, and Adrian Gallardo. 2015. Managing Groundwater Contamination at the Daiichi Nuclear Plant. *International Journal of Environmental Research and Public Health* 12:8498–8503.

Masanori, Kikuchi. 2015. Rebuilding Onagawa: An Interview with Suda Yoshiaki. Nippon.com, June 29. http://www.nippon.com/en/in-depth/a04305/.

Matanle, Peter. 2011. The Great East Japan Earthquake, Tsunami, and Nuclear Meltdown: Towards the (Re)construction of a Safe, Sustainable, and Compassionate Society in Japan's Shrinking Regions. *Local Environment: The International Journal of Justice and Sustainability* 9:823–847.

Matanle, Peter, and Anthony Rausch, eds. 2011. *Japan's Shrinking Regions in the 21st Century: Contemporary Responses to Depopulation and Socioeconomic Decline*. NY: Cambria Press.

Matsui, Nozomi. 2018. Local Government Response to 3.11: Staff Perceptions. In Yutaka Tsujinaka and Hiroaki Inatsugu, eds., *Aftermath: Fukushima and the 3.11 Earthquake*, 277–302. Australia: TransPacific Press.

Matsushita, Tomoko. 2013. *Higashi daishinsai no shinsaichi no kyojū ni kansuru ikō chosa bunseki* [An analysis of the goals related to residences in disaster struck areas after the 3.11 disasters]. 47th Conference on Planning, Hiroshima University.

Mayhew, David. 1974. *Congress: The Electoral Connection*. New Haven: Yale University Press.

McAvoy, Gregory. 1999. *Controlling Technocracy: Citizen Rationality and the NIMBY Syndrome*. Washington, DC: Georgetown University Press.

McCormack, Gavan. 1996. *The Emptiness of Japanese Affluence*. New York/London: M. E. Sharpe.

MercyCorps. 2014. *Mid-Term Evaluation of Tohoku Small Business Recovery Programs*. With Planet Finance and New Frontier Services.

Michishita, Narushige, and Andrea Pressello. 2015. *Jieitai to beigun no kyōdō sakusen no seika to kyōkun* [Lessons and outcomes from the joint operations of Japanese SDF and US troops]. In Keiichi Tsunekawa, ed., *Daishinsai genpatsu kiken shita no kokusai kankei* [The international relations of great disaster and nuclear plant hazards], 39–62. Tokyo: Toyozeikai.

Midford, Paul. 2014. The Impact of 3–11 on Japanese Public Opinion and Policy Toward Energy Security. In Espen Moe and Paul Midford, eds., *The Political Economy of Renewable Energy and Energy Security*, 67–96. New York: Springer.

Mimura, Satoru. 2015a. Sharing Experiences of Fukushima. Presentation at the Victoria University of Wellington. http://www.victoria.ac.nz/sef/about/pdf/mimura.pdf.

———. 2015b. Recovery in Fukushima from Integrated Disasters. In Rajib Shaw, ed., *Tohoku Recovery: Challenges, Potentials, and Future*, 165–179. New York: Springer.

Miska, Horst. 2016. Evaluation of the Response to the Fukushima Accident. *Health Physics* 111 (2): 218–222.

Miyagi Prefecture. n.d. *Overview and Characteristics of the Great East Japan Earthquake*. http://www.pref.miyagi.jp/pdf/kiki/2digest.pdf.

MLIT (Ministry of Land, Infrastructure, Transport and Tourism). 2005. *Sosharu kapitaru wa chiiki no keizai seichō wo takameru ka*. MLIT Working Paper 61. https://www.mlit.go.jp/pri/houkoku/gaiyou/pdf/kkk61.pdf.

Mollenhorst, Gerald, Beate Volker, and Hank Flap. 2014. Changes in Personal Relationships: How Social Contexts Affect the Emergence and Discontinuation of Relationships. *Social Networks* 37:65–80.

Montgomery, Roy. 2013. Filling the Gaps from the Christchurch Earthquakes 2010–2013. *Community, Environment and Disaster Risk Management* 14:43–78.

Morioka, Rika. 2015. Gender Difference in Risk Perception following the Fukushima Nuclear Plant Disaster. Fukushima Global Communication Program Working Paper Series no. 12. United Nations University.

SOURCES

Morris, John. 2012. Recovery in Tohoku. In Jeff Kingston, ed., *Natural Disaster and Nuclear Crisis in Japan*, 33–50. New York: Routledge.

Murakami, Kayo, and David Wood. 2014. Planning Innovation and Post-disaster Reconstruction: The Case of Tohoku, Japan. *Planning Theory and Practice* 15 (2): 237–242.

Murakami, Michio, Kyoko Ono, Masaharu Tsubokura, Shuhei Nomura, Tomoyoshi Oikawa, Tosihiro Oka, Masahiro Kami, and Taikan Oki. 2015. Was the Risk from Nursing-Home Evacuation after the Fukushima Accident Higher than the Radiation Risk? *PLOS One*, September 11. https://doi.org/10.1371/journal.pone.0137906.

Muramatsu, Michio. 1986. Center-Local Political Relations in Japan. *Journal of Japanese Studies* 12:303–327.

———. 1997. *Local Power in the Japanese State*. Los Angeles: University of California Press.

Murao, Osamu. 2015a. Regional Comparison of Temporary Housing Construction Processes after the 2011 Great East Japan Earthquake and Tsunami. In Rajib Shaw, ed., *Tohoku Recovery: Challenges, Potentials, and Future*, 37–50. New York: Springer.

———. 2015b. Recovery after Sanriku Tsunamis in 1896 and 1933, and Transition of Housing Location before the 2011 Great East Japan Earthquake and Tsunami. In Rajib Shaw, ed., *Tohoku Recovery: Challenges, Potentials, and Future*, 93–105. New York: Springer.

Nadesan, Majia. 2013. *Fukushima and the Privatization of Risk*. New York: Palgrave Macmillan.

Nagamatsu, Shingo. 2014. Are Cash for Work Programs Effective to Promote Disaster Recovery? Evidence from the Case of Fukushima Prefecture. *Journal of Disaster Research* 9 (2): 161–175.

———. 2018. Building Back a Better Tohoku after the March 2011 Tsunami: Contradicting Evidence. In Vincente Santiago-Fandino, Shinji Sato, Norio Maki, and Kanako, Iuchi, eds., *The 2011 Earthquake and Tsunami: Reconstruction and Restoration*, 37–54. New York: Springer.

NAIIC (Nuclear Accident Independent Investigation Commission). 2012. The official report of the Fukushima Nuclear Accident Independent Investigation Commission. https://www.nirs.org/wp-content/uploads/fukushima/naiic_report.pdf.

Naito, Kaoru. 2016. Security Implications of the Fukushima Accident. In Edward Blanford and Scott Sagan, eds., *Learning from a Disaster: Improving Nuclear Safety and Security after Fukushima*, 58–79. Stanford, CA: Stanford University Press.

Nakajima, Akiko. 2012. Issues of People in Shelters and Temporary Housing after the 3.11 Great East Japan Earthquake from the Perspective of Gender. Presentation for Conference on Disasters, Sendai, November 29.

Nakane, Chie. 1978. *Tateshakai no rikigaku*. Tokyo: Kodansha.

Nakao, Koichi. 2014. Higashi Nihon Daishinsai kara no fukkō katei ni okeru soshuru kapitaru no sōzo sayō: Iwanuma-shi no jirei kara. [Interactions

of Social Capital in the reconstruction process from the Great East Japan Earthquake: The case of Iwanuma city]. *Chiiki seikatsu kenkyū* 5:317–326.
Nakayachi, Kazuya. 2015. Examining Public Trust in Risk-Managing Organizations after a Major Disaster. *Risk Analysis* 35 (1): 57–67.
Nateghi, Roshanak, Jeremy Bricker, Seth Guikema, and Akane Bessho. 2016. Statistical Analysis of the Effectiveness of Seawalls and Coastal Forests in Mitigating Tsunami Impacts in Iwate and Miyagi Prefectures. *PLOS One*, August 10. https://doi.org/10.1371/journal.pone.0158375.
National Police Agency of Japan. 2018. Damage Situation and Police Countermeasures Associated with the 2011 Tohoku District. https://www.npa.go.jp/news/other/earthquake2011/pdf/higaijokyo_e.pdf.
Newman, Oscar. 1996. *Creating Defensible Space*. Washington, DC: U.S. Department of Housing and Urban Development.
Newton, Kenneth, and Pippa Norris. 1999. Confidence in Public Institutions: Faith, Culture, or Performance? Paper prepared for presentation at the Annual Meeting of the American Political Science Association, Atlanta, September 1–5.
Nishide, Junro. 2018. The Practical Realities of Volunteer Activity in a Time of Disaster. In Yutaka Tsujinaka and Hiroaki Inatsugu, eds., *Aftermath: Fukushima and the 3.11 Earthquake*, 303–321. Australia: TransPacific Press.
Nishikawa, Satoru. 2011. Japan's Preparedness and the Great Earthquake and Tsunami. In Yoichi Funabashi and Heizo Takenaka, eds., *Lessons from the Disaster: Risk Management and the Compound Crisis Presented by the Great East Japan Earthquake*, 17–46. Tokyo: Japan Times.
Normile, Dennis. 2012. One Year After the Devastation, Tohoku Designs Its Renewal. *Science* 335 (6073): 1164–1166.
———. 2016. Five Years after the Meltdown, Is It Safe to Live near Fukushima? *Science*, March 2. doi:10.1126/science.aaf4136.
NTT East. 2012. Recovering from the Great East Japan Earthquake. https://www.ntt-east.co.jp/info/detail/pdf/shinsai_fukkyu_e.pdf.
Oguma, Eiji. 2013. Nobody Dies in a Ghost Town. *Asia-Pacific Journal*, 11 (44), no.1, November 3.
Okuyama, Naoko, and Yoji Inaba. 2017. Influence of Natural Disasters on Social Engagement and Post-disaster Well-Being: The Case of the Great East Japan Earthquake. *Japan and the World Economy* 44:1–13.
Oldenburg, Ray. 1999. *The Great Good Place: Cafes, Coffee Shops, Bookstores, Bars, Hair Salons, and Other Hangouts at the Heart of a Community*. New York: Da Capo Press.
Oliver, J. Eric, Shang Ha, and Zachary Callen. 2012. *Local Elections and the Politics of Small-Scale Democracy*. Princeton, NJ: Princeton University Press.
Oliver-Smith, Anthony. 1999. What Is a Disaster? Anthropological Perspectives on a Persistent Question. In Anthony Oliver-Smith and Susanna Hoffman, eds., *The Angry Earth*, 18–34. New York: Routledge.
Onagawa chō kassei-ka shien dantai [Support group for galvanizing Onagawa]. 2012. Chiiki saseai junkan moderu jigyo hikitsugi keikaku [The

project continuation plan for the regional support circulation model]. Presentation.

Osnos, Evan. 2011. The Fallout. *New Yorker*, October 17.

Otake, Midori, and Takashi Sakata, eds. 2014. *Borantia ni yoru shien to kasetsu jūtaku* [Support and temporary housing by volunteers]. Tokyo: Kenpakusha.

Otani, Junko. 2012. Ageing Society, Health Issues, and Disaster: Assessing 3/11. In Jeff Kingston, ed., *Natural Disaster and Nuclear Crisis in Japan*, 237–254. New York: Routledge.

Parry, Richard. 2017. *Ghosts of the Tsunami: Death and Life in Japan's Disaster Zone*. New York: Farrar, Straus, and Giroux.

Peace Boat. 2014. *Annual Report*. https://pbv.or.jp/en/news/pbv-annual-report-20132014/.

Pekkanen, Robert. 2000. Japan's New Politics: The Case of the NPO Law. *Journal of Japanese Studies* 26 (1): 111–148.

Pekkanen, Robert, Yutaka Tsujinaka, and Hidehiro Yamamoto. 2014. *Neighborhood Associations and Local Governance in Japan*. New York: Routledge.

Pharr, Susan, and Robert Putnam, eds. 2000. *Disaffected Democracies: What's Troubling the Trilateral Countries?* Princeton, NJ: Princeton University Press.

Phelan, Stephen. 2016. The Fall and Rise of Onagawa. *New Yorker*, March 18.

Pronyk, Paul M., Trudy Harpham, Joanna Busza, Godfrey Phetla, Linda A. Morison, James R. Hargreaves, Julia C. Kim, Charlotte H. Watts, and John Porter. 2008. Can Social Capital Be Intentionally Generated? A Randomized Trial from Rural South Africa. *Social Science & Medicine* 67: 1559–1570.

Putnam, Robert. 1995. *Making Democracy Work: Civic Traditions in Modern Italy*. Princeton, NJ: Princeton University Press.

———. 2000. *Bowling Alone: The Collapse and Revival of American Community*. New York: Simon and Schuster.

Ramseyer, J. Mark. 2015. Nuclear Power and the Mob: Extortion, Construction, and Social Capital in Japan. Discussion Paper no. 817, Harvard John M. Olin Discussion Paper Series.

Ranghieri, Federica, and Mikio Ishiwatari. 2014. *Learning from Megadisasters: Lessons from the Great East Japan Earthquake*. Washington, DC: World Bank.

Raschky, Paul. 2008. Institutions and the Losses from Natural Disasters. *Natural Hazards and Earth System Sciences* 8: 627–634.

Reconstruction Agency (Fukkōchō). 2013. *Current Status and Path toward Reconstruction*. May.

———. 2015. *Current Status of Reconstruction and Challenges*.

Reconstruction Promotion Committee. 2012. *FY 2012 Interim Report*. Tokyo. http://www.reconstruction.go.jp/english/topics/20121228_FAINAL_CHUKAN.pdf.

Reed, Steven. *Political Outcomes across Japan* [database].

Reed, Steven, Ethan Scheiner, and Michael Thies. 2012. The End of LDP Dominance and the Rise of Party-Oriented Politics in Japan. *Journal of Japanese Studies* 38 (2): 353–376.

Reiher, Cornelia. 2016. Food Safety and Consumer Trust in Post-Fukushima Japan. *Japan Forum* 29 (1): 53–76.

Rencoret, Nicole, Abby Stoddard, Katherine Haver, Glyn Taylor, and Paul Harvey. 2010. *Haiti Earthquake Response: Context Analysis*. Humanitarian Outcomes.

Ritchie, Liesel, and Duane Gill. 2007. Social Capital Theory as an Integrating Theoretical Framework in Technological Disaster Research. *Sociological Spectrum* 27 (1): 103–129.

RJIF (Rebuild Japan Initiative Foundation). 2015. *Anatomy of the Yoshida Testimony*. Tokyo: RJIF.

Roasa, Dustin. 2013. The D.I.Y. Disaster Plan: How Informal Networks Battled Bangkok's Worst Flood. *Next City* 1 (1): 1–12.

Roberts, Patrick. 2013. *Disasters and the American State: How Politicians, Bureaucrats, and the Public Prepare for the Unexpected*. New York: Cambridge University Press, 2013.

Rofi, Abdur, Shannon Doocy, and Robinson Courtland. 2006. Tsunami Mortality and Displacement in Aceh Province, Indonesia. *Disaster* 30 (3): 340–350.

Rose-Ackerman, Susan. 2004. The Challenge of Poor Governance and Corruption. In Bjorn Lomborg, ed., *Global Crisis, Global Solutions*, 301–362. New York: Cambridge University Press.

Safecast. 2016. *The Safecast Report*. Vol. 2: March.

Sagara, J. 2011. Critical Cause Analysis of Delayed Evacuation in the Great East Japan Earthquake and Tsunami. Presentation at IRDR International Conference, Beijing, November 1.

Saito, Jun. 2010. Local Government Reform and the Demise of the LDP. Paper prepared for presentation at the Conference on Japanese Political Economy, University of Tokyo, August 19–20.

Sakai, Sasuke. 2012. Social Capital and Regional Economy: Empirical Analysis Using Individual Data from Questionnaire Survey. *Public Policy Review* 8 (5): 705–736.

Samuels, Richard. 1983. *The Politics of Regional Policy in Japan: Localities Incorporated*. Princeton, NJ: Princeton University Press.

———. 2013. *3/11: Disaster and Change in Japan*. Ithaca, NY, and London: Cornell University Press.

Sanderson, David, and Anshu Sharma. 2008. Winners and Losers from the 2001 Gujarat Earthquake. *Environment and Urbanization* 20 (1): 177–186.

Sasakawa Peace Foundation. 2012. *The Fukushima Nuclear Accident and Crisis Management*. Minato ku, Tokyo: Sasakawa Peace Foundation.

Sawada, Yasuyuki, and Yusuke Kuroishi. 2015. How Does a Natural Disaster Affect People's Preference? The Case of a Large Scale Flood in the Philippines Using the Convex Time Budget Experiments. In Yasuyuki Sawada and Sothea Oum, eds., *Disaster Risks, Social Preferences, and Policy Effects: Field Experiments in Selected ASEAN and East Asian Countries*, 27–56. ERIA Research Project Report no. 34. Jakarta: ERIA.

Sawada, Yasuyuki, and Satoshi Shimizutani. 2008. How Do People Cope with Natural Disasters? Evidence from the Great Hanshin-Awaji (Kobe) Earthquake in 1995. *Journal of Money, Credit and Banking* 40 (2–3): 463–488.

Scheiner, Ethan. 2005. Pipelines of Pork: Japanese Politics and a Model of Local Opposition Party Failure. *Comparative Political Studies* 38 (7): 799–823.

Shifleen, Aminath. 2015. *The "Great Wall" of Japan—A Shield against Tsunamis.* Sanriku Fukkōu, November 20. https://sanrikufukkou.com/2015/11/20/the-great-wall-of-japan-a-shield-against-tsunamis/.

Shigemura, Jun, Takeshi Tanigawa, Azura Aziz, Rethy Chhem, Soichiro Nomura, and Aihide Yoshino. 2016. Psychosocial Challenges of Fukushima Nuclear Plant Workers. In Jun Shigemura and Rethy Chhem, eds., *Mental Health and Social Issues Following a Nuclear Accident*, 119–130. New York: Springer.

Shimada, Go. 2014. A Quantitative Study of Social Capital in the Tertiary Sector of Kobe: Has Social Capital Promoted Economic Reconstruction since the Great Hanshin Awaji Earthquake? JICA-RI Working Paper no. 68. Japan International Cooperation Agency Research Institute.

Shimizu, Nanako. 2015. *Ishi kettei to jendā fubyōdō* [Gender equality and decision making]. Fukushima Global Communication Program Working Paper Series no. 9. United Nations University.

Shiozaki, Yoshimitsu, Eichi Nishikawa, and Shunichi Deguchi. 2012. *Fukkō no Seigi to Rinri* [Justice and Ethics of Reconstruction]. Tokyo: Creative Kamogawa.

Siembieda, William J. 2012. Transactions and Friction as Concepts to Guide Disaster Recovery Policy. *International Journal of Disaster Risk* 3 (1): 38–44.

Siembieda, William J., and Haruo Hayashi. 2015. Japan's Megadisaster Challenges: Crisis Management in the Modern Era. In Frank Baldwin and Anne Allison, eds., *Japan: The Precarious Future*, 139–166. New York: Social Science Research Council and NYU Press.

Singleton, John. 2016. *Economic and Natural Disasters since 1900.* Cheltenham, UK: Edward Elgar.

Sinha, Anil. n.d. *The Gujarat Earthquake 2001.* Asian Disaster Reduction Center.

Slater, David, Keiko Nishimura, and Love Kindstrand. 2012. Social Media in Disaster Japan. In Jeff Kingston, ed., *Natural Disaster and Nuclear Crisis in Japan*, 94–108. New York: Routledge.

Snider, Leslie, Sonia Chehil, and Douglas Walker. 2012. Psychological First Aid. In *Mental Health and Psychosocial Support in Disaster Situations in the Caribbean: Core Knowledge for Emergency Preparedness and Response*. Washington, DC: Pan American Health Organization/WHO.

Soga, Kengo. 2016. Responses of the Central Government to the Great East Japan Earthquake. In Keichi Tsunekawa, ed., *Five Years After: Reassessing Japan's Responses to the Earthquake, Tsunami, and the Nuclear Disaster*, 33–56. Tokyo: University of Tokyo Press.

Solnit, Rebecca. 2009. *A Paradise Built in Hell.* New York: Penguin Books.

Sōmushō [Ministry of Internal Affairs and Communications]. 2016. *Shakai seikatsu kihon chōsa* [Basic survey on social activities]. Tōkeikyoku [Statistics Bureau]. http://www.stat.go.jp/data/shakai/2016/rank/index2.htm.
Sone, Yasunori. 2012. Deliberative Polling about Japanese Energy Policy. Presentation prepared for UNU-ISP Symposium-Rebuilding after 3/11: Vulnerability and Empowerment, Tokyo, November 30.
Sorace, Christian. 2017. Be Grateful to the Party! How to Behave in the Aftermath of a Disaster. *Made in China Journal* 3 (1): 52–61.
Storr, Virgil, Stefanie Haefelle-Balch, and Laura Grube. 2015. *Community Revival in the Wake of Disaster*. New York: Palgrave.
Strömberg, David. 2007. Natural Disasters, Economic Development, and Humanitarian Aid. *Journal of Economic Perspectives* 21 (3): 199–222.
Strusińska-Correia, Agnieszka. 2017. Tsunami Mitigation in Japan after the 2011 Tohoku Tsunami. *International Journal of Disaster Risk Reduction* 22:397–411.
Sugimoto, Amina, Stuart Gilmour, Masaharu Tsubokura, Shuhei Nomura, Masahiro Kami, Tomoyoshi Oikawa, Yukio Kanazawa, and Kenji Shibuya. 2014. Assessment of the Risk of Medium-Term Internal Contamination in Minamisoma City, Fukushima, Japan, after the Fukushima Dai-ichi Nuclear Accident. *Environmental Health Perspectives* 122 (6): 587–593.
Suppasri, Anawat, Natsuki Hasegawa, Fumiyasu Makinoshima, Fumihiko Imamura, Panon Latcharote, and Simon Day. 2016. An Analysis of Fatality Ratios and the Factors That Affected Human Fatalities in the 2011 Great East Japan Tsunami. *Frontiers in Built Environment* 2:1–13.
Suzuki, S. 2016. Childhood and Adolescent Thyroid Cancer in Fukushima after the Fukushima Daiichi Nuclear Power Plant Accident: 5 Years On. *Clinical Oncology* 28 (4): 263–271.
Suzuki, Shiho, and Taro Miura. 2014. The Librarians of Fukushima. *Journal of Library Administration* 54 (5): 403–412.
Suzuki, Tatsujiro. 2011. The Fukushima Accident and Implications for Nuclear Energy Policy. Presentation at Temple University Japan, November 25.
———. 2015. Japan's Contaminated Fukushima Debate Four Years On. *East Asia Forum*, March 8.
Sweet, Stephen. 1998. The Effect of a Natural Disaster on Social Cohesion. *International Journal of Mass Emergencies and Disasters* 16 (3): 321–331.
Szreter, Simon, and Michael Woolcock. 2004. Health by Association? Social Capital, Social Theory and the Political Economy of Public Health. *International Journal of Epidemiology* 33 (4): 650–667.
Taft-Morales, Maureen, and Rhoda Margesson. 2010. Haiti Earthquake: Crisis and Response. Congressional Research Service, January 15.
Tagawa, Hiroyuki. 2016. Corporate Influence and the Fukushima Daiichi Nuclear Accident: How Has TEPCO Survived? In Keichi Tsunekawa, ed., *Five Years After: Reassessing Japan's Responses to the Earthquake, Tsunami, and the Nuclear Disaster*, 81–112. Tokyo: University of Tokyo Press.

Takahashi, Sho, Mikihito Ishiki, Naoki Kondo, Aaiko Ishiki, Takeshia Toriyama, Shuko Takahashi, Hidenori Moriyama, Masahiro Ueno, Masaaki Shimanuki, Toshio Kanno, Tomoharu Oki, and Kiyoshi Tabata. 2015. Health Effects of a Farming Program to Foster Community Social Capital of a Temporary Housing Complex of the 2011 Great East Japan Earthquake. *Disaster Medicine and Public Health Preparation* 9 (2): 103–110.

Takeda, J., K. Tamura, and S. Tatsuki. 2003. Life Recovery of 1995 Kobe Earthquake Survivors in Nishinomiya City: A Total-Quality-Management-Based Assessment of Disadvantaged Populations. *Natural Hazards* 29 (3): 567–585.

Takenaka, Heizo. 2011. The Great Disaster and the Japanese Economy. In Yoichi Funabashi and Heizo Takenaka, eds., *Lessons from the Disaster: Risk Management and the Compound Crisis Presented by the Great East Japan Earthquake*, 117–146. Tokyo: Japan Times.

Takezawa, Shoichiro. 2013. *Hisaigo wo ikiru: Kirikiri Otsuchi Kamaishi Funtoki*. Tokyo: Chuokoronsha. Translation 2016. *The Aftermath of the 2011 East Japan Earthquake and Tsunami: Living among the Rubble*. Lanham, MD: Lexington Books.

Tamba, Fuminori, and Masafumi Yokemoto. 2013. The Evacuation of Residents after the Fukushima Nuclear Accident. In Miranda Schreurs and Fumikazu Yoshida, eds., *Fukushima: A Political Economy Analysis of Nuclear Disaster*, 89–107. Sapporo: Hokkaido University Press.

Tanigawa, Koichi, Yoshio Hosoi, Nobuyuki Hirohashi, Yasumasa Iwasaki, and Kenji Kamiya. 2012. Loss of Life after Evacuation: Lessons Learned from the Fukushima Accident. *Lancet* 379 (9819): 889–891.

Tatsuki, Shigeo. 2013. Old Age, Disability, and the Tohoku-Oki Earthquake. *Earthquake Spectra* 29 (S1): S403–S432.

Tilly, Charles. 1992. *Coercion, Capital, and European States*. Cambridge: Blackwell.

Thaler, Richard, and Cass Sunstein. 2008. *Nudge: Improving Decisions about Health, Wealth, and Happiness*. New York: Penguin Books.

Thiruppugazh, V. 2007. What Has Changed after the Gujarat Earthquake of 2001? Paper prepared for the Asian Science and Technology Forum.

Thompson, Nevin. 2017. Six Years On: How Fukushima, Miyagi, and Iwate Are Recovering from the Tsunami. *Global Voices*, April 3. https://globalvoices.org/2017/04/03/six-years-on-how-fukushima-miyagi-and-iwate-are-recovering-from-the-tsunami/.

Toba, Futoshi. 2013. *Ganbapesshi!* [Try hard!]. Tokyo: Yamato.

Tolan, Casey. 2015. Disasters Happen When We Forget: The Slow Rebuilding of a Tiny Japanese Town Destroyed by a Tsunami. July 10, 2015. Fusion.net. http://fusion.net/story/207610/onagawa-japan-tsunami-rebuilding/#mail-share.

Tomita, Hiroshi. 2012. Reconstruction of Tsunami Devastated Fishing Villages in the Tohoku Region of Japan and the Challenges for Planning. *Planning Theory and Practice* 15 (2): 242–246.

———. 2015. Resilience Enhancement of Traffic and Distribution Network That Sustains Invaluable Human Lives and Day to Day Live. Presentation prepared for UN World Conference on Disaster Risk Reduction, Sendai, March 15.

Tomodachi Initiative. 2014. *Annual Report*. Tokyo: US Embassy.

Truitt, Allison. 2012. The Viet Village Urban Farm and the Politics of Neighborhood Viability in Post-Katrina New Orleans. *City & Society* 24 (3): 321–338.

Tse, Chun Wing, Jianwen Wei, and Yihan Wang. 2013. Social Capital and Disaster Recovery: Evidence from Sichuan Earthquake in 2008. Center for Global Development Working Paper no. 344.

Tsuboya, Toru, Jun Aida, Hiroyuki Hikichi, S. V. Subramanian, Katsunori Kondo, Ken Osaka, and Ichiro Kawachi. 2016. Predictors of Depressive Symptoms Following the Great East Japan Earthquake: A Prospective Study. *Social Science & Medicine* 161:47–54.

Tsuchiya, Tomoko, Shinetsu Sugawara, and Taketoshi Taniguchi. 2015. Kikiji no gabanansu [Governance during crisis]. In Hideyaki Shiroyama, ed., *Fukushima genpatsu jiko to fukugō risuku gabanansu* [Shared risk governance in the Fukushima nuclear accident], 119–148. Tokyo: Toyokeizai Publishers.

Tsuda, Toshihide, Akiko Tokinobu, Eiji Yamamoto, and Etsuji Suzuki. 2016. Thyroid Cancer Detection by Ultrasound Among Residents Ages 18 Years and Younger in Fukushima, Japan: 2011 to 2014. *Epidemiology* 27 (3): 316–322.

Tsujinaka, Yutaka, and Hiroaki Inatsugu. 2018. Introduction. In Yutaka Tsujinaka and Hiroaki Inatsugu, eds., *Aftermath: Fukushima and the 3.11 Earthquake*, 1–25. Australia: TransPacific Press.

Tsujiuchi, Takuya. 2015. Mental Health Impact of the Fukushima Nuclear Disaster: Post-Traumatic Stress and Psycho-Socio-Economic Factors. Fukushima Global Communication Program Working Paper Series no. 8. United Nations University.

Tsunekawa, Keiichi, ed. 2015. *Daishinsai genpatsu kiken shita no kokusai kankei* [The international relations of great disaster and nuclear plant hazards]. Tokyo: Toyozeikai.

———. 2016. *Five Years After: Reassessing Japan's Responses to the Earthquake, Tsunami, and the Nuclear Disaster*. Tokyo: University of Tokyo Press.

———. 2018. Radioactive Contamination and Japan's Foreign Relations. In Yutaka Tsujinaka and Hiroaki Inatsugu, eds., *Aftermath: Fukushima and the 3.11 Earthquake*, 382–400. Australia: TransPacific Press.

Ueda, Yasutaka, and Rajib Shaw. 2015. Community Recovery in Tsunami-Affected Area: Lessons from Minami-Kesennuma. In Rajib Shaw, ed., *Tohoku Recovery: Challenges, Potentials, and Future*, 131–146. New York: Springer.

UNICEF. 2010. *Sichuan Earthquake: Two Year Report*. Beijing.

UNISDR (United Nations International Strategy for Disaster Reduction). 2013. *Private Sector Strengths Applied: Good Practices in Disaster Risk Reduction from Japan*.

UNU (United Nations University). 2016. *Fukushima Global Communication Programme Final Report*. Tokyo: United Nations University Institute for the Advanced Study of Sustainability:.

Useem, Michael, Howard Kunreuther, and Erwann Michel-Kerjan. 2015. *Leadership Dispatches: Chile's Extraordinary Comeback from Disaster*. Stanford, CA: Stanford University Press.

Varshney, Ashutosh. 2001. Ethnic Conflict and Civil Society: India and Beyond. *World Politics* 53 (3): 362–398.

Vatsa, Krishna. 2001. *The Bhuj Earthquake District of Kutch, State of Gujarat (India): A Reconnaissance Report Identification of Priority Issues*. Prepared for DRM: World Institute for Disaster Risk Management.

Veszteg, Robert, Yukihiko Funaki, and Aiji Tanaka. 2014. The Impact of the Tohoku Earthquake and Tsunami on Social Capital in Japan: Trust Before and After the Disaster. *International Political Science Review* 36. https://doi.org/10.1177/0192512113509501.

Wada, Akiko. 2018. Service and Support by Local Governments outside the Disaster Zone. In Yutaka Tsujinaka and Hiroaki Inatsugu, eds., *Aftermath: Fukushima and the 3.11 Earthquake*, 262–276. Australia: TransPacific Press.

Waddington, I., P. J. Thomas, R. H. Taylor, and G. J. Vaughan. 2017. J-Value Assessment of Relocation Measures Following the Nuclear Power Plant Accidents at Chernobyl and Fukushima Dai-ichi. *Process Safety and Environmental Protection* 11:16–49.

Waltz, Kenneth. 1999. Globalization and Governance. *PS: Political Science and Politics* 32 (4): 693–700.

Wei, Jiuchang, Dingtao Zhao, and Dora Marinova. 2013. Disaster Relief Drivers: China and the US in Comparative Perspective. *China: An International Journal* 11 (2): 93–116.

Wein, Anne, Laurie Johnson, and Richard Bernknopf. 2011. Recovering from the ShakeOut Earthquake. *Earthquake Spectra* 27 (2): 521–538.

Weitzdorfer, Julius. 2014. Liability for Nuclear Damages under Japanese Law: Key Legal Problems Arising from the Fukushima Daiichi Nuclear Accident. In Simon Butt, Hitoshi Nasu, and Luke Nottage, eds., *Asia-Pacific Disaster Management: Comparative and Socio-Legal Perspectives*, 119–138. Berlin: Springer.

Westlund, Hans, and Federica Calidoni-Lundberg. 2006. Social Capital and the Creative Class. Swedish Institute for Growth Policy Studies Working Paper 1.

WHO (World Health Organization). 2010. Public Health Risk Assessment and Interventions: Earthquake-Haiti. January.

Winchester, Simon. 2017. The Nature of Catastrophe. *New York Review of Books*, November 9.

Wood, Robert Muir. 2016. *The Cure for Catastrophe: How We Can Stop Manufacturing Natural Disasters*. New York: Basic Books.

World Bank. 2017. *Implementation and Completion Results Report on a Loan in the Amount of $710 million to the People's Republic of China for a Wenchuan Earthquake Recovery Project*. Report no. ICR00003783.

WREMO (Wellington Region Emergency Management). 2012. *Community Resilience Strategy*. Wellington, New Zealand: WREMO.

———. n.d. *It's Easy: Get Prepared for an Emergency*. Wellington, New Zealand: WREMO.

Xu, Bin. 2017. *The Politics of Compassion: The Sichuan Earthquake and Civic Engagement in China*. Stanford, CA: Stanford University Press.

Yamashita, Fumio. 2008. *Tsunami tendenko: Kindai nihon no tsunami shi* [History of Modern Japanese tsunami]. Tokyo: Shin Nihon Shuppansha.

Yamashita, Shunichi, Shinichi Suzuku, Satori Suzuki, Hiroki Shimura, and Vladimir Saenko. 2018. Lessons from Fukushima: Latest Findings of Thyroid Cancer After the Fukushima Nuclear Power Plant Accident. *Thyroid* 28 (1): 11–22.

Yamashita, Yusuke, and Hiroshi Kainuma, eds. 2012. *Genpatsu hinan ron* [Theories of Nuclear Evacuation]. Tokyo: Akashi Publishers.

Yamato. 2012. Great East Japan Earthquake Living and Industrial Base Reconstruction and Recovery Fund. http://www.yamato-hd.co.jp/english/information/info/data/description01.pdf.

Yilmaz, Senol. 2011. Fukushima Nuclear Disaster: A Study in Poor Crisis Communication. S. Rajaratnam School of International Studies, NTU RSIS Commentaries no. 93.

Yoshida, Fumikazu. 2013. Fukushima Nuclear Disaster: One of the World's Worst Cases of Pollution. In Miranda Schreurs and Fumikazu Yoshida, eds., *Fukushima: A Political Economic Analysis of a Nuclear Disaster*, 21–60. Sapporo: Hokkaido University Press.

Yoshida, Katsuhiko. 2012. *Fukushima ni aru mondai no kaiketsu* [Solutions to the problems of Fukushima]. *Japanese Journal of School Counseling* 6:82–89.

Yoshioka, Kaori. 2015. Residents of Fukushima's Iitate Village File Petition for Nuclear Damage Compensation to Restore Home Village. Nuke Info Tokyo no. 164. Citizens' Nuclear Information Center.

Young, Laura. 2013. The Evolution of Society and War. Ph.D. dissertation, Department of Political Science, Purdue University.

Yun, Mani Yi, and Masanori Hamada. 2015. Evacuation Behavior and Fatality Rate during the 2011 Tohoku-Oki Earthquake and Tsunami. *Earthquake Spectra* 31 (3): 1237–1265.

Zhang, Qiang, Qibin Lu, Yameng Hu, and Jocelyn Lau. 2015. What Constrained Disaster Management Capacity in the Township Level of China? *Natural Hazards* 77:1915–1938.

Index

3/11 triple disasters. *See* earthquakes; Fukushima Dai-ichi nuclear power plant; Tōhoku tsunami
77 Bank, xii–xiii

@Rias, 116
Abe, Shinzō, 138, 148–49, 152, 227n146
Abukuma River, 31
Agency for Natural Resources and Energy (ANRE), 135
agriculture: and contamination stigma, 122, 181; cooperatives, 20; damaged by 3/11 disasters, 113; Hamarassen Farm, 19, 189; repair and rebuilding, 130; revitalization, 122–23, 183; rezoning, 141; in Watari, xii
Ai Weiwei, 168–69
AKB48, 99
Akimoto, Yasushi, 99
American Association for the Advancement of Science, 9
Amnesty International, 176
Aneyoshi, 76, 186
Arahama, 14, 29–32
Asian Development Bank, 170
Australia, 109

Bahrain, 167
Ban, Shigeru, 99
Belgium, 131, 186
Beteran Mama no Kai (Veteran Moms' Group), 116

bonding social capital: definitions, 14–15; effect on disaster outcomes, 18, 77–78, 100, 175, 177; *kizuna*, 136; programs to strengthen, 189; in temporary housing, 47, 56–57
BP, 135
Brazil, 161
bridging social capital: definitions, 15–16; effect on disaster outcomes, 175; and governance, 82, 96; programs to strengthen, 189
Brookings Institution, 90
building codes, ix, xiii, 5, 159, 162–63, 169, 171–74, 179
buses. *See* mass transit
businesses, small and medium-sized: damaged by 3/11 disasters, 47, 58, 89; food distribution plans, 107; government funding for, 113, 115, 193; as index of recovery, 90, 94; reopenings, xi, 60–61, 111; temporary locations, xiv; zoning laws protecting, 67

Canada, 82, 131, 173, 211n71, 230n41
Cash for Work Japan, 116
Center for Research and Training on Community Health Services during Disaster, 110
Center for the Development of Power Supply Regions, 145
Chengdu, China, 167

259

INDEX

Chernobyl meltdowns. *See* nuclear disasters and accidents
Chiba, 75
Chicago heat wave of 1995, 77
children: disaster survival, x–xi, 76; disaster training, 209n6; financial incentives, 117–18; health effects of radiation exposure, 64, 153; outdoor play, 123, 209n44; scholarships, 119; in Sichuan earthquake, 168; support programs, 116, 134, 190. *See also* schools
China: bridging social capital in, 16; building codes, 163; disaster management, xiii, 28, 163, 166–70; earthquakes in (*see* earthquakes); governance, 166–70, 179; nuclear facilities, 186; repression in, 166, 228n18; volunteers from, 61
Chisso company, 70
Chubu Electric Power Company, 6
Citibank, 99
citizen science: and distrust of government, 132, 150–51; government threats to prosecute, 148; open-source radiation data, 23, 148, 150–51, 154, 175, 179. *See also* Kizuna; Minna no Data; Safecast
City Network, 96; Disaster Volunteer Center, 96; fund-raising, 98–99; governance, 24; housing, 95, 97; raising downtown, 72–73, 95, 97–99; recovery and reconstruction process, 95–99, 194; relationship with central government, 95–99, 178; relationship with civil society/NGOs, 96, 98–99; relationships with foreign governments, 98–99; tsunami damage, 96; wave heights, 95
civil society organizations and NGOs: author's interviews with, xvi; in China, 167; and contamination stigma, 46; and democratic governance, 163–64; effect on disaster outcomes, 159; family reunification efforts, 116; fund-raising and financial assistance, 99, 111, 116, 132, 159; housing efforts, 69; in India, 170–71; neighborhood associations, 35; partnerships with government, 22, 96, 116–17, 124–25, 133, 138–39; radiation monitoring, 150–51, 164, 175, 179; registration laws, 138; and renewable energy, 152; slogans, 132; social activities, 62–63; social capital creation, 188–89; third-party verification of decontamination, 154–55; volunteer efforts, 57–58, 61–63, 71, 99, 114, 116, 132, 134, 162, 181. *See also* citizen science; *individual organizations*
Clean Government Party (CGP), 87, 98, 137
Coastal Town, Japan, 16
comics, xii, 192, 230n30
communications infrastructure: FM radio, 41, 98, 178–79, 212n2; and governmental communications, 106, 121; internet, 111; mobile phones, 2, 4, 33, 37, 108, 111; social media, 41; telephone service, xii, 106; television, 37, 106. *See also* NTT East; warning systems
construction industry: bid rigging, 60; costs, 60, 67, 141–42, 153; government funding for, 113, 139, 188; jobs, 140, 188; local builders, 69; swamped with reconstruction projects, 24. *See also* building codes; emergency shelters and temporary housing
corruption and clientelism: in China, 168–69; in construction industry, 168, 188; in Japan, 24, 84, 89, 100, 212n75; misdirection of reconstruction funds, 141; in New Orleans, 21. *See also* linking social capital
crime: crime rates as proxy for social capital, 77–78, 80–81, 218n13, 220n50; effect on social networks, 17; looting, 48, 163
Cuba, 158–59
culture, xii–xiv, 13, 48, 131, 180, 208n30

Date (town), 46, 150
death tolls and mortality rates: effect of governance on, 158–63; effect of immediate evacuation on, 37; effect on recovery process, 92–93; effect of seawalls, 17, 79–81; effect of social ties on, 177; effect of wave heights on, 74–75; of elderly and infirm, 4; of Great Sichuan Earthquake, 167–68, 173–74, 228n18; of Gujarat Earthquake, 170, 173–74; of Haiti Earthquake, 172–74; and local government outreach, 84–85; official, 5; of Tōhoku tsunami, ix, 5, 32, 49, 58, 72, 173–74; variation in, x, 11, 25–27, 72–81, 86, 99–101, 121

260

decontamination: of buildings, 10, 64–65; costs, 182; effect on recovery process, 118; effectiveness, 10, 64–65, 115, 152–53; government assistance with, 46, 64–65, 111; as job source, 66, 102–3; Josen Tokubetsu Chiiki (Special-Case Decontamination Zones), 115; public relations, 123; reuse of radioactive soil, 148, 153; of soil, xi, 10, 64–65, 148, 153–55, 182; third-party verification, 154–55; waste disposal, 129; worker safety, 154–55

Deepwater Horizon oil spill, 135

Democratic Party of Japan (DPJ), 78, 87, 92, 98, 100, 137–38

disabled people. *See* elderly and infirm people

disaster planning: by central government, 26–28, 128, 180, 187; Disaster Basic Countermeasures Act, 108; "disaster culture," 28, 194; faulty maps, 104–5; at Fukushima Dai-ichi nuclear power plant, 6–7, 104; for hospitals, 5, 149; in India, 170–71; after Kobe earthquake, 133, 138–40; legal frameworks, 128; mitigation strategies, 117; at municipal level, 78; for nuclear disasters, 104–5, 128, 132, 184; by prefectural governments, 85, 104–5, 121; reciprocal aid agreements, 22, 85; in Tōhoku post-3/11, 117; for tsunami, 174–75, 180

disaster training and drills: and disaster outcomes, 159, 174–75; "Disaster Prevention Day," 3, 104; financial factors, 92; at Fukushima Dai-ichi nuclear power plant, 6–7; by prefectural governments, 104–5; in schools, 2–3; *tsunami tendenko*, 2–3, 17, 33, 37, 76–77, 174–75

Dispute Resolution Committee for Nuclear Damage Compensation, 151

Dominican Republic, 158

Earthquake Engineering Research Institute (EERI), xvi

earthquakes: 1700s Portugal earthquake and tsunami, 13; 1978 Miyagi-Oki Earthquake, 104; 1995 Great Hanshin-Awaji (Kobe) Earthquake, 16, 22, 109, 133, 137–38, 169, 179, 182–83; 2001 Gujarat Earthquake, 170–71, 173; 2003 Northern Miyagi Earthquake, 104; 2008 Great Sichuan Earthquake, 16, 163, 166–70, 173; 2008 Iwate-Miyagi Nairiku Earthquake, 104; 2010 Haiti Earthquake, xiii, 163, 171–74; 2011 Great East Japan Earthquake, ix, 1, 29–30, 100, 102, 138, 154, 173 (*see also* Tōhoku tsunami); 2013 Hong Kong Earthquake, 168; prediction, 104

Ebina, 22

"eco-towns," 117, 123–24

elderly and infirm people: and bonding social capital, 14–15, 18; community gardening programs, 19; desire to return home, 58–59, 65–66; difficulties with electronic governance methods, 69; difficulties evacuating, 4, 32–37, 45, 76; difficulties receiving disaster warnings, 4; disaster mortality rates, 4, 76; disaster survival, x–xi; health outcomes of evacuation, 18, 45; housing, 40–41, 54–55, 144–45, 153–54, 193; lists for future evacuations, 149; loneliness and *kodokushi*, 15, 18–19, 40–41, 54–58, 62, 144–45; and medical personnel shortages, 114; returnees, 103; social ties, 61–62, 177, 211n54; support programs, 116, 134, 189–91; and trust, 17

EM-DAT. *See* International Disaster Database (EM-DAT)

emergency shelters and temporary housing: bureaucracy and red tape, 69; communal, 54; conditions, 38–39, 53–58; continued use, x, 69, 90, 130–31, 153, 179; designation process, 104; distance from social networks, 54–55; flooded by tsunami, 105; food supplies, 39, 107, 121; frequent moves, 39, 229n7; fuel supplies, 133; within Fukushima Prefecture, 46; government-owned, x, 39, 112, 130; government-subsidized, 54, 111–12, 120; after Haiti earthquake, 172–73; as index of recovery, 90, 179; lack of sites for, 112; lotteries, 40, 193; moving to permanent housing, 12, 40, 54, 69, 129, 141; new permanent construction, 67, 97, 111, 130, 141, 144; NGO assistance, 62–63; with relatives, x, 40; in schools, 5, 31, 33, 38–39, 45, 49; self-governance in, 47–49; after Sichuan earthquake, 167–68; and

261

INDEX

emergency shelters and temporary housing (*continued*)
social networks, 15, 19, 62–63; speed of construction, 95; supplemented by private sector, 112; telecommunications in, 111
ethnic diversity, 15
evacuation: and bonding social capital, 77; by bus, 147; by car, 37–38; delays, 3–5, 31, 36–38, 79, 81, 187; "deliberate" vs. mandatory, 9, 41–47; designated evacuation sites, 5, 30–31, 147 (*see also* schools); effect on mortality rates, 86–87, 114; of elderly and infirm, 37; by helicopter, 106; orders, 9–10, 21, 40, 43, 146–47; poor planning of, 44; and radioactive plume, 146–47; role of neighborhood associations, 35–36; routes (*see* roads); scale, 38; and self-organization, 77; "voluntary" vs. "forced," 46–47, 120, 148. *See also* disaster planning; *individual municipalities*
evacuees from 3/11 disasters: assistance by volunteers, 57–58, 61–63; bureaucracy and red tape, 66–70; compensation for, ix, 46–47, 53, 57, 59, 68, 142, 148, 207n6, 215n109; divorce rates, 114, 120, 188; domestic abuse rates, 53; likelihood of return to homes, xi, 50, 58–61, 65–66; loneliness, 18, 40; reentering workforce, 57; registration, 21–22, 59–60; resettlement in faraway areas, 18, 47; stigma against, 45–47, 120. *See also* elderly and infirm people; emergency shelters and temporary housing

Fair Trade Commission, 60
Federal Emergency Management Agency (FEMA), 40, 53–54, 112
Federation of Electric Power Companies of Japan (FEPC), xvi
Finland, 131
first responders: Coast Guard, 107–8; firefighters, 2, 25, 38, 105, 107–8, 135, 159, 179; negative interactions with residents, 15; from other parts of Japan, 25, 110, 133, 135; police, 2, 25, 105, 107–8, 162, 217n189 (*see also* National Police Agency [Keisatsu chō]); supply shortages, 107

Fisheries Agency, 66
fishing industry and aquaculture: and contamination stigma, 70, 181; damaged by 3/11 disasters, 113; effect on mortality rates, 76; recovery and reconstruction process, 12–13, 66, 98, 130; and seawalls, 24, 140, 143–44, 187; volunteer assistance, 181
flooding: in China, 167; at Fukushima Dai-ichi nuclear power plant, 6–7; inland, 31, 73, 79, 142. *See also* Tōhoku tsunami
food: and community, 62–63; at evacuation shelters, 39; from Fukushima (*see* agriculture; fishing industry and aquaculture); government distribution, 106, 124, 231n53; helicopter drops, 25, 106; local produce, xii, 216n133 (*see also* agriculture); private-sector aid, 111; radiation safety standards, 132; riots, 163, 172; self-organized distribution, 25, 48; shortages, 107
Forest Act (Shinrinhō), 67; tsunami damage, 96; as tsunami mitigation strategy, 17, 23, 117, 140, 142, 187
forests: clearance for housing, 138; decontamination, 65
France, 163, 165, 210n31
Fudai, 12, 72, 75, 79
Fukushima City, 10, 123, 138, 151
Fukushima Dai-ichi nuclear power plant: continued evacuation around, xi, 41–42, 115, 213n43, 214n70 (*see also* evacuation; Fukushima Prefecture); cost of meltdowns, ix, 148; effect on public opinion about nuclear power, 146, 183–84, 230n41; efforts to restart, 120; emergency shutdown (SCRAM), 6–7, 210n21; events of meltdowns, 6–10; radioactive contamination, 41–43, 64–65, 121, 146–48; reactor decommissioning, xi, 65, 103, 121, 148; water storage, 8, 65, 210n34; worst-case scenario, 133–34. *See also* decontamination
Fukushima Dialogue Initiative, 120
Fukushima Ecotech Clean Center, 120–21
Fukushima Prefecture: ban on nuclear energy, 185; births after 3/11 disasters, 64; central government assistance with disaster response, 106; civil servants,

102; Council of Social Welfare, 116; depopulation, 103, 117–21, 181–83, 212n89; disaster headquarters, 108; disaster planning, 104–5; evacuation, 9, 37; financial incentives for returnees, 46, 117–18, 122; housing efforts, 131; librarians, 116; Prefectural Disaster Task Force, 106–7; quality of temporary housing, 69; Reconstruction Agency field office, 138; recovery and reconstruction process, xii, 93–95, 119, 121–24, 152, 178; relationships with foreign governments, 123; remaining industries in, xi; scale of tsunami in, x, 74–75; unique challenges to reconstruction, 114–17, 122–24, 181–82; work with NGOs and foreign aid groups, 22, 110, 125. *See also* prefectural governments

Fukushima Renewable Future Fund, 152

Fukushima University, 116, 123

Futaba: decontamination, 64; evacuation, xv, 41; mental health of residents, 51–52; potassium iodide pills, 147; speed of recovery, 91; Tokyo Electric Power Company (TEPCO) in, 44. *See also* Fukushima Prefecture

Germany: disaster aid, 110; energy policy, 185–86; federal system, 19, 211n71; governance in, 82, 161; renewable energy pact with Fukushima, 123

governance: bureaucracy and red tape, 66–71, 82; citizen participation, 22–23; civil service personnel shortage, 67–68, 85; definitions, 19–24; and disaster outcomes, 158–63; effect of triple disaster on, 178–79, 191–94; electronic, 69; extractive capacity, 164–66; in Germany, 19, 82; input structures, 166, 175; in North America, 82; and social safety nets, 20–21, 161, 163, 167; and social ties, 70, 81–85, 211n62; state capacity, 164–66, 175; and trust, 10, 77, 131–32. *See also* Japanese central government; linking social capital; municipal governments; prefectural governments

Great East Japan Earthquake, ix, 1, 29–30, 100, 102, 138, 154, 173. *See also* Tōhoku tsunami

Great Hanshin-Awaji (Kobe) Earthquake. *See* earthquakes

Greenpeace, 9–10

Gujarat, India, 15, 170–71, 173–74

Gunma, 152

Haiti, xiii, 28, 158, 160–63, 166, 171–74, 179

Hamarassen Farm, 19, 189

Hamatte-kerain kadatta-kerain, 189

Hasegama, 56

health: cancer, xv; cholera, 172; communal healing, 116; diabetes, xv, 188; effects of radiation exposure, xiii, 64, 103, 114, 119–20, 146, 214n70; effects of stress (*see* mental health); at evacuation shelters, 39; hypertension, xv; infectious disease, 172; obesity, xv, 123, 188; potassium iodide pills, 21, 147; screenings and surveillance, xv, 23, 64, 119; and social capital, 211n64; of TEPCO employees, 64; thyroid abnormalities, 64, 119; and variation in disaster death rates, 93. *See also* hospitals and medical facilities; mental health

Higashidori nuclear facility, 184

Higashimatsushima, 75

Hirono, xi, 59, 75, 103

Hiroshima atom bomb, 1

historical disasters. *See* earthquakes; hurricanes; tornadoes; tsunamis

Hokkaido, 22, 141

Hokuriku Electric Power Company, 6

Hong Kong, 168

Hosono, Goshi, 43

hospitals and medical facilities: Disaster Medical Assistance Teams (DMATs) and field hospitals, 105, 109–10; disaster plans (*see* disaster planning); evacuation, 45, 214n61; funding for, xiii; Minamisoma, 114; mobile clinics, 114; patient deaths, 5, 45, 214n61; personnel shortages, 114, 156; radiation exposure on the job, 147–48; rebuilding and new construction, 115, 117; South Miyagi Medical Center, 36; staff from other parts of Japan, 110; supply shortages, 107; Tōhoku University Hospital, 50

House of Representatives, 88, 137

housing. *See* emergency shelters and temporary housing
hurricanes: Gustav, 158–59; Harvey, 13; Katrina, x, 13, 54, 90, 140, 158, 169, 221n36; Sandy, 13
Hyogo Prefecture, 22

Ibaraki, 75
Ibasho, xvi, 18–19, 63, 189–91
Iitate: depopulation, 64; as evacuation destination, xv, 147; evacuation order lifted, xi; lawsuits by residents, xiii, 151; radiation exposure, xv, 10, 42, 147; "shelter indoors" order, 9–10; voices of residents, xv
Ikarigawa, Yutaka, 24
Inagaki family, 16, 35–36
India: bridging social capital in, 15; building codes, 171; disaster management, xiii, 28, 163, 170–71; earthquakes in, x; governance, 166, 175, 179; social safety nets, 170; state capacity, 166
insurance, 51–52, 138, 160
International Disaster Database (EM-DAT), 160
International Nuclear Event Scale (INES). *See* nuclear disasters and accidents
Ishinomaki: deaths in, xii, 5; housing, 55, 62; Ogatsu hospital, 5; rebuilding port, 66; recovery and reconstruction process, 141; tsunami mitigation strategies, 144; wave heights, 75
Ishinomaki 2.0 (NGO), xvi
Israel, 110
Italy, 98–99, 131, 164–65, 186
Itochu, Inc., 99
Iwaizumi, 75, 91
Iwaki, 38, 75
Iwanuma, 4, 56, 75, 98
Iwate Prefecture: airports, 106; betweenness centrality, 124–25; Center for Research and Training on Community Health Services during Disaster, 110; civil servants from other prefectures, 110; degree centrality, 124; depopulation, 117–21, 212n89; disaster headquarters, 108; disaster planning, 85; evacuation, 37; housing efforts, 121; Iwate Disaster Relief Welfare Support Team, 117; previous tsunami, 104; public opinion about government, 96;

public works, 113; recovery and reconstruction process, xii, 93–95, 118–19, 122, 178; relationships with municipal governments, 96; scale of tsunami in, x, 74–75; work with NGOs and foreign aid groups, 22, 110, 117. *See also* prefectural governments

Japan Atomic Energy Agency, 136
Japan Atomic Energy Relations Organization, 145
Japan Atomic Power Company, 184
Japan Communist Party (JCP), 87
Japan International Cooperation Agency, 176
Japan Platform, 124
Japan Self Defense Forces (SDF): burying bodies, 217n189; collaboration with Miyagi Prefecture, 107–9, 124; disaster planning, 109; food distribution, 231n53; triple-disaster rescue work, 25, 33, 36, 38, 105–9, 134, 162
Japan Trucking Association, 111
Japanese central government, 128–29: ad hoc Disaster Management Headquarters, 20, 136–37; bureaucracy and red tape, 82, 105–6, 112–13, 217n189; Cabinet Office, 2, 16, 20, 92, 96, 100, 133, 136, 178; citizen trust levels, 10, 126, 129, 131–32, 147–57, 179–80, 191–94; cleanup efforts, xi; as "construction state," 118, 141–45; corruption and clientelism (*see* corruption and clientelism); electoral system, 83; emphasis on signs of recovery, x, 11; encouraging relocation of towns, xi; energy policy, xi, xii, 135, 145–49, 152, 155–57, 185; evacuation orders, xv, 9–10, 146–47; failure to distribute potassium iodide, 147; health care system, 20; held back information about radiation and meltdowns, 9–10, 23, 42–45, 128, 132, 146–54, 179, 192; input structures, 166; lawsuits and claims for compensation against, ix–x, ix–xii, 151; nuclear regulation (*see* nuclear power industry); official exposure limits (*see* radioactive contamination); prime minister's role, 20, 133, 208n14; public hearings on nuclear power, 136; relationship with Tokyo Electric Power Company

INDEX

(TEPCO), 135, 146, 148, 150; relationships with municipal governments, 19, 82, 84–89, 92, 141–42, 178–79; repopulation efforts, xi, 10; seawall requirements (*see* seawalls); speed of disaster response, 133, 162; structure of, 19–21, 111, 211n71, 212n72; substituting for Fukushima Prefecture government, 106; taxation, 111, 145, 156; transportation infrastructure (*see* mass transit; roads); underrepresentation of women, 23; work with NGOs and foreign aid groups, 133–34. *See also* Japanese laws; Japan Self Defense Forces (SDF); *individual agencies*

Japanese economy, xiii

Japanese laws: Act on Support for Reconstructing Livelihoods of Disaster Victims, 138, 142; Disaster Relief Act, 79, 112; Emergency Acts to Improve Depopulated Areas, 182; Family Registration Act, 217n189; Law to Promote Municipal Mergers, 78–79; Mountain Village Promotion Act, 182; Special Law for Preparedness for a Nuclear Power Accident, 146

Japanese Meteorological Agency (Kishōchō, JMA), 2

Kamaishi, 2–4, 75, 83, 116, 144
Kaminoseki, 152
Kan, Naoto, 132, 137, 225n52
Kanagawa Prefecture, 22
Kansai Electric Power Company, 6
Kashiwazaki-Kariwa nuclear facility, 185
Katada, Toshitaka, 2–3
Katsurao, 42, 64
Kawamata, 44
Kawauchi, xi, 41, 43–44, 66, 147
Kerobe, 144
Kesennuma, 5, 69, 75, 131, 162–63
Kimura, Masayuki, 58, 60–61
Kirikiri, 48
Kiyomi, Tsujimoto, 133
Kizuna, 116
Kobe. *See* earthquakes
Kodama, Tatsuhiko, 154
Koizumi, Junichiro, 100, 139
Koriyama, 45
Kuji, 75
Kuwait, 110

labor unions, 20, 88, 144
Liberal Democratic Party (LDP): advocacy for restarts and new nuclear plants, 184; and Coastal Town, 98; and construction industry, 139, 188; effect of electoral support on subsidies, 78, 80, 92, 100; electoral results, 78, 137–38; and linking social capital, 87. *See also* Abe, Shinzō

linking social capital: and clientelism, 89–90, 94, 100; definitions, 16–17; effect on assistance to municipalities, 73, 77–78, 81–85; "Iron Triangle," 139; and recovery process, 100–101, 178. *See also* governance

Maebashi District Court, 152, 184–85
Makoto, Yuasa, 133
Masato, Ebihara, 83
mass transit: buses, 89; damaged by 3/11 disasters, ix, 83, 134; railroads as tsunami mitigation strategy, 23, 143; rebuilding and reopening, xi, xiv, 70, 90, 94, 110, 122, 130; and tourism, 99
media, xii, xiv, 43–44, 169, 174, 221n6
mental health: access to care, 116; alcoholism, xv, 114, 188; anxiety, 17–18, 47–53, 55–56, 120; depression, xv, 18, 47–53; effects of radiation exposure, xv, 17–18, 50–53, 114; happiness and altruism, 131–32; and job loss, 50; litigation about, xiii; loneliness and *kodokushi*, 15, 18–19, 40–41, 54–58, 62, 144–45; of parents, 116–17; personnel shortage, 114; post-traumatic stress disorder (PTSD), 13, 49–53, 120, 215n105; and risk behaviors, 53, 114, 120, 188; and social ties, 177; and stresses of evacuation, 45, 47–53, 177; suicide, xv, 56, 114; survivor guilt, 50. *See also* elderly and infirm people; health
MercyCorps, 176
Merkel, Angela, 185
Minamata, 70, 218n208
Minamisanriku, 98
Minamisoma: community identity, 79; evacuation, 41–42; hospital, 114; lack of nuclear disaster plans, 104; mayor, 21; returnees, 10; speed of recovery, 91; temporary shelters near, 15; wave heights, 75

INDEX

Ministry of Agriculture, Forestry, and Fishing (MAFF), 141
Ministry of Defense, 109. *See also* Japan Self Defense Forces (SDF)
Ministry of the Economy, Trade, and Industry (METI), 20, 135–36
Ministry of Education, Culture, Sports, Science and Technology (MEXT), 42–43, 136, 141, 148–49, 213n44. *See also* System for the Prediction of Environment Emergency Dose Information (SPEEDI)
Ministry of Foreign Affairs, 213n44
Ministry of Health, Labor, and Welfare, 20, 40, 148
Ministry of Internal Affairs and Communications, 20
Ministry of Land, Infrastructure, Transport, and Tourism (MLITT), 20, 67, 83–84, 96–98, 133
Minna no Data (Everyone's Data), 150
Mitsubishi, 111
Miyagino, 75
Miyagi Prefecture: agriculture, xii; airports, 117; betweenness centrality, 124–25; city planning, 113; death toll, 102; degree centrality, 124; depopulation, 117–21, 130, 212n89; Emergency Response Disaster Management Headquarters, 107–10; evacuation, 37; housing efforts, 112, 117; lack of contamination, 103; mental health of residents, 56, 62; recovery and reconstruction process, xii, 93–95, 103, 122, 178; scale of tsunami in, x, 32–35, 74–75; spending on construction, 113; Victim Support 4-Way Liaison Council, 109; work with NGOs and foreign aid groups, 22, 117. *See also* prefectural governments; Watari
Miyako, 4, 74–75, 143, 185
Montblanc, 99
Morioka, 96, 138
municipal governments: 1999 Law to Promote Municipal Mergers, 78–79; in China, 169–70; citizen trust levels, 126; disaster planning, 78; effect on mortality rates, 78; electoral system, 83, 86; helping evacuees, 21–22, 69–71; individual civil servants, 84–87, 219n40; and linking social capital, 16–17, 84–85, 178, 191; mayors, 9, 21, 99, 141; radiation exposure of civil servants, 151; reciprocal aid agreements, 22, 134–35, 179; relationship with central government, 19, 82, 84–89, 92, 141–42, 178–79 (*see also* linking social capital); relationship with civil society/NGOs, 88, 96; relationship with prefectural government, 86–89; taxation, 84, 103; terraforming and relocation projects, 72–73, 95–99, 153; tsunami damage to, 85; zoning, 67, 72, 141. *See also individual municipalities*

Nagamatsu, Shingo, 188
Nagin, Ray, 21, 158
Nagoya, 22
Namie: depopulation, 64, 66; evacuation, xi, 41, 146–47; radioactive contamination, 65; returnees, 58–59; speed of recovery, 91; taxation, 103; wave heights, 75
Naraha: decontamination, 64; depopulation, 153, 181–83; evacuation order lifted, xi, 66; returnees, 66; speed of recovery, 91; wave heights, 75
National Diet, 20, 24, 84, 92, 131, 137, 192
National Institute of Population and Social Security Research, 117
National Police Agency (Keisatsu chō), 5, 56, 134
National Policy Unit, 155
Natori, 4, 69, 72, 75
Nepal, 191
networks: analysis data, 22; betweenness centrality, 124–25; bonding social capital (*see* bonding social capital); bridging social capital (*see* bridging social capital); and community self-organization, 17, 24; consequences of disconnection from, 54–58; degree centrality, 124; digital (*see* social media); effect on mortality rates, 17, 75; governmental, 13, 24, 26; health effects, 18; horizontal vs. vertical, 25, 73, 98–101; linking social capital (*see* linking social capital); programs to strengthen, 18–19, 189–91 (*see also* Ibasho); and resilience, xiv, 14, 53–61; in temporary housing, 59, 62–63, 70, 189–91; and "third spaces," 63, 189–91
New Orleans, LA, 21, 54, 90, 158–59,

221n36. *See also* Federal Emergency Management Agency (FEMA); hurricanes
New Zealand, 109, 188
Nicaragua, 188
Nigeria, 164–65
Nihonmatsu, 44, 153
Nishikigura, 35–36
Noda, 75
Noda, Yoshihiko, 137–38
North Korea, 167
Norway, 131, 164–65
NTT East, xii, 2, 111
Nuclear Damage Compensation Dispute Resolution Center (NDCDRC), 151
nuclear disasters and accidents: Chernobyl meltdowns, 9, 105, 119–20, 145, 147, 156, 192, 221n6; International Nuclear Event Scale (INES), 9, 105; Monju reactor leak, 183; Three Mile Island, 105, 145, 221n6; Tokai plant worker deaths, 183 *See also* Fukushima Dai-ichi nuclear power plant
Nuclear Emergency Response Headquarters, 9
Nuclear and Industrial Safety Agency (NISA), 43, 136
nuclear power industry: economic dependence on, 120–21, 146; efforts to restart facilities, 120, 136, 149–55, 184, 186, 192; future expansion in Japan, 63, 227n162; in Germany, 185–86; government support for, 148–49; incentives for host communities (Dengen Sanpō), 145, 182; and Japanese central government, xi–xii, 135, 145–49; jobs, 121; lack of safety checks and "safety myth," 64, 104–5, 145, 180, 183–84, 210n31, 210n44; legal and regulatory frameworks, 6, 20, 128, 132, 135–36, 146, 151–52, 155, 175, 180 (*see also* Japanese central government; Japanese laws); lobbying efforts, 145; in North America, 155; public opinion about, 6, 63, 136, 145–46, 149–57, 183–85, 225n52; radiation exposure on the job, 147–48, 210n44; radiation-proof robot manufacturing, 121; relationship with *yakuza*, 150; waste cleanup businesses, xi, 63, 65–66, 120–21. *See also* Tokyo Electric Power Company (TEPCO)

Nuclear Regulation Authority (NRA), 20, 136, 139, 178, 184
Nuclear Safety Commission, 136

Ochakko, 189
Ofunato, 3, 18, 63, 75, 91, 143, 190
Ogatsu, 191
Ōgawara, 36
oil, 110, 133, 135, 164–65
Okawa Elementary School, xii
Okinawa, 141
Ōkuma, xi, 41, 65–66, 75, 91
Olympic Games (2020), x, 10–11, 60, 123, 141, 207n10
Onagawa: community opposition to seawalls, 144; death toll, xii–xiii, 5, 11, 72–73; fishing industry, 70; grieving family members in, 49; insurance compensation for residents, 51–53; memorials to tsunamis, 186; recovery and reconstruction process, 12, 98–99; social capital in, 189; tourism, 99; tsunami damage, 4–5; wave heights, 2, 11, 75
Onagoe, 59–60
Ono, Yoshikuni, 82, 85
Osaka, 22, 181
Otsuchi: death toll, 72; depopulation, 117; emergency shelters, 47–48; evacuation, 37; public servants, 24; schools, 49; support programs, 116; wave heights, 2, 75
Otsu District Court, 151

Peace Boat, 231n53
Philippines, 191
PlanMiyagi, xvi
Poland, 147, 161
politicians: personal characteristics, 84–85; role in recovery process, 91–92, 94–95. *See also* Japanese central government; Liberal Democratic Party (LDP); municipal governments; prefectural governments; *individual politicians*
Port-au-Prince, Haiti, 171–74
ports, 4, 21, 66, 75, 130, 140, 182–83
prefectural governments: bypassed by municipal-national connections, 96; citizen trust levels, 126, 150; governors, 84; housing efforts, 21, 111, 141; lack of communications during disaster,

prefectural governments (*continued*) 106; as "middlemen," 111; post-disaster workloads, 102; public opinion about, 96; relationship with central government, xiv, 103, 106; relationships with municipal governments, xiv, 96, 103; search-and-rescue efforts, 105–9; spending decisions, xiv; work with NGOs and foreign aid groups, 22, 109–10, 116–17, 124–25

protest: antinuclear, 132, 136, 152, 180, 184, 192, 230n30; in China, 168–69; as governance input channel, 166; in Haiti, 175

Putnam, Robert, 78

Qiang people, 167

radioactive contamination: cesium, x, 8, 10, 65, 153; from Chernobyl, 9; citizen data on (*see* citizen science, 23); and depopulation, 119; around Fukushima Dai-ichi nuclear power plant, 41–42, 64–65; within Fukushima Dai-ichi nuclear power plant, 8, 65; iodine, x, 8, 65; official exposure limits, 41–42, 128, 132, 147–48, 154; and personnel shortages, 115; public fears about, 63, 114–15, 209n44 (*see also* mental health); spread of, x, xv, 42, 44, 65, 147; strontium, 65; tritium, 8, 65, 210n36; uranium, x; of water, 8, 65. *See also* decontamination; evacuees from 3/11 disasters; health; mental health; nuclear power industry

railroads. *See* mass transit

Reconstruction Agency, 20, 65–66, 113, 130–31, 136–38, 142, 168, 178. *See also* Japanese central government

Reconstruction Design Council, 136, 187

recovery and reconstruction process: bureaucracy and red tape, 66–70; citizen-directed, 156; costs, x, 60, 67–68; debris removal, 86, 90, 129, 153, 182; decontamination (*see* decontamination); demographic factors, 92–93; economic, xi–xii, 69–70, 90–91, 98–99, 115–17; effect of geographic conditions, 92–93; financial factors, 92–93, 113; frameworks of central government, 128–29; housing (*see* emergency shelters and temporary housing); importance of social networks in, xiv, 93; independent efforts by cities, xii; National Institute for Research Advancement (NIRA) index, 90–95; New Orleans Index, 90; Special Zones for Reconstruction, 156; terraforming and relocation projects, xi, 68, 72–73, 82, 95–99, 130, 138; theories, 11–14, 92–93; variation among Japanese cities, x, 11

Red Cross, 109–10, 125

religious groups, 20, 38, 62–63, 88, 159

renewable energy, 123, 152, 185–86

Rifu, xi, 12, 72, 75

Rikuzentakata: bureaucratic issues with reconstruction, 67; death toll, 11, 37, 58, 72; depopulation, 117, 181; housing, 145; mental health of residents, 51–52, 55; reciprocal aid agreements, 22; small businesses, 58, 60–61, 63; social networks, 63, 162–63; speed of recovery, 91; tsunami damage, 4–5; wave heights, 11, 75. *See also* Toba, Futoshi

roads: damaged by 3/11 disasters, ix, 106, 134; evacuation routes, 76, 98, 143, 184; governance, 19, 21; as index of recovery, 90; on levees, 144; repair and rebuilding, 111, 122, 129–30, 142, 153, 182; as tsunami mitigation strategy, 144, 187; use of radioactive building materials, 153

Roos, John, 9

Rugby World Cup, x

Russia, 186. *See also* Soviet Union

Safecast, 23, 150–51, 164, 175. *See also* citizen science

Saitama Prefecture, 44–45

Sakurai, Katsunobu, 21

Sanaburi Foundation, 134

San Francisco, 188

Sasebo, 9

Saudi Arabia, 161

Sawada, Yasuyuki, 77, 79

schools: and bridging social capital, 15; colleges and universities, 123; consolidation, 141; cram schools, 119; deaths in, xii, 5; decontamination, 153; disaster training and drills, 2–3; enrollment, 64, 123, 208n26; as evacuation sites, 5, 31, 33, 38–39, 45, 49; in Fukushima, 50;

funding for, xiii; as index of recovery, 90–91, 94; reopenings, 12, 46, 49, 89, 129–30; after Sichuan earthquake, 168
seawalls: breached by tsunami, 4–5; community opposition to, 12, 18, 24, 70, 97, 113, 136, 142–44, 187; dikes, 117; economic effects, 24, 73, 140, 143–44, 187; effect on mortality rates, 17, 78–81, 187; environmental effects, 140; false sense of security, 3, 79, 143, 187; at Fukushima Dai-ichi nuclear power plant, 6–7; funding for, 21, 98, 140, 142–44, 207n11; heights, 79, 81, 126–27; new construction, 130, 142–44, 186–87; planned by communities, 24, 97; preventing residents from seeing tsunami, 143; role in attracting residents, xi, 122; uniform government requirements for, 12, 79, 113, 126–29, 140, 142–44, 156, 182, 193
Self-Defense Forces. *See* Japan Self Defense Forces (SDF)
Sendai: city council, 83; effects of earthquake in, 1–2; Ministry of Land, Infrastructure, Transport, and Tourism (MLITT) office, 98; population growth, xi, 72, 117, 181; Reconstruction Agency field office, 138; recovery and reconstruction process, 11, 67; staffed by civil servants from Yokohama, 22; temporary housing, 69; wave heights, 75
Shichigahama, 61, 69, 75
Shiga Prefecture, 151
Shimizutani family, 14, 29–32, 194
Shinchi, 75, 91
Shinkin Bank, 116
Shinto shrines, 30, 63, 65, 186, 191
Shiogama Port, 4, 75
Shiroishi, 22
Singapore, 98–99
Smith, Tilly, 3
social capital. *See* networks
Social Democratic Party (SDP), 87
SocialHearts, 116
social media, 21, 41, 108, 166, 211n60
SoftBank, 2, 111
Soka Gakkai, 38, 137. *See also* religious groups
Soma, Fukushima, 54, 75
Somalia, 165
South Africa, 188

South Korea, 109
Soviet Union, 156, 192. *See also* Russia
Spain, 131
Suda, Yoshiaki, 99
Supreme Court, 20
Sweden, 131
Switzerland, 186
System for the Prediction of Environment Emergency Dose Information (SPEEDI), 43, 147

Tagajo, 69, 181
Taihaku, 75
Taiwan, 110
Takaya elementary school, 31–32
Takayoshi, Kikuchi, 83
Tamaura-Nishi, 98
Tanaka, Kakuei, 84
Tanaka family, 32–35
Tanohata, 11, 74–75
Taro, 4, 143
Thailand, 3, 211n63. *See also* tsunamis
Three Mile Island. *See* nuclear disasters and accidents
Toba, Futoshi, 67
Togichi Prefecture, 46
Tōhoku sanken. *See* Fukushima Prefecture; Iwate Prefecture; Miyagi Prefecture
Tōhoku tsunami: damage to housing and infrastructure, ix, 4–5, 33, 47, 53, 58, 85, 89, 96, 106, 113, 134; effect of geographic conditions, 75–76; effects inland, 73, 79; incorrect forecasts, 2–3; personal accounts, 30–36; wave heights, x, 2, 4–5, 11, 58, 74–75, 80, 95, 152
Tōhoku University, 181
Tokyo: effects of earthquake in, 1–2; evacuees from Fukushima in, 47, 181; political/financial dominance, 90, 101, 183; possibility of evacuating, 133–34; US personnel in, 9. *See also* Japanese central government
Tokyo Electric Power Company (TEPCO): "clean coal" facilities, xii; compensation payments, 57, 216n148; employees, xii, 44, 64, 184; evacuation of command center, 106; faulty disaster management, 6–10, 106; government bailout, 148, 150, 184; held back information about radiation and meltdowns, 23, 43–44, 148, 192; indict-

INDEX

Tokyo Electric Power Company (*continued*) ments of officials, 184; lack of nuclear disaster plans, 104–5, 132, 146, 152, 180; lawsuits and claims for compensation against, ix–x, ix–xii, 150–52; as local job provider, 59; market pressures on, 135; public opinion about, xii, 44, 120, 126; relationship with central government, 135, 146, 148, 150
Tokyo Engineering University, 96
Tokyo University, 96, 165
Tomiichi, Murayama, 133
Tomioka, 41, 43–44, 64, 75, 146–47
Tomodachi Initiative, 99
tornadoes, 7, 13
Toshiba, 186
tourism: in China, 167, 228n22; damaged by 3/11 disasters, 113; and recovery process, 99, 103, 121, 183; and seawalls, 24, 143, 187; wildlife, 183
Transparency International, 166, 176
transportation infrastructure. *See* mass transit; ports; roads
tsunamis: 1700s Portugal earthquake and tsunami, 13; 1854 Ansei-Nankai tsunami, 209n6; 1896 Meiji Sanriku tsunami, 3, 104; 1933 Ofunato tsunami and fires, 3; 1960 Chile tsunami, 3; 2004 Indian Ocean tsunami, 3, 76; ancient, 76, 180, 186; monuments, 76, 98, 180, 186. *See also* Tōhoku tsunami
Tsuruga nuclear facility, 184

Uchibori, Masao, 150
Ukraine, 9. *See also* nuclear disasters and accidents: Chernobyl meltdowns
United Kingdom, 176
United Nations, xvi, 96, 158, 172
United States: 9/11 terror attacks, 137–40; Agency for International Development (USAID), 176; antinuclear sentiment, 230n41; Bilateral Coordination Mechanism, 139; Department of Homeland Security, 137; disaster aid, 98–99, 109; embassy in Japan, 9, 147; Federal Emergency Management Agency (FEMA), 16, 20 (*see also* hurricanes); federal system, 82, 211n71; governance in, 19; immigrant communities, 173, 221n36; lawsuits against Tokyo Electric Power Company (TEPCO), 151–52; media coverage of disasters, 169; NGOs, 99; nuclear facilities, 7, 186, 210n21; Nuclear Regulatory Commission, 9; offshore gas and oil drilling, 135; Operation Tomodachi, 134; radiation maps, 42; Three Mile Island nuclear disaster, 105, 145, 221n6. *See also* Chicago heat wave of 1995; *Deepwater Horizon* oil spill; hurricanes; New Orleans, LA; tornadoes
USS *George Washington*, 9
USS *Ronald Reagan*, 151
utilities: electricity, 12, 30, 89–91, 94, 129, 149; gas, 12, 89–91, 129; regional monopolies, 135; water, 129. *See also* nuclear power industry; Tokyo Electric Power Company (TEPCO)

Wakahayashi, 75
warning systems: ancient, 186; Area Mail Disaster Information System, 4; and disaster outcomes, 159, 162; earthquake damage to, 4; for earthquakes, 1, 209n1; financial factors, 92; and linking social capital, 77; loudspeakers, 37, 209n1; mobile phones, 37; saigai (disaster) radio, 37, 41; television, 30, 37; for tsunamis, 2–4, 30, 81, 174–75, 180, 186. *See also* communications infrastructure
Watari: agriculture, xii; depopulation, 181; elementary school, 30–31; housing, 145; personal accounts, 29–32; seawalls, 187; social stability, 162–63; speed of recovery, 91; wave heights, 75
Weber, Max, 165
Wellington, New Zealand, 188
Westinghouse, 186
World Bank, 166–67
World Health Organization, 172
WorldVision, 176
World War II, 20

Yamada, 51–52, 75, 91, 117, 143
Yamaguchi Prefecture, 152
Yamamoto, 75
Yamato Transport, 111
Yingxiu, China, 167
Yokohama, 22, 46
Yoshida elementary school, 33
Yume-Chan, 98